To Marion + Morag
With love from Sarah
Jan/95

This copy of
PATHFINDERS: Canadian Tributes
which contains the
story of

is presented with the compliments of

® HORN ABBOT

Horn Abbot Ltd.

Pathfinders
Canadian Tributes

Charles J. Humber

Editor-in-Chief

HEIRLOOM PUBLISHING INC.

CANADA HEIRLOOM SERIES
Volume I   *CANADA: From Sea Unto Sea*
Volume II *CANADA's Native Peoples*
Volume III *ALLEGIANCE: The Ontario Story*
Volume IV *PATHFINDERS: Canadian Tributes*

HEIRLOOM PUBLISHING INC.
6509B MISSISSAUGA ROAD NORTH
MISSISSAUGA ON L5N 1A6

Tel: (905) 821-1152
Fax: (905) 821-1158

Chairman William E. Melbourne
Publisher Charles J. Humber
President Angela Dea Cappelli Clark
Secretary-Treasurer Phyllis L. Melbourne

Research, Editorial, Sales, and Support Staff
Jo Daly, Helen de Verteuil, Patricia Eden, Christine Hebscher,
Jo-Ann Lamb, Danielle White, Hughes Winfield. Also,
Alexandrea Clark, Jamie Clark, Charlie W. Humber,
Scott Humber

Cover Design Hart Broudy
Book Design Amstier Communications: Peter Reitsma,
             Patricia Kruger
Film Linotext Mississauga Inc.
Printing Annan & Bird Lithographers

PATHFINDERS: Canadian Tributes
Printed and bound in Canada

Copyright 1994 by Heirloom Publishing Inc.
All Rights Reserved

Canadian Cataloguing in Publication Data
Main entry under title:
PATHFINDERS: Canadian tributes

(Canada heirloom series ; v. IV)
Includes bibliographical references and index.
ISBN 0-9694247-2-8
I. Canada — Biography.   I. Humber, Charles J.
II. Title   III. Series
FC25.P37 1994   920.071   C92-094201-6
F1005.P37 1994

This book is set in Stone Informal

Printed on *Luna Matte*, 80lb text, manufactured in Canada
by Island Paper Mill

OPPOSITE: Photograph, *The Walk to Paradise Garden*, 1946, W. Eugene Smith
Courtesy, Jane Corkin Gallery, Toronto

*Dedicated to
the Pathfinders of
the 21st Century...*

CONTENTS

Contributors 6

Introduction *Spotlighting Pathfinders* 7

Prime Minister's Introductory Messages 8

Insulin
Saving Millions of Lives Worldwide MVJ 10

Georges-Édouard Desbarats
Pictures for the Press MVJ 14

Québec Wood Sculpture
A Triple-Century Tradition DBW 16

Canadian Comic Creators
Superman, Tarzan, and Prince Valiant MVJ 20

Inuit Art
Responding to a Spiritual World IH 24

Canadian Pacific Railway
Linking Canada JMSC 28

John McCrae *"...lest we forget..."* ADC 32

Sandford Fleming
Canada's First Renaissance Man DMS 34

Gilles Villeneuve
Canadian Sporting Legend MVJ 38

Reginald Fessenden
"...greater than Marconi..." MVJ 42

Louis Cyr
The Strongest Man in the World DMS 46

Pauline Johnson *Bridging Cultures* JMSC 48

Billy Bishop VC
Warrior Knight of the Air AJB 50

Paul Peel
Artist with Poetic Paintbrush MVJ 54

Norman Bethune
"The spirit of absolute selflessness" DMS 58

Mohawk Skywalkers *Walking on Air* JMSC 64

The Hospital For Sick Children
For the Love of Children DMS 66

Frederick Tisdall & Pablum
Saving the Children MVJ 72

Canada's Bush Pilots *Eagles of the North* MVJ 76

Edward "Ned" Hanlan
Canada's First International Sports Hero DMS 82

The Massey Legacy *Farming the World* LC 84

Joseph E. Atkinson
Publisher for Social Reform DMS 88

Leslie McFarlane
"The Ghost of the Hardy Boys" MVJ 92

Festivals
Three Stages in Canadian Life JMSC 96

Thomas Charles Longboat
World Champion Iroquois Marathoner DMS 100

Joseph B. Tyrrell
Peer of Darwin, Huxley, and Agassiz MVJ 102

John Tuzo Wilson *Master of Plate Tectonics* DMS 106

The McIntosh Apple *Canada's "Big Apple"* MVJ 110

Maude Abbott
Pioneering Heart Research DMS 112

John Peters Humphrey
"Creating a Magna Carta for Mankind" DMS 114

Yousuf Karsh *Greatness Exposed* MVJ 118

John McLennan
Pioneering Canadian Physicist DMS 122

Andrew McNaughton
Scientist, Military Commander, and Diplomat JMSC 126

William Osler *International Doctor* DMS 128

Gustave Gingras
"...a travelling salesman for rehabilitation..." HSH 132

Abraham Gesner
Lighting up the Nineteenth Century DMS 136

Norman McLaren *Innovative Film Genius* MVJ 140

Oscar Peterson *"Maharajah of the Piano"* MVJ 144

Frederic Newton Gisborne
Linking Continents by Cable DMS 148

Paul-Émile Cardinal Léger
Living the Servant Principle DMS 152

William Edmond Logan
"He formed a rock group and toured the country" DMS 156

Battle of Amiens and Gen. A.W. Currie
A Greater Triumph... SG 160

Elizabeth Arden *"Creator of Beauty"* MVJ 162

William Maxwell Aitken *"Lord Beaverbrook is
at his very best when things are at their very worst"* DMS 166

Glenn Gould *Keyboard Genius* MVJ 170

Kenneth Colin Irving *Industrial Caesar*	DMS	174
Marshall McLuhan *Oracle of the Electronic Age*	JMSC	178
Samuel Cunard *Merchant Prince of the Oceans*	DMS	180
Clifford Sifton *Opening Canada's Breadbasket to the World*	JMSC	184
Harold Elford Johns *Creating a Bomb of a Different Kind*	DMS	186
William Thornton Mustard *Giving Life to "Blue Babies"*	MVJ	188
Thomas "Carbide" Willson *Inventing the Acetylene Torch*	JMSC	192
Ring Champions *Dixon, Burns, McLarnin and Langford*	MVJ	194
Women's Rights *Women Liberating Men*	DMS	200
Pierre Beauchemin *Mining Quebec's Klondike*	DMS	206
Bernard Lonergan *Honoured Thinker*	DMS	208
Alexander Graham Bell *At Brantford and Baddeck*	MVJ	210
Trivial Pursuit *"... what mighty contests rise from trivial things"*	MVJ	216
Maple Syrup *Thousand-Year-Old Recipe*	JMSC	220
Hans Selye *Understanding Stress*	DMS	222
Joseph-Armand Bombardier *Creator of the Snowmobile*	DMS	224
Lester B. Pearson and the United Nations as Peacekeepers *Planting Seeds for World Peace*	JMSC	228
L.M. Montgomery Anne of Green Gables	VC	230
Wilfred G. Bigelow *From Cooling Hearts to Pacing Them*	MVJ	234
Hugh MacLennan *Dramatizing Canadian Culture*	DMS	238
Gratien Gélinas *In the Tradition of Chaplin and Molière*	MVJ	240
Charles Saunders *The Wheat that Won the West*	MVJ	242
Jean Vanier *Changing the World One Heart at a Time*	DMS	246
Adelaide Hunter Hoodless *Visionary Social Reformer*	DMS	250
Northrop Frye *World-Leading Literary Theorist*	JMSC	252
Franc R. Joubin *Finding New Wealth for Nations*	DMS	254
The Electron Microscope *Travelling the Unknown World of Inner Space*	MVJ	258
Gordon Murray *The Story of Heparin*	RJB	262
The Underground Railroad *The Hidden Road to Freedom*	JMSC	264
Nickel *Serving the World*	DMS	268
Thayer Lindsley *Visionary Mining Developer*	DMS	272
James Y. Murdoch *Creative Mining Executive*	DMS	274
John Patch *Propeller of Ships*	MVJ	278
Dr. James Naismith *Inventor of Basketball*	DMS	280
Stephen Leacock *Monarch of Wit*	DMS	286
Charles Fenerty *Paper Maker*	MVJ	290
Wallace Rupert Turnbull *A Most Prolific Genius*	MVJ	292
Harry Botterell, John Counsell, and Al Jousse *Revolutionaries in Spinal Cord Injury Management*	MT	296
Omond Solandt *Insightful Interpreter of Scientific Research*	DMS	300
Before Edison *Two Canucks Beat Edison to the Light Bulb*	WS	304
H.R. MacMillan *Pacific Timber Baron*	MVJ	308
Hollywood Stars *The Original Canadian 3-peat*	MVJ	312
Adam Beck *The Power Behind Electrical Power*	MVJ	318
Ice Hockey *Creating Canada's Game*	DMS	322
John E. (Jack) Hammell *Giving Wings to Prospectors*	DMS	328
Wilder Graves Penfield *Mapping the Brain*	DMS	330
Edward Samuel Rogers *Plugging in the World*	DMS	334
Canadian Corporate Achievers		336

CONTRIBUTORS & ACKNOWLEDGEMENTS

JMSC **J.M.S. Careless**, O.C. (1981), Order of Ontario (1987), Ph.D. (Harvard Univ.), F.R.S.C., Born, Toronto, Ontario; Professor Emeritus, Univ. of Toronto; Author, *Canada: A Story of Challenge* (1953); *Brown of the Globe* (1959; revised, 1963); *The Union of the Canadas* (1967); *Colonists and Canadians* (1971); *Rise of Cities in Canada to 1914* (1978); *Pre-Confederation Premiers* (1980); *Frontier and Metropolis* (1989); Contributor, *CANADA: From Sea Unto Sea* (1986; revised, 1988); *ALLEGIANCE: The Ontario Story* (1991); Chief Historical Consultant, *Chronicle of Canada* (1990); Chairman, Board of Ontario Historical Studies Series; Special wartime assistant, Dept. of External Affairs, Ottawa, 1943-45

MVJ **Melbourne V. James**, Born, Montreal, P.Q.; Former Director of Information, Bell Canada's Public Affairs Department (Ontario Division); Public Relations writer with Bank of Montreal and CNR; Journalist; Eighteen years on Board of Couchiching Institute on Public Affairs (CIPA) and President, 1975-77; President, Canadian Public Relations Society (CPRS) 1974-75 and Chairman of its Foundation 1988-91; Former PR Chairman, Toronto Board of Trade, The United Way, and Family Services Association; Awarded life membership in both CIPA and CPRS and recipient of the 25th anniversary medal of Her Majesty Queen Elizabeth's Coronation

DMS **D. McCormack Smyth**, Ph.D. (Univ. of Toronto) Born, Toronto, Ontario; Senior official, International Trade Fair which played a major role in transforming Toronto into a cosmopolitan centre; Director of Admissions, Univ. of Toronto, 1958-60; First Fellow Commoner and first Canadian senior member of Churchill College, Cambridge, the international memorial to Sir Winston Churchill; Professor, Political Science, York University, 1962; Appointed Dean, Atkinson College, York University, 1963; Executive member, the Council of Regents for Colleges of Applied Arts and Technology, 1966-73; Founding Chairman, the Canadian Institute for Radiation Safety (CAIRS) and the Churchill Society for the Advancement of Parliamentary Democracy; International lecturer, writer and contributor to many publications; Author, *The Cybernetic Age* (1969), *Government for Higher Learning* (1970), *The House that Ryerson Built* (1984), *Not For Gold Alone* (1989)

RJB Ronald J. Baird, M.D., F.R.C.S. (C) Professor of Surgery, University of Toronto; Senior cardiovascular surgeon, The Toronto Hospital, Toronto General Division; Chairman Emeritus of the Divisions of Cardiovascular Surgery, University of Toronto, Toronto Western Hospital, and the Toronto General Hospital

AJB Group Captain A.J. Bauer, RCAF Raised near Owen Sound, Ontario; Spent career as pilot in Canada's Air Force; Founded Billy Bishop Heritage, 1987, which purchased the Bishop home in Owen Sound and converted it into a museum; Originated the RCAF Pilots Club, 1972; National President, RCAF Association, 1981-83

LC Lynn Campbell, M.A. (McMaster University, Hamilton) Born, Freelton, Ontario; Historical Researcher, Ontario Agricultural Museum, Milton, Ontario; Contributor, *Dictionary of Canadian Biography*, numerous magazines, and newspapers

VC Virginia A.S. Careless, M.A. (University of British Columbia) Curator of History, Royal B.C. Museum, specializing in domestic, social, and cultural history with an emphasis on clothing, textiles, and household wares

SG Strome Galloway Colonel, Canadian Army (ret'd); Colonel, The Royal Canadian Regiment (app't, 1989); Author of numerous articles and books about World War II

IH Ingo Hessel, B.A. (Carleton University) Co-ordinator, Inuit Art Section, Indian & Northern Affairs Canada; Author, *Canadian Inuit Sculpture*, and of numerous articles and essays on Inuit Art

HSH H. Shirley Horne, B.A. (University of P.E.I.) Freelance journalist; Author of children's biography on Dr. Gustave Gingras; Contributed to national and international publications

WS Walter Stefaniuk Born, Sault Ste. Marie, Ontario; Newspaper reporter and editor for various newspapers; Produces *You Asked Us* column for *The Toronto Star*

MT Mary Tremblay, Ph.D., O.T. (C) Associate Professor, Faculty of Health Sciences, School of Occupational Therapy, McMaster University, Hamilton, Ontario

DBW Donald Blake Webster, M.A. (University of Rhode Island) Curator and Head, Canadiana Depart-ment, Royal Ontario Museum; Well-known author of numerous publications on Canadiana

ACKNOWLEDGEMENTS: Among the many others whose time and assistance shall not go unnoticed are Dr. Bill Bigelow, Toronto; Mr. William J. Hardie, Vancouver Bookbinding; Aynsley MacFarlane, Alexander Graham Bell National Historic Site, Nova Scotia; Irma Coucill, artist, Toronto; Microscopists Dr. F.W. Doane, Toronto, Dr. J.H.L.Watson, Detroit, Dr. James Hillier, Princeton, N.J. and Dr. Albert Prebus, Columbus, Ohio; Rev. Frederick E. Crowe, S.J., St. Regis College, Toronto; Kenneth Molson; former curator, National Aviation Museum, Ottawa; John Hobbins, Associate Director, Libraries, McGill University; Jim Ware, President Horn Abbott; The Naismith Foundation; Billy Bishop Heritage, Owen Sound; Mrs. Grant Davidson, Toronto; Angelo Savelli, Hamilton; Mr. J.V. Brady, Goderich; Linda Coates, Public Relations, Bombardier Inc.; and Fred Gaskin, Cambridge, Ontario

INTRODUCTION

Spotlighting Pathfinders

For much of this century, contemplating the Canadian identity has been a Canadian preoccupation. Canadian journalists such as Bruce Hutchison have labelled Canadians "hewers of wood," figuratively identifying those living north of the 49th parallel as hardworking beavers.

Others have suggested that Canadians, collectively, constitute a coat of many colours, a colourfully woven mantle attracting a multitude of newcomers from around the world. Such glossography has prompted Margaret Atwood to muse that "we are all immigrants to this place."

While commentators and media mushers note that Canadians, more than anything else, are burdened by a huge inferiority complex, mainly because geography registers Canada next-door to a star player on the world stage, in actual fact, Canadians are anything but inferior.

Canadians are an unassuming people whose singular achievements, disproportionately high to their small population, have impacted with positive consequences upon the "global village." Unfortunately their accomplishments have, for the most part, significantly gone unappreciated, unrecognized and unapplauded far too long....

A major purpose of *PATHFINDERS: Canadian Tributes* has been to overcome this malaise by spotlighting stories of Canadian achievement in an appropriate format. From the outset, Heirloom Publishing's approach was to identify 125 of these achievements, commission their respective stories and celebrate the series of vignettes in a major publication. This task was a privilege but it was also a challenge in that the selection process was made difficult because there were so many inspiring stories from which to choose.

This fourth volume of the *CANADA Heirloom Series*, nevertheless, attempts with unabashed passion to fulfil this mandate. The Publishers now take this opportunity to thank the Rt. Hon. Jean Chrétien, Canada's 26th Prime Minister, for graciously accepting our invitation to write the special message introducing this production. The Prime Minister's message, as well as the warm remarks by Liu Zhongde, Minister of Culture, the People's Republic of China, and Maurice Strong, Chairman, Ontario Hydro, have greatly assisted in making *PATHFINDERS* a distinguished "cultural ambassador."

Without the generous support, moreover, of some 70 Canadian business establishments strongly believing in Canada's future as a great land of opportunity, Heirloom would never have succeeded in launching *PATHFINDERS,* thus fulfilling a determined vision to generate heritage awareness by promoting Canada's "pathfinders".

Heirloom is also deeply grateful to Professor J.M.S. Careless, Mr. Mel James and Professor D. McCormack Smyth for undertaking the huge responsibility of writing the majority of the stories. Their contributions, plus the contributions of some 12 other personalities, have assisted Heirloom in generating unprecedented heritage awareness.

Gratitude is also extended to Amstier Communications, especially Peter Reitsma, for insisting on a design commensurate with the subject material. To *The Toronto Star,* Heirloom also extends grateful appreciation for their generous support especially by providing extensive access to research and library files.

Finally, Heirloom would be very remiss in not acknowledging the immense contribution to this visionary project made by both William and Phyllis Melbourne, our colleagues. Their mentorship and business acumen steadfastly guided all of us to strive, to focus and to be of heart....

July 14, 1994

Publisher

President

The Right Honourable Jean Chrétien, P.C., Q.C., M.P., Prime Minister of Canada
Le très honorable Jean Chrétien, P.C., Q.C., M.P., Premier ministre du Canada

CANADA

We Canadians do not make a habit of brashly advertising our accomplishments. Perhaps this is due to modesty. Or, perhaps it is a residue of the pragmatic, pioneering spirit of our forebearers: we tend to want to move on to the next challenge as soon as one is overcome. However in-born our national tendency to understatement may be, with a history as rich in stories of tremendous individual and collective achievement as ours is, I have always believed we must be careful to guard against forgetfulness.

That is why I was very pleased to be asked to contribute a special introduction to *PATHFINDERS: Canadian Tributes*.

The fourth in a series of books dedicated to raising the awareness among Canadians of their unique heritage, *PATHFINDERS: Canadian Tributes* celebrates the tremendous contributions that individual Canadians — and indeed Canadian society as a whole — have made to the betterment of people everywhere.

This handsome volume recounts, in colourful detail, 125 stories of accomplishments as compelling and diverse as the piano virtuosity of Glenn Gould, the ground-breaking work in battlefield medicine by Norman Bethune, Canadian involvement in the evolution of women's rights, and the daring feats of Gilles Villeneuve.

Taken together, they paint a picture of a visionary and energetic people, with a capacity for innovation and creativity that belies our modest self-image. And by chronicling these singular achievements in one volume, *PATHFINDERS: Canadian Tributes* gives all Canadians readier access to the tradition of innovation and excellence that is very much a part of our national heritage — and which will continue to keep us in the forefront of nations as we work to meet the challenges of the coming century.

Les Canadiens ne font pas grand étalage de leurs mérites. Ils sont tout en modestie. Peut-être parce que, dans la foulée de leurs ancêtres, ils relèvent les défis un à un, sans s'attarder. La retenue est une propension nationale, elle fait partie de notre spécificité. Mais on ne saurait laisser sombrer dans l'oubli les plus belles pages de notre histoire.

Je suis donc privilégié de signer l'avant-propos de cet ouvrage qui rend hommage aux grands pionniers canadiens.

Le quatrième volume de ce recueil qui fête l'exception canadienne fait revivre les hauts faits de Canadiens qui ont contribué au mieux-être du monde entier.

Il s'agit d'un merveilleux ouvrage, qui regorge de détails sur 125 vies aussi diverses que remarquables. On y retrouve, pour ne nommer que ceux-là, Glenn Gould, le pianiste virtuose, Normand Bethune, le médecin qui a réinventé les antennes chirurgicales, les Canadiennes qui ont fait progresser la condition féminine, Gilles Villeneuve, le grand coureur automobile.

Ensemble, ces vies composent une fresque à la gloire d'un peuple qui sait voir loin et déployer toutes ses forces vives, sous ses dehors modestes. En retraçant nos grandes réalisations, cet ouvrage tisse le destin canadien aux couleurs de l'inventivité et du dépassement, il décline sur tous les tons une certaine idée du Canada, qui rayonne dans le monde et qui est prise sur le XXIe siècle.

Jean Chrétien

INSULIN

Saving Millions of Lives Worldwide

THE Egyptians described diabetes 4,000 years ago and a Greek physician named the disorder some 2,000 years later, but how to control this devastating condition was unknown until Frederick G. Banting had an idea that led to the discovery of insulin in 1921.

A part-time instructor at the University of Western Ontario's medical school, Banting was preparing a lecture on the pancreas when he read that an American researcher had tied the pancreatic ducts of animals and found that, although the pancreas withered, the animals did not develop diabetes. He knew that the pancreas produces two secretions: one helps the body digest protein, starch and fat; the other is absorbed directly into the bloodstream. Banting wondered whether the blockage of the pancreatic ducts had stopped only the digestive secretions and whether the other secretions, possibly created by the spots on the pancreas known as the Islets of Langerhans, were still being produced. At 2:00 a.m. he wrote out his idea: "Ligate pancreatic ducts of dogs. Wait six or eight weeks. Remove the residue and extract."

A week later he discussed his idea with a diabetes expert, Professor J.J.R. Macleod, head of physiology at the University of Toronto. Macleod was not impressed with Banting's idea, asking frankly why he thought he had the answer when others far more experienced had failed.

Banting nonetheless persisted. He wrote a more detailed outline, and Macleod finally, in the spring of 1921, agreed to provide a laboratory. He also gave Banting two physiology graduate students to take turns doing the analytical work while he, himself, was vacationing in his native Scotland.

Banting, born on a farm near Alliston, Ontario, and a University of Toronto medical school graduate, began his work with Charles Best as his first assistant. The pancreatic ducts of some dogs were tied and in others removed to create diabetic animals.

Late in July an operation on a dog with tied ducts showed a pancreas about one-third normal size. It was removed and ground in a solution of sand and saline. The extract was then injected into a diabetic dog near death. The blood sugar decreased so dramatically that the dog lived weeks longer than expected.

When the other graduate student was unable to keep the commitment to replace Best, Best remained. He and Banting worked feverishly over the next two months to confirm their findings and improve the extract which they called "isletin."

On returning from Scotland, Macleod was impressed but insisted they repeat their experiments to confirm that the results were consistent and that the extract proved beneficial over time. Also, another means of obtaining enough extract had to be found, and Banting recommended using the pancreas of unborn calves obtained from beef cattle at the local abattoir. This proved effective. Later, the glands of fully grown cows and pigs were used as they are today.

Problems still remained. There was a need to improve the solvent used in the preparation of the extract in order to reduce its toxicity before it could be tested clinically. Moreover, if the extract was successful, how to mass produce it would be important since there were an estimated one million diabetics in North America.

Macleod, who renamed the extract "insulin," enlisted the support of his staff, notably Dr. J. Bertram Collip, a University of Alberta biochemist then working with him, to find a less toxic and more effective product. Working with others, particularly the University of Toronto's Connaught Laboratories, Collip produced a clinically acceptable insulin, and in January 1922, Banting was able to administer it to a patient, 14-year-old Leonard Thompson, whose health improved almost miraculously. Other diabetics were treated over the next several months with similar dramatic results.

Diabetes causes excessive thirst, urination, weight loss, fatigue and eventual emaciation, coma and death. Treatment with insulin corrects the body's deficiency of this hormone. With daily

In several magazine polls during his lifetime, Sir Frederick Banting was judged the most famous living Canadian. Co-discoverers of insulin, Banting and Professor J.J.R. Macleod of the University of Toronto were co-recipients of the Nobel Prize for Medicine in 1923. Banting, knighted in 1934, seven years before he tragically died in an airplane crash, was the first Canadian to be awarded a Nobel Prize

The Toronto Star

Professor J.J.R. Macleod, left, was a Professor of Physiology at the University of Toronto in 1923 when he was awarded the Nobel Prize along with Dr. Banting; assigned to work as an assistant with Dr. Banting in the spring of 1921, Charles Best was an integral member of the team discovering insulin. Banting shared his prize money with Best. Macleod, similarly, shared his prize money with J.B. Collip

insulin injections, patients recover their normal state; growth and vigor are regained.

The awesome success of insulin was first made known in medical journals based on remarks made by Professor Macleod. Some reports credited him with the discovery, implying that Banting and Best were assistants. Banting, already feeling that Macleod had taken over, resented the inference. When *The Toronto Daily Star* made the story public in a front-page article in March 1922, a subheading read "Banting Gives His All on the Result."

From then on Banting's name became synonymous with the discovery. This was later reinforced when Professor Macleod issued a statement indicating that reports crediting him with the discovery were wrong and that the idea was entirely Banting's.

Honours were heaped on Banting. The University of Toronto made him a full professor of medical research and later established the Banting Institute in Toronto. Governments rewarded him with research grants, he was in great demand as a speaker, numerous medical societies presented him with medals, universities bestowed honorary degrees, and learned societies made him a member of their organizations. He was also the first Canadian to win the Nobel Prize (1923). Later he was knighted.

The fact that the Nobel Prize was shared with Professor Macleod didn't please him as he felt it was Best who deserved this. Consequently, he gave half his prize money to Best; Macleod split his with Dr. Collip, a move later considered appropriate when it was realized all four had played a major role in the development of insulin.

Banting sold the patent to the University of Toronto for one dollar proposing that Connaught Laboratories produce the extract. They did, but the demand was so great that Eli Lilly Company (Canada) Limited, which had worked on the purification of the insulin in 1922, was awarded a contract and produced the first commercial supply in 1923. This company is today a major producer of insulin.

In 1928 Dr. Macleod returned to work in Scotland. Dr. Collip was later Dean of the University of Western Ontario's medical school and Charles Best, graduating in medicine in 1925, served as chairman of the University of Toronto's Physiology Department from 1929 to 1965. Dr. Banting continued to do research but also spent much of his time encouraging young scientists with their discoveries.

At the outbreak of World War II, Banting succeeded in assisting an RCAF doctor, W.R. Franks, to develop the world's first anti-G suit designed to prevent pilots from blacking out. Asked to conduct research on seasickness, Banting boarded a bomber flying to England but, tragically, died of a punctured lung when the plane crash-landed near Musgrave Harbour, Newfoundland, in February 1941.

MVJ

Before the discovery of insulin in 1921, juvenile diabetes was a dreaded and deadly disease. Made available in late 1922, insulin, a means of controlling this more serious form of diabetes, must be injected by syringe on a daily basis. While not a cure, insulin has saved the lives of millions worldwide. Banting did not take out a patent on insulin but assigned the rights to the University of Toronto

Connaught Laboratories

Georges-Édouard Desbarats

BOTH the United States and Germany claim credit for being the first to reproduce photographs on a printing press. But Georges-Édouard Desbarats was doing so in Canada for roughly a decade before either of those countries introduced a similar process. And while the *New York Daily Graphic* can rightly claim that it, in 1880, was the first daily paper to print photographs, its publisher was the same Georges-É. Desbarats.

Pictures for the Press

Georges-Édouard was born into a family of distinguished printers who had settled in Canada in 1799 when his grandfather Pierre-Édouard left Pau, France, to become King's Printer at Quebec City.

Pierre's son succeeded him and Georges-Édouard, although admitted to the Quebec Bar at age 19, became the third generation in the family business. On succeeding his father, he continued to serve as Queen's printer until a major fire at his Ottawa plant in 1869 caused severe financial losses.

To recoup his loss, Georges launched his publishing career, establishing in Montreal the weekly *Canadian Illustrated News*, Canada's first national news magazine. In its introductory edition on October 30, 1869, he published a letterpress half-tone Notman photograph of Queen Victoria's son, Prince Arthur. This was eight years before the Jaffe Brothers of Vienna produced half-tone plates and nine years before Frederick Ives of the United States patented his half-tone letterpress in 1878.

Desbarats' half-tone process was actually developed by his engraver, William Leggo, who discovered a way to virtually re-photograph the picture through a fine screen which breaks the picture into thousands of dots of different sizes: the larger outline the shadows of the photograph and the smallest provide the highlights.

Desbarats printed 6,000 copies of this first edition, distributed it free of charge, inviting the public to subscribe to it for four dollars per year or ten cents per issue. He stressed the value of its illustrations, writing, "At least seven pages will be handsomely illustrated by the beautiful and wonderful process of Leggotype, which being in result the transformation of a photograph into a relief engraving by purely chemical appliances, ensures accuracy as well as beauty of effect."

Describing itself as a "weekly journal of Current Events, Literature, Science and Art, Agriculture and Mechanics, Fashion and Amusement," the 16-page paper sometimes published poems and stories, had a portrait gallery of outstanding personalities, and numerous pictures of the country's important commercial, religious, government, and educational buildings.

Its success prompted Desbarats in January 1870 to launch *L'Opinion publique*, a French language news journal. Consisting initially of eight pages, it had distinctive editorial content, but its photographs were mostly those that had already appeared in the *Canadian Illustrated News*. The first two editions were distributed free to 5,200 addresses with a notice that "All those not returning the paper will be considered subscribers" at a rate of $2.50 in Canada and $3 in the US. The sales technique was obviously successful as by 1871 the paper had grown from eight to sixteen pages and by 1874 had reached a circulation of 12,000.

In 1873 Desbarats and Leggo founded the *New York Daily Graphic*. By 1880 it had become the first daily paper to use their half-tone process. Later, Desbarats also published the *Dominion Illustrated*, *Canadian Patents Office Record*, and *Mechanics Magazine*.

Under various ownerships over the years, both the *Illustrated* and *L'Opinion* continued until the year of Desbarats' death in 1893, when, due to their elitism and deteriorating quality, they were shut down with the blunt explanation that not enough people were subscribing.

As the publisher who introduced illustrated journalism to the world and as the founder of several news magazines, Desbarats was truly a media pioneer. His intense energy revolutionized the entire publishing industry worldwide. *MVJ*

Publishers before Desbarats resorted to engravings, woodcuts and lithography to illustrate publications. This photograph of a lacrosse tournament team was reproduced in the inaugural edition of the Canadian Illustrated News. *Published by Desbarats, October 30, 1869, this important edition used for the very first time the technique of half-tone reproduction. It heralded the day when the photographer would replace the illustrator reporting news events in print publications*

QUÉBEC WOOD SCULPTURE

A Triple-Century Tradition

FROM the earliest settlement of Québec in the seventeenth century, the Roman Catholic Church was both the official church and an integral part of Québec's cultural life.

The Church had always preferred its premises to be both elaborate and ornate. Witness the grand cathedrals and churches of medieval and post-medieval Europe. The rationale, probably the same as that of modern-day law firms or financial houses wanting good and tasteful interior design, was the desire to create an atmosphere of respectability, prosperity, and prestige. The colonial churches, though perhaps not as opulent as those of Europe, were still as ornate as could be achieved by expatriate and native craftsmen. And, since the Church required builders, stonemasons, carpenters, joiners, carvers, sculptors, gilders, glassworkers, and silvermakers, the Roman Catholic church became the greatest single patron and employer of artisans and craftsmen.

In an age when all material goods were individually produced by skilled artisans, craftsmanship flourished. Whole families often pursued the same craft for many generations. Rigid apprenticeship — learning by doing — is a practice going back to the Middle Ages.

Wood sculpture was a highly specialized and respected craft. In Québec, the Church was by far the largest, and in some areas, the only employer for wood sculptors and carvers. By the 1670s, because woodworkers, generally, were in short supply, Bishop François de Laval brought a shipload of craftsmen from France in 1675 to teach and train apprentices in New France.

ABOVE The wooden crucifix has been sculpted in Québec ever since Bishop Laval brought a shipload of wood artisans from France to Quebec in 1675. This view shows a wood-sculpted, nineteenth century hearse cruicifx (Royal Ontario Museum, Canadiana Gallery)

Among the earliest of the woodworkers and sculptors to arrive in New France was Guillaume Jourdain, dit Labrosse (c. 1630-90), whose descendants were major figures in the craft for over a century. As well as providing sculpted crucifixes, madonnas, reliquary figures, and decorative carvings, the Labrosse family carved and panelled entire church interiors.

Another seventeenth century progenitor of a long line of master cabinetmakers and wood sculptors was Jean le Vasseur (or Levasseur) (1622-86), who arrived in Québec in 1660 and whose great-grandson Pierre-Noël was still active through the 1760s. The greatest of the Québec church carvers emerged after 1700. The rococo and baroque style introduced into France during the Louis XV period emphasized very elaborate and often asymmetrical carving and because it coincided with the increasing wealth of the church, this style survived in Québec churches into the 1830s, far longer than in France.

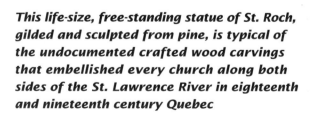

Although cabinetmakers and carvers depended on church commissions, they were also engaged in carving and ornamenting the interiors of private homes as well as crafting individual pieces of furniture.

One of the greatest of the eighteenth century woodworkers was sculptor and architect Jean Baillairgé (1726-1805), who founded a dynasty: his sons François (1759-1852) and Pierre (1761-1812) and his grandson Thomas (1791-1859) continued in the trade. Renowned for churches and church carvings, the Baillairgés are also known for crafting furniture in later English fashions.

Another of the greats was Louis Amable Quévillon (1749-1823). Quévillon, virtually a general contractor, with a large team of cabinet makers and carvers, was responsible for the complete interiors of many well-known churches, and for carved figures including the magnificent altar of Montréal's Église Notre-Dame.

This life-size, free-standing statue of St. Roch, gilded and sculpted from pine, is typical of the undocumented crafted wood carvings that embellished every church along both sides of the St. Lawrence River in eighteenth and nineteenth century Quebec

Attributed to Louis Amable Quévillon (1749-1823), this console table in carved pine can be dated to the last decade of the eighteenth century

Courtesy, Royal Ontario Museum, Canadiana Gallery

One of the last of the classical Quebec wood sculptors, Louis Jobin (1845-1928), specializing in large religious statues, especially angels, as viewed here, spent a lifetime serving a religious clientele

Royal Ontario Museum, Canadiana Gallery

Wood sculpture and many other crafts began slowly to decline by the 1830s. The Québec woodcarvers, as commercial craftsmen, had enjoyed a constant market for their skills as long as they were the only producers. Time was money, however, then as now. Individual craftsmanship was laborious, time-consuming, and expensive. With the coming of new techniques of mechanized mass-produced wood carving, moulded gesso, and cast decorative plasterwork — all much less expensive — the individual artisan was being forced out of the market.

Although church carving, with its strong, traditional base, continued for decades, it was increasingly restricted to larger free-standing pieces such as madonnas and large crucifixes not easily produced by the newer techniques. During the nineteenth century wood carving for church interiors and domestic furniture had all but disappeared.

As sons failed to follow fathers, the surviving carvers gained a greater share of a declining market. Fortunately, the craft itself held on and never really died out. In fact, the last of the great church carvers, Louis Jobin (b. 1845) worked until his death in 1928. Jobin is memorialized at such places as the basilica at Ste.-Anne de Beaupré where a number of his works grace the magnificent interior of this world-famous shrine.

In the mid-1930s Québec experienced a craft revival that continues to the present. The impetus was not the Church or wealthy individual patrons but collectors, a sympathetic tourist market, and a growing international interest. In fact, a few superb studio wood sculptors continue to be active. And although wood carving in Québec has not disappeared, the craft as a whole will never return to the high levels achieved in Québec by the great church carvers of the eighteenth and nineteenth centuries.

DBW

Because of upbeat demand, wood sculpture is still being produced in Québec. St.-Jean Port-Joli, the wood-carving capital of Québec, is located some 60 miles east of Québec City. As many as 60 different wood-carving families, led by Médard Bourgault and brothers, André and Jean-Julien, eked out a living in the 1950s. But the craft, as a whole, has never returned to the high levels achieved by the magnificent carvers of New France whose works still embellish and decorate so many interiors of the early parish churches still standing along the St. Lawrence River. Representing contemporary wood sculpting in Québec is this objet d'art by Benoi Deschênes of St.-Jean Port-Joli. Called Les Voyageurs, *it won "Best of the Show" in 1978 at the annual Woodcarving Exhibition sponsored by the Canadian National Exhibition. Carved in basswood and 48 inches long, it demonstrates the interests of modern-day wood carvers in Québec in that the subject matter no longer is restricted to religious iconography but rather reflects the secularization of the contemporary Québecois whose roots extend back to the days of Bishop Laval, Louis XV, even Samuel de Champlain....*

Courtesy, Benoi Deschênes

Superman, Tarzan, and Prince Valiant

WHEN "Superman" made his debut as a comic strip sensation in 1938, the newspaper employing reporter Clark Kent was *The Daily Star.* The fictional name was suggested by its first illustrator, Joe Shuster, because, as a paperboy, young Joe had delivered *The Toronto Daily Star.* By the time the newspaper was named *The Daily Planet* in 1940, "Superman" had become a super hit across North America.

Shuster, however, was not the first Canadian to illustrate a comic strip. A decade earlier, Harold R. Foster, a native of Halifax, Nova Scotia, working for a Detroit advertising agency, was hired to create realistic illustrations for the Tarzan stories of Edgar Rice Burroughs. His original ten-week trial is "the most reprinted, most imitated and most important Tarzan strip of all." But Foster is even better known and honoured for his work as author and illustrator of "Prince Valiant," which premiered one year before "Superman."

There is little similarity between the two illustrators who entertained millions of readers for more than half a century. Joe Shuster, a shy introvert with poor eyesight, was born into a family of limited means who had emigrated to Canada from Rotterdam. He often scrounged paper from local shops, being given, on one occasion, rolls of wallpaper left over from a neighbourhood job. "The backs were blank naturally. So it was a gold mine for me, and I went home with every roll I could carry," he recalled in a 1992 interview for *The Toronto Star*, a paper he had delivered in Toronto when only nine years old. A year later, in 1924, Joe moved to Cleveland with his parents and became a high-school classmate of

The Toronto Star

Comic strip creator Hal Foster was born in Halifax, raised in Winnipeg and became one of the most famous comic strip illustrators upon moving to the United States at age 28

DC Comics is the pioneer of the comic book industry and inventor of the Super-hero genre. Its Action Comics, *published since June 1938, was made successful by its Superman series. Joe Shuster, shown, right, a year before his death, illustrated Superman numbers 1,7,10,13,17,19-24,83,88,97. The younger image of Shuster (below) was taken shortly after he left Toronto for the United States*

The Toronto Star

Jerry Siegel, his later collaborator.

Hal Foster, born in 1892, the son of a seafaring family, was sailing a 30-foot sloop solo at age ten. When the family business failed in 1906, the Fosters moved to Winnipeg where young Hal, besides turning to boxing, enjoyed sketching, hunting, and fishing.

His ability to sketch landed him a job as a staff artist for a mail-order house until the depression of 1913. He then freelanced but, on marrying in 1915, moved to Ontario where he worked as a hunting guide. Foster added prospecting for gold to his skills, struck a "million dollar claim" at Rice Lake, Ontario, in 1917, and worked it for three years before the claim was jumped and passed out of his control.

Foster thought again about art but, with a wife and two children to support, decided he needed to improve his skills if he were to be successful. At age 28, he made a 1,000-mile bicycle trip to Chicago to enroll at the Art Institute. More courses followed at both the National Academy of Design and the Chicago Academy of Fine Arts before he landed a job with a Detroit advertising agency. In 1928 he was introduced to Tarzan author Edgar Rice Burroughs and was

The Toronto Star

Prince Valiant
IN THE DAYS OF KING ARTHUR
WRITTEN AND ILLUSTRATED BY HAROLD R FOSTER

Our Story: MERLIN AMBROSIUS, CALLED WIZARD BY SOME, A DEMON BY OTHERS. BUT LEGEND HAS IT THAT HIS FATHER WAS A DEMON, HIS MOTHER A SAINTLY WOMAN. HIS POWERS CAME FROM HIS SIRE BUT FROM HIS MOTHER CAME VIRTUE THAT WOULD NOT LET HIM USE THOSE POWERS FOR EVIL. SO IT WAS SAID IN THE OLD DAYS BEFORE EVER CAMELOT WAS BUILT.

commissioned to illustrate a venture new to a newspaper syndicate — a comic strip based on a serious adult adventure story.

The ten-week series drawn by Foster was a success but he had other commitments and gave up the comic strip to another illustrator. In 1931, however, he agreed to do the illustrations for the Sunday colour strip of "Tarzan" and he continued to do so until he stopped in 1937 to write and illustrate "Prince Valiant."

Joe Shuster and Jerry Siegel, meanwhile, were still struggling to make their mark with "Superman." After leaving high school, they eventually sold, in 1934, their first two stories to DC Comics. One was about a swashbuckling hero called Henry Duval; the other was about a magician, Dr. Occult. The former was illustrated on the back of Toronto wallpaper. The syndicate thought that the concept of Superman was just too far out, one owner claiming the idea "ridiculous." There were already comic strip heroes in costume — futuristic characters such as "Flash Gordon" and "Buck Rogers," but a costumed "man of steel" fighting battles on the planet Earth in the present century was beyond comprehension until Action Comics took a chance in June 1938.

The response was incredible! Within months the comic book featuring a Superman adventure was selling more than half a million copies. By 1939, *Superman* became a comic book in itself, and soon a daily comic strip. In 1940, the Mutual Radio Network began a tri-weekly 15-minute radio serial.

Shuster and Siegel's creation, however, was not a personal financial success for the two friends. After years of rejection, they finally sold the first 13 pages for a total of $130 or $10 a page, signing the customary release form that, unfortunately for them, relinquished all rights to the character. When they later protested, they were told they were "grossly exaggerating" the importance of "Superman" and that instead they should each put their energies into working "with zest and ambition to improve."

By 1941 Superman was appearing in 230 newspapers with an estimated circulation of 25 million. There were overseas translations and spin-off products as well that earned some $1.5 million dollars annually. The creators of "Superman" split $150,000 among themselves and a small staff of five artists working in one room in Cleveland! They won a partial court victory in 1947, sharing $100,000 for the newly created character, "Superboy," but were denied their claim to the ownership of "Superman" and were fired when the contract for the daily comic strip they were

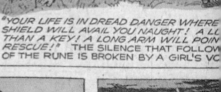

Tarzan

by EDGAR RICE BURROUGHS

RK TARZAN SPED
SYBIL'S FATE
ED APE

BUT AS HE APPROACHED HE WAS SURPRISED TO SEE SYBIL SAFE; AND THE APE WAS PEERING AT HIM ANXIOUSLY ACROSS THE WATER.

SUDDENLY THREE M

AS THE SEA-BEASTS PRESSED UPON HIM, TARZAN CAUGHT THE VINE AND BOHGDU JERKED HIM VIOLENTLY FROM THE JAWS OF DEATH.

D FOR THE
LACED A VINE
T TO HIM

producing ran out in 1948. By then, Shuster was no longer illustrating because of his failing eyesight.

By contrast, "Prince Valiant" enabled Foster to take trips to Europe where he carefully studied medieval history to re-create accurately the scenes for his strip which won kudos from historians and teachers alike. In 1946, Eagle Lion Pictures produced a full-length movie starring Robert Wagner. Foster also received awards from several groups including the National Cartoonists Society before he retired fully from the field in 1979. He died three years later at the age of 90.

Shuster and Siegel continued to struggle to gain recognition for their creative effort which continued to enrich DC Comics, but little happened until 1975 when a $20-million-dollar *Superman* movie was announced. There had been earlier Grade B movies, but this time Siegel wrote and distributed widely a nine-page press release to make Superman fans and comic industry leaders better aware of both his and Shuster's claim and plight. By then Siegel was working in a mailroom, and Shuster, legally blind, was living with a brother in a Los Angeles suburb.

A peace offering was made by the owners of "Superman." They gave the partners, in exchange for an end to the feud, an annual pension of $20,000 each as well as life-long medical coverage and a promise, in the event of their deaths, to take care of Siegel's wife and Shuster's brother. Their names were also re-instated on the comic strip.

Shuster died in 1993, a year after his interview with *The Toronto Star* and 52 years from the time of his last visit to the city of his birth where he was best man for still another Canadian achiever, his cousin Frank of Wayne and Shuster fame.

HE SAW THE FIRST SHARK
R YOU, HIS MADNESS VANISHED.
RIL SHOCKED HIM BACK TO HIS SENSES."

TARZAN SMILED AND ORDERED THE REMAININ FOOD TO BE DIVIDED BETWEEN THE GIRL AND THE APE. FOR HIMSELF HE ASKED NOTHING.

MVJ

Courtesy,
Estate of
Edgar Rice
Burroughs

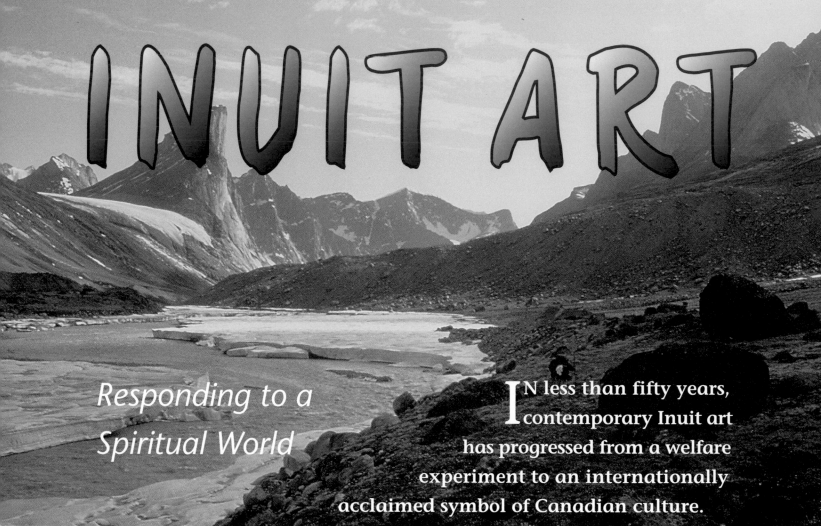

INUIT ART

Responding to a Spiritual World

IN less than fifty years, contemporary Inuit art has progressed from a welfare experiment to an internationally acclaimed symbol of Canadian culture.

1

Industry Canada

Canadian Inuit art has humble and surprisingly recent beginnings. The notion that it is the culmination of thousands of years of artistic development is somewhat of a myth. The prehistoric Dorset culture (500 B.C. - 1000 A.D.), which produced ruggedly expressionistic animal and human figures in ivory, bone, wood, and antler for magico-religious reasons, was probably wiped out by a wave of immigrants from Alaska around 1000 A.D. The art of this more recent Thule culture included some amulets and ritual carvings but concentrated more on the decorative embellishment of utilitarian objects.

The Thule are true ancestors of Canada's Inuit, but their culture was disrupted by the Little Ice Age of the sixteenth century and the simultaneous arrival of Europeans in the Arctic. Art produced from the late eighteenth to the mid-twentieth century (known as Historic Period art) was based on declining Thule traditions but quickly adapted itself to the tastes of Europeans — explorers, traders, whalers and missionaries. Primarily a souvenir art, it illustrated Arctic themes and subjects but

1. The Pangnirtung Pass, majestically passing through Auyuittuk National Park on Baffin Island, is guarded by soaring mountains revered for centuries as regenerative terrain by Canada's Inuit
2. John Tiktak's timeless stone figures and heads were shown in the first one-man public exhibition of Inuit art in 1970. "Man" (1965) illustrated here is now part of the national collection at Ottawa's Canadian Museum of Civilization

2.
Canadian Museum of Civilization
courtesy, the estate of John Tiktak

4.

Reproduced with permission,
West Baffin Eskimo Cooperative

also created miniature replicas of European items. Non-traditional objects such as cribbage boards and cigarette boxes, exquisitely fashioned in ivory, were eagerly traded for tobacco, guns, and other goods.

The birth of the Contemporary Period of Inuit art can be precisely dated to 1949 because of an historic exhibition and sale of Inuit art held at the Canadian Guild of Crafts in Montreal that year. James Houston, a young Toronto artist, had visited Arctic Quebec the previous summer and excitedly showed the Guild the carvings he had purchased. The Guild sponsored a buying trip for Houston. The hundreds of carvings he purchased sold out in three days! The Hudson's Bay Company, the Federal government, and the northern cooperative movement all encouraged art production across the Canadian Arctic. Initially the Federal government viewed art production as a means to supplement welfare payments to Inuit.

Carvings from the early 1950s were somewhat tentative and naive in conception, but changes occurred rapidly. Stone replaced ivory as the preferred material; consequently, sculptures grew in scale and complexity. Today, carvers work in a wide variety of stone types as well as in ivory, antler, and whalebone. Regional and community differences flourish, and

3.

Canadian Museum of Civilization
courtesy, the estate of Karoo Ashevak

3. From Taloyoak (Spence Bay), Karoo Ashevak's brilliant surrealistic whalebone compositions, such as "Whalebone Face," 1974, won international acclaim before his tragic death
4. Osuitok Ipeelee's elegantly sculpted caribou and birds have earned him the medal of the Royal Canadian Academy. "Kneeling Caribou," 1970, represents the best of Cape Dorset craftmanship and is part of the permanent collection of the Canadian Museum of Civilization

Jessie Oonark, from Baker Lake, sewed boldly coloured, hieratic images into wallhangings. "Untitled" was crafted 1973/74, and is hanging in the permanent collection of Ottawa's National Gallery

Arctic Quebec realism, Cape Dorset stylized naturalism, Keewatin abstraction, and Central Arctic expressionism have become stylistic "schools" of Inuit sculpture.

Drawing and printmaking (Southern art concepts first introduced in Cape Dorset in 1957) were quickly and masterfully adapted by Inuit artists. Graphic art programs spread to Povungnituk, Holman, Baker Lake and Pangnirtung. Pangnirtung also became famous for its woven tapestries, Baker Lake for its appliqué wall hangings.

As individual artists gained confidence and skill, many became stars in the Southern art world. John Tiktak's timeless stone figures and heads were shown in the first one-man public exhibition of Inuit art in 1970. Osuitok Ipeelee's elegantly sculpted caribou and birds have earned him the medal of the Royal Canadian Academy. Kenojuak Ashevak's celebrated print "Enchanted Owl," has become an icon of Inuit art. Jessie Oonark sewed her boldly coloured, hieratic images into wall hangings; others translated her drawings into prints. Karoo Ashevak's brilliant surrealistic whalebone compositions won him international acclaim in the four short years before his tragic death.

That such a small population (30,000), so thinly spread across the Canadian Arctic, has produced such a richly diverse art is a testament to the talent and ingenuity of Inuit. Within the constraints of a severe climate, chronic shortages of raw materials, economic forces beyond their control, and (until recently) primitive tools, Inuit artists have created works which are eagerly sought by collectors and public institutions in Canada and abroad. The production of art is not only a major economic force in the North but also has become a source of cultural identity and pride for the Inuit and Canadians as a whole. Both at home and abroad, Inuit sculptures and prints are probably more closely identified with Canada than even the paintings of the Group of Seven.

Perhaps no other art form can boast such wide popularity. The secret of Inuit art's success is its ability to strike a responsive chord in almost anyone from the museum curator or art collector to the average person looking for a souvenir or gift. There is something for everyone, in almost any price range. Inuit art is refreshingly straightforward in a world where much art is political, elitist, or difficult to appreciate in aesthetic terms.

Contemporary Inuit art is one of those happy accidents of history. Essentially an acculturated art form prompted by outsiders, Inuit art has nonetheless captured the essence of Inuit spirituality and strength. Inuit artists have immortalized their traditional culture through their work and in the process have preserved their culture and values for their grandchildren. But as their traditional customs and lifestyle become only memories, will Inuit artists be able to rely on nostalgic themes and subjects or will they explore new paths? The future of Inuit art is uncertain, but its achievements to date will be a source of pride for Inuit and Canadians for all time.

IH

NAC/PA/140297

Kenojuak Ashevak, from Cape Dorset, is recognized worldwide for her colourful prints, primarily of birds, characterized by a strong sense of composition, colour, design and draughtsmanship

Kenojuak Ashevak's hunting print, "Arrival of the Sun," 1962, is part of the permanent collection of the Canadian Museum of Civilization

Reproduced with permission, West Baffin Eskimo Cooperative

CANADIAN PACIFIC RAILWAY

1.

Canadian Pacific Limited

THE CANADIAN PACIFIC RAILWAY achieved the dream of a transcontinental Canada in 1885. Chugging up and down the ragged pre-Cambrian shield of Northern Ontario, slipping across 1,500 kilometres of Canada's western plains, and piercing British Columbia's rugged Cordillera, it linked the settled eastern cities with the Pacific.

The story of this world-famous line began earlier, in 1871, when British Columbia joined Canadian Confederation on the promise of a Pacific railway within ten years. Such a railway was chartered by Parliament at Ottawa in 1872. The next year, however, the "Pacific Scandal" revealed that the group that was granted the charter had supplied election funds to the then Conservative government of Sir John A. Macdonald. The company collapsed and Macdonald was driven from office. Thereafter the Liberals under Alexander Mackenzie, facing a world depression, tried to build the line as a public project but made scant headway, much to the discontent of British Columbia.

In 1878 Macdonald regained power and again espoused the Pacific railway this time as a private enterprise with public assistance. By 1881 a new syndicate had received the charter along with a grant of 25 million dollars and 25 million acres of land in addition to other benefits such as the 900 miles of track already built chiefly between the Lakehead and the prairies. This new CPR company was headed by George Stephen, president of the Bank of Montreal, and Donald Smith, financial tycoon of the Hudson's Bay Company. Its general manager was the hard-driving and efficient William Cornelius Van Horne, who in 1882 took on the enormous task of construction. At Callander, outside North Bay, Ontario, tracks came up from Ottawa and Montreal, and soon from Toronto as well. The workers blasted, hacked, and bridged the ancient rock north of Lake Superior, filling in

Linking Canada

deep muskeg, too. Costs rose steadily. On the prairies, track-laying from Winnipeg to Regina and Calgary leapt ahead. By 1884 the railroad was literally climbing the Rockies. At the same time, in Western British Columbia still other crews composed mainly of Chinese workers were thrusting east, building through steep canyons, tunnelling stubborn mountains, and sometimes being caught in murderous rock slides.

At last, in November 1885, work crews from east and west met in the Gold Range of the B.C. interior. Here at Craigellachie, in Eagle Pass, Donald Smith, now Lord Strathcona, drove in "the last

4. Courtesy, Irma Coucill

spike" as Van Horne, Chief Engineer Sandford Fleming, and all the construction gangs looked on. By mid-1886, regular trains were running through to the Pacific shores, thereby enabling Vancouver to emerge as the new West Coast terminus.

In years to follow, the CPR carried settlers and supplies into the west and far west Plains, took their products out to market, and prospered both on its land sales and mounting western traffic. In sum, this engineering triumph, with no rivals in all of North America, opened one of the most rewarding pathways in Canada's history.　　*JMSC*

Hudson's Bay Company

5.

2. *Following penetration of the formidable Canadian Rockies by the CPR in the early 1880s, and the eventual driving of "The Last Spike" at Craigellachie on November 7, 1885, commissioned and itinerate photographers travelling the line captured with their lenses the awesome landscape surrounding them everywhere. They reproduced and sold the best of their images in albums and stereoscopics. This particular view suggests not only the rugged terrain confronting railway engineers in the Selkirk Range, but exposes the raw beauty of a new land opened up by the railway. Taken by Charles McMunn in 1887, this dramatic image depicts Albert Canyon, part of the Illecillewaet River valley which the CPR struggled to follow. Note the two natives dwarfed by the jagged cliffs in the lower forefront*

When not blasting rock or shaping mountain inclines or building rock beds for railway ties, engineers were spanning canyons and river valleys with trestle bridges as illustrated in these three views depicting the CPR line: 1.crossing the Nipigon River by wooden trestle bridge in northern Ontario, and 3.and 4.spanning the Selkirks, east of Craigellachie in western British Columbia

5. *Donald A. Smith, First Baron Strathcona and Mount Royal, financed much of the construction of the CPR. He was given the honour of driving "The Last Spike" at Craigellachie, British Columbia, November 7,1885*

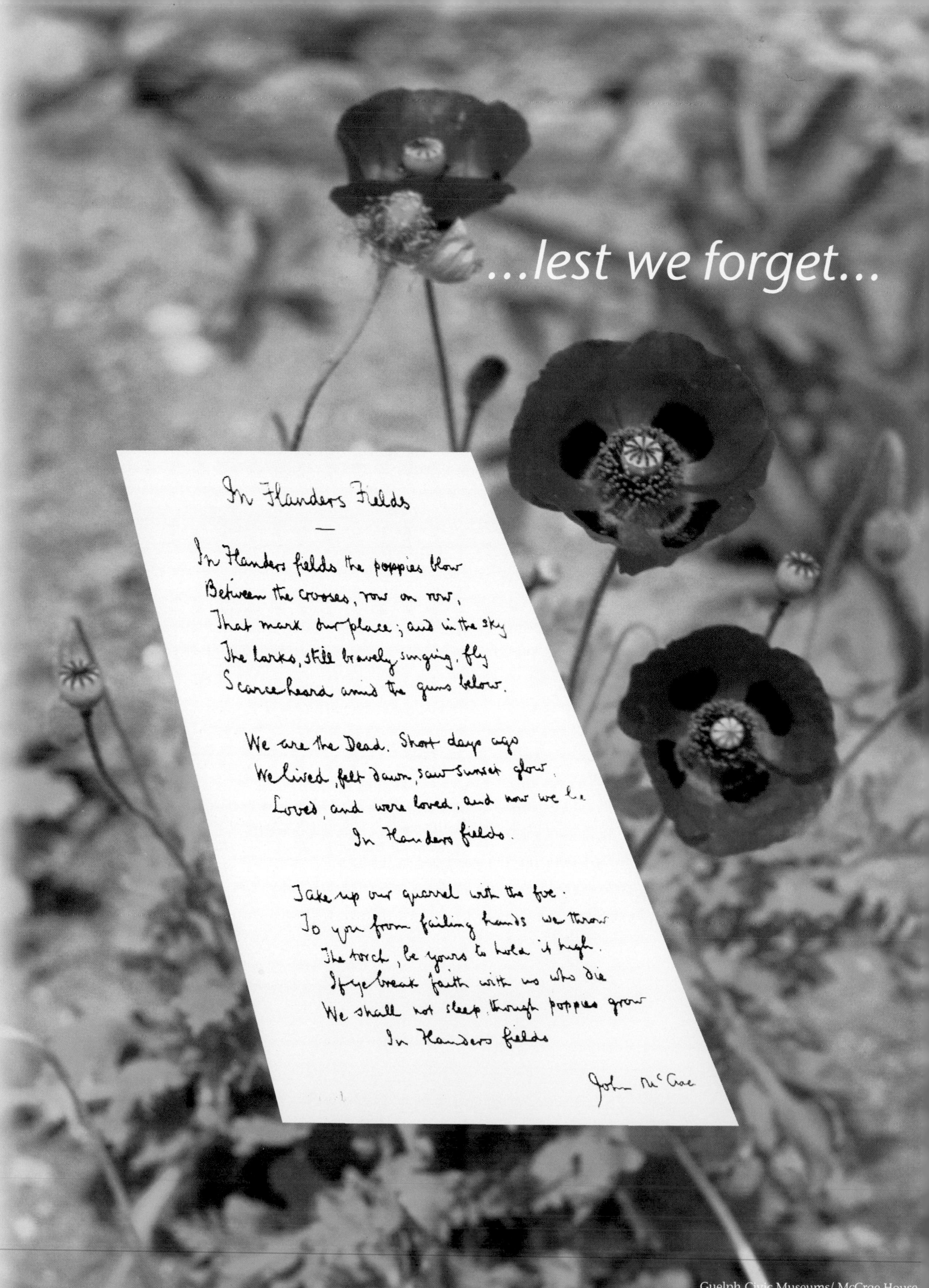

...lest we forget...
In Flanders Fields
In Flanders fields the poppies blow
Between the crosses, row on row,
That mark our place; and in the sky
The larks, still bravely singing, fly
Scarce heard amid the guns below.
We are the Dead. Short days ago
We lived, felt dawn, saw sunset glow,
Loved, and were loved, and now we lie
In Flanders fields.
Take up our quarrel with the foe:
To you from failing hands we throw
The torch; be yours to hold it high.
If ye break faith with us who die
We shall not sleep, though poppies grow
In Flanders fields
John McCrae

Guelph Civic Museums/ McCrae House

John McCrae

THE BEST-KNOWN and most widely read lyric of the English language, this century or any century, "In Flanders Fields" has immortalized the red poppy as the universal symbol for remembering soldiers who lost their lives in war.

First published in *Punch*, December 1915, this memorial poem was written by Dr. John McCrae, a man of high principles and strong spiritual values. Born at Guelph, Ontario, November 30, 1872, John McCrae attended medical school at the University of Toronto, receiving the Gold Medal for his Bachelor of Medicine Degree. Interning at Johns Hopkins, Maryland, he and his brother, Thomas McCrae, were close associates of Dr. William Osler and both were major contributors to Osler's ten-volume textbook, *Modern Medicine.*

Guelph Museums

Dr. McCrae, who had already served from 1899 to 1900 in the Boer War, was in his early 40s when World War I broke out. In spite of his reputation as a highly respected medical authority, leading pathologist, author, and teacher at McGill University, McCrae enlisted, stating, "I am rather afraid but more afraid to stay at home with my conscience."

Although his services as a surgeon were invaluable in the trenches, McCrae himself fought as an artilleryman and was subsequently gassed at Ypres, Belgium, in 1915.

As a diversion from the daily horrors, McCrae wrote letters to his mother and family members and composed poetry. His haunting poem, "In Flanders Fields," was composed the day after a grief-stricken McCrae witnessed a dear friend blown apart by an enemy shell.

A commissioned officer, Lt.-Col. John McCrae succumbed to meningeal-pneumonia in January 1918, days after being made senior consulting physician to the British Army. No other Canadian doctor had been so highly promoted. He was buried with full military honours not far from the fields of Flanders so poignantly immortalized in his poem. *ADC*

CPR Archives

Canada's First Renaissance Man

Standing next to Cornelius Van Horne (left) and behind Lord Strathcona striking "the last spike" is Sir Sandford Fleming who was "the greatest man who ever concerned himself with engineering"

AN extraordinarily gifted engineer, inventor, scientist, designer, and author, Sir Sandford Fleming was Canada's most creative polymath in the last quarter of the nineteenth and the early years of the twentieth century.

Fleming contributed in numerous ways to the development of Canada and it was he, more than any other person, who was responsible for the development and world adoption of the system of international standard time.

Born in Scotland on January 7, 1827, at Kirkcaldy, an industrial town and seaport on the north shore of the Firth of Forth, Fleming received his preliminary education and experience in technology and science there before coming to Canada in 1845. When he arrived, Canada was in its early stages of railway development. Intelligent, far-sighted leaders were urgently needed at the time to organize, build, and operate the railways and related systems needed for the economic, industrial, political and social development of Canada. Fleming who became one of Canada's primary railway builders, made the first practical suggestion for a Canadian railroad to the Pacific Ocean.

Early in his career he worked as an engineer for the Ontario, Simcoe and Huron Railway. By 1857 he had become the chief engineer of the Northern Railway which earlier had taken over the Ontario, Simcoe and Huron. In 1863 the Canadian government appointed him chief surveyor of the initial part of the proposed railway to link Quebec City with Halifax, Nova Scotia, and Saint John, New Brunswick. For this railway, known later as the Intercolonial, Fleming was Chief Engineer.

In the 1870s he became the engineer for the proposed construction of Canada's national railway from Montreal to Vancouver with special responsibility for the surveying of routes across the prairies

SANDFORD FLEMING

1827-1915

Sir Sandford Fleming was Chancellor of Queen's University for 35 years

and Rocky Mountains. He eventually recommended a route through Edmonton, Yellowhead Pass, and then south beside Burrard Inlet to the Pacific. While another route through Kicking Horse Pass was chosen when the main line of the Canadian Pacific Railway was built, the extensive surveying of various routes by Fleming and his staff was of great value in Canadian railway development. The Canadian Northern Railway was built early in the twentieth century along the northern route he had originally proposed for the Canadian Pacific.

But Sanford Fleming was much more than a railway builder. Increasingly, after 1881 when the Government of Canada entrusted the construction of the first North American transcontinental railway system to the Canadian Pacific Railway Company, Fleming devoted himself to the development of solutions to broader problems. In particular, he dedicated his efforts to the unification of time-reckoning systems throughout the world as well as to the installation of transoceanic cable systems.

Sir Sandford Fleming designed Canada's first postage stamp, the threepenny beaver, first issued in April 1851

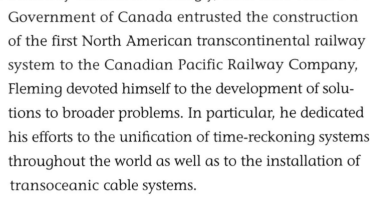

Through his involvement in the planning and development of Canadian railways, Fleming became acutely aware of the inadequacies of traditional means of establishing the correct time, especially because people began to travel longer distances in shorter periods of time. As railways were built, the owners devised their own particular solutions for dealing with problems created by time zones and they individually put them into place. A more comprehensive, all-embracing system was obviously needed. Therefore, in 1878 Fleming began publishing a series of papers for the Royal Canadian Institute of which he was a founder. In these papers he advocated his ideas for an international standard time system.

He proposed that there should be a prime median which would be the base geographical line from which all nations would measure time. His plan was based on twenty-four standard time zones for the entire earth with each zone covering 15 degrees in longitude. Within each time zone all clocks would be set to the same time. By 1883 all railways in North America had incorporated his innovative system. In 1884 Fleming convened an International Prime Meridian Conference in Washington, D.C., and succeeded in getting his proposal accepted. By the beginning of the twentieth century his concept of international standard time had been adopted throughout the civilized world.

Fleming's influence continued to be felt worldwide. Early in the twentieth century, Fleming's plans to link Canada and Australia by a trans-Pacific undersea communications cable were realized. He had struggled with this for a quarter of a century at financial cost to himself.

It was in Canada, however, that his influence was felt most directly. Fleming designed the first Canadian postage stamp, the threepenny beaver issued in 1851. So obviously superior to any other engineer, he actually held down no fewer than three of the biggest railway jobs in the country. In his prolific writings over the years he initiated and promoted ideas that were enormously influential in his adopted homeland.

In 1847 he completed a book on railway inventions. Another on the International Railway appeared in 1876. His volume, *Canada and British Imperial Cables*, was published in 1900.

This plaque once stood near Richmond St. E. and Bertie St. in downtown Toronto

For his many contributions to Canada and British traditions around the world, Fleming received a variety of honours including a knighthood. Perhaps the honour which brought him greatest satisfaction was his appointment as Chancellor of Queen's University in which position he served with distinction for 35 years. His genuine modesty is revealed in his diary entry: "This is the strangest thing in my life. What made them elect a man to the highest position, who has never been in his life at college?" He would doubtless also have been gratified when the new community college established in Peterborough, Ontario, in the late 1960s was named in his honour.

During his 70 years in Canada, Fleming, a vigorous explorer, had come to know it well. He crossed Canada by foot, snowshoe, dog team, canoe, wagon, raft, and dug-out log more than once. Canadians respected him highly; his reputation for integrity inspired all who knew him and many who have read of his life and work.

He was a world figure and benefactor, a friend to royalty and ordinary citizen alike. His personal friends included Rudyard Kipling and Cecil Rhodes. His death in Halifax on July 22, 1915 was mourned by many. A great Canadian achiever had come and gone. Sir Andrew Macphail, a man of letters at McGill University, said of Sir Sandford Fleming: "He was the greatest man who ever concerned himself with engineering .... His hands were clean, his eye was single, his heart was pure."

DMS

GILLES VILLENEUVE

1950-1982

Canadian Sporting Legend

"GILLES was the perfect racing driver ... with the best talent of all of us." This was the assessment of Niki Lauda whom Gilles replaced in 1977 as a member of the Ferrari team of Formula One drivers. He was referring to Gilles Villeneuve of Berthierville, Quebec, and this opinion was shared by many other Grand Prix drivers and veteran journalists who covered the sport.

Born January 18, 1950, Gilles is still idolized by race-car fans throughout the world. He was taught to drive by his father, and his love of cars and driving at high speeds was evident even in his teens. At 17, he bought a Mustang, replaced the engine, and entered drag racing. He also raced snowmobiles for two manufacturers over

Villeneuve's approach to racing was simple: drive as hard as you can all the time. "I have never got out of a car and said I could have tried harder," he maintained. Off the track, the slightly built, youthful-looking Gilles was unpretentious and casual

several winters, eventually winning both Quebec and Canadian championships.

Auto racing, however, was his first interest. In 1973 he enrolled in a driving course, obtained a licence to race, and was declared rookie of the year in the Quebec provincial Ford championships that same year. In 1974 he was asked to join the Ecurie Canada Formula Atlantic team and had to put up some money for vehicles. Gilles promptly sold his young family's mobile home and entered the Player's Challenge series. Midway through the season he broke his leg in a crash at Ontario's Mosport track but resumed racing five weeks later while still wearing a cast.

Skiroule, his snowmobile sponsor, agreed to help finance his Formula Atlantic cars in 1975 — the first year he competed against top European drivers. The following year Gilles had victories throughout the USA and Canada, winning both the Canadian and IMSA Formula Atlantic championships. His win at Trois Rivières so impressed some European drivers and media people that he was offered a contract to drive selected races with the European Marlboro McLaren team.

His first two races on that circuit were unimpressive and the option was dropped. Before the year was over, however, he won his second consecutive Atlantic Formula point title and signed a contract with Enzo Ferrari. He made his debut with the famed Italian automaker on October 19, 1977, at the Labatt Grand Prix at Mosport in a race in which 20 of the 25 cars starting the race failed to finish, Gilles among them. Two weeks later, in Japan, he was involved in a spectacular crash when his Ferrari ran into the right rear wheel of another car, soared skyward, and cartwheeled into the crowd. Two were killed and 25 injured, but he escaped unharmed.

The 1978 season was not much better. Gilles had three accidents and one DNF (did not finish) in his first five races. Some experts blamed the Ferrari vehicles which were not considered easy to handle or as efficient as the other competing vehicles, while others suggested Ferrari had erred in hiring an untried driver and openly speculated on who would replace him.

Ferrari, however, recognized the young French Canadian's determination and his driving skills against the world's top drivers. His faith paid off when

The Toronto Star

One of Canada's greatest international sporting heroes was Gilles Villeneuve. His racing exploits were better known in South America and Europe than in his homeland. A new racing star was born in 1994 when Jacques Villeneuve, only 10 years old when his famous father died, placed second at the world's premier racing event, the Indianapolis 500

Gilles won the last race of the year at Ile Notre Dame in Montreal. On that occasion Ferrari said, "Gilles represents a daring hope which has come true," while the winner simply told his home crowd, "This is the greatest day of my life."

His friendly and unpretentious attitude endeared him to the media and the public alike. Journalists marvelled at his daring and skill on the track but used words like polite, sincere, unassuming and likable to describe his character. "I found him unbelievably charming and friendly," wrote Peter Windsor of Britain. "He loved the physical act of driving, but beyond that he was a very sensitive and warm person who cared about people and was never rude to anyone."

In 1979, with a new teammate, Jody Scheckter, Gilles, early in the year, won races in South Africa, California, and Britain and in seven races recorded the fastest single lap time. His race against René Arnoux of France became one of the classic and breathtaking battles of all time as their vehicles clashed numerous times on the way to the finish line, Gilles winning second place 24/100ths of a second ahead of the much superior Renault vehicle. By year's end, he finished just four points behind his teammate, Scheckter, in the world point-scoring title.

Gilles renewed his contract, but the success of 1979 was not to be repeated in 1980 as it included three accidents and three DNF races. In 1981, with a new teammate, Didier Pironi of France, he won at Monaco and at the Spanish Grand Prix but finished well back in the total point standings mainly, many felt, because of the weight of the Ferrari vehicles that year. With a new car in 1982, he and Pironi were cruising to victory at Italy's Imola track in April when the Ferrari pit signalled them to go slow to conserve gas for the finish. Gilles complied but, on the final lap, Pironi suddenly darted past his teammate to win.

Gilles was stunned, and furious at Pironi's duplicity, vowing he would never speak to him again. He didn't, for 13 days later in a qualifying heat at the Zolder Track in Belgium, Gilles, driving furiously — to prove himself against his teammate, many believe — came over a hill and slammed into a slow-moving car heading for a pit stop. His own vehicle again cartwheeled, strewing wreckage for 200 metres along the track. That evening he died of his injuries.

At the funeral in Berthierville, former teammate, Jody Scheckter, delivered a simple but moving eulogy and prophecy. "I will miss Gilles for two reasons. First, he was the fastest driver in the history of motor racing. Second, he was the most genuine man I have ever known. But he has not gone. The memory of what he has done, what he has achieved, will always be there."

More than a decade later, Scheckter's prophecy remains true. There is still a huge demand for Villeneuve memorabilia at the race-track shops, and several books have been written about him. There is a bronze bust of him at the entrance to the Ferrari test track; a challenging corner at the Imola Track, site of the San Marino Grand Prix, is named Curva Gilles Villeneuve; a Canadian flag is painted on the spot where he started his last race. In Berthierville, a museum was opened in 1992 and a lifelike statue stands in a nearby park named in his honour. *MVJ*

Reginald Fessenden

1866 - 1932

A CANADIAN, Reginald Aubrey Fessenden was the first person to prove that voices and music could be heard over the air without wires. Yet some books ignore him, others mistakenly call him an American, and one Canadian encyclopedia cites his mother as the principal founder of Empire Day but overlooks her eldest son's accomplishments. Marconi, on the other hand, is given credit for radio even though his theory on sound waves was wrong and even though he was still sending only Morse code signals when Fessenden made his first "broadcast."

"...greater than Marconi..."

The reasons for the oversight are many. Although born in the Eastern Townships of Quebec in 1866, Fessenden left Canada at 18. He later worked for Edison, was a professor at two American universities, and was working with an American company when he proved his theories for broadcasting. In addition, lacking the showmanship of Marconi and Edison, Fessenden had difficulty marketing himself or his inventions.

A brilliant student at Trinity College School, Port Hope, at 14 he was granted a mathematics mastership to Bishop's College in Lennoxville, Quebec. This gave him a small income and a credit for a college year if he passed the exams. He did, but a growing interest in science caused him to tire of study of the classics, and thus at 18 he accepted a teaching position in Bermuda.

Two years later he was hired for Thomas Edison's machine shop where he so impressed his superiors that Edison invited him to work in the labs. At 24 he was chief chemist, but financial difficulties forced Edison to lay him off. He was hired almost at once by George Westinghouse, and two of his inventions helped Westinghouse fulfil his contract to light the 1892 Columbian Exposition in Chicago. Fessenden then became professor of electrical engineering at Purdue University, and a year later Westinghouse arranged that he become chief of electrical engineering at Western University of Pennsylvania and conduct research for him.

At the university, Fessenden explored his major interest, the study of Hercules sound waves. Marconi believed waves were generated by creating a spark that caused a whiplash effect, but Fessenden rejected this concept, theorizing correctly that sound waves continuously rippled outward — like water when a stone is dropped into it. Further experiments led him to suggest that, if the waves could be sent at a high frequency, it would be possible to hear only the "variations due to the human voice."

In 1900 he joined the US Weather Bureau on the understanding that the bureau could have access to any devices he invented but that he would retain ownership. This suited Fessenden perfectly. Within months he improved their Morse code systems for weather forecasting, and in his own experiments transmitted voice a mile away for the first time. In 1902, however, a Bureau superior demanded a share of his patents. Rather than submit, Fessenden complained to President Theodore Roosevelt, but his letter was returned to the Bureau and he was forced to resign.

A larger-than-life eccentric genius, Reginald Aubrey Fessenden, often arrogant and cutting, was also respected as a warm and loyal colleague

PAC/PA 93160

Seen with his staff outside Brant Rock Station, Fessenden, seated, was born in Quebec where he attended Bishop's University. He made the first public radio broadcast of music and voice on Christmas Eve, 1906

North Carolina Division of Archives and History

In 1906, Fessenden achieved 2-way voice transmission by radio between Machrihanish, Scotland, and Brant Rock Station, Massachusetts (Marconi had sent radio signals from England to Newfoundland in 1901, but only one-way and in Morse Code). In this view he is seen, right, in his laboratory at Brant Rock with operators Parmill and Wescoe

North Carolina Division of Archives and History

Two Pittsburg millionaires joined with him to form the National Electric Signaling Company (NESCO) to develop Morse code services between Brant Rock, Massachusetts, and several American points and to carry on his own research. In 1903 he sent a voice message to an assistant 50 miles distant, and another was heard at his experimental towers in Scotland. In 1904 he was also hired to help engineer the Niagara Falls power plant for the newly formed Ontario Power Commission, and in 1906 he opened his own Canadian company in Montreal.

His greatest achievement that year, however, occurred at 9 p.m., Christmas Eve, 1906, when wireless operators of several United Fruit Company ships in the Atlantic, tipped off to expect something unusual on their NESCO-provided sets, heard Fessenden transmit a recording of Handel's "Largo" on an Ediphone, play "Oh Holy Night" on the violin, and read from the Bible before wishing them a Merry Christmas.

Marconi's theory still prevailed, however, and even Fessenden's own backers were not interested in voice or music communication. The partnership began to sour, and this eventually led to the seizure of his patents as his sponsors believed they did not need him any more. Fessenden sued.

For the next two years he invented various gadgets in order to earn a living and to pay legal fees before joining the Submarine Signal Company in Boston. There he developed a wireless system for submarines to signal each other, and a device — to avoid another Titanic disaster — that could "bounce radio waves off icebergs miles away." Later he sent sound waves to the bottom of the ocean to accurately tell its depth. He was eventually to have some 500 patents to his credit.

At the outbreak of World War I, Fessenden volunteered his services to Canada, went to London, and developed a device to detect enemy artillery and another to locate enemy submarines. But the military bureaucracy was not interested in pursuing many of his ideas; therefore, he returned to Boston in 1915 and perfected his ocean depth device — he called it a fathometer — which gave him enough financial security to live comfortably and spend summers visiting friends and relatives in Canada.

The phenomenal interest in radio in the 1920s increased his demands for settlement of his lawsuit, and he finally gained recognition for his pioneer work. The Institute of Radio Engineers presented him with its Medal of Honour, and Philadelphia awarded him a medal and cash prize for "one whose labors had been of great benefit to mankind." Finally, in 1928, he won an out-of-court settlement for $500,000 for his patent lawsuit.

Fessenden, then 62 and with a heart condition, decided to return to Bermuda where he had met his wife, Helen, more than 40 years earlier. There, the man called by the head of General Electric Laboratories "the greatest wireless inventor of the age — greater than Marconi," died in January 1932, largely a forgotten man.

MVJ

LOUIS CYR was one of the strongest men who ever lived. His amazing feats of physical strength were comparable to those of Samson, the Israelite hero of ancient times.

Cyr's awesome strength first gained public attention in 1882 when, for a brief period, he was a policeman. On one particular occasion, after arresting three men he was forced to carry all of them to the local police station. He did so with one man under each arm and the third held securely between them. This was the beginning of his career as a strongman.

Louis Cyr was born on October 10, 1863 at St. Cyprien-de-Napierville, Quebec. His family moved to the United States and he worked as a lumberjack in New England before returning to Canada in 1882 to begin work as a policeman. Recognizing the commercial potential of his unusual strength, he resigned from the police force, opened a gymnasium and restaurant, and began giving demonstrations of his phenomenal strength.

Although Cyr was not unusually tall — only 5 feet 10 inches — in 1896 he weighed about 365 pounds. His chest measured 60.5 inches and his biceps 22 inches. These measurements and his astounding demonstrations of strength gained international attention. In the late nineteenth century, feats of strength were of great popular interest. Cyr soon became a living legend! At that time, public competitions were held before large crowds and Cyr, never defeated by his challengers, became the North American "weightlifting" champion in 1885.

In 1892 Cyr began a 26-month tour of Europe. While in London, England, he gave a demonstration before a packed hall. The Prince of Wales was front and centre as Cyr won the world's "weightlifting" championship and set seven astonishing records. That evening he lifted onto his back a platform holding eighteen men whose combined weight was 3,665 pounds. He also lifted from the ground to his shoulder, without bending his knees, a 374-pound barrel of cement. The Prince of Wales was so impressed with the performance that he sponsored the strong man's tour of England, Scotland, Ireland, Germany, and Italy.

On his return to Canada, Cyr proudly brought back with him one of the Marquess of Queensbury's horses after he had won a bet that he could hold two horses to a standstill, one tied to each of his massive arms.

Cyr was featured for five years with circuses such as Ringling Brothers and Barnum & Bailey. During his circus career he performed many phenomenal stunts such as lifting 552 pounds with one finger. In 1895 in Boston he lifted on his back a platform with 18 men weighing a total of 4,337 pounds. At the time, this feat was believed to be the heaviest weight ever lifted by one man.

Louis Cyr, the French-Canadian strongman and idol of his people in Quebec, died of Bright's disease on November 10, 1912 at St. Jean-de-Matha, Quebec. His celebrated feats of strength have been commemorated in Canada's Sports Hall of Fame. DMS

Modern-day Samson, Louis Cyr, was born in Quebec in 1863 and died there in 1912

LOUIS CYR.

JOHN ROBINSON'S
$25,000 CHALLENGE FEATURE,
LOUIS CYR

THE WONDER OF THE WORLD, THE CANADIAN GIANT,

THE STRONGEST MAN ON EARTH.

Europe and America Held Spell-Bound by His Miraculous Performances.
Now Appearing for the First Time with Any Circus.

ACTUALLY LIFTING THE TREMENDOUS WEIGHT OF 4,300 LBS.

Carrying on his Shoulders a Platform upon which 25 Men are Supported.
Picks Up With One Hand 987 Lbs.

LIFTS 552½ LBS. WITH HIS LITTLE FINGER.

LIFTING 4300 LBS

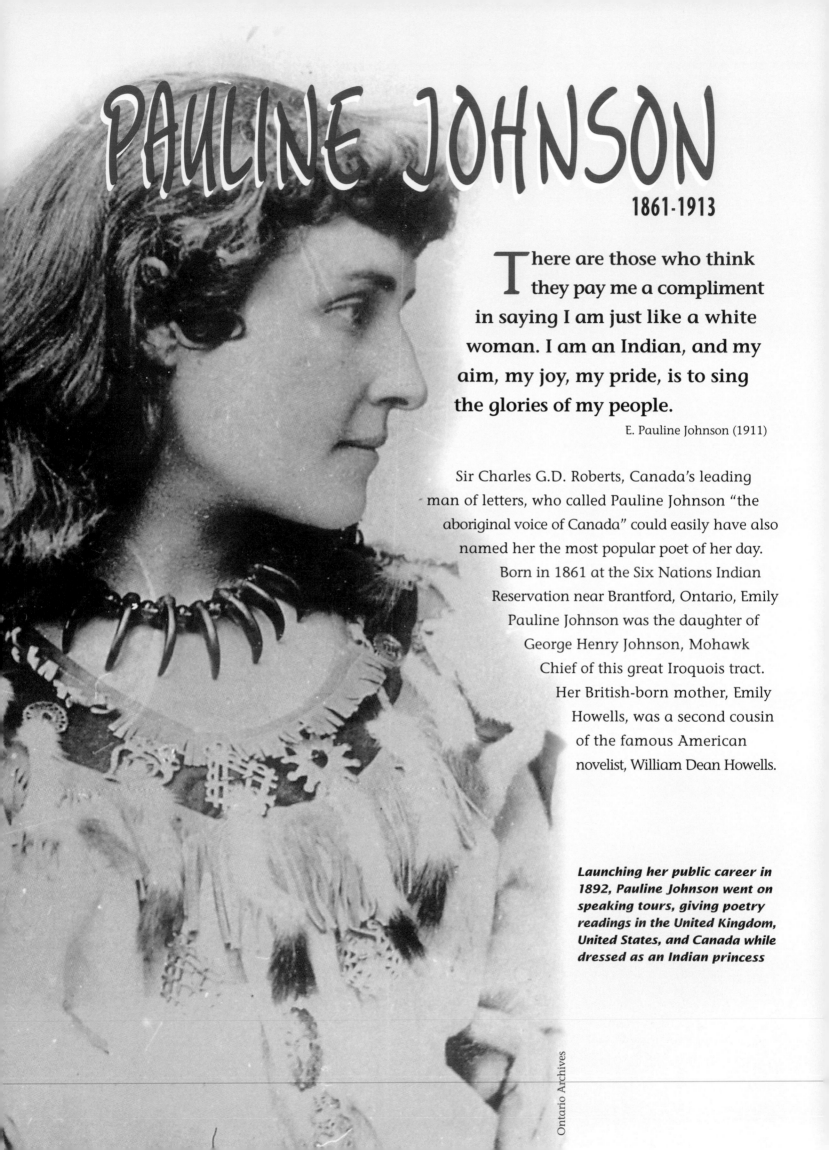

PAULINE JOHNSON

1861-1913

There are those who think they pay me a compliment in saying I am just like a white woman. I am an Indian, and my aim, my joy, my pride, is to sing the glories of my people.

E. Pauline Johnson (1911)

Sir Charles G.D. Roberts, Canada's leading man of letters, who called Pauline Johnson "the aboriginal voice of Canada" could easily have also named her the most popular poet of her day. Born in 1861 at the Six Nations Indian Reservation near Brantford, Ontario, Emily Pauline Johnson was the daughter of George Henry Johnson, Mohawk Chief of this great Iroquois tract. Her British-born mother, Emily Howells, was a second cousin of the famous American novelist, William Dean Howells.

Launching her public career in 1892, Pauline Johnson went on speaking tours, giving poetry readings in the United Kingdom, United States, and Canada while dressed as an Indian princess

Ontario Archives

Today, *Chiefswood*, the magnificent home of her birthplace is an historic landmark near Ohsweken, a village on the Six Nations Indian Reserve.

A cultured woman, Pauline Johnson was educated at the nearby Model School at Brantford. Early in life, recognizing most deeply the importance of her own Native ancestry, she adopted the Native name "Tekahionwake" or "Double Wampum."

Contributing poetry to periodicals at an early age, she launched her public career in 1892 to a sold-out audience at Toronto's Association Hall. Focusing on Native myth and legend, her poems generated ongoing public awareness of and a sensitive response to her people's Native heritage.

By 1895 Pauline Johnson had launched her first collected volume of verse. Called *White Wampum*, it was followed in 1903 by *Canadian Born*. Her most famous work, *Flint and Feather*, was published in 1912. Others followed, including *Legends of Vancouver* (1911) and a collection of short stories, *The Shagganappi* (1913).

While such works created for her a literary reputation throughout England and the United States as well as in Canada, this celebrated Mohawk poetess was just as famous for the dramatic readings of her poems. Audiences packed the halls to listen, hushed, to an unforgettable performance.

Poems such as "The Song My Paddle Sings" sensitively draw on the Indian past but are no less meaningful to any canoer familiar with the vast and silent beauty of Canada's lakes. Her writings, even today, by interlinking Native and non-Native feelings from coast to coast are expressions of Canadian nationalism. Although she grew up in Ontario, Pauline Johnson later moved to Vancouver. Following her untimely death there in 1913, at age 51, a memorial plaque was erected in Vancouver's Stanley Park as a memorial to a Mohawk poet whose heritage sings in her verses.

Pauline Johnson was a cultural ambassador, a link between an ancient, native Canada and a modern, largely European community. She knew and could represent both. Bringing two very different but strong-rooted cultures into closer contact and understanding, she was a powerful literary influence. JMSC

Dressed conventionally here, Pauline Johnson adapted Indian dress for her dramatic recitations which she began in 1892

BILLY BISHOP VC

Warrior Knight of the Air

1894-1956

BORN on February 8, 1894, William Avery Bishop attended schools in Owen Sound until 1911 when he enrolled in Canada's Royal Military College in Kingston, Ontario.

He was an active young man, known more for *joie de vivre* than for academic accomplishment. When he graduated from RMC in 1914, the overall assessment of Billy's RMC career was "conduct good."

He enlisted in the Mississauga Horse at the outbreak of war in 1914 and was posted to England with the 7th Canadian Mounted Rifles. Bishop saw his first aircraft while trying to extricate his horse from the mud of the Aldershot plain. Captivated by the concept of freedom of flight, and relative cleanliness, Billy decided to transfer from the cavalry to the Royal Flying Corps.

He was trained as an observer and did a full tour of duty in France with 21 Squadron of the Royal Flying Corps. Unfortunately, from his point of view, the Squadron was based in the northern part of France where, in 1916, there was little aerial fighting.

Toward the end of his observer tour he was injured in a landing accident. Because the injury to his knee became a problem again while he was on leave in England, he entered hospital for repairs and while there, initiated action to be trained as a pilot. In March 1917, he joined the RFC's 60 Squadron in France to fly Nieuport 17 Scout aircraft. He was soon promoted to Captain and took charge of "C" Flight.

Billy Bishop was extremely keen on flying and in relatively short order was given a "roving commission" that permitted him to fly his Nieuport serial number B1566 wherever and whenever he chose.

Colonel William A. Bishop, premier ace of the Royal Flying Corps in London, England, 1917

Robert Bradford is one of Canada's foremost aviation artists. **Dawn Attack,** *his rendition of Billy Bishop's Victoria Cross mission of 1917 shows Bishop in his Nieuport passing an Albatros D III of the German Air Force at the moment the Albatros "crashed into some trees near the aerodrome." The Albatros shown was the second of the three credited to Bishop during his daring and imaginative raid behind enemy lines. Bishop's aircraft is already damaged, presumably from rapid-firing airfield defence machine guns. This acrylic on canvas work was donated by the artist, Robert Bradford, to the Billy Bishop Heritage and was unveiled on June 25, 1987 at the Billy Bishop Museum in Owen Sound, Ontario*

Billy shot down three enemy aircraft over Vimy Ridge in April 1917 and won the Military Cross. His mechanic, Freddie Bourne, affixed a blue spinner to the propeller of B1566 and from that time Billy was feared on the German front as the "blue-nosed devil." In May he was awarded the Distinguished Service Order in recognition of his outstanding aerial efforts.

By the end of May he had scored 22 confirmed victories. On June 2, flying alone as usual, he attacked an airfield some 12 miles behind enemy lines. The event was unusual in that it was the first time an aircraft had been used in enemy territory to attack a force on the ground.

Four enemy Albatros aircraft rose in sequence to deal with Billy's raid. The first was shot down on the airfield; the second was attacked on its take-off roll and crashed into some trees; the third was pursued and shot down not far from the airfield while the fourth escaped despite the fact that Billy had fired a complete drum of ammunition into it.

In 1983 Canada's National Film Board presented a documentary entitled "The Kid Who Couldn't Miss." Disregarding Bishop's acclaimed record of confirmed victories, the film suggests that many of his successes were imaginary and further suggests that his celebrated dawn attack on the enemy airfield did not actually happen. In a misleading, simulated interview with Bishop's mechanic, the late Freddie Bourne, the film portrays Bourne as clearly doubting Bishop's claims. In fact, positive evidence exists that Bourne had no doubt at all concerning Bishop's exploits.

His dawn attack won Billy Bishop a Victoria Cross which was presented by King George V at Buckingham Palace, August 1917. In addition, Billy received the Military Cross and Distinguished Service Order awarded earlier. At the time, Bishop had 42 enemy aircraft to his credit. Late in August, with his score at 47 and with another DSO award, he was returned from France to England.

Billy Bishop was assigned as commander of an Aircraft Gunnery School being established at the time in England. However, since the new airfield was not yet completed, Billy returned to Canada on authorized leave and married Margaret Eaton Burden, a granddaughter of retailer Timothy Eaton. Bishop was then attached to the British Embassy in Washington, D.C., where he lobbied for an increase in U.S. aircraft and aircrew production.

Keen to get back into the air, Billy was transferred to England in January 1918 and given command of a newly forming squadron, No. 85. In France in June of 1918, he shot down a further 25 enemy aircraft and was awarded the Distinguished Flying Cross.

After World War I, Billy Bishop VC and Billy Barker VC formed Bishop-Barker Aeroplanes Limited. They operated HS2L flying boats between Lake Muskoka and Toronto Lakeshore. Eventually, Bishop returned to England to become involved with considerable success in several business ventures until the stock market crashed in 1929. Having lost his fortune, Billy returned to Canada to become director and vice president for sales of McColl-Frontenac Oil Company (later Texaco) in Montreal.

Appointed to Canada's Air Advisory Committee in the mid-30s, Bishop was part of the team responsible for development of the British Commonwealth Air Training Plan, preparing some 136,000 commonwealth aircrew in Canada for action over Europe and around the world during World War II.

Billy Bishop, left, and Billy Barker, born, Dauphin, Manitoba, standing in front of German-made D VII Fokker shortly after dissolution of Bishop-Barker Airplanes Ltd., the company established following World War I by the two Victoria Cross winners to photograph Canadian towns and villages from the sky

As director of recruiting for the Royal Canadian Air Force, Bishop travelled extensively, presenting wings or certificates to many graduating courses, and serving as a national inspiration.

Billy retired from business in the early 1950s having been bothered for some time with minor heart problems. He died in his sleep in Florida in September 1956, only 62 years old. In Toronto, following the largest Canadian funeral to that time, Billy's body was cremated and his ashes interred in Owen Sound's Greenwood Cemetery.

The late John Fisher ("Mr. Canada"), in one of his famous radio vignettes on remarkable Canadians, gave an example of how Billy Bishop had underlined Canada's influence in the first Air War. As commander of the fledgling Canadian Air Force in August 1918, Billy had a large red maple leaf painted on the tail of each of his aircraft to signify the national identity of his organization. "Mr. Canada" concluded his vignette by saying, "Thanks, Billy."

AJB

Paul Peel

Artist with Poetic Paintbrush

WHEN the Hungarian government needed money following its defeat in World War I, it sold a number of art treasures. Among them was a painting by a Canadian artist that is now a prize possession of the Art Gallery of Ontario. Titled "After the Bath," it was painted by Paul Peel, a native of London, Ontario.

Peel won third prize for it at the Paris Salon in 1890 and, in 1891, sold it to the Hungarian government for 8,000 francs despite more lucrative offers from well-known patrons of the arts because he wanted it hung in a public institution. French actress Sarah Bernhardt declared, "I would have been willing to pay any price for it because the little girl with the red top-knot reminded me so much of myself when I was little."

That is one of the reasons the painting became one of the most reproduced works in the world. As early as 1895, one critic wrote that "His work had the misfortune of being too popular, so that cheap reproductions of his rosy youngsters warming themselves after a bath ... have become quite common, and have been used as advertisements of soap, powder and the like."

Capitalizing on this were companies such as Seeman & Co. of Leipzig, Braun of Germany, the French firm of Florillo in cabinet card photographs and the Artotype Company in the United States. One photographer in New York even posed children the same way Peel had, photographed them, and sold the photograghs as "living pictures."

Paul and a sister, Mildred, four years his senior, were two of five children of John R. Peel, a marble cutter interested in the arts who came from England with his wife to London, Ontario, in 1856 and eventually opened a successful monument business in that city.

At an early age, Paul, the youngest, showed a remarkable talent. His father, who also taught art at the Old Mechanics Institute and held classes at the back of his shop, encouraged him. For two years

"After the Bath" brought Paul Peel international recognition when it was awarded a bronze medal in 1890 by the judges of La Société des Artistes Français, Paris. The following year it was purchased by the Hungarian government

Paul also studied under an English painter, William Lees Judson, who had settled in London before becoming founder and first dean of the College of Fine Arts in Los Angeles. By 1877 Paul, then 17, had won prizes at the city's Western Fall Fair and had been accepted as a student at the Pennsylvania Academy of Fine Arts in Philadelphia where he studied for three years.

Returning to Canada, he briefly set up a studio in Toronto but soon left for England and thence to France in 1881 where he first painted in Brittany and then moved to Paris to study under such eminent artists as Boulanger, Gerome, and Constant at the Ecole des Beaux-Arts and the Académie Julian.

National Gallery of Canada, Ottawa, #15184

"Self-portrait," 1892

Handsome with a well-trimmed Van Dyke, Peel was an accomplished fencer. His friendly, outgoing personality and fluency in French made him a popular member of France's artistic community that included many Canadians and Americans. In 1882 he married Isaure Verdier from Denmark, a student painter of miniatures, whom he met through his sister Mildred while she was visiting him in Brittany.

He kept in constant touch with his family, sending many of his paintings home. At the Western Fall Fair in 1883, he won six firsts but some complained that his father, as manager of the Fair's art exhibit, had rigged the jury panel — all local clergymen. That year he also had his first painting accepted by the Paris Salon.

Peel worked hard. Unlike many young artists, he managed, through the sale of his paintings, to support a wife and two children: Robert, born in 1884, and Marguerite, born in 1886. In 1889 he won an honourable mention at the Paris Salon for a child study, "The Modest Model," and the following year he painted his most famous work, "After the Bath," which established him as one of the truly outstanding painters of young children. That same year he sold a pastel study to Princess Alexandra of England.

As his mother was seriously ill, Peel returned to Canada in July 1890 to visit his family. He stayed until November painting various Canadian scenes from London to Quebec City. Before returning to Europe after the death of his mother, he held an exhibition and auction in Toronto of more than 60 of his paintings. Although many of the city's leading citizens attended, the sale of 57 of the paintings realized only a disappointing $2,746.

The single highest bid was $325 for "The Venetian Bather," which was then loaned to a Yonge Street barroom and may thereby have been the first nude on display in Toronto. It was purchased by the National Gallery five years later. An article at the time of the auction reported, "There was a great deal of curiosity and a large attendance at the sale but the pictures were sacrificed at ridiculous prices." It suggested that Peel would have been wiser to have auctioned them in Paris.

"Paul Peel in his Studio, Paris." **The unknown photographer captured the Canadian artist in 1889 surrounded by several of his best-known works including "Venetian Bather," left/centre, and "The Modest Model," right/centre, the latter winning honourable mention by the judges of the Paris Salon, 1889**

National Gallery of Canada, Ottawa

On his return to Paris, Peel worked on a number of new paintings that continued to reflect traditional academic techniques in studio settings as well as landscapes and portraits. They included another nude entitled "La Jeunesse," a portrait of his son, and "The Dancing Doll." A month before his 32nd birthday he suddenly became ill and died of a lung disorder.

In the years since his death, Peel's work has undergone criticisms and popularity. At the time of his death, the impressionist painters were sweeping aside the more traditional painters like Peel and, in the decade following the return of "After The Bath" to Canada in 1922, Canadians took greater interest in the fresh and dramatic paintings of the Group of Seven.

In 1970, however, Canadian interest in Peel was revived when 34 works and 12 reproductions were exhibited in Ontario at the London Public Library and Art Museum. Four years later a comprehensive study of Peel's work listed more than 200 of his paintings in galleries and private collections. And as Virginia Baker, author of a 1987 catalogue depicting more than 70 of his paintings for an exhibit at the London Regional Gallery and the Royal Ontario Museum, observes, "... he emerges, distanced from us by almost a century, as a painter of considerable authority who accomplished much during his brief professional life."

NORMAN BETHUNE

1890-1939

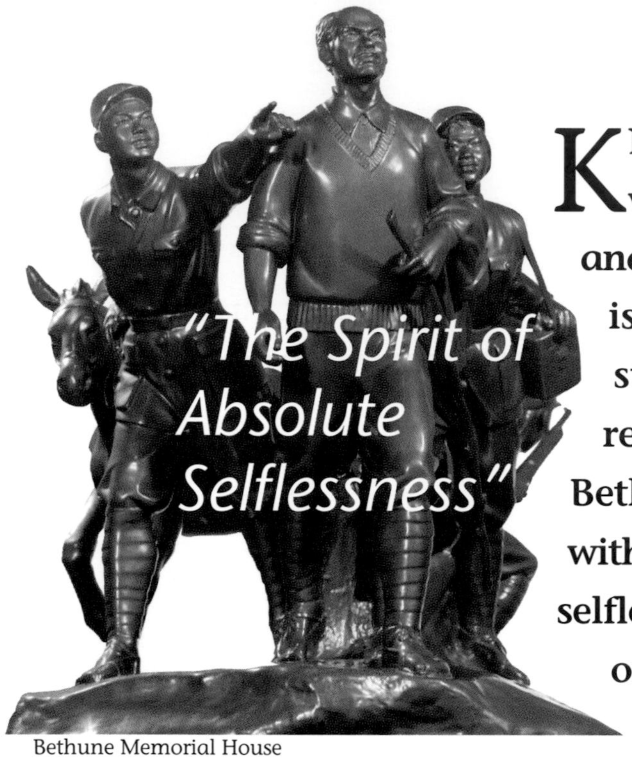

"The Spirit of Absolute Selflessness"

Bethune Memorial House

KNOWN widely as an innovative thoracic surgeon, a vigorous advocate of democratic medical services, and an international humanitarian, Norman Bethune is revered in China as a hero in the successful struggle for the establishment of its first united republic in 5,000 years. Mao Zedong, who received Bethune after his arrival in China early in 1939, wrote with great appreciation of Bethune's spirit of absolute selflessness as proven dramatically in his tragic death on the battlefront in northwestern China from blood poisoning on November 12, 1939. His spirit and Mao's tribute to his life and work became primary sources of inspiration in the new China.

Bethune's unique contributions in China were the culmination of his family's long tradition of dedication to altruistic human service and his personal experiences as a medical doctor in the First World War, the Spanish Civil War, and among the sick and destitute in both Canada and the United States. A descendant of French nonconformist Christians who emigrated from France to Scotland in the sixteenth century and to North America in the eighteenth century, he was born on March 3, 1890, into a deeply religious family in Gravenhurst, Ontario, the "Gateway to the Muskoka Lakes" a hundred miles north of Toronto. Curious, independent, and sometimes stubborn in his youth, he prepared for his medical career through study at the University of Toronto.

As a university student he began to demonstrate the compassion and commitment to helping less fortunate people that later became dominant features of his unorthodox but highly creative

As a martyr, Bethune is memorialized in China by a larger-than-life statue next to his tomb in Shih-chia Chuang, in northern China. Nearby is a pavilion, a museum, and the Norman Bethune International Peace Hospital. A different statue, depicted above, was presented as a gift to the people of Canada by a Chinese delegation attending the official opening of the Bethune Memorial House in Gravenhurst, Ontario, on August 30, 1976

Painting of Dr. Norman Bethune, presented by a delegation of 17 Chinese diplomats and officials attending the official opening of the Bethune House in Gravenhurst, Ontario, on August 30, 1976

medical work. He consciously delayed his university studies on two separate occasions. In 1911-12 he worked as a lumberjack and as a teacher at Frontier College, a unique Canadian adult education agency dedicated to meeting the educational needs of men labouring in lumber and mining camps and other remote locations. When Canada entered the First World War in August 1914, he enlisted immediately as a stretcher bearer.

Badly wounded by shrapnel at Ypres, he spent six months in hospitals, first in France and then in England, before being invalided home. On completing his university studies and qualifying for his medical degree, he re-enlisted and served as a surgeon in the British navy. During the last six months of the First World War, he was a medical officer with Canadian airmen in France.

After the war he completed his internship at the Hospital for Sick Children and the Fever Hospital in London, England, financing himself in a variety of enterprising ways including the buying and selling of art. Overcoming many distractions, he completed his internship and, in 1923, wrote and passed the difficult examination to qualify as a Fellow of the Royal College of Surgeons. A few months later, despite the resistance of her parents, he married Frances Campbell Penny, eleven years his junior. Theirs was a tempestuous and ultimately tragic marriage.

Bethune and his wife travelled through much of western Europe in 1924. He observed the work of leading surgeons in Paris, Vienna, and Berlin. By the end of that year they were settled, with little money, in a rented apartment in a busy but, unknown to them, somewhat disreputable section of Detroit, Michigan.

During the two years he and his wife lived in Detroit, they gained first-hand, personal knowledge of poverty, then affluence, and finally tragedy. Bethune's initial practice in Detroit put him in close daily contact with the less fortunate and their never-ending medical and financial problems. Increasingly, however, as his skill as a surgeon became known in Detroit, new patients came and paid handsomely, sometimes for what he regarded as trivial services. Gradually he began to appreciate the extent to which money was corrupting the medical system. He was greatly troubled by the unattended suffering among the poor. Then personal tragedy struck.

Tuberculosis had infected his left lung! After treatments in Detroit and at the Gravenhurst Sanatorium, he was sent in late 1926 to a sanatorium at Saranac Lake, New York. After reading an article on a surgical procedure for the treatment of tuberculosis of the lung, Bethune underwent this risky operation. Two months later, following careful examination, he was pronounced fit to leave.

For two years he worked at a tuberculosis hospital in Ray Brook, New York, and in 1929 began to specialize in thoracic surgery at the Royal Victoria Hospital, Montreal, and later at the Sacré Coeur Hospital in Cartierville, north of Montreal. More dedicated than ever to the practice of medicine, he wrote articles for medical journals setting out new surgical techniques and suggesting improvements based on his research.

In the late summer of 1935, Bethune participated in the International Physiological Congress in the Soviet Union. He returned to Canada convinced that democratic societies must be much more aggressive in their development of publicly financed medical care and health systems. Earlier he had set up a free clinic for the unemployed in Montreal. After his return, he organized "The Montreal Group for the Security of the People's Health." This group championed the idea that in democratic societies the primary duty of medical doctors must be to secure and to maintain the health of all citizens.

During this time Bethune continued to develop and refine surgical instruments. He invented or improved a dozen such instruments that soon were being used by thoracic surgeons throughout Canada and in other countries. The experience he gained in the development of new means for the delivery of medical services prepared him for an assignment he agreed to accept in Spain where civil war had broken out in mid-July 1936.

Soon after his arrival in Spain, Bethune organized and put into operation a pioneering mobile blood transfusion service in Madrid. Later he collected blood from donors in various cities and transported it wherever needed, along a front of over 600 miles.

"Spain," Bethune wrote later, "is a scar on my heart." He knew, however, that the blood transfusion method he had introduced in Spain had drastically reduced fatalities among the wounded, in some sectors as much as 75 percent. When he had accomplished all that he felt he could in Spain, he returned to Canada to undertake a cross-country speaking tour to raise money for the continuance of humanitarian efforts among the Spanish people.

His lectures stimulated a moral and financial response far beyond all expectations. His tour was barely under way, however, when the Japanese launched a new attack on China. A growing sense of urgency was noted in Bethune's speeches. He was aware, of course, that Japan had invaded Manchuria in 1931 and that earlier, throughout the nineteenth century, Western nations had contended for privileges and concessions within China. In addition, he knew that China had been grossly exploited during the Opium Wars. It was obvious that China needed help even more urgently than Spain.

Completing arrangements with the China Aid Council in New York, Bethune left Vancouver for China on January 2, 1938. Writing from Hong Kong he explained why he had come: "I refuse to condone, by passivity, or default, the wars which greedy men make against others. Spain and China are part of the same battle. I am going to China because I feel that is where I can be most useful."

When Mao received him, Bethune enquired concerning the number of mobile medical units then functioning with the Eighth Route Army. Learning that there were none and that many soldiers were dying because of the lack of facilities to treat them, Bethune emphasized the need to organize mobile medical services at once.

Early in May 1938, Bethune left Yenan for the mountain ranges in the

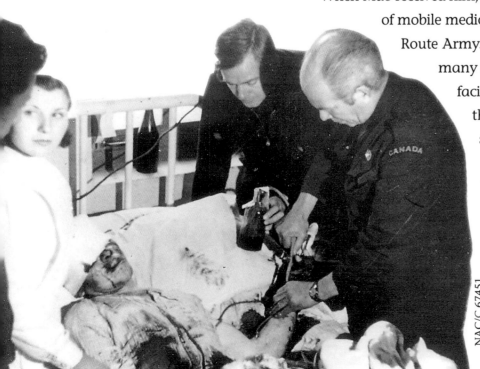

Dr. Norman Bethune, performing a blood transfusion during the Spanish Civil War (1936-1938), is assisted by Henning Sorensen and other hospital staff. Bethune's innovation created mobile blood banks enabling the wounded to be cared for on fields of action

NAC/C 67451

isolated border region about two hundred miles to the north. Fighting was extremely fierce and there were only a few qualified doctors to care for the 13 million people in the area. One of the most pressing needs was to train individuals to provide basic first aid and sanitation services and to carry out simple surgical procedures. Illustrated manuals were necessary. Modest hospitals were essential. Sick peasants as well as wounded soldiers required immediate attention. Bethune sought to deal with all of these matters.

Despite many problems, Bethune established over twenty teaching and nursing hospitals. None of the young doctors supervising these hospitals had received training in a modern hospital. Whenever it was necessary Bethune operated, sometimes at a prodigious rate. He once operated for sixty-nine hours continuously to attend to the urgent needs of 115 individuals.

Word was passed from mouth to mouth among those led by Mao Zedong of the amazing Canadian doctor who shared his clothes, his food, and even his blood with wounded soldiers and civilians.

Late in October 1939, while operating on a wounded soldier barehanded because there were no surgical gloves, Bethune accidentally cut his left hand with his scalpel. Immediately he plunged his hand into an iodine solution to disinfect the cut but continued operating. It wasn't the first time he had cut himself in an operation. He was sure this would heal, given careful attention. But the cut did not heal.

Despite their best efforts to drain the infection, it spread. His hand and then his arm became badly swollen. Amputation of his arm was suggested, but Bethune rejected the idea. He knew his death could not be long delayed. Blood poisoning had set in; his whole body was infected. In America and Europe there were drugs that might have saved him. But there were none in that remote, war-torn northwest corner of China.

Exhausted by his poisoned system, Bethune wrote — in Chinese — one final letter setting out his last will and testament. In it he requested that some money be provided by the Chinese Aid Council to his divorced wife. His responsibility to her, he wrote, "is undeniable." He also listed the basic pharmaceuticals his group needed. He concluded: "The last two years have been the most significant, the most meaningful years of my life.... I have found my highest fulfilment here among my beloved comrades."

Bethune died on November 12, 1939. His affection for, and devotion to his Chinese colleagues were fully reciprocated. Mao Zedong wrote *In Memory of Norman Bethune*. It became one of Mao's most famous essays. "Comrade Bethune and I met only once.... I am deeply grieved over his death. Now we are all commemorating him, which shows how profoundly his spirit inspires everyone. We must all learn the spirit of absolute selflessness from him. With his spirit everyone can be very useful to the people. A man's ability may be great or small, but if he has this spirit, he is already noble-minded and pure, a man of moral integrity and above vulgar interest, a man who is of value to the people."

Mao's short essay on Bethune later became required reading in China. Bethune's picture appeared on posters and postage stamps. Quotations of even a small portion of that essay were enough to identify him.

Dr. Norman Bethune's unceasing and inventive work as a surgeon, teacher, founder, and administrator of hospitals for Chinese people, whose cause he had made his own, established a lasting bond between his adopted people and this heroic, outstanding Canadian. DMS

中 华 人 民 共 和 国 文 化 部

加拿大传家宝出版公司：

　　欣闻贵公司即将出版的《传家宝》丛书的第四部《开拓者》收入了介绍白求恩大夫事迹的文章，我谨以此信祝贺该书的出版。

　　白求恩大夫是中国人民的老朋友，是一位高尚的国际主义和人道主义者。他为中国人民的解放事业作出了重要贡献，他的事迹在中国家喻户晓。他爱好和平、无私奉献的崇高品格永远值得中、加两国人民为之骄傲。

　　《开拓者》一书编入介绍白求恩大夫的文章，必将使更多的加拿大人得以了解白求恩大夫的事迹，也必将增进中、加两国人民的相互了解和友谊。为此，感谢所有为该书的出版作出努力的人们。

　　祝愿中、加两国人民友谊世代长存！

中华人民共和国文化部部长
一九九四年二月二十五日

The Chinese people remember Dr. Norman Bethune as an international humanitarian. Mao Zedong praised Bethune's "boundless sense of responsibility," recalling his sense of brotherhood as heroic. These sentiments are reflected in the thoughtful message of Liu Zhongde, Minister of Culture, the People's Republic of China

中 华 人 民 共 和 国 文 化 部
MINISTRY OF CULTURE
PEOPLE'S REPUBLIC OF CHINA

To Heirloom Publishing Inc. of Canada:

It is a pleasure for me to offer my congratulations on the publication of *PATHFINDERS: Canadian Tributes*, the fourth volume of the *Canada Heirloom Series*, which carries an article about Dr. Norman Bethune.
A revered internationalist and humanitarian, and an old friend of the Chinese people, Dr. Norman Bethune is known to almost every household in China for his important contributions to the liberation cause of the Chinese people. His love of peace and spirit of selflessness bespeak a loftiness of character which should inspire pride in Canadians and Chinese alike.

Featuring Dr. Norman Bethune in *PATHFINDERS: Canadian Tributes* will surely help more Canadians to learn of his good deeds, thus enhancing the mutual understanding and friendship between the two peoples of China and Canada. Therefore I wish to thank all who have lent their efforts leading to the publication of this special volume.

May the friendships between the peoples of China and Canada endure from generation to generation!

Liu Zhongde
Minister of Culture
People's Republic of China

Mohawk Sky Walkers

Walking on Air

CANADIAN Mohawks from the Caughnawaga Indian Reserve on the St. Lawrence near Montreal truly are skywalkers. These descendants of one of the main tribes of the historic Iroquois Confederacy took readily to working on aboveground high-steel construction, in particular on the giant skyscrapers that soared over New York City during the twentieth century. Theirs were careers of thrill and daring — and distinctive achievements by a native people still very much alive in Canada today.

The story of these Mohawks goes back to the days of New France. In 1667 Mohawk Christian converts moved north from their nation homelands in what is now upstate New York to the vicinity of Montreal. Under the auspices of French Catholic Jesuit priests, they settled at Caughnawaga ("By the Rapids") on the south shore of the St. Lawrence across from Lachine. This mission settlement flourished, for the Mohawks had originally been farmers. They had also been enterprising traders who, during peace years, easily moved north to south, from Montreal to Albany in English New York Province or helped protect the frontiers of New France in time of war. Later, however, after Britain, by 1763, had won the French empire in America the Caughnawaga Mohawks, always realists, came quickly to accept the all-British connection. In fact, they would go on to play a notable part in defending Canada from American attacks, especially at the Battle of Beaver Dams in the Niagara Peninsula of Upper Canada during the War of 1812.

Yet what led these Mohawk farmer-trader-fighters to become erectors of the steel frames for skyscrapers? Perhaps their aptitudes were suggested early when an English traveller, John Lawson, noted in 1714 that the Caughnawaga Mohawks crossed rushing streams "on the smallest of poles" or ran sure-footed "along the ridge of barn or house." More significant, by the later nineteenth century, was the coming of the age of iron and steel to Montreal and the St. Lawrence, particularly in the form of great bridges being built across the river. In 1886, for instance, when a big new railway bridge was being erected above the rapids between Caughnawaga and Lachine, Mohawk children were seen scrambling over it while fearless youths and men found employment in shifting, linking, and bolting great beams high in the air.

Hitherto, seamen had been primarily engaged on lofty bridge construction. But the Caughnawaga Mohawks showed such sure and fearless efficiency that their reputation as high-steel specialists spread far and wide. Soon they were enticed to New York City where tall buildings were about to rise above the jam-packed streets of a booming, central Manhattan.

Mohawks sought well-paid jobs in this high-steel work, often settling into cheap flats in Brooklyn within good reach of employment in Manhattan. One needs to keep in mind that these Caughnawagas operated in small, cousinly tribal crews, spoke fluent English, were prepared to live in downtown conditions, and did not mind commuting by subway. When their gruelling steel years inevitably ended, most would then retire to the Caughnawaga Reserve and its traditional family ties — having seen more of big-city living than a lot of Canadian small-town dwellers who thought they knew all about "native" ways.

Furthermore, through decades of construction centred mainly in New York, these First Canadians shared in creating many far-famed structures. Among these were the Woolworth Building which, when completed in 1915, was the world's tallest in its own day; its still more celebrated successor, the Empire State Building of the 1930s; the splendid RCA Tower in Rockefeller Plaza, New York; the sumptuous Waldorf Astoria Hotel; the grand United Nations Assembly Building of the 1950s. The list could go on and on. Overall, however, these testify to the remarkable accomplishments of the Caughnawaga high-steel men who functioned in small, deft units, where each man knew and fully trusted his comrades and where the safety of all, on wind-blown beams 50 stories up, depended on each individual. There is surely something to be said here for the strength and value of age-old tribal bonds.   JMSC

Rockefeller Center,© Rockefeller Group, Inc.1994

Mohawks from the Caughnawaga Indian Reserve, south of Montreal, have assisted in erecting many buildings across North America. This view depicts two skywalkers on narrow beams high above Manhattan. They are part of a Mohawk crew that helped build the Rockefeller Center's French Building. In the background is New York's famous former RCA Building, now named the GE Building, which they also assisted in erecting

OPPOSITE
In the 1930s, Mohawks helped build the Empire State Building. In 1951 the fearless skywalkers from Canada added the 222-foot communications tower to the same building

⊞ The Hospital

For the Love of Children

ON March 23, 1875, a group of dedicated Christian women led by Elizabeth McMaster opened a small hospital for sick children in an 11-room house in a central but poor section of Toronto. Ten days later Maggie, a three-year-old child who had been terribly scalded in an accident in her nearby home, was carried, bundled up in a coat, by her ten-year-old sister to the front door of the new hospital. A kindly lady in a long dress and starched white apron opened the door to admit Maggie, the first patient of the Hospital for Sick Children (HSC).

Those who cared for Maggie were determined to ensure that she would receive the medical treatment necessary to restore her to full health and strength. Facilities were severely limited and the building had a leaky roof and several broken windows. But, it was well located on a small portion of the present site of the Toronto General Hospital. The rent was $320 a year!

The dedication and sensitive work of founder Elizabeth McMaster and her friends and supporters made possible the establishment and development of the hospital in the early days. Their efforts and those of their successors, particularly the medical, nursing, and support staffs, to provide the highest quality of medical treatment for children, are the primary sources of its continuing power and strength. Equally vital are the knowledge, skill, and compassion of its medical specialists.

The first club foot operation at HSC on a child over two years old was

For Sick Children

performed in 1886. Gradually, so many crippled children were brought to HSC for this operation that it was necessary to set up an orthopaedic department in 1898. By 1901 correction of body deformities had become a leading specialty at the hospital. The head of orthopaedics, Dr. Clarence Starr, became one of the world's leading orthopaedic surgeons and teachers. A long line of equally brilliant surgeons followed, including Dr. Robert Salter whose arrival in 1955 led to a new era in orthopaedics. His operation to correct the dislocated hips of infants is widely acclaimed. The outstanding success achieved in orthopaedics at HSC is only one example of the brilliant accomplishments of members of the various medical departments at HSC.

The list of specialists who have made and are making HSC known and respected is long and impressive. Among them are Dr. John Keith, the cardiologist; Joe Bower, the Superintendent; Harry Balmford, who "manufactured" iron lungs during the polio epidemic in the late 1950s; Dr. Stewart Thomson, who introduced into Canada the new treatment for club feet in infants; Dr. D.E. Robertson who, in 1940, performed the first "blue baby" operation at HSC to correct "a hole in the heart"; Dr. William T. Mustard, Dr. Laurie Chute, and Dr. William Keith who, in 1951, developed a heart-lung machine.

Dr. Mustard first used the heart-lung machine in 1963 to bypass the heart and circulate and oxygenize blood during heart surgery. The "Mustard Operation" revolutionized heart surgery: it became standard

Built for $100,000.00 and officially opened in 1892 by its instigator, Mrs. Elizabeth McMaster, the great building at Toronto's College and Elizabeth Streets was the Hospital for Sick Children until 1951

procedure at HSC and was later used with great success in the Great Ormond Street Hospital in London, England.

In 1966 Dr. J. Simpson and his team separated the first set of Siamese twins at HSC. One survived. In 1971 a second set underwent the operation with both surviving.

Those to whom specific reference has been made include only a small, albeit a highly significant, group from the large company of devoted and highly gifted men and women who have contributed and are contributing to the high esteem in which HSC is held around the world.

When HSC was established, there was only one major children's hospital in the world — that on Great Ormond Street in London. Since then, many hospitals devoted to the needs of children have been established. But wherever and whenever medical specialists meet, there is knowledge of the work of members of HSC in the treatment of children's diseases.

Specialists at HSC have earned international renown through their research and innovative procedures. The reputation HSC has gained is based, however, not just on the skill of such individuals and the groups in which they work. As a teaching hospital, HSC has a long tradition of service to the Canadian medical profession and the many communities dependent on it.

In 1901 HSC established the first "in hospital" plant for the pasteurization of milk in Toronto to which parents could come to purchase milk for their babies at cost. Pablum and Sunwheat biscuits were developed at HSC. For children hospitalized for long-term treatment, programs for visiting school teachers were arranged so that the children might continue their education. A team of visiting nurses was established to monitor, when needed, the health of patients on their return home. An out-patient department gradually expanded to include a large number of special out-patient services.

The original 2-to 14-year age limit for children admitted for treatment was gradually extended to include newborn children and young people up to 18 years of age.

H THE HOSPITAL FOR S

With more and more children coming from increasingly distant places, there was need for a special service to ensure that parents who could not come to Toronto were advised concerning the health of their children. In 1930 the Parents Personal Service was inaugurated with Nurse Alice Boxhill in charge. Her loving concern for parents of children in HSC was greatly appreciated by those who received letters and photographs of their children while they were in hospital.

In 1950 Dr. A.L. Chute, then physician-in-chief, suggested to his wife, Dr. Helen Reid, that she organize a group to raise funds for the further development of the hospital's library. Dr. Reid's group secured the necessary funds and thus contributed to the improvement of the library's resources which subsequently became quite extensive. The group that Dr. Reid brought together became the nucleus of the HSC Women's Auxiliary. Its members now serve in virtually every department of the hospital and the auxiliary is regarded as indispensable in the effective operations of the hospital.

One of the services staffed by the Women's Auxiliary is the Parents Postoperative Information Service which provides, to parents and family anxiously waiting for reports from the doctors, information on the progress of children undergoing surgery and/or special tests.

A major source of the hospital's strength and of its capacity for development is the financial support it receives from a wide variety of individuals and organizations. The first recorded donation was "some English coins" — about ten dollars in Canadian money. Among early benefactors, one of the most generous was John Ross Robertson, founder and publisher of *The Evening Telegram*, one of Toronto's leading newspapers for many years. He became Chairman of the Board of Trustees in 1891 and served in that capacity for 27 years. During his chairmanship, financial support for the hospital was secured from many prominent individuals and organizations in Toronto. Before he died in 1918, Robertson had provided in his will that revenue from the major

A second new building, again constructed specifically for HSC, was opened at Gerrard Street and University Avenue, not far from the earlier site. This new facility had nearly doubled the accommodation of the earlier building

K CHILDREN

Hospital for Sick Children

portion of his estate be paid to the hospital provided that it continued to be independent and was "maintained and kept exclusively as a Hospital for Sick Children, and for no other purpose...."

John Ross Robertson's altruism encouraged others to make similar contributions. One of these was J.P. Bickell, a mining executive, whose charitable foundation has provided continuing support.

After Robertson became Chairman, the women who had worked with Elizabeth McMaster in the founding of HSC turned their attention to the development of a home for children for whom the doctors could do little. First called The Home For Incurable Children, it later became the Bloorview Children's Hospital.

As HSC developed, it was regularly in need of better facilities and more space. In

The healing, renewal, and prevention achieved day by day through the work of members of the hospital more than fulfil the hopes and practical aspirations of its founder, Elizabeth McMaster

1892 an entirely new building at the corner of Elizabeth and College Streets, designed specifically for the Hospital, was opened. It became the home of HSC for 60 years. For over half of that time, from 1919 until 1951, Dr. Alan Brown served as physician-in-chief. During his time the hospital survived attempts to phase it out. He and his colleagues at HSC were resolutely committed to its continuance as an independent hospital of the highest quality devoted exclusively to the care and treatment of sick children and to the training of medical and nursing specialists who would devote themselves to that objective.

In 1951, not far from where Mary Pickford of Hollywood fame grew up, a second new building, again constructed specifically for HSC, was opened at Gerrard Street and University Avenue, not far from the earlier site. This new facility had nearly doubled the accommodation of the earlier building. In the early 1990s about 500 rooms were staffed and in service. Over 15,000 patients were being treated annually. They were coming from more than 30 countries by car, train, and aeroplane.

Improvements to the hospital's building in the early 1990s have made it one of the world's most attractive and efficient centres for the treatment of the illnesses of children and for research into the diseases that afflict them. The healing, renewal, and prevention achieved day by day through the work of members of the hospital more than fulfil the hopes and practical aspirations of its founder, Elizabeth McMaster, and those pathfinders who worked with her. Their idealism, compassion, and intelligent attention to the medical needs of children continue to animate the hospital to which they gave birth.

DMS

Dr. Alan Brown served as Physician-in-Chief at The Hospital for Sick Children from 1919 to 1951

The Toronto Star

Frederick Tisdall & Pablum

Saving the Children

THE name Frederick F. Tisdall is not a household word in Canada but the product he was most responsible for developing over 60 years ago still strikes a responsive chord with millions of people around the world. That's because they either ate it as an infant or fed it to their offspring. It is Pablum, the cereal that saved thousands of children from death and disease and helped build one of today's outstanding children's research facilities at Toronto's Hospital for Sick Children.

The genesis of Tisdall's career as the developer of Pablum can be traced to the appointment of Dr. Alan Brown of Toronto as physician-in-chief of the Hospital for Sick Children (HSC) in 1919. Brown, a graduate of the University of Toronto Medical School, on returning to Toronto from post graduate studies in Europe in 1914, promised that he would reduce infant deaths by 50 percent. Upon his appointment five years later, he hired a number of bright young medical people to accomplish his goal.

Tisdall was one of them. Born in 1893 in Clinton, Ontario, he had won the silver medal in medicine at the University of Toronto in 1915, the same year classmate Frederick Banting won the gold. He was joined by still another young doctor, T.G.H. (Theo) Drake, of Webbwood, Ontario, who, like Tisdall, was an army medical corps veteran of World War I. They had, following the war, done post-graduate work at Johns Hopkins and Harvard Universities, respectively, and were anxious to carry out research on childhood diseases.

In 1921 Tisdall's first papers on deficiency diseases such as rickets and tetany were published and his desire to find nutritional methods not only to cure but also to prevent such diseases increased. In 1929 he was named director of the hospital's nutritional research laboratories and early in 1930 announced the first major product based on experiments carried out by him and his colleagues, Drs. Alan Brown, T.G.H. Drake, Pearl Summerfeldt, Gladys Boyd, and Elizabeth Chant Robertson, all of

*Dr. Frederick Tisdall was named director of the nutritional research laboratories at Toronto's Hospital for Sick Children in 1929. By 1931 Tisdall and his team at the world-famous hospital had formulated **Pablum**, an infant cereal that not only supplied energy but also furnished the necessary minerals and five of the six known vitamins*

Some co-discoverers of Pablum, *left to right, were Dr. Frederick Tisdall, Dr. Pearl Summerfeldt, Dr. T.G.H. Drake, and technician Ruth Herbert*

whom experimented with rats housed on the roof of the hospital.

The product was a biscuit called Sunwheat that Tisdall described as containing whole wheat, wheat germ, milk, butter, yeast, bone meal, iron, and copper. It was baked under conditions that conserved its vitamin content which included A, B1 and B2, D, and E.

Known as McCormick's Sun Wheat Biscuit, it was sold for 52 years with the royalties being given to the Toronto Paediatric Foundation which was established by Tisdall to provide further research funds for the hospital.

Six months later Dr. Tisdall, collaborating with Drs. Brown and Drake, submitted a second paper about an even more important food product that was later given the name Pablum.

While admitting that little was known about the exact requirement of vitamins for humans of any age, the new paper observed that most cereal products were consumed primarily for their energy-producing value but were deficient in many minerals and virtually all vitamins. It suggested that many infants and children receive diets containing an insufficient amount of some of the necessary minerals and vitamins. It then announced that "an infant breakfast cereal mixture had been devised which, in addition to supplying energy, furnishes the necessary minerals and five of the six known vitamins in appreciable amounts."

The five vitamins — A, B1 and B2, D, and E — were produced from a mixture of wheat, oats, corn, and bone meal plus wheat germ, dried brewer's yeast, and alfalfa. This was all ground, mixed, and dried at a temperature of 70 °c. for 30 minutes so that "the mixture will keep indefinitely."

Tisdall, who also took on the marketing job, was on his way to Chicago with Drake to see a major cereal producer when he met some friends from Mead Johnson who suggested their firm should sell it. Further experiments in pre-cooking the cereal reduced the cooking time from half an hour to seconds, and in 1931, the cereal was launched in Canada and the United States as Mead's Cereal. Drake later suggested the name Pablum from the Latin word *pabulum*, meaning food. Tisdall also arranged to have Faxo manufacture and market it in the United Kingdom.

For the 25 years that the patent was in effect, Pablum was spoon-fed to infants and royalties were fed to the Paediatric Foundation established earlier. Meanwhile, Tisdall and Drake introduced the "sunshine" vitamin D into bread flour, and in 1934, Dr. Drake announced in a medical paper that he, Tisdall, and Brown had eliminated the need for daily doses of cod liver oil by adding Vitamin D in milk.

On becoming chairman of the Committee on Nutrition for the Canadian Medical Association in the 1930s, Tisdall prompted the life insurance companies of Canada to sponsor the publication of millions of copies of booklets on healthy foods. Later he published his own book, *The Home Care of The Infant and Child*, which was praised by doctors in both Canada and the United States. One Boston practitioner wrote, "I think it is a very good book and of the type I would expect Tisdall to write."

Wartime saw him back in uniform, first as advisor on nutrition for the Department of National Defence, and then as group captain in the RCAF serving in both Canada and Britain. He established the nutritional content of Red Cross food parcels sent to Canadian, United Kingdom and United States prisoners of war, and developed a new highly nutritional flour used in Canada that contained the husks of the wheat berry. In recognition for his work, he was awarded the OBE in 1943.

Tisdall returned to "Sick Kids" to continue his research activities and teach as associate professor of Paediatrics at the University of Toronto. He also took part as a key member with British and American doctors to conduct a nutritional survey of Newfoundlanders and, in 1946, launched a study of the school meal program in Toronto — the first in Canada.

In the immediate postwar years, the Hospital For Sick Children, terribly overcrowded and in need of new facilities, announced plans for the construction of a new building. Tisdall enthusiastically took part in the fund-raising efforts by inviting community leaders from business, the professions, and others to visit his department where he gave them personalized tours and was on hand when the cornerstone for the new building was laid on April 22, 1949.

It was to be his last visit to the new site: the following morning he died suddenly at age 55 while testing a new sit-down lawn mower at his farm north of Toronto.

When the hospital wing was opened in 1951, a plaque summarizing his accomplishments was mounted at the entrance to the new research laboratories. It reads: "His outstanding achievements in the field of nutritional research brought great good to humanity and worldwide fame to this Hospital. Through his efforts these research laboratories were created."

The Foundation which raised more than $1.5 million for research was dissolved in 1952. Seven years later Dr. Drake died followed by Dr. Brown in 1960. As for Pablum, it is now sold only in Canada and, because of changes made to the formula in the 1970s, is no longer given to the children at the hospital where it was developed.

MVJ

WHAT THEY EAT TO BE FIT is Good for the Health of all Canadians

Dr. Tisdall, acting as advisor to the Department of National Defence, was responsible for many booklets advocating proper nutrition for those serving their country during World War II as well as for those at home

CANADA'S BUSH PILOTS

C.J. Humber Collection

Junkers *much like this one photographed at Sept-Îsles, Quebec, 1931, were durable workhorses for Canada's intrepid bush pilots*

ON New Year's Eve 1928, word was received at Edmonton that a diphtheria epidemic had broken out at Fort Vermillion 600 miles to the north. Sending the antitoxin by rail to Fort McMurray and from there by dog sled would, tragically, be too late. It was then decided to ask Wilfred ("Wop") May, a barnstorming pilot who had just spent the summer as instructor of the local flying club, if he would fly the much-needed medicine to Fort Vermillion.

May agreed and took off in sub-zero weather on New Year's Day with Vic Horner, a club member who owned the only plane available — an open cockpit *Avro Avian* two-seater with no skis! A blizzard forced them to land en route. They arrived next day frostbitten and bleeding from wind cuts. In fact, they were so cold they had to be helped out of the plane.

That mercy flight, and two more by May that winter, added lustre to the exploits made by Canada's early bush pilots whose skill and daring in flying over vast, unmapped areas of Canada's north made them legends in their own lifetime.

When Clennell Dickins, for example, landed his aircraft with bags of mail at Aklavik, Northwest Territories, on July 1, 1929, one old Eskimo found it unbelievable "because the wings didn't flap." To Dickins, known to everyone as "Punch," it was just another experience that had already included winter-testing Siskin fighter planes for the RCAF, flying furs from a trading post 1,600 miles north of Edmonton to an auction in Winnipeg, and completing an aerial survey of the Dubawnt River system in 37 hours of flying time over 12 days — much of it along the same route that had taken Joseph Tyrrell seven months to complete by canoe in 1893.

Harold ("Doc") Oaks, like May and Dickins, learned to fly while serving overseas in World War I with the Royal Flying Corps. On his return he studied mining engineering and flew for Ontario's Provincial Air Service, leaving it to stake claims at Red Lake where gold had just been discovered in 1925. He exchanged these claims for a minority interest in Patricia Airways where he served both as manager and pilot of its lone two-passenger, open cockpit *Lark*. Before the end of 1926, he had flown 260 passengers and 70 tons of freight from Sioux Lookout to Red and Woman Lakes in Ontario and had won the backing of James A. Richardson of Winnipeg to form Western Canada Airways. That winter he flew men and tons of equipment not only to Fort Churchill, where the government was undertaking feasibility studies to determine its suitability as a railroad terminus, but also to Cold Lake, Manitoba, for Sherritt-Gordon Mines.

Much of the early demand was to fly prospectors and trappers to mine and hunting sites. When Dickins was flying Gilbert Labine from Great Bear Lake in the Northwest Territories, Labine spotted the pitchblende deposits over Great Slave Lake that led to his discovery of radium and uranium in 1930.

In January 1929, when Doc Oaks and T.M. ("Pat") Reid were making the first winter flight to Richmond Gulf on the east side of Hudson Bay to pick up 13 prospectors, a treacherous storm forced them to land. Because of the fierce winds it was necessary for Reid and his mechanic to freeze the skis to the surface ice in order to prevent the plane from blowing away. Oaks, sheltered along the shore, used a blow torch to cook emergency rations for himself, the mechanic, and an Anglican missionary couple on their honeymoon. Next day he walked miles in search of help which came

This **Fokker Super Universal, representing the new trend in arctic transportation, quickly replaced husky dog teams which, for centuries, were the only mode for winter travel in Canada's northern regions**

Photo, courtesy, Ken Molson

1. **S.A. Cheesman, left, was a well-known Arctic bush pilot. He was invaluable as a plane mechanic, especially to H.A. ("Doc") Oaks, right, one of Canada's most famous bush pilots who won the Distinguished Flying Cross as a World War I fighter pilot. He convinced James Richardson to finance Western Canada Airways, Canada's first major airline service. Later he formed his own air service company to search for and discover mineral deposits in Canada's unmapped northern territories**

2. **The legendary ("Punch") Dickens was the first pilot to fly the full length of the Mackenzie River (2,000**

about midnight as the result of their plight being reported at Rupert House by an Indian trapper. A few days later they picked up the prospectors as planned.

That same month Dickins attempted his first mail delivery to Aklavik, but the attempt ended when he wrecked the undercarriage and damaged the propeller while landing on rough ice at Fort Resolution. Before flying back to their base, he and his mechanic rebuilt the undercarriage using pieces of pipe and repaired the propeller by cutting back the blade tips and straightening the entire propeller.

While in charge of two aircraft flying a mining company president and seven others from Baker

4.

miles in two days!). As well, he was the first to fly prospectors to Great Bear Lake in the Northwest Territories where uranium was discovered in the 1930s. Before retiring from professional flying, this "snoweagle" had flown more than 1,000,000 miles across unchartered landscape in weather unforgiving of human error

3. During World War I, W.R. ("Wop") May was an ace air pilot. At war's end, his daring exploits as a Canadian bush pilot united people through air transport. He became world famous for delivering serum in sub-zero temperatures to scattered arctic outposts experiencing a widespread diphtheria epidemic

4. Grant McConachie was only 22 years old when he bought his first plane. Viewed here in his Fokker Universal, he would inaugurate regular airmail service to the Yukon and pioneer passenger service between Edmonton and Whitehorse. After Canadian Pacific Airways bought out his firm in 1941, he would, by 1947, be its president. He linked continents and bridged forbidden barriers, making him an outstanding Canadian pathfinder

Lake to Bathurst Inlet in September 1929, pilot Tommy Thompson caused the decade's biggest air search. When his plane failed to arrive within 10 days, a search party involving Dickins and 14 other pilots flew almost 30,000 miles before word was received in early November that a storm had forced Thompson's party to land. With insufficient fuel to continue, the entire party had been forced to wait until the winter freeze-up made it possible to walk some 50 miles across Dease Straight to the Cambridge Bay trading post.

About the same time George W. ("Grant") McConachie was doing odd jobs for pilots like Dickins and May at the Edmonton airport in return for a chance to fly with them. He also worked for the CNR to pay for flying lessons at which he was considered "a natural." After an aerobatics course in the United States, he went into business with his own plane when in 1931 an uncle arranged financial backing for him. He was 22 years old.

The depression made McConachie take every job he could get, including flying fresh fish out of northern Alberta and Saskatchewan. His first mercy flight mission to pick up two badly burned men at Pelican Rapids required him to land on a stretch of beach only 13 feet wider than the plane's wingspan. Shortly thereafter a crash that hospitalized him for two months forced him to close his first company.

By 1933 McConachie was barnstorming the circus routes offering joyrides to locals and tourists alike. He charged one cent for every pound they weighed! By that August he had become a partner in a new firm called United Air Transport. The company transported tons of fresh fish, flew men and materials to mine sites, and expanded into mail and charter flights so successfully that, by 1935, McConachie flew east to buy a *Ford Tri-motor* monoplane — the first multi-engined aircraft in western Canada.

To veteran bush pilots, McConachie and others like him were "airborne garbagemen." But air

Photo, courtesy, Ken Molson

When planes were not flying during severe winter months, tarpaulins were used to protect engines from severe weather conditions. In this view, a Fokker Universal *is being refuelled while the portable nose hanger covers the engine. The gasoline blowpot used to heat engines would not be in use during refuelling*

travel everywhere was changing: companies and planes were getting larger; runways were being extended; wireless systems kept track of planes and weather conditions; and some of the early pioneers were taking desk jobs.

Dickins became a general superintendent for CPR airline division, was named director of operations for the Atlantic Bomber Ferry Service and then a vice-president of CP AirLines before joining DeHavilland Aircraft to market the world-famous and versatile Beaver and Otter aircraft, both made extremely desirable because of short-takeoff-and-landing (STOL) capacities. Oaks worked for aircraft companies during World War II, eventually becoming a mining consultant in Toronto. May, during World War II, headed the Air Observation Schools out west and was repair depot manager for CP Air at Calgary when he died of a heart attack in 1952. Grant McConachie, who became president of CP Air in 1947, was instrumental in the company's becoming a major international airline with worldwide connections before a heart attack ended his life in 1965.

Many of the early pioneering bush pilots have come and gone. Although their saga is inspirational, even romantic, they each served a major purpose in that, as pathfinders, they exploded the myth that Canada's hinterland was inaccessible.   _MVJ_

Photo, courtesy, Ken Molson

This Bellanca Pacemaker *is being salvaged after going through ice. It could cruise at 110 mph with either floats or skis. It had an 850-mile range. In the 1930s, bush pilots like "Wop" May flew such planes, bringing the Royal Mail to isolated settlers in sub-zero conditions, while jeopardizing their own safety to bring others comfort*

Edward "Ned" Hanlan
1855 - 1908

Canada's First International Sports Hero

EDWARD "NED" HANLAN, often described as the best sculler of all time, began his sculling career in 1874. In 1880, in London, England, he became the world's professional rowing champion.

Hanlan was born in Toronto, Ontario. When his parents moved to Toronto Island, where his father was a hotelkeeper, he had to cross Toronto Harbour to attend George Street Public School on the mainland. The only way to reach the mainland was by boat. This daily crossing in all kinds of weather in his first boat, a scooped out wooden plank, gave the young Hanlan great confidence on the water.

By the time he was 16, Hanlan was competing in local regattas on Toronto Bay. When he was 18, he rowed his first shell and won the Toronto amateur sculling championship. At age 21, in 1876, Hanlan won in the Philadelphia Centennial Regatta, on the Schuylkill River, against 15 professionals and established a new world's record over a three-mile course for single sculls competition.

Hanlan developed his own particular rowing style even though he never weighed more than 155 pounds during his racing career and was only 5'8" tall. Much lighter and shorter than many of his competitors, Hanlan became a most finished sculler with an exceptionally long slide, a smooth sweeping stroke, and a sharp clean "catch." His every stroke seemed almost to lift his racing shell which nevertheless always travelled gracefully on an even keel. During races Hanlan would occasionally stop, wave impishly to spectators, wash his face, even bend over to sponge water from his shell until competitors caught up to him. Then he would put on a sprint and win easily.

In 1878 Hanlan won the U.S. title on the Allegheny River, defeating all the best challengers. The following year he triumphed over the English champion, William Elliott, on the Tyne River in England, winning by an astonishing eleven lengths.

By this time sculling events were popular worldwide and drew huge crowds. Results were given to the crowds of people along the course through loud speakers. The ever-present press were quick to publish their stories. Although the English media lectured Hanlan on his flamboyancy, they appreciated his graceful rowing style.

On November 15, 1880, Hanlan defeated the world professional champion, E.A. Trickett of Australia, on England's Thames River course and became the world's champion sculler. Over the next several years Hanlan successfully defended his title six times — in Canada, the United States, and England.

After giving demonstrations in Honolulu, he went to Australia in 1884. For two months he was feted with receptions and banquets and sculled only in warm-up races. On the Paramatta River in Sydney he finally lost his crown to the Australian sculler, William Beach.

Hanlan continued to row well into the 1880s winning more than 300 races. He died in January 1908 at the age of 52. Later, on the grounds of Toronto's Canadian National Exhibition, a monument was erected honouring Hanlan as "the most renowned oarsman of any age," an athlete with the "spirit of true sportsmanship." A north western section of one of the Toronto Islands is named "Hanlan's Point." *DMS*

Rare image and early tobbacco card (Allen & Ginter's) illustrating world champion sculler, Toronto's own Ned Hanlan, circa 1880

BELOW
Artist Frederic Marlett Bell-Smith painted the skyline in the background of this 1880 view depicting the new world champion sculler Ned Hanlan in the Toronto harbour as photographed by Thomas Hunter

The Massey

A PROGRESSIVE FARMER, Daniel Massey was fascinated by the new labour-saving machinery that was beginning to appear in Upper Canada (Ontario). In 1844 he turned over the management of his Grafton area farm to his son Hart so that he could devote all of his time to tinkering with these new machines in a small workshop on the farm. Convinced of his ability to produce better machines, in 1847 he opened his own agricultural implement company in Newcastle, Ontario. From this modest beginning sprang one of the largest and most important firms in Canada's history, the Massey Company.

The Massey Manufacturing Company grew very quickly under the direction, in succession, of Daniel, his son Hart, and Hart's sons — Charles, Chester, Walter, and Fred. All of the Masseys were skilled businessmen who understood the importance of producing the most up-to-date machinery. Frequent trips to the United States allowed them to secure production rights to new machines that they then modified, even improved. The Masseys also believed in promoting their products: Massey machines won prizes at fairs and exhibitions all over North America and later in Europe. Soon Massey began to sell products worldwide.

Other factors also helped to promote the growth of the company. The National Policy under Sir John A. Macdonald in 1879 gave Massey a secure home market. A shortage of labour on Canadian farms also meant that farmers were looking to invest in machines that would reduce labour involved in harvesting. Additionally, continued emphasis on wheat production in Canada was a boon to Massey since it specialized in grain-harvesting equipment.

Massey's biggest competitor was the A. Harris Company of Brantford. Founded by Alanson Harris of Beamsville in 1880, this firm was engaged in a "binder war" with Massey, with each

Legacy

Farming the World

company struggling to produce the best and lowest-priced machine. By 1891 the two firms arrived at a creative solution to their mutual problem. They merged!

The new company, Massey-Harris, which already boasted a 50 percent market share in grain-harvesting machinery, was quick to acquire similar manufacturing companies. For example, the Wisner Company, specializing in seed drills, and the Verity Plow Company and the Bain Wagon Company, both specializing in other agricultural equipment, came under the Massey-Harris umbrella. Now Massey-Harris could offer a full line of agricultural machinery to farmers and had the sales and distribution network to support the various products.

In the twentieth century, the Massey-Harris Company forged ahead. It led the world in developing the first self-propelled combine in the 1930s, a machine that enabled farmers to harvest grain quickly and efficiently. During World War II, the Harvest Brigade, a fleet of Massey-Harris combines played a key role in the Allied victory by helping harvest the North American grain crop.

Massey-Harris also became a leader in tractor technology. In 1953, efforts in this area culminated in a strategic merger with Harry Ferguson, the eccentric Irish genius who developed the Ferguson system. This was a vital new technological innovation that allowed tractors to operate much more efficiently. The name of the firm was changed to Massey-Ferguson and, under this new banner, it continued to be a world leader in the production of agricultural machinery.

Today the name Massey is still synonymous with agricultural machinery. Reorganized in 1986 under the Varity Corporation, the tractor division of Massey-Ferguson still sells tractors and agricultural machinery all over the globe.

In other ways, too, the Massey family has enriched Canadian life. The Masseys strongly believed in giving something back to their country. Hart Massey personally endowed many charitable organizations. He built Massey Hall and the Fred Victor Mission in Toronto and in his will established the Massey Foundation which endowed the University of Toronto's Hart House and Massey College.

The last Masseys to be associated with the company were Daniel's great-grandsons Vincent and Raymond. Each chose to pursue other careers: Vincent, a diplomat, climaxed his career by becoming the first Canadian-born Governor-General; Raymond, an actor, became one of Canada's most outstanding stars of screen and stage. Both contributed in their own way to the family's legacy. LC

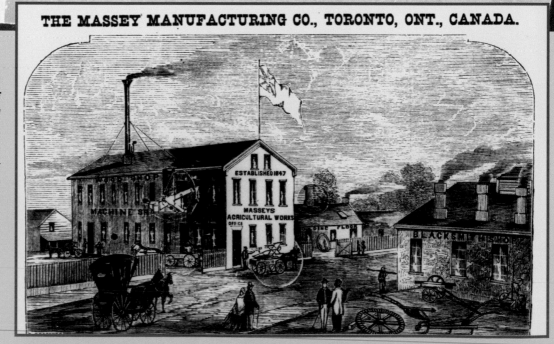

МАССЕЙ-ГАРРИСЪ

After a Massey harvester won grand prize at the 1876 Paris National Exhibition, the Massey Manufacturing Co. began exporting farming implements worldwide, moving its headquarters to Toronto in 1879. By 1892, the company merged with rival A. Harris and became known as Massey-Harris Co. Ltd., exporting farming equipment worldwide to such places as the Ukraine and France, as these 1911 Massey-Harris catalogues indicate. It was at this time the largest manufacturer of its kind in the British Empire

The old Newcastle Works, east of Toronto, as printed from an old stereotype view. These shops were totally destroyed by fire in 1864

THE MASSEY MANUFACTURING CO., TORONTO, ONT., CANADA.

ESTABLISHED 1847

MASSEYS AGRICULTURAL WORKS OFFICE

MACHINE SHOP

BLACKSMITH SHOP

MASSEY-HARRIS

138, Rue d'Allemagne, PARIS

Joseph E. Atkinson

1865-1948

*T*HE EVENING STAR was the least promising of Toronto's six daily newspapers when Joseph Atkinson became its manager and editor in December 1899. Under his leadership, it became Canada's largest-circulation newspaper and one of its most successful and influential publications.

Originally created by a group of striking printers eager to establish a paper for working people, *The Star* began publication in 1892. Financial difficulties soon arose and ownership changed four times in seven years. In late 1899 a group

Publisher for Social Reform

The first transatlantic call from **The Toronto Star** offices was made in 1927 by publisher Joseph E. Atkinson to **The Star's** London correspondent

of prominent Toronto businessmen purchased the paper.

Several of *The Star's* new owners wanted it to be a purely political organ controlled by the Liberal Party. Atkinson had a different view. He knew that a newspaper could be a good ally of a political party but that many citizens would not trust it if it were purely partisan. In Atkinson's view, *The Star*, to be successful, had to be independent — free from both partisan and financial control.

When the new purchasers of *The Star* approached Atkinson he had already been in the newspaper business for sixteen years. He had worked for the *Port Hope Times*, had moved to the *Toronto World* and then had spent eight productive years with the *Globe*. In 1897 he had become the managing editor of the *Montreal Herald*. Two years later he was invited to assume the same position at the *Montreal Star*, then Canada's leading English language daily newspaper. Instead, on December 13, 1899, he presciently joined *The Evening Star*, which became *The Toronto Daily Star* the following month.

The new owners agreed that Atkinson would manage *The Star* solely as an independent newspaper. Given this independence, which he regarded as absolutely essential, Atkinson embarked on the daunting task of making *The Star* a success. He believed that the ordinary citizen needed a champion. *The Star* would be that champion. He understood the needs of the ordinary people. He had grown up among them.

When Joseph was six months old, his father was killed in an accident. Destitute, his widowed mother moved to Newcastle, Ontario, with her eight children of whom Joseph was the youngest. There Mrs. Atkinson ran a boarding house for workers in the Massey foundry and later for workers in the local woollen mill. Young Joe Atkinson listened to them talk and learned of the problems of labouring people. He remembered what he heard. He was just fourteen when his mother died.

Consequently he quit school to work in the woollen mill. Within weeks it burnt down and young Joe lost his job. The fire was a community calamity, particularly for the older workers, since there were no other jobs for them in Newcastle.

Joe Atkinson never boasted about the poverty and hard work of his early years. But he did not conceal his humble origins. He remembered his mother's struggles and crises and, throughout his life, was conscious of the day-by-day trials of ordinary people. From his early youth, he had definite objectives: he strove to broaden his personal knowledge, to be a man of courage, to invigorate his religious faith, to foster self-reliance, to be compassionate especially to the unfortunate, and to be guided by his intuitive business sense.

Perhaps the most significant event in Atkinson's adult life was his marriage, in 1892, to Elmina Elliot of Oakville, Ontario. Her career as a writer had begun with occasional contributions to *Saturday Night* magazine. About 1890 she became editor of the woman's page of the *Globe*. There she and Atkinson met. A person of outstanding intellect and literary gifts, Mrs Atkinson has been described as "Joe Atkinson's conscience." She was a primary influence on her husband and through him the policies of *The Star* and *The Toronto Star Weekly* which he established in 1910.

Mrs. Atkinson's kindliness and social concern, like her husband's and later their children's, were reflected in *The Star's* two major charities — The Star Fresh Air Fund and The Star Santa Claus Fund — which softened, in some measure, the hardships of families in distress. It is not surprising that she was called "Atkinson's good angel."

The Atkinsons had two children. Their daughter, Ruth, was born about the same time as *The Star* began publication and their son, Joseph Story Atkinson, in early April 1904. Both daughter and son became members of *The Star* family early in their lives.

Another major source of strength and influence in Joseph E. Atkinson's life was his friendship with Mackenzie King, Canada's Prime Minister for 21 years between 1921 and 1948. During the 1896 Canadian Federal election, Atkinson and King shared a desk as reporters at the *Globe.* Through their collaboration on various election articles, they found they shared an interest in, and had similar views on, social problems and their resolution. A lifelong bond of friendship united them as they worked to make life better for Canadians.

Unlike Mackenzie King, who studied at three universities — Toronto, Chicago, and Harvard — and earned four university degrees, Atkinson gained his education through his day-by-day experience and through independent study. He knew from his own experience that the task of self-education is so difficult that few could hope to become well-educated on their own. They needed help. And society, in its own interest as well as in the interest of its citizens, needed to help them.

Throughout his life as a journalist, J.E. Atkinson was a 'radical' in the best sense of that term. He constantly urged governments in Canada, through their humanitarian, educational, economic, and social programs, to care for less fortunate Canadians, to help individuals develop their abilities to the highest possible levels, and to implement policies that would ensure the ongoing development of Canada. His progressive attitude and detailed attention, particularly to those matters that influenced the lives of individual human beings, gave his newspapers their distinctive character. *The Star*, under Atkinson's direction, was unique among North American newspapers in its consistent, ongoing advocacy of the interests of ordinary people.

The friendship of Atkinson, the publisher, with Mackenzie King, the prime minister, was a major influence on the development of Canadian social policy. Atkinson was considerably in advance of King in his advocacy of federal funding of old-age pensions, unemployment insurance, and family allowances. Nonetheless, many of the humanitarian ideals they shared had been embodied in the laws of Canada by the time of Atkinson's death in 1948.

The remarkable development of *The Star*, and its gradual emergence as Canada's leading English language newspaper reflected the high level of ability and acumen of Joe Atkinson and those who joined him at *The Star*. A large number of gifted individuals contributed to its success. Some of them became well-known celebrities — Ernest Hemingway, Morley Callaghan, Foster Hewitt and Gordon Sinclair. None of the many talented individuals who have worked for *The Star*, however, has made a more significant contribution to its success and development than Beland Honderich who joined the paper in 1943, became its editor-in-chief in 1955, and president and publisher in 1966. The success

Mrs Ruth Hindmarsh, daughter of The Toronto Star *founder, Joseph E. Atkinson, celebrated her one hundreth birthday in 1993 with John Honderich,* The Toronto Star *editor*

The Star enjoyed during its first half century was sustained, in considerable measure through Honderich's efforts, during its second half century when the bases for its ongoing development were strengthened and broadened.

After Mr. Atkinson's death, *The Star* continued in the tradition he had established. Its influence on the formulation of public policy in Canada continues. It is quoted widely in other newspapers and magazines around the world. The Atkinson Charitable Foundation, created under the terms of Joe Atkinson's will, carries forward his efforts to effect social reforms that will benefit the people of the province of Ontario.

The Atkinson Charitable Foundation was incorporated in 1942. During its first half century of operations, the Foundation made grants of $44 million in support of religious, charitable, and educational projects in Ontario. Throughout that half century, Ruth Atkinson Hindmarsh devoted herself unreservedly to the Foundation established by her father. Her husband, Harry Hindmarsh, and her brother, Joseph Story Atkinson, devoted their entire professional careers to *The Star*. With them she expanded the compassionate, altruistic work of the Foundation and of the newspaper which, in 1992, celebrated its first hundred years of service to the people of Canada. DMS

Leslie McFarlane

Leslie McFarlane

1903-1977

"The Ghost of the Hardy Boys"

IN 1926, Canadian-born Leslie McFarlane responded to an advertisement in *Editor and Publisher* magazine which read: "Experienced fiction writer wanted to work from publisher's outlines." He got the job. Forty-eight years later, when the same man wrote his autobiography entitled *The Ghost of the Hardy Boys*, he humorously revealed how he thus became, beginning in 1926, the writer of one of the most successful series for juveniles in the history of world publishing and eventually one of Canada's most prolific writers for magazines, radio, television, and films.

McFarlane had sold his first story when he was only 17 and had, from age 21, published a number of adventure stories as a freelance writer. In response to the 1926 advertisement, McFarlane was sent an outline and plot for 20 chapters in the "Dave Fearless" series by Edward Stratemeyer, an American publisher. The author's *nom de plume* would be Roy Rockwood, and payment would be one hundred dollars!

McFarlane was at that time working for the *Springfield Republican* in Massachusetts after having failed to convert one of his earlier-published adventure tales into a New York stage play. He now produced his first book for Stratemeyer in a matter of days. Weeks later he was sent the outline for still another "Fearless" tome. Subsequently Stratemeyer asked McFarlane if he would accept an assignment a month and "be available for work on other series."

McFarlane left the *Republican* and returned to northern Ontario. McFarlane had been born at Carleton Place near Ottawa in 1903, but his family had moved to northern Ontario when he was eight years old. His father had been appointed principal of Haileybury High School in 1910, and, following graduation from there at 17, young Leslie had become a reporter for several papers including the *Sudbury Star* and the *North Bay Nugget*. At 21, he rented a cottage on Ramsey Lake near Sudbury and began freelancing full-time.

Leslie McFarlane, also known as Franklin W. Dixon, was the writer of one of the most successful series for juveniles in the history of world publishing

McFarlane had written several more "Fearless" books before Stratemeyer asked him to author the first three books for a new series, *The Hardy Boys* — stories about the two teenage sons of a famous detective living in Bayport on the Atlantic seaboard of the United States. The boys' names were to be Frank and Joe; the titles were to be *The Tower Treasure, The House on the Cliff* and *The Mystery of the Old Mill*; the author's name was to be Franklin W. Dixon; and under no circumstances was McFarlane ever to reveal his authorship or to receive royalties. He would be paid $125 for each volume.

"They were called breeders," McFarlane later recalled. "Each book had references to the other two volumes." If they caught on, more would be published; if not, the series would be dropped. McFarlane thought there might be ten volumes in all, but "This merely proves I wasn't Thinking Big," he wrote in his 1974 autobiography. Over the next 20 years, McFarlane wrote 21 volumes. Since then, another 40 have been published by the Stratemeyer Syndicate that has been called the Henry Ford of juvenile fiction.

The Syndicate was founded by Stratemeyer who had begun writing juvenile adventures in 1889. After turning out dozens of books personally, he struck upon the idea of hiring writers to produce stories based on his outlines and plots. Between 1900 and 1930 he created more than 1,300 juvenile novels in 125 different series, some of the best known besides *The Hardy Boys* being *Nancy Drew, Tom Swift, The Rover Boys,* and *The Bobbsey Twins.* When Edward Stratemayer died in 1930, his daughter Harriet Stratemeyer Adams took over, creating more series such as *The Dana Girls.* For this series McFarlane wrote the first three breeders using the name Carolyn Keene. Adams also began updating the Hardy books.

McFarlane was not asked to do the rewrites. He had bowed out of the series in 1946, by then a proven and successful freelancer. While writing the Hardy breeders, he had entered a *Maclean's* short story contest and shared first prize with Mazo de la Roche, a Canadian writer whose *Jalna* series had achieved international acclaim. He continued to write primarily for magazines in Canada, the United States, and England until 1942. In the mid-thirties he also wrote radio scripts for a series called the "Canadian Theatre of the Air."

In 1942 he was turned down for war service but joined the public relations branch of the Department of Munitions and Supply. A year later, he was asked by the National Film Board to direct a script he had written about aircraft production. Over the next 14 years he wrote, produced, and directed some 50 films for the NFB. He also wrote and directed "The Boy Who Stopped Niagara" for the J. Arthur Rank organization of England and scripted a documentary drama, "Herring Hunt," which won a nomination for an Oscar in 1951. He received a British Film Award for a documentary on the 1951 Royal Tour. A 1954 film about hockey won an international award in Venice.

McFarlane left the NFB in 1957 for the CBC as editor of "The Unforseen" series that won the Liberty Award as the best new series of the year. He was also story editor of the General Motors shows but gave this up to return to freelancing and win the Liberty Award as Canada's best TV playwright in 1960-61.

In 1968-69 he went to Hollywood to write several scripts for "Bonanza," the famous TV western series for television starring a fellow Canadian, Lorne Greene. McFarlane also scripted for "U.S. Steel Hour" and the "Jane Wyman Show." On returning to Whitby, which had become home in 1936, he continued to write scripts for CBC radio which he called "one of his first loves." By 1974 he had written *The Ghost of the Hardy Boys* recalling his life as a reporter, a *Hardy Boys* writer, the author of four novels, 100 novelettes, 200 short stories, 75 TV plays, 50 movie scripts, and countless articles.

McFarlane never complained about the poor payment he received from the Stratemeyer Syndicate which ultimately sold an estimated 50 million *Hardy Boys* volumes. He did not think of them as his — Stratemeyer had invented the series and outlined the plots — and he thought of his role as that of foster father. In fact, when his son, Brian, saw the volumes in his father's workroom and asked if he had read them, he was astounded when his father replied, "Read them? I wrote them. At least I wrote the words."

McFarlane also felt no pangs about the updating of his stories until he realized during an interview for a magazine exactly how far the Syndicate had gone in rewriting the originals. Looking through three copies with the writer who was doing the story, he realized that nearly all his favourite scenes, especially those with crusty Aunt Gertrude, had been slashed. "My God, they've been gutted," he said, and while admitting the Syndicate had the legal right to do what it wished with them, he felt that a literary fraud was being perpetrated. "Hell," he added "even a ghost has some pride." MVJ

Courtesy, Brian McFarlane

More then 20 volumes of The Hardy Boys *series were written by Leslie McFarlane. This famous series has competed with Tom Swift, The Rover Boys, The Bobbsey Twins *and* Nancy Drew *as the most popular books for juvenile reading*

Festivals
Three Stages in Canadian Life

EACH WINTER, subscribers by the thousands, worldwide, eagerly wait to learn what plays will be performed during the forthcoming season by three respected and distinguished Canadian Institutions: the Stratford, Shaw, and Charlottetown Festivals.

Each is held every summer, but extends from early blossom time into the falling of the leaves in late autumn. The first, located at Stratford on the beautiful Avon River in southwestern Ontario, has been producing the classic plays of William Shakespeare since 1953; the second, at Niagara-on-the-Lake, has been staging the works of the Irish wit, George Bernard Shaw, since 1962; the third, at Charlottetown, Prince Edward Island, has been showcasing Canadian musical talent since 1964.

The Stratford Festival, which opened in a giant tent on grassy parklands that edge the placid Avon, was the brainchild of Tom Patterson, a young man from Stratford. Back in his hometown after World War II service, he had dreamed of using this attractive setting for a Canadian Stratford offering Shakespeare. And his dream-on-a-shoestring won backing not only from local businessmen but also from the world-renowned director, Tyrone Guthrie, and the famed actor, Alec Guinness. This subsequently led to a six-week season, in 1953, with Guinness performing splendidly in *Richard III*. This triumph led to longer, more varied seasons featuring not only Shakespearean plays but also comic opera and musical concerts from symphony to jazz. In 1957 the Tent Theatre was replaced by a permanent building, designed by Canadian architect Robert Fairfield, that featured an innovative apron stage, devised by Tanya Moiseiwitsch, that projected into the audience. Thereafter, the Festival grew apace. It drew first-rate directors and actors, many of them developed at Stratford, many internationally renowned such as Sir Lawrence Olivier, Sir John Gielgud, and Canada's own Christopher Plummer. Other types of drama and more music were added; two more theatres, an arts museum, new hotels, and quality restaurants now cater to the needs of the enthusiastic audiences that throng

Canadian actors Lorne Greene and William Shatner performed as Brutus and Lucius, respectively, in Shakespeare's Julius Caesar, produced during the Stratford Festival's third season in 1955

in from Toronto, Detroit, and beyond. Thus the Festival was no mere cultural "frill" to be sneered at by hard-headed businessmen. Drawing annually close to 500,000 theatregoers, the Stratford Theatre has become a money-maker as well as a great enjoyment for all who could see that Shakespeare's plays just might prove more lasting than the Ringling Brothers or P.T. Barnum.

The Shaw Festival at Niagara-on-the-Lake similarly grew from the drive and devotion of a local lawyer and producer, Brian Doherty. Begun as an amateur summer happening, it developed into a professional, international event, particularly under Paxton Whitehead, its dedicated artistic director from 1966 to 1977. Set as it was in a two-hundred-year-old picturesque community, it readily drew

George Bernard Shaw's Pygmalion *was produced at the Shaw Festival in 1992. Col. Pickering was played by Michael Ball and Seana McKenna played a strong and biting Eliza Doolittle*

visitors and tourists from Buffalo or upstate New York as well as from Toronto and other Canadian centres. Accordingly, by 1973, after eleven years in the venerable Niagara Courthouse, the Festival moved into a superb new Ronald Thome-designed Festival Theatre. The "Shaw" now has three theatres, drawing annual audiences of some 250,000. It has widened its offerings to include revues and musical comedies that are in keeping with its mainly Edwardian focus. Overall, it has contributed richly and originally to Canada's artistic life — no less than has Stratford.

The Charlottetown Festival, Prince Edward Island's showcase of original Canadian musical theatre, started in 1964, thanks in large part to the efforts of Mavor Moore, actor, playwright, producer, professor, and public servant. By 1968, Alan Lund had been chosen as artistic director and has continued to direct, to date, Canada's best-known and most successful musical, *Anne of Green Gables*. This annual, all-Canadian production has made beautiful Charlottetown, provincial capital of Prince Edward Island, a household name across Canada. The festival, in fact, is internationally acclaimed, and the annual production of *Anne of Green Gables* has gone on the road to such places as London, England; Osaka, Japan; and Broadway, New York City. Because of an enthusiastic following, *Anne of Green Gables* (based on Canada's Lucy Maud Montgomery's famous novel), and two additional musical productions selected to highlight each new season, the Charlottetown Festival has become a premier all-Canadian attraction drawing upon an international audience of some 250,000 fans who trek each summer to the island capital, the setting of Canada's birthplace in 1867. *JMSC*

Each summer a musical rendition of Lucy Maud Montgomery's Anne of Green Gables *is played to packed houses at the Charlottetown Festival in Prince Edward Island*

1887 - 1949

Thomas Charles Longboat

TOM LONGBOAT, who became Canada's most celebrated marathon runner, grew up in a world stimulated by the revival of the Olympic Games. In 1896, when he was nine years of age, the first marathon of the modern era took place at the Olympics held in Athens, Greece.

C.J. Humber Collection

The Greatest runner in the World Mr Indian Longboat.

LONGBOAT AND MARSH IN 5 MILE RACE, IRISH-CANADIAN GAMES, HAMILTON, ONT.

C.J. Humber Collection

World Champion Iroquois Marathoner

Labelled by a cross-section of international sportswriters as one of the greatest marathon runners prior to World War I, Tom Longboat, an Onandagan from Ohsweken, Ontario, dominated long distance races between 1906 and 1912

Before winning the world famous Boston Marathon in 1907, Tom Longboat was unsuccessfully challenged by Lewis Edwin Marsh at Hamilton's popular Irish-Canadian Games as this view indicates. A former aid and coach of Longboat, Marsh is best remembered each year as Canada's top male and female athletes are presented with the annual Lou Marsh Trophy

Early in his life it became clear that Longboat had the ability to become a great runner. By 1910 he was widely recognized as one of Canada's leading athletes. His crowning achievement came in 1909 when he was proclaimed Professional Champion of the World after winning a marathon in New York's Madison Square Gardens in which he defeated the world's best runners including Alf Shrubb from Great Britain.

Longboat was born at Ohsweken, on the Six Nations Reserve near Brantford, Ontario, on July 4, 1887. His Onondaga Indian name was Cogwagee. When he began to race competitively, he developed the ability to call upon an energy reserve that enabled him to sprint just before the finish line. This became the outstanding feature of his racing style.

Longboat's first important road race took place in 1906 when he won the "Around the Bay" marathon in Hamilton, Ontario. Winning that event made him an instant celebrity and clearly established him as one of the favourites for any long-distance race he would enter. When he won the 1907 Boston Marathon in the record time of 2:25:004, he became the world's premier marathoner. He also won Toronto's famous Ward's Island Marathon from 1906 through 1908.

He entered the Olympic marathon in London, England, in 1908 but unfortunately collapsed after twenty miles as did a second runner, Dorado Pietri. Rumours spread that they had been using drugs to improve their performance, especially since Longboat's handlers had told numerous people that their runner was certain to win.

Returning to Canada, Longboat determined to take personal charge of his training. This led to conflict with his managers. However, Longboat stuck to his own training regime despite racist criticisms. He bought out his own contract and began to run better than ever. For him, his way of training was obviously superior. In 1912, after turning professional, he set the record of one hour, eighteen minutes and ten seconds for 15 miles — seven minutes faster than his old amateur record!

In racing there are always rivals. Alf Shrubb was Longboat's. When Shrubb immigrated to Canada from Great Britain in 1909, he held every record in 2-mile to 10-mile distance running. In 1905 Shrubb had been declared a professional and thus disqualified himself for the Olympics. However, Shrubb and Longboat raced against each other ten different times. Longboat won three times when the distance was longer than 20 miles; Shrubb won the distances between 10 and 16 miles. Longboat's ability to call on his reserve after the 20-mile mark obviously set him apart from Shrubb, the recognized professional world champion middle-distance runner of his day.

During World War I Longboat served as a dispatch runner in France and raced professionally as often as possible. After the war Longboat returned to Canada and settled in Toronto where he worked until 1944. He retired to the Six Nations Reserve and died of pneumonia on January 9, 1949.

Longboat's achievements as a marathoner, prior to World War I, brought him recognition as one of Canada's greatest athletes. On July 17, 1985, Parks Canada unveiled a plaque at the Six Nations Sports Centre commemorating his superb career as one of the world's premier Marathon runners.

DMS

Joseph B. Tyrrell

1858-1957

Peer of Darwin, Huxley, and Agassiz

Royal Tyrrell Museum of Palaeontology

A Royal Tyrrell Museum dig at a dinosaur bone bed near Drumheller, Alberta

WHILE exploring Black Lake, Manitoba, in 1892, Joseph B. Tyrrell learned from Chipewyan Indians that beyond their hunting ground to the north was a major river flowing into the area then known as the Barren Lands. He at once devised a plan to explore it, a move that ultimately elevated him from anonymous clerk with the Geological Survey of Canada to global headline maker.

The greatest land explorer of his day, Tyrrell had already achieved considerable fame with his employer since joining the Survey a decade earlier. In the space of three days, in 1884, he discovered dinosaur skeletons to prove that the prehistoric beasts once roamed Alberta and identified the coal mine near present-day Drumheller. The first discovery was the most important find of its kind in North America; the second would become the largest coal deposit in Canada.

Both were outstanding achievements for the then 25-year-old native of Weston, Ontario, who overcame severe deafness and poor eyesight to graduate from Upper Canada College and the University of Toronto before articling in law. He found law boring; therefore, to pursue his love of the outdoors, he had his aristocratic Irish father help him land a job with the Survey unit.

In 1883 he made his first trip west mapping the Kicking Horse Pass area. Between 1884 and 1892, he surveyed the breadth of Alberta between Calgary and Edmonton spending six summers heading up teams to map and explore the vast, unknown areas of both northern Saskatchewan and Manitoba. Winters were spent writing reports in Ottawa where he also enjoyed many social events at Government House.

Studying Samuel Hearne's journeys from Fort Churchill made between 1770 and 1772 and examining a crude map he had obtained from a Chipewyan, Tyrrell carefully planned his 1893 trip

Opening in 1985, the Royal Tyrrell Museum of Palaeontology is located at Drumheller, Alberta, some 100 km east of Calgary. It displays over 200 dinosaur specimens, the largest number under one roof anywhere in the world. This huge museum complex is named after the Canadian geologist, dubbed in his day the greatest living land explorer in the world

to the Barren Lands. The expedition included his younger brother, James, also an experienced explorer, three brothers, canoeists from the Caughnawaga Indian Reserve, and three Metis from northern Saskatchewan as bearers — "a group," Tyrrell later wrote, "who knew the value of teamwork."

Leaving Fort Chipewyan in mid-June, Tyrrell recorded each day's route. Naming a number of lakes after people he knew, he named one "Carey" for his future father-in-law at a place where they replenished their food supplies from a herd of caribou "for as far as the eye could see." Another lake, at the point where the Dubawnt River veers eastward towards Hudson Bay, was called "Aberdeen" in honour of the Governor General.

The explorers reached Hudson Bay in September but their adventures were not over. Still 400 miles north of Fort Churchill, they canoed along the shoreline, but furious gales, food shortages, fatigue, and delays almost cost them their lives.

After three weeks in Churchill, they left in early November for Winnipeg 900 miles distant and once again encountered bad weather and food shortages before reaching Oxford House. At Norway House the Metis headed home to Saskatchewan while the Tyrrell party carried on to reach Selkirk on New Year's Day 1894. They were three months overdue. The press headlined their achievement — one that was not to be repeated for another 60 years.

That February, Tyrrell married Mary Edith but, with the financial help of an adventurous Scot and aide-de-camp of the Governor General, he left in the Spring for a second seven-month journey into the Barren Lands to explore the Kazan River.

In 1884, at present-day Drumheller, Alberta, James B. Tyrrell, in the space of three days discovered the largest coal deposits in Canada and the single most important remains of dinosaurs on the continent. J.B. Tyrrell devoted his whole life to the exploration and development of Canada's natural resources

The following summer he was assigned to survey the Lake Winnipeg area but found it "rather monotonous." In 1896 he went north of the Saskatchewan River to examine the mineral content of Huron rock deposits, that later, at Flin Flon and Thompson, were to become one of Canada's richest mining areas.

Reading a paper in Toronto to the British Association for the Advancement of Science, Tyrrell hypothesized that the ice age was not a single iceberg mass, as had been generally believed, but the "result of glaciation that had formed and radiated out to cover vast stretches of the continent on several occasions," a concept that subsequently gained universal acceptance and firmly established his reputation in the scientific community.

By then, however, he was disenchanted with his employer. Because he was still classified as a clerk making less than $1,800 a year, his financial circumstances forced him to resign as an aide-de-camp at Government House. He was further annoyed when the maps of his Barren Lands travels were changed and his name removed from them.

In 1898, however, he went on one more trip to the Klondike to survey an area between the Yukon River and the Alaska border. It was at this time that he briefly visited the Klondike to compare the two areas. The gold rush was at its height: he saw a single pan of gravel yield gold worth more than a third of his annual salary. This was one of the factors prompting him to quit the Survey when he learned, on his fortieth birthday, that he was not in line for a promotion.

Through friends, he arranged a $2,000 loan and announced he was returning to the Klondike as a consultant. By March, Tyrrell was in Dawson City where he later became involved with several enterprises including ownership of a gold mine.

By 1906, however, it was clear the boom was over. Returning east, he visited Northern Ontario where cobalt and silver had been discovered three years earlier. He set himself up as a consultant, first in Ottawa, then in Toronto where his reputation as an explorer and his work in the Klondike quickly assured his success.

Between 1910 and 1924 he also served as resident agent for a British mining company, a post that enabled him to hone his business skills with the same dogged determination that he had shown both as explorer and geologist. This also afforded him an opportunity to visit England where he confronted company officials who had earlier ignored his investment and mining proposals.

When he learned in 1924 that the owners of the Kirkland Lake Gold Mine did not have sufficient funds to dig beyond the 1,000-foot level, Tyrrell arranged new financing, becoming, in his 65th year, its president and general manager.

Following a major heart attack four years later, he retired as general manager but remained president until 1955, even attending board meetings up to the age of ninety-eight, one year before his death in 1957. By then the company had yielded almost $40 million in gold bullion.

Most of his advanced years were spent on a farm he bought near the present Metropolitan Toronto Zoo, where he experimented with orchids and wrote about mining, geology, and his ancestors in Ireland. For the Champlain Society he edited the journals of David Thompson and Samuel Hearne, Canadian explorers whose diaries and maps he had carefully studied in preparing for his own explorations.

The distinctions bestowed upon him were numerous and varied. He was a Member or Fellow and often Officer in some 15 learned and scientific bodies throughout the world. He was ranked with Darwin, Thomas Huxley, and Agassiz by London's Royal Geological Society when it awarded him the rare Wollaston Palladium Medal in 1947, the Society's most prestigious award for lifetime achievement.

A mountain and lake in Canada that bear his name also honour a man who devoted his whole life to the exploration of Canada's natural resources. MVJ

John Tuzo Wilson

Master of Plate Tectonics

JOHN TUZO WILSON is celebrated throughout the world by geologists and geophysicists for his insights concerning, and analysis of, the motions of the outer rocky surface of the earth. In the 1960s he was a leading contributor to the development of the theory of plate tectonics that has revolutionized the study of geophysical sciences.

Through his research on glaciers, the geology of oceans, mountain building, and the structure and location of continents, Wilson gained international renown. In recognition of his contributions to the advancement of scientific understanding, mountains in Antarctica and an extinct volcano on the floor of the Pacific, off Canada's west coast, have been named in his honour.

Born in Ottawa in 1908, Wilson studied physics and geology at the University of Toronto. After graduation he continued his study of these subjects and of mathematics at the University of Cambridge.

One of his academic tutors there was physicist John Cockcroft. While Wilson was studying under his supervision, Cockcroft was engaged in research on the artificial acceleration of atom particles for which he and his colleague, Ernest Walton, later received the Nobel Prize for Physics. The two years during which Wilson was a Cambridge undergraduate was a time of great intellectual stimulation for young scientists. Cockcroft later described the year 1932, when Wilson graduated, as that

OPPOSITE
Throughout his career Wilson enjoyed travelling to unusual and remote places. In the mid-1930s, for example, when he was a doctoral student at Princeton University, he took time to become the first person known to have scaled Mount Hague (12,328 ft.) in Montana. When he was in Moscow in the summer of 1958 for the final meeting of the special committee which had organized the International Geophysical Year, he decided to travel to Beijing by the Trans-Siberian Railway. This led to his publication of One Chinese Moon *(1959),* IGY, The Year of the New Moons *(1961), and* Unglazed China *(1973)*

"miraculous year" in the history of the Cavendish Laboratory, the centre for the study of physics in Cambridge. Upon graduating from Cambridge, Wilson went to Princeton University.

As a graduate student there, Wilson again found himself in the midst of brilliant scientists. One of them was John von Neumann, the Hungarian mathematician who, although trained initially as a chemist and mathematician, gained international renown for his work in quantum physics, logic, meteorology and computer science. Von Neumann's interest in large questions left its impress on Wilson who received his doctorate from Princeton in 1936.

After three years as an assistant geologist with the Geological Survey of Canada and four years of overseas service with the Royal Canadian Engineers, Wilson was appointed Director of Operational Research at Canadian Army Headquarters in Ottawa. In 1946-47, while searching for unknown Arctic islands, he was the second Canadian to fly over the North Pole.

While professor of Geophysics at the University of Toronto (1946-1974) Wilson mapped glaciers in Northern Canada. His research and writing on mineral occurrences, mountain building, continental drift and plate tectonics brought him international stature as a geophysicist. In the late 1950s he was elected President of the International Union of Geodesy and Geophysics.

Through lectures and papers such as "Continental Drift" published in *Scientific American* in 1963, Wilson contributed to the renewal of interest in the theory of continental drift. This theory had been formulated earlier by the German meteorologist and geophysicist Alfred L. Wegener. He argued that 250 million years ago the continents had all been joined together in one supercontinent that he claimed had gradually broken up as the continents known to us today had drifted apart over long periods of time. Through the gradual separation of the continents, the Atlantic and Indian Oceans had been formed. While Wegener gained some support, his ideas were generally rejected by many authorities because he had not provided conclusive scientific evidence.

Through the study of earthquakes and the careful analysis of the results of seismic wave testing, much information was accumulated concerning the composition and state of the crust and of the interior of the earth after Wegener published his ideas in 1915. A new theory emerged in the 1950s called plate tectonics to which Wilson was a key contributor.

Plate tectonics is a modification of Wegener's earlier theory of continental drift which assumed that the individual continents moved separately through stationary ocean floors. Wilson and other proponents of plate tectonics accepted Wegener's view that the separate continents had originated through the breakup of one supercontinent. Plate tectonic theorists, however, concluded that continents are not entities or plates in themselves. The evidence they accumulated brought them to the conclusion that continents, along with the ocean floors, are incorporated in about a dozen enormous moving plates. These plates together constitute the surface of the earth.

This outer region of the earth, known to geologists and geophysicists as the lithosphere, includes both the outside crust of the earth and the upper part of the earth's mantle. This lithosphere ranges in thickness from about 30 to 90 miles. Below the lithosphere is a weaker and hotter section of the mantle known as the asthenosphere which is presumably partially molten. It is on this hotter soft section of the earth's mantle that the plates move somewhat like enormous rafts. Earth scientists are not precisely certain as to what it is that moves plates at an estimated 0.8 inches per year.

To Wilson, the acceptance of the idea that the continents, rather than being fixed, are mobile and have collided and separated, is helpful to mankind. It provides a thoughtful explanation "for the transfer of living forms that evolved on one continent to another continent, and shows that all continents are in effect mosaics of many fragments." Wilson also believed that the movement of continents had influenced climates and had caused periodic ice ages. He noted that "if one continent becomes isolated, with currents flowing around and not toward it (eg. modern Antarctica), that continent loses much heat, the world's climates are uneven and an ice age results."

It was also clear to Wilson that the replacement of earlier ideas concerning a relatively stable earth with a more dynamic view would profoundly influence traditional ideas concerning the origin, sources, and distribution of ore bodies and petroleum deposits. Such new ideas have major implications for those with particular interests in the evolution of geological regions, the elements that have gone into them, and the sources from which they have been derived. Regions of the earth now separated by great distances may have been linked to one another in distant periods of geologic time. Features that demand attention in one particular area may merit careful study in still other areas.

Perhaps Wilson's most significant contribution to the acceptance of plate tectonics resulted from a 1965 paper called "A new Class of Faults and Their Bearing on Continental Drift." Here Wilson argued that plates could also slide over or under each other in addition to converging and diverging. His arguments in this regard were widely accepted and contributed to the revolution of geophysical thinking in the 1970s.

Wilson set out his ideas on continental drift and plate tectonics in a variety of papers and several important volumes. Among these are *Physics and Geology* (1959, 1973), *A Revolution in Earth Science* (1967), *Continents Adrift* (1973), and *Continents Adrift and Continents Aground* (1978).

When Wilson retired as Professor of Geophysics at the University of Toronto in 1974, he became Director General of the Ontario Science Centre in Toronto. This novel scientific museum through its push-button exhibits and hands-on demonstrations gave Wilson an opportunity to utilize his jovial and thoughtful approaches to science.

Two years before Wilson died in 1993, his article "Continental Drift," originally published in the April 1963 issue of *Scientific American*, was republished in a special issue entitled "Science in the 20th Century." It was dedicated to this century's five greatest scientific breakthroughs.　DMS

The McIntosh Apple

Canada's "Big Apple"

MORE than 3,000,000 McIntosh apple trees flourish throughout North America, all of them literally stemming from one single tree discovered in undergrowth on a farm near Prescott, Ontario, in 1811.

The discovery was made by John McIntosh, who, before 1800, came to Canada as a teenager after quarrelling with his Scottish Highland parents then living in the beautiful Mohawk Valley of upper state New York. John took up farming in Canada, married, and eventually swapped his property for a small farm owned by his brother-in-law at Dundela, Ontario.

While clearing land at Dundela he discovered several young apple trees on his property. As apples were important to pioneers — it was one of the few fruits available to them — he carefully transplanted the trees to a garden near the pioneer home he had built on his property. One tree produced a particularly red, sweet-tasting, crisp apple.

Originally called Granny Apples, they were enjoyed by friends and neighbours, but no one knew how to produce more trees like that one, a situation that challenged John's son, Allen, born in 1815 as the ninth child in a family of 13. He learned that planting the seed from the core would not produce the same fruit nor could bees carrying pollen.

While still young, Allen became a weekend Methodist preacher or circuit rider, preaching in and around Dundela and nearby communities. As his reputation grew, he was invited by homesteaders in more distant settlements to preach to them. Invariably he packed not only religious tracts but also homegrown apples. This led to discussions about apple trees and rumours that there were itinerant Yankees roaming the countryside who knew how to grow good trees.

By chance a farmhand hired at the McIntosh homestead in 1835 was one of them, and Allen, discovering this, quickly put him to work. He carefully watched him cut small tree branches called scions and tightly tie or graft them to another apple tree. The farm hand also showed him a second method — budding — in which he could remove a bud from the host tree and insert it into another branch of an entirely separate tree.

McIntosh variety makes up nearly half of Canada's annual crop of apples.

(Below) Standing, circa 1890, next to the original McIntosh apple tree, Allen McIntosh extensively propagated the McIntosh apple for world use. Today the McIntosh is the only variety grown in all five apple-growing districts in Canada

Ontario Ministry of Agriculture & Food

Ontario Ministry of Agriculture & Food

That winter Allen, along with his father and a younger brother, Sandy, inserted the scions into crab apple seedlings, packed them in sawdust, and stored them for planting that spring. He also sold some to neighbours and took others in his saddle bags on his weekend jaunts to other settlements where he not only conducted prayer meetings but also sold seedlings and taught farmers how to graft so that they could grow these trees for themselves.

When Allen took over his father's farm in 1845, Sandy became the salesman and teacher of grafting techniques throughout much of Eastern Ontario. By 1867 — the year of Confederation — a few farmers had given up mixed farming to develop apple orchards and some prospered for the next two decades from the sale of what became known as McIntosh Reds.

The survival of the variety and its ultimate popularity almost 200 years after its chance discovery was the long-time effort of several generations of the McIntosh family. Sandy's son, Harvey Austin, expanded the small nursery by marketing thousands of trees throughout the province and into the northern United States. By 1910 the McIntosh had reached British Columbia and was the parent used in breeding such varieties as Cortland, Joyce, and Melba. Dr. P.A. McIntosh of Spencerville, Ontario, carried on the nursery activities by sending trees to England, Scotland, and Rhodesia.

When a fire swept through the McIntosh farm in 1895, Allen managed to nurse back to health the badly singed original tree that was still producing apples. In fact the tree outlived him. Allen died in 1899, but the tree continued to bear fruit until 1906. It was left standing as a memorial to a true Canadian ambassador.

MVJ

Maude Abbott

Osler Library of the History of Medicine/McGill University

1869-1940

ADVANCES in medical knowledge in recent decades have been amazing. Historically, however, women faced major difficulties if they wished merely to become medical doctors. Almost insurmountable barriers of entrenched traditions and prejudice stood in their way until the closing years of the nineteenth century.

Despite such historic obstacles, numerous talented and determined women made outstanding contributions to the science and practice of medicine before World War I. Maude Abbott, born in 1869 in St. Andrews East, Quebec, was one of these gifted contributors.

Abbott was stimulated by the ideas of Sir William Osler, known for his outstanding work in a variety of clinical fields and as a professor at McGill, the University of Pennsylvania, Johns Hopkins, and Oxford. Through Abbott's careful classification of congenital heart defects — heart problems with which individuals may be born — she became widely known as a pathologist. In her *Atlas of Congenital Cardiac Disease* she set out in detail hundreds of such cases of heart disorders.

Abbott's chapter on that subject in Osler's text, *Modern Medicine* published in 1908, was recognized as the definitive statement at that time. These writings are accepted as important contributions to the development of cardiac surgery. Almost to the end of the nineteenth century it was agreed that the heart could not be treated surgically. Through her careful classification and documentation as a pathologist, Abbott provided basic scientific data of strategic value to those who pioneered in the development of surgical procedures for the treatment of heart problems. Had she not been a highly motivated and determined person, she would never have gathered and organized that data.

When she graduated in Arts from McGill University in 1890, Maude Abbott applied to study medicine there but was refused because she was a woman. To deal with her refusal, she sought help from her influential relative, John Abbott, a McGill graduate, who had been dean of its law faculty from 1855 until 1880 and who was to become Prime Minister of Canada in 1891-1892. He urged her to gain public support for the admission of women to Canadian medical schools and, in due course, she did. But she wished also to complete her own medical studies. She went to Bishop's, one of the first Canadian universities to admit women as medical students, and graduated in 1894 with the chancellor's prize and the senior anatomy medal.

Early in her career Abbott developed an abiding appreciation of the important roles a medical museum could play in the teaching program of a medical faculty. She was appointed assistant curator of McGill's medical museum in 1898 and curator in 1901. She reluctantly retired from her long career as curator in 1936. During these years, as a lecturer and, later, assistant professor of pathology, she helped many medical students.

From 1907 until 1938 she served as the international secretary and editor of the Journal of the International Association of Medical Museums. Through this work and her writing of histories of medicine and nursing and her many professional papers, she became recognized as a pathologist and author of international renown. Given the high esteem in which she was held by pathologists around the world, it is surprising, though perhaps understandable because of the continuing prejudice against women academics, that McGill did not grant her the senior professorial status she had earned.

After she retired from McGill, the Carnegie Foundation gave her a grant to draw together all she had learned concerning heart disease. Unfortunately this work was never completed. She died of a cerebral hemorrhage on September 2, 1940.

Maude Abbott is remembered as an indefatigable authority on heart disease who enabled countless "blue babies" who would otherwise have died, to become normal children and to grow up to enjoy healthy lives. Also remembered are the key contributions she made in the gradual removal of long-standing barriers to women seeking to enter the medical profession. DMS

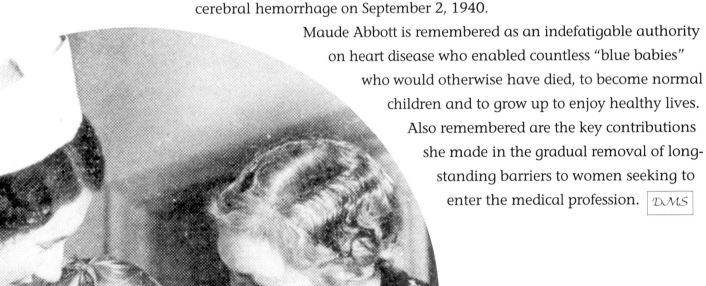

Osler Library of the History of Medicine/McGill University

Much of the dramatic improvements in the life expectancy of "blue babies" and infants with similar disorders is based directly on Dr. Maude Abbott's painstaking work on congenital heart disease over several decades of intense medical research

JOHN PETERS HUMPHREY

" Creating a Magna Carta of Mankind"

JOHN PETERS HUMPHREY, born in Hampton, New Brunswick, and educated at Mount Allison and McGill Universities, played a primary role in the preparation of the *Universal Declaration of Human Rights* and in its adoption by the General Assembly of the United Nations on December 10, 1948. Eleanor Roosevelt referred to this Declaration as "The Magna Carta of Mankind"

The adoption of the Declaration was the culmination of a long and difficult process. From April 25 to June 26, 1945, an international conference of 50 nations met in San Francisco to develop the much-needed global organization that was formally established as the United Nations on October 24 of the same year, many delegates lobbied for the inclusion of human rights provisions in its Charter.

Although seven explicit references were made to such rights in the Charter, it became clear that the wide variety of cultural, legal and philosophical perspectives from which conference participants viewed such matters would prevent the inclusion of a comprehensive human rights statement in the Charter. Thus it was decided that a universal declaration on such rights, which would gain allegiance as well as respect, should be written and, when adequate agreement was reached at the committee stage, should then be presented to the UN General Assembly. When John Humphrey was appointed Director of the Human Rights Division of the Secretariat of the United Nations in 1946. He was well prepared to undertake the formidable task of preparing the draft for an international bill of rights. The request was made by the Executive of the Human Rights Commission consisting of Eleanor Roosevelt (Chairman), P.C. Chang(Vice-Chairman) and Charles Malik (Rapporteur).

He had studied law at both McGill University and the University of Paris and had practised law in Montreal from 1930 until 1936 when he was appointed Lecturer in Roman Law at McGill. Subsequently he studied international law at the University of Paris as a Carnegie Foundation Fellow and then, beginning in 1937, served as Secretary of McGill's Faculty of Law. In 1946 he became

OPPOSITE
John Peters Humphrey, in 1948, was the Director of the Human Rights Division that created the code of human rights for the United Nations. Called The Universal Declaration of Human Rights, *an unprecedented step was taken in human history when it was adopted by the United Nations. The 1948 UN poster shows, left to right: P.C. Chang (Vice-Chairman, Human Rights Commission); Henri Langier (Assistant Secretary-General, Social Affairs); Eleanor Roosevelt (Chairman, Human Rights Division); Unidentified U.S. State Dept. aide (face partially covered); John Humphrey (Director, Human Rights Division, U.N. Dept. of Social Affairs); James Hendrick (U.S. State Dept. aide, background); two unidentified State Dept. aides (background); Charles Malik (Rapporteur, Human Rights Commission); V.M. Koretsky (Russian Representative, Human Rights Commission)*

Director and Chairman, respectively, of the Human Rights Division, the United Nations, John Peters Humphrey and Eleanor Roosevelt meet in New York in 1951 to discuss "The Magna Carta of Mankind"

photos courtesy of John Hobbins/McGill University Library

Professor of Roman Law and was asked to become Dean of the Faculty of Law at McGill. That same year, he went from McGill to the United Nations.

During his two decades of work as Director of the UN Division of Human Rights, Humphrey drew on the theoretical, historical, and practical understanding of the law that he had gained in his earlier career. After the United Nations adopted the Universal Declaration of Human Rights, Humphrey and his UN colleagues prepared two international covenants on human rights to give binding legal effect to the rights proclaimed in the declaration. These — the International Covenant on Economic, Social, and Cultural Rights; the International Covenant on Civil and Political Rights and the Optional Protocol to the International Covenant on Civil and Political Rights — were adopted unanimously by the UN General Assembly on December 16, 1966.

Humphrey completed his full-time work as Director of Human Rights in 1966, but the efforts in which he had been engaged bore fruit later. The International Covenant on Economic, Social and Cultural Rights came into force on January 3, 1976; the International Covenant on Civil and Political Rights and the Optional Protocol on March 23, 1976.

These steps taken by the United Nations were major events in human history. They resulted in the first ever comprehensive international agreement concerning such basic rights as freedom of movement; equality before the law; freedom of association, conscience, expression, opinion, peaceful assembly, political participation, and religion. Approval of these agreements by the United Nations led to revolutionary changes in the theory and practice of international law.

Although the principles set out in the Universal Declaration are often violated by member states of the UN, its adoption has resulted in its provisions becoming fundamental features of customary law of nations in the modern world.

Thus, through the efforts of John Humphrey and his Human Rights colleagues and the action taken by the United Nations concerning human rights, an unprecedented step was taken. It was finally agreed that the rights and duties of States towards their own citizens logically require the acknowledgment of certain equally important human obligations of States to one another and to citizens of all other States as well as their own.

When he completed his full-time work with the United Nations, Dr. Humphrey returned to McGill University to serve as Professor of Law and Political Science from 1966 until 1971. Since then he has engaged in a wide variety of ongoing human rights issues and related activities, including compensation from Japan for the Canadian Hong Kong veterans and Korean "comfort" women. He has been honoured by many organizations and has served on important international boards and committees. He has written many articles on international political and legal subjects and has lectured at leading universities while serving around the world as a special advisor to private and public agencies concerned with human rights.

While it is difficult to measure the full worldwide impact of the human rights code, Canadians should be proud of this native son who played a leading role in its creation and implementation. DMS

Yousuf Karsh

Greatness Exposed

FOR 60 years, people world famous in politics, theology, royalty, the arts and sciences, and the military have posed for a "Karsh of Ottawa" portrait. A sitting with Karsh, in fact, has become a meeting between two world-renowned people — the subject and the photographer. Following his sitting, Field Marshal Sir Bernard Law Montgomery of El Alemain fame described the process succinctly: "I've been Karshed," he said.

In his first book, *Faces of Destiny* (1946), Karsh said that his purpose was to use the camera to portray the famous "both as they appeared to me and as they impressed themselves on their generation." Seeing his work as "contemporary historical documents," he cited three portraits in that acclaimed volume as meeting that objective: those of Churchill, George Bernard Shaw, and Eleanor Roosevelt.

It was the portrait of Winston Churchill visiting Ottawa in 1941 that catapulted Karsh into international fame as a portrait photographer. Canada's Prime Minister Mackenzie King arranged for Karsh to set up his equipment in the speaker's chamber and to photograph Churchill following Churchill's speech in the House of Commons. Not forewarned, Churchill lit up a cigar and growled, "Why was I not told of this?" but consented to a brief session. Karsh asked him to remove the cigar and, when he didn't, stepped forward and gently removed it with the comment, "Forgive me, Sir." Churchill glowered as the shot was taken, then permitted Karsh to take still another, jokingly commenting, "You can even make a roaring lion stand still to be photographed."

When, in 1932, the now famous photographer set up his studio in Ottawa, MacKenzie King was one of Karsh's early mentors. Born of Armenian parents at Madrin, Armenia, Turkey, in 1908, he remembers scenes of brutality as the Turks uprooted Armenians in 1915. Two of his uncles died.

When Yousuf was 15, his parents and two younger brothers were allowed to leave Turkey for Syria via caravan providing they took nothing with them. Once settled in Apello, they decided to send Yousuf to his uncle who had volunteered to sponsor his nephew in Canada. His uncle, George Nakash, was a successful photographer at Sherbrooke, Quebec.

In his 1962 biography, *In Search of Greatness*, Karsh recalls his trip through the streets of Halifax on New Year's Day, 1924. "We went up from the dock to the station in a taxi — a sleigh taxi drawn by horses with bells on their harness which never stopped tinkling. Everybody looked happy and I was intoxicated by their joy."

He attended Sherbrooke High School, intending to be a doctor, but in working around the studio found "the art of photography captivated my interest and energy." This interest was further enhanced when Nakash arranged for Karsh to be apprenticed with a friend, John H. Garo of Boston, a noted photographer who not only taught Karsh the technical processes used by photographic artists of the period but also "prepared me to think for myself and evolve my own distinctive interpretations."

The six-month apprenticeship developed into a three-year stay with Garo, whose studio became a meeting place for noted musicians and artists of the period. Karsh often served as bartender, in that prohibition period, serving people such as Arthur Fiedler, Serge Koussevitzky, and others from the world of music and theatre, an experience that led him to resolve that he would photograph "those men and women who leave their mark on the world."

In 1934 Karsh chose Ottawa as the place in which to open a modest studio partly because of his early experiences in Canada, but primarily because the capital was the crossroads for many important visitors. Shortly afterwards he was invited to join a local drama group where he not only learned new skills in lighting but also befriended the son of Canada's then Governor General, who prevailed on his parents, Lord and Lady Bessborough, to sit for Karsh. The subsequent photograph was used by several British publications and newspapers in Canada.

One of the first in Canada to commission Karsh was B.K. Sandwell of *Saturday Night* magazine. It was, in fact, Sandwell whom Karsh contacted about the Churchill portrait, asking his advice how best to offer the negative to other sources for future publication. Sandwell suggested that he get an agent. Some time later *Life* magazine "offered $100 which I accepted, being then very naive about the value of anything — all I wanted was for the photograph to be published."

Life first printed the photograph on an inside page but later used the same print on its cover. It was then published in England and throughout the Commonwealth to become, Karsh happily admits, "one of the most frequently published photographic portraits of any person in history."

This also led the Canadian government to arrange for Karsh to sail overseas early in 1943 to photograph wartime leaders and others in England. In 60 days he took 43 portraits which became the basis for his first book in 1946. These included sittings with King George VI, King Hakkon of Norway, numerous military leaders as well as George Bernard Shaw, Noel Coward, and H.G. Wells.

Photographed in 1932, Yousuf Karsh (left) is seen with his tutor and mentor, John H. Garo of Boston

The Toronto Star

Soon after, *Life* magazine commissioned him to do a smaller series of portraits in Washington. Other assignments were quick to follow.

Ever since, Karsh has roamed the world photographing primarily the famous. While he has made "countless photographs of people of all kinds" and "my personal interest in ordinary people is unlimited," he confesses that he continues to feel more challenged when "portraying true greatness adequately with my camera." In preparation, he reads as much as he can about the person before the sitting, but avoids having a "preconceived idea of how I will photograph any subject." Rather he seeks, as he wrote in his 1967 volume, *Karsh Portfolio*, to capture the "essential element which has made them great," explaining, "All I know is that within every man and woman a secret is hidden, and as a photographer it is my task to reveal it if I can."

He admits he does not really know what enables him to capture the secret so often and, in a 1992 interview, said, "and I am not going to make inquiries. The magic and the mystery are very comforting to me. The unknown is very welcome."

The year 1992 was a momentous one for Karsh: he not only published *American Legends* which features 73 portraits taken between 1989 and 1991 but also closed his Ottawa studio after its 60 years of existence. He still maintains an apartment in Ottawa and an apartment/studio in New York but stopped accepting commercial assignments. "Now I just photograph the people I want to," says Karsh.

Karsh has had exhibitions of his work in Canada, Great Britain, Australia, China, and, in 1994, the United States. A number of portraits are also on display at numerous museums throughout the world. The bulk of his work, however, amounting to some 250,000 negatives, 12,000 colour transparencies, and 50,000 original prints was sold in 1987 to the National Archives of Canada at Ottawa.

MVJ

John McLennan

1867-1935

Pioneering Canadian Physicist

JOHN CUNNINGHAM McLENNAN was one of Canada's most distinguished scientists in the first half of the twentieth century. From 1906 until 1932 he was the Director of the Physics Laboratory at the University of Toronto. Under his direction it gained international recognition for its advanced research in spectroscopy and low-temperature physics.

Born in Ingersoll, Ontario, on April 14, 1867, McLennan taught for several years in southwestern Ontario before enrolling in physics and mathematics at the University of Toronto. Upon graduation in 1892, he received an appointment as a demonstrator in the physics department there. Later he went to the Cavendish Laboratory in the University of Cambridge, England.

In 1897, the year before McLennan went to England, J.J. Thomson, Cavendish Professor of Physics, discovered the electron. This was a highly significant event in the advancement of knowledge concerning the atomic structure of matter. McLennan was greatly stimulated by the intellectual environment of Cambridge and became engaged in research on ionization and electric charges.

After his return to the University of Toronto, from which he received the first doctorate in physics in 1900, he became the leading member of its physics department. Under his direction, during the next thirty years, it gained international recognition as an outstanding research centre.

When McLennan assumed responsibility for the physics department in 1906, its facilities for scientific research had just begun to develop. Step by step he improved and extended its research capability. Through his own research and publications he contributed greatly to growing realization that the earth is continually bombarded by high-energy, fast-moving particles now known to come from all directions and from far beyond the atmosphere. These particles, known as "primary" cosmic rays, were correctly believed to interact with the atoms and ions of the air. Both the earth's magnetic field and the ground produce "secondary " cosmic rays that have much lower energy and differ substantially from the "primary" in composition.

Greatly stimulated by the intellectual environment at the University of Cambridge, John McLennan, during a thirty-year career at the University of Toronto, was instrumental in developing closer cooperation among scientists, industrialists, and senior government officials in the advancement of scientific research

Through his research on atmospheric conductivity and cathode rays, McLennan made other important contributions. His specific research interests began to shift, however, after the Danish physicist, Niels Bohr, in 1913 propounded a new atomic model in place of the earlier concept of an atom as consisting of a tiny nucleus, a positively charged heavy core surrounded by light, orbiting planetary negative electrons of arbitrary radii. Bohr's model presented the properties of atomic electrons in terms of a set of allowable or possible values. Thus the atoms changed their states only when the electrons abruptly jumped between allowed or stationary states.

In essence, Bohr's new model of the atom dealt dramatically with the activity of atomic electrons and was based on a fundamentally new principle involving quantum theory. This theory had been developed at the beginning of the twentieth century by Max Planck, the German physicist. Planck had argued convincingly that, even though light appears to be emitted in a continuous stream, on the submicroscopic level it may safely be regarded as being transmitted and absorbed in discrete packages of energy or "quanta." These are determined by the frequency of the radiation and the value of what is known as Planck's constant, often defined as the elementary quantum of action.

The ideas of Bohr and Planck led McLennan to devote increasing attention to spectroscopy — the study of the sources, measurement, analyses, and uses of spectra. As he became active in the study of light rays and optics and was recognized for his work, he was able to secure the best research apparatus available. By the beginning of the First World War, the physics laboratory at the University of Toronto had perhaps the world's best-equipped spectroscopic laboratory.

McLennan, freed from teaching responsibilities because of the outstanding quality of his work, produced fundamental research of the highest order. During the First World War when the British Admiralty sought effective systems for the electromagnetic detection of enemy submarines, McLennan was engaged. He also investigated the potential of natural gas as a source for helium, which, as a light, non-inflammable gas was advantageous for use in observation balloons and airships as a substitute for hydrogen, a flammable and thus much more dangerous substance.

A team of research physicists brought together at the University of Toronto by McLennan developed a system for extracting helium from natural gas which there was in abundant supply near Calgary, Alberta. Before the end of the First World War, production at the Calgary plant had reduced the price of helium from $7,000 per cubic foot to just 11 cents. Although this work did not result in direct advantages for Canadian industry, the successful completion of this project under McLennan's direction further enhanced his scientific reputation. The donation by the British Admiralty of the supply of helium remaining in Canada, as well as the equipment used to make it, enabled McLennan and his associates to establish at the University of Toronto the first low-temperature laboratory in Canada.

In the 1920s McLennan and some of his students, one of whom was a future Chancellor of Simon Fraser University, Gordon M. Shrum, developed a helium liquefier, an essential apparatus for the production of helium. At that time, it was necessary to liquefy all the other components of natural gas and by this means separate helium from them. The helium liquefier developed by McLennan and his research group was the first of its type in North America.

Work by McLennan and his colleagues encouraged the early development of Canadian research on superconductors, the solid materials that abruptly lose their resistance to the flow of electrical currents when they are cooled below their characteristic temperatures. Because superconductors lack resistance to electric currents, they have the ability to prevent external magnetic fields from penetrating their interiors. The research in these fields under the direction of McLennan had considerable impact on Canadian industry.

McLennan gained additional renown as a scientist in the mid 1920s when, again with the assistance of Gordon Shrum, he contributed to clearer understanding of the spectrum of the *Aurora Borealis*, popularly known as the Northern Lights. McLennan and Shrum showed that the unique yellow-green line in the spectrum of the Northern Lights was due, not to nitrogen as had been formerly thought, but rather to atomic oxygen.

By 1915, McLennan had already been elected to the Royal Society of London. In 1928 he received its highest award, the gold medal. Four years later he retired as director of the physics laboratory at the University of Toronto and moved to England where he continued his research. For his many contributions to the advancement of science, he was knighted by King George V in July 1935. He died in Paris, France, in October 1935.

McLennan was one of a relatively small group of native-born Canadians who established the bases for scientific research in Canadian universities during the first quarter of the twentieth century. Evidence of his permanent contributions to Canadian life is widespread but known to only a few.

While McLennan's work is still remembered at the University of Toronto, few of its members know today of the key roles he played in securing the funds necessary to build Convocation Hall and the Physics Building on University of Toronto's main campus in downtown Toronto. Similarly, it is not widely known that McLennan was the person primarily responsible for the founding in 1916 of the Advisory Council for Scientific and Industrial Research which, in 1928, became the National Research Council, Canada's national laboratory at Ottawa. *DMS*

Professor John McLennan of the University of Toronto sits at the apparatus which he and G.M. Schrum used to discover the origin of the yellow-green line in the spectrum of the Aurora Borealis (Northern Lights) in 1925

University of Toronto Archives

Scientist, Military Commander, and Diplomat

A.G.L. McNaughton became a compelling public figure for almost two decades after World War II. Slated to become the first Canadian-born governor general, McNaughton instead became the Canadian representative on the U.S. Atomic Energy Commission as well as the permanent Canadian delegate to the United Nations. This view was taken when McNaughton was president of the United Nations Security Council, 1949

NAC/C-18123

I N war or peace, whether as a scientist, an army commander, or an international diplomat, General A.G.L. McNaughton left a legacy that reaches far beyond his homeland.

Born in 1887 in that part of the Northwest Territories today called Moosomin, Saskatchewan, Andrew McNaughton joined the militia when only 18 years old. By 1912 he had obtained a Master's degree in electrical engineering from McGill University. Two years later he led the Fourth Battery of the Canadian Expeditionary Forces overseas to fight in France "for King and Country."

ANDREW GEORGE LATTA MCNAUGHTON 1887-1966

In World War I, McNaughton applied science to military gunnery. Twice wounded in action, by war's end he was commander of Canada's artillery in France. Following the armistice, he entered permanent military service, becoming Deputy Chief of the General Staff in Ottawa by 1922 and full Chief from 1925 to 1935, all the while modernizing and mechanizing Canadian forces. In 1935 he became president of the National Research Council of Canada, the main federal scientific authority. While at the NRC, he promoted research into radio and ballistics and, with Col. W.A. Steel, in 1925 developed a cathode-ray tube direction finder that led directly to the development of radar. Radar, permitting the early tracking of enemy air attacks, would prove vital to Britain in meeting the on-slaughts of the German Luftwaffe in World War II.

McNaughton's contributions to science were significant, but he nevertheless left his position at the outbreak of World War II to return to military affairs as Major-General. He was named commander of the First Canadian Infantry Division, which crossed the Atlantic to Britain in the fall of 1939.

By 1942, as Canadian units increasingly arrived in Britain, McNaughton had risen to command a full Canadian army. Training the army for a scientific war, he strove to keep it together as a unified fighting force, always resisting political pressures from Ottawa to dispatch units for service with other allied commands. The resulting friction with his superior, Minister of Defence J.R. Ralston, led to McNaughton's dramatic resignation late in 1943.

Back in Canada he nevertheless became Minister of Defence in 1944-45. He was brought into the Cabinet by Prime Minister Mackenzie King to replace Ralston, who had been lobbying for conscription: King still hoped to head off that controversial issue through the appointment of a highly regarded military figure such as McNaughton who still supported voluntary enlistment. But the General met little success in politics, and conscription was carried. Nonetheless, McNaughton went on to important diplomatic posts before his death in 1966.

In the late forties he represented Canada on the UN Atomic Energy Commission, while presiding over Canada's own Atomic Energy Board. He served as president of the UN Security Council in 1949 and was Canadian chairman of the International Joint Commission, 1950-62, and of the Canadian-American Permanent Joint Defence Board, 1950-59. Altogether, "Andy" McNaughton — uncompromising in his independent views but foresighted as a scientist, devoted as a military commander, and widely respected as a diplomat — left an outstanding mark on Canadian and world affairs. JMSC

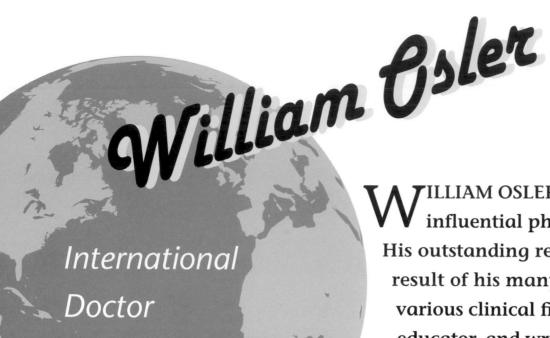

William Osler

International Doctor

WILLIAM OSLER was one of the most influential physicians in history. His outstanding reputation was the result of his many contributions in various clinical fields as a researcher, educator, and writer; and the mutual respect and affection he shared with his many talented pupils who made lasting contributions to the practice and science of medicine. He was renowned for his integrity and kindness.

William Osler was born on July 12, 1849, in Bond Head, Ontario, one of the eight children of an Anglican cleryman. Upon completion of his undergraduate studies at the University of Toronto and then his medical degree at McGill University, Montreal, which he received in 1872, he studied in London, Berlin, and Vienna. During this time he did research on blood platelets. Returning to Canada he joined McGill's medical faculty as a lecturer on medicine and pathology.

Osler published extensively while at McGill and gained wide respect for his scientific and humanitarian activities. Constantly in the hospital ward, the library, or laboratory, he was appointed a full professor at age 25, teaching physiology and microscopic anatomy.

Osler's great work, *The System of Medicine,* comprised seven volumes and became a primary source of medical information throughout the medical world. Through his speeches and publications, Osler became widely known as a cultured, witty, articulate, and highly principled physician. He gave major impetus to the study of the history of medicine in the United States.

Widening appreciation of his abilities led in 1884 to his acceptance of an invitation to join the faculty of the University of Pennsylvania. Five years later he became the first Professor of Medicine at Johns Hopkins University founded that year in Baltimore, Maryland. At age 42 he married Grace Revere Gross, widow of his former colleague, the surgeon Samuel Gross. Osler and his wife, a direct

NAC/C7105

Sir William Osler's description of the inadequacy of treatment methods for most disorders, as outlined in his The Principles and Practice of Medicine (1892), *was a major factor leading to the creation of the Rockefeller Institute for Medical Research in New York City*

descendant of Paul Revere, had two children. One child died at birth; the other, son Revere Osler, died in the First World War.

Johns Hopkins Medical School became the most advanced centre of medical education in the United States. There, Osler's reputation as a teacher, medical doctor, and author continued to develop. The Johns Hopkins Hospital was established specifically to facilitate not only the care and recovery of patients but also teaching and research by members of the medical faculty. Osler effected strategic changes in medical education and increased the time devoted to direct consultation with patients during his career at Johns Hopkins.

In 1892 Osler published *The Principles and Practice of Medicine* which became the standard text in its field for more than 30 years and was translated into several languages. Throughout his career Osler listened carefully as his patients told him of their illnesses and he urged his students also to listen carefully to their patients. Believing that the patient's state of mind was of strategic importance in effecting a cure, Osler instilled hope in his patients with his vivacious manner and practical joking. The detached method of lecturing employed by medical schools in the United States was

Professor of Medicine at McGill, Johns Hopkins, and Oxford Universities, Sir William Osler was internationally renowned in both the 19th and 20th centuries as a medical writer, researcher, and teacher

courtesy/ Dr. Charles G. Roland

replaced by Dr. Osler's bedside examinations which were the basis for instruction in his native Canada.

Osler's description of the inadequacies in the prevailing systems of medical treatment in the United States in the late nineteenth century contributed to the establishment in 1901 of the Rockefeller Institute for Medical Research in New York City. In 1905 the Oslers left for England where he became the Regius Professor of Medicine at Oxford University. Many honours were conferred upon him and he was created a baronet in 1911.

Throughout his life Osler had worked extremely hard, intelligently striving for excellence. At Oxford, however, he had more time to devote to his writing, to the collection of medical books, and to the preparation and delivery of scholarly addresses on various subjects particularly the roles and responsibilities of physicians. He also devoted much time to the encouragement of students such as Dr. Wilder Penfield, who made such an outstanding contribution as a neurosurgeon in Montreal. Dr. Penfield later observed that Osler was "a sort of John the Baptist in a wilderness of medical superstition."

When Osler died of pneumonia in 1919, one of his disciples, an American, Fielding Garrison, wrote: "What Osler meant to the medical profession ... what he did for us, can never be adequately expressed ..." He lives on through his writings and the treasured memories of those who knew him and wrote of his sterling life and influence.

His farewell message to the medical profession of America was the sincere expression of a fine and generous nature:

"It may be that in the hurry and bustle of a busy life I have given offence to some — who can avoid it? Unwittingly I may have shot an arrow o'er the house and hurt a brother. If so, I am sorry, and I ask his pardon. So far as I can read my heart I leave you in charity with all. I have striven with none, not, as Walter Savage Landor says, because none was worth the strife, but because I have a deep conviction of the hatefulness of strife, of its uselessness, of its disastrous effect, and a still deeper conviction of the blessings that come with unity, peace and concord. And I would give to each of you my brothers — to you who hear me now, and to you who may elsewhere read my words, to you who do our greatest work labouring incessantly for small rewards in towns and country places, to you the more favoured ones who have special fields of work, to you teachers and professors and scientific workers, to one and all through the length and breadth of the land, I give you a single word as my parting commandment. It is not hidden from thee, neither is it far off. It is not in heaven that thou shouldst say, 'Who shall go up for us to heaven and bring it unto us that we may hear it and do it?' Neither is it beyond the sea that thou shouldst say, 'Who shall go over the sea for us and bring it unto us, that we may hear it and do it?' But the word is very nigh unto thee, in thy mouth and in thy heart, that thou mayest do it — *charity*."   D.M.S

Gustave Gingras

"...a travelling salesman for rehabilitation..."

Dr. Gustave Gingras likes to joke that he has been "a travelling salesman for rehabilitation." This is, in fact, quite an accurate statement. Throughout his life he has worked tirelessly to promote rehabilitation for the handicapped, not only in Canada but in many countries around the world.

Gustave Gingras was well-prepared for this role. He was educated at Querbes School, Brebeuf College, Joliette Seminary, and Bourget College where he received a BA. He enjoyed his years at school but was occasionally guilty of reading, debating, acting in plays or playing the organ when he should have been working on mathematics. Math was his stumbling block; however, with the help of a kind teacher, he finally conquered it. Young Gustave was good at sports, especially lacrosse. Following graduation from college he entered the Faculty of Medicine of the Université de Montréal.

Even before he graduated with his MD, he was wearing the khaki. In 1942 Dr. Gingras joined the Royal Canadian Army Medical Corps. As a young lieutenant he suffered through basic training where everything was done "on the double." He was impatient to get overseas where he perceived the action to be. However, it was several postings later before he finally sailed for England. Having interned in neurosurgery, Dr. Gingras was posted to The Canadian Neurosurgical & Plastic Surgery Hospital in Basingstoke, England. Of his service in Basingstoke, he said, "Working closely with such dedicated professionals was the best medical training of my career." In 1945 Dr. Gingras volunteered for service in the Far East but the war ended before he could serve.

Following World War II, he fully intended to carry on in neurosurgery when he returned to Canada. A conversation with Dr. Wilder Penfield changed his plans. Dr. Penfield asked him to coordinate the rehabilitation of 50 veterans at Ste.-Anne-de-Bellevue Hospital in Montreal. How could he refuse his brothers-in-arms who were paraplegics and quadriplegics? Thus began Dr. Gustave Gingras' career in physical medicine and rehabilitation.

Physical medicine — later called physiatrics — was a new branch of medicine at that time. His more

A salesman for spinal cord rehabilitation since 1945, Dr. Gustave Gingras founded in 1949 the Rehabilitation Institute in Montreal. In the 1960s, he was instrumental in establishing at the Institute a prosthetic and orthotic workshop and laboratory for children with physical handicaps. This view captures the amicable relationships Dr. Gingras has had with his patients, many of whom were young people needing prosthetic and orthotic treatment

conservative colleagues would ask, "What is it? Is it some kind of witch doctoring?" But Dr. Gingras was convinced that rehabilitation could play a major role during convalescence from certain diseases and injuries.

At Ste.-Anne's, working with physical and occupational therapists, social workers, psychologists and dedicated nurses, Dr. Gingras was able to pioneer rehabilitation techniques. Many of the 50 handicapped veterans, rehabilitated to wheelchairs, attended sporting events and concerts; many returned to their homes and jobs — even to careers in medicine and law.

By this time Dr. Gingras was working with patients from the private sector. He opened his first clinic with assistance from the Montreal Rotary Club. It was held in what had been the billiard room of the old Viger Hotel. Here he attended patients two afternoons per week. To fill the growing need, the clinic was soon moved to larger quarters in the basement of The Montreal Convalescent Hospital. It then became The Rehabilitation Institute of Montreal and a bona fide clinic where physiatrics were trained. It was a proud moment for Dr. Gingras when the Institute was recognized by the College of Physicians & Surgeons.

It was during this period, at the invitation of the Faculty of Medicine at the Université de Montréal, that Dr. Gingras became the first professor of physical medicine and rehabilitation.

It was fortunate that the Institute had the knowledge and expertise to help when the polio crisis struck in the 1950s and when the tragic thalidomide babies were born in the 1960s. Dr. Gingras was asked to coordinate the treatment and rehabilitation of the thalidomide victims in Quebec and the Atlantic Provinces.

In 1953 the United Nations called for his help in the rehabilitation of victims of work-related accidents in Venezuela. (Venezuela had had an oil boom and there were many accidents on the job: in 1953 there were 10,000.) This was the first of his 15 international missions.

In carrying out his missions for rehabilitation, Dr. Gingras would first assess the situation in the particular country. Then, in consultation with local physicians who were usually appointees of the government, he would bring in trained personnel — usually from Canada — so that rehabilitation could begin immediately. Realizing that local and regional personnel would eventually have to take over upon his return to Canada, he would, in consultation with local health officials, initiate training programs for local personnel to assure the establishment of necessary rehabilitation centres.

He was also asked to visit such additional South American countries as Brazil, Argentina, Chile, Bolivia and Columbia to assess the need for rehabilitation.

In 1959 The League of Red Cross Societies and the World Health Organization requested his assistance when a mysterious paralysis struck in Morocco. Here the mission was unique in that he coordinated, from 21 countries, health personnel who spoke diverse languages. Eventually it was discovered that the paralysis that afflicted as many as 10,000 had been caused by machine oil that had been unscrupulously sold as cooking oil.

In 1965, at the request of the Canadian International Development Agency (CIDA), Dr. Gingras

Mr. Lorenzo Robichaud (left) presents Dr. Gustave Gingras with the Canadian Paraplegic Association's Distinguished Service Citation in 1985. A Companion of the Order of Canada, Dr. Gingras was the president of the Canadian Medical Association in 1973

travelled to South Vietnam to coordinate the rehabilitation of wounded victims of the war, many of whom were children. In 1968, again at the request of CIDA — via Cardinal Leger — he went on a mission to the African country of Cameroon as a consultant for the building of rehabilitation centres and the establishment of training programs.

As president of the Canadian Medical Association (CMA), in 1973 he led a 13-member delegation on a tour of China to observe the practice of medicine. Following Canada's recognition of the People's Republic of China in 1971, his was the first Canadian group to visit mainland China.

Dr. Gingras is now a senior citizen but he continues to work diligently on what he says "may be my last mission." For several years he has been lobbying along with the War Amputations of Canada, of which he is chief consultant, to gain compensation for Canadian veterans who were prisoners of war in Hong Kong in 1941-45. Dr. Gingras has collected information about the medical situation and has reviewed and compiled many interviews that document the cruelty suffered by these veterans as war prisoners.

Dr. Gustave Gingras, in failing health, now sits in a wheelchair himself at his oceanside home in Glen Green in Prince Edward Island. Reflecting on his life, he is modest about the many honours bestowed upon him, honours too numerous to recount but that include several honorary degrees, Companion of the Order of Canada, Knight of Malta. These acknowledge Dr. Gingras' vital rôle in studying the causes and effects of various handicaps and his impressive pioneering work in the areas of physical medicine and rehabilitation.

HSH

Abraham Gesner

1797-1864

Lighting Up the Nineteenth Century

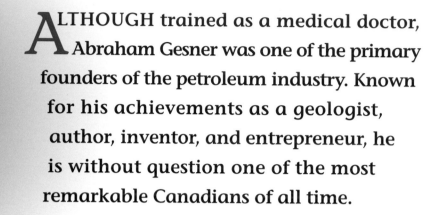

ALTHOUGH trained as a medical doctor, Abraham Gesner was one of the primary founders of the petroleum industry. Known for his achievements as a geologist, author, inventor, and entrepreneur, he is without question one of the most remarkable Canadians of all time.

After receiving his medical degree in England, in 1827, and practising medicine there for a time, Gesner returned to his native Nova Scotia. While working as a country physician and surgeon in Parrsboro, above the north shore of the Minas Basin, south of Amherst, he took a particular interest in the natural history and geology of the immediate region. Geologically fascinating deposits, known later as the Cumberland and Joggins coal formations, were observed nearby. He carefully studied these and other geological features in Nova Scotia.

Gesner explored on foot, by boat, and on horseback. In 1836, he published a remarkable volume, *Remarks on the Geology and Mineralogy of Nova Scotia*, which included a detailed geological map giving information on the main formations and deposits of iron ore and coal in Nova Scotia. Soon he was asked to undertake a similar geological survey of New Brunswick.

Gesner's acceptance of this responsibility made him the first government geologist appointed in any of the British colonies. Through his work from 1838 until 1843 as New Brunswick's first geologist and through his annual reports, Gesner created great interest in the potential mineral wealth of the province. This interest subsided after many investors, including Gesner himself, lost money, and he unfairly became the scapegoat. His appointment as New Brunswick's geologist was terminated. To pay his debts, Gesner had to forfeit his mineral collection and other personal artifacts. His collection became the initial component for what is now called the New Brunswick Museum, Canada's oldest public museum.

A fortunate result of his work in New Brunswick was his discovery in 1839 of a large deposit of a

Abraham Gesner invented Kerosene, popularly known as "coal oil." Before the introduction of the incandescent electric light bulb, households across north America were lit up with kerosene

Father of the petroleum industry, Abraham Gesner incorporated the Kerosene Gaslight Company in Halifax in 1850. This view, circa 1860, demonstrates a streetlamp in Halifax operated by Gesner's company. Its kerosene light brightened Haligonian streets after sundown

pitch-like, bituminous substance called "albertite" after Albert County where he had discovered it.

In the mid 1840s Gesner began to search for a mineral oil to use as an illuminant. By carefully distilling a few lumps of coal, he was able to produce several ounces of a clear liquid. When this liquid was placed in an oil lamp equipped with a flat absorbent wick and cautiously lit, it produced a clear bright light. It was much superior to the smoky light produced through the burning of whale oil and other animal and vegetable oils, then the primary fuels used to produce artificial light.

Successful public demonstrations of the new light included a spectacular event in a church hall in Charlottetown, Prince Edward Island, in 1846. These displays of the high quality of bright light produced by Gesner's new illuminating fuel stimulated great interest in it. He called his fuel kerosene — from the Greek words for wax and oil. Gesner then organized the Kerosene Gaslight Company. One of its first major contracts, beginning in 1850, was the lighting of homes and streets in Halifax, Nova Scotia. To increase his production, Gesner wished to use the albertite he had discovered in 1839 in New Brunswick. Legal opposition to his access there forced Gesner to resort to other plans.

In Halifax, Gesner had met Admiral Thomas Cochrane, the tenth Earl of Dundonald and Commander of the British Naval Forces stationed there. Cochrane had extracted an illuminant from Trinidad asphalt and in 1813 had been granted a British patent on a lamp designed for its use. Encouraged by this adventurous British admiral and inventor, Gesner in 1854 sought and soon obtained patents for the distillation of bituminous rock from which he could obtain kerosene that he purified by treating it with sulphuric acid and lime and then redistilled.

The illuminant Gesner produced sold readily. By the mid 1850s he was convinced it could and would surpass whale oil. The problem, however, was supply. That difficulty was overcome when it was established that kerosene could be extracted from petroleum. Gesner learned this after he had established the North American Kerosene Gas Light Company on Long Island, New York in 1854. With an assured supply of petroleum following its discovery in both Ontario and Pennsylvania in the late 1850s and demand for kerosene increasing, Gesner believed that his future was secure. Problems arose, however, concerning his patents. Forced to pay royalties to another patent holder, Gesner eventually had to sell his patents and return to Nova Scotia.

While in the United States, Gesner had written a variety of scientific articles, reports, and books. His volume, *A Practical Treatise on Coal, Petroleum and Other Distilled Oils* published in 1861, became a standard reference in its field. On his return to Halifax, Gesner became Professor of Natural History at Dalhousie University. But the years had taken their toll and he died on April 29, 1864.

Throughout his life, Gesner demonstrated exceptional creativity and resourcefulness. His inventiveness resulted in millions of individuals in the United States, Canada, and elsewhere enjoying better artificial light. During the first half century in the petroleum industry, kerosene was the major product of refineries. Later, growing popular demand for gasoline-powered vehicles gradually made the production of gasoline and lubricants the principal concern. Then in the second half of the twentieth century, kerosene took on new significance as the fuel for jet aircraft.

Gesner made other less visible but highly significant scientific and technical contributions in addition to those he made in the petroleum industry. His work as a pioneering government geologist attracted the attention of other geologists in Canada and overseas. Prominent among these was William Logan, Founding Director of the Geological Survey of Canada. Another was Charles Lyell, the foremost English geologist for nearly half of the nineteenth century. Lyell's interest in turn stimulated that of J.W. Dawson, who carried forward Gesner's study of the geology of Nova Scotia before he, Dawson, became the highly influential principal of McGill University for 48 years. Dawson's son, in his time, also became a distinguished geologist.

The United States corporation that Gesner founded, the North American Kerosene Gas Light Co., was purchased by the Standard Oil Company and became part of the Rockefeller group. In 1933 another company in that same group, Imperial Oil, originally a Canadian-controlled corporation, erected a memorial in Camp Hill Cemetery in Halifax to honour Gesner. *DMS*

Norman McLaren

1914-1987

National Film Board of Canada

Innovative Film Genius

NORMAN MCLAREN never made a full-length feature movie or documentary but his work with Canada's National Film Board has won more than 100 international awards — including a Hollywood Oscar and prizes at numerous global film festivals. Most of his productions, in fact, are no more than ten minutes in length, yet he is considered to have been an artist, animator, filmmaker, scientist, inventor, and technical genius.

Although Neighbours won an Academy Award for Norman McLaren as best documentary short subject film in 1952, Pas de deux (1965) is McLaren's masterpiece. Using as many as ten multiple exposures per frame, McLaren's virtuosity in this film shaped the movement of two ballet performers into a fantasy of his own creation. His film is a brief peek into a world where dancers are transformed into an abstraction of movement which would be impossible to create live on any ballet stage. The 13-minute short was voted the Outstanding Film of the Year by the London Film Festival and was judged Best Animation Film by the British Film Awards. In all Pas de deux won more than 20 international awards from 11 different countries following its release in 1965. It was also nominated for an Academy Award as "Best Live Action Short"

Born in Stirling, Scotland, in 1914, McLaren, the youngest of three children, became interested in film while studying interior design at the Glasgow School of Art. Lacking the funds to purchase equipment, Norman obtained a used 35mm film from a local moviehouse, washed off the emulsion, and used coloured inks to create a short sequence of dancing colour patterns.

Encouraged by his teachers, McLaren then produced two documentaries at the school that impressed judges at a local film festival and won him some financial support from the school to create two more productions. These were shown at another local film festival where they were seen by the legendary John Grierson, head of the General Post Office film unit, who offered McLaren a job that he accepted before graduating in 1936.

Later that year McLaren was loaned as a cameraman for a film expedition covering the Spanish Civil War, an experience that increased his already firm views about the futility and misery of war. Returning to England, he made several more films for the post office before emigrating to New York in 1939.

Jobs were hard to come by but he eventually managed to attract the attention of the director of the Guggenheim Museum of Non-Objective Art who financed McLaren to make several abstract films using cameraless animation and hand-drawn sound. Later he landed a job with an industrial film company until Grierson, now in Canada as head of the government-backed National Film Board (NFB), recruited him in 1941 to set up an animation unit. At age 27 McLaren moved to Ottawa and thence to Montreal where he spent the rest of his life.

His first films at the NFB encouraged the purchase of war bonds, promoted early mailing at Christmas, and condemned war gossip. He also taught young artists animation techniques, created illustrations for a series of popular French-Canadian folk songs, and, in 1949, worked with jazz pianist Oscar Peterson to make *Begone Dull Care*. The film won top prizes at festivals in Venice, Italy, and Durban, South Africa as well as awards in Canada, Germany, and the United States.

At the request of UNESCO, McLaren went to China in 1949 to teach animators how to create films that would teach illiterate villagers about health and sanitation. While he was there, Communist forces overran the village; this gave McLaren his second taste of the horror and futility of war and led inexorably to his creation of *Neighbours* in 1952 as a protest to the Korean conflict.

Neighbours contrasted sharply with McLaren's normally whimsical and humorous approach. A political fable using his innovative technique of stop-motion cinematography called "pixilation," *Neighbours* involves two men building homes beside each other, erecting a fence, and planting a flower that winds around the fence and ultimately leads to conflict that culminates in the violent killing of their wives and children as well as each other.

McLaren included the murder of the families to emphasize the killing of innocent women and children in war, but distributors in the USA and Europe refused to show the film unless that sequence was removed. At first McLaren refused, but when the distributor for US schools showed McLaren a revised version, he relented and *Neighbours* went on to win an Academy Award as the best short

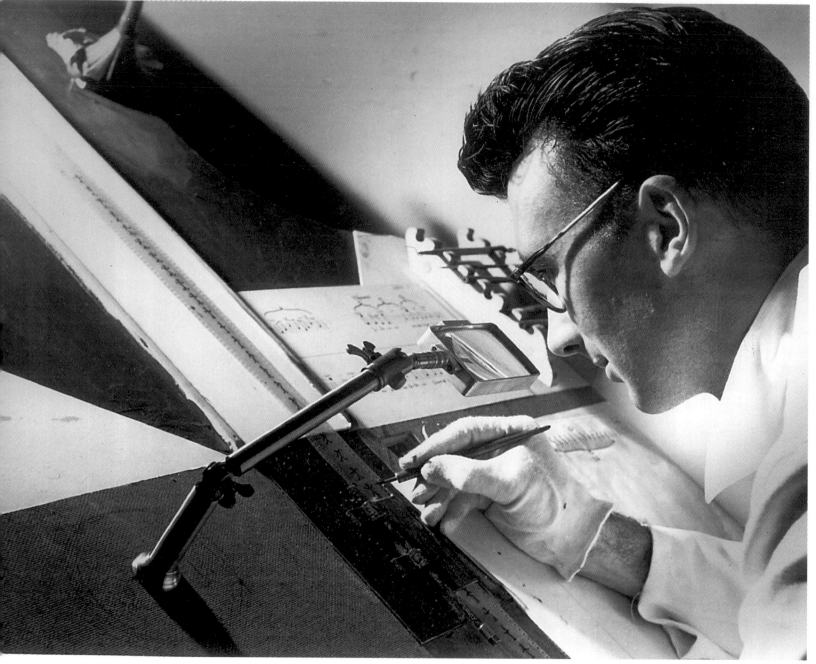

Norman McLaren was a film pioneer who was also an accomplished artist whose genius lay in his practice of drawing directly onto each frame of the film to be projected. Individual frames of some of McLaren's short films are worthy of any art gallery. This sophisticated innovation was accomplished by McLaren's use of a magnifying glass

subject of 1952/53 as well as numerous other prizes in the USA, Italy, and Canada. Following the outbreak of the war in Vietnam, demands were made to include the offending footage. That sequence is retained in the versions shown today.

In 1953, McLaren again went on a UNESCO assignment, this time to teach animation in India.

On his return he produced *Blinkety Blank* (1954) in which he varied his technique of drawing on every frame by consciously skipping some to create a subliminal effect and firmly establish his reputation as a "manipulator of motion." Awards were showered on the production from Germany, Great Britain, South Africa, Uruguay, the United States, and Italy, and more were heaped on other McLaren-made NFB productions such as *Rythmetic* (1956), *A Chairy Tale* (1957), *Le merle* (1958), *Lines Vertical* (1960), *Lines Horizontal* (1962), and *Mosaic* (1965). For over thirty years he produced approximately one film per year.

A Chairy Tale was considered another work reflecting McLaren's pacifist views, but like most of his work, it was interpreted many ways. This witty, humorous story is about a chair that refuses to be sat upon until the actor, played by noted Canadian filmmaker Claude Jutra, allows it to sit on his lap. Students of one high-school classroom felt it represented a student-teacher relationship that "makes it clear the teacher has to give more consideration to the pupil." McLaren, after having made it, realized "it was a kind of therapy to overcome the feeling that I was being sat upon by friends too much."

In 1967, McLaren turned his genius to a totally new animation concept when he photographed two ballet dancers performing a *pas de deux*, and then, according to biographer Maynard Collins, shaped "each movement into a fantasy of his own creation." Collins further explained that "The technical virtuosity of this film, its ethereal beauty, its lovely Roumanian pan-type music, made it a joy to watch, even if — perhaps especially if — you do not care for ballet."

Awards for *Pas de deux* were even more worldwide than for his thematic productions of *Neighbours* and *A Chairy Tale*. Film festivals held in various countries of Europe, Asia, North and South America all recognized it with various awards and honours for its creator who, five years later, made a second film using ballet dancers.

Ballet Adagio was originally intended to illustrate the movements of ballet to students through slow-motion photography. McLaren's ingenious skill created, according to Collins, "an aesthetic experience," one that showed not only the concentration demanded by formal dance but also examined "the human soul and found it beautiful."

Ballet Adagio was one of McLaren's last major works with the National Film Board. Always somewhat frail in health and gentle in demeanour, he eased his way out of the demanding role of constantly being sought out by visitors from around the world to teach his animation skills or discuss his concept and objectives for productions. "He was a kind of good will ambassador at the NFB," recalls Herb Taylor, a former colleague and friend, pointing out that for two years after his death on January 26, 1987, the External Affairs Department was constantly asked to send an expert to numerous film festivals around the world so that the creativity and genius of Norman McLaren and his animated films could be discussed. *MVJ*

Oscar Peterson

Maharajah of the Piano

WHEN Dizzy Gillespie was playing in Montreal, in response to the crowd's urgings, the late, great jazz trumpeter invited a local pianist to play a set with his jazz band. The band opened the set with "What is This Thing Called Love?" and, as one observer recalls, "Dizzy's eyes were like saucers with disbelief."

The pianist who so impressed one of the most important figures of the jazz world was Oscar Peterson. He also impressed Duke Ellington, who dubbed him "the maharajah of the piano." And Coleman Hawkins exclaimed, after a gig at Montreal's Cafe St. Michel, "I'd like to take you back to New York and have a whole bunch of cats hear you."

A trip to New York occurred in September 1949 and, when Oscar was introduced to an audience as a visitor from Canada, Mike Levin of *Down Beat* magazine recalls that the Montreal pianist "stopped the Norman Granz 'Jazz at the Philharmonic' concert dead cold in its tracks."

Four decades later, jazz pianist Roger Kellaway met Oscar at Milan, Italy, and told his biographer, Gene Lees, "One of the reasons I revere Oscar is that ... he's a total musician. He's absolutely complete as a pianist."

Peterson established his love for and his skill with the piano at an early age. It was recognized that, at age five, he had perfect pitch. His musical father, a railroad porter, virtually sat him at the piano with orders to play. Oscar had no difficulty in obliging and recalls that he would, when possible, practise from nine until noon, eat lunch, practise from one until six, and after dinner, practise again from 7.30 p.m. until his mother dragged him away to bed.

One of Oscar's teachers, Lou Hooper, on his first visit when Oscar was 11 years old, was astonished

Oscar Peterson, one of the world's greatest jazz pianists, was Chancellor, York University, from July 1991 to January 1994

"not only at what I was hearing but [at] the intelligent interpretation, the easy and adequate technique while playing entirely from memory." Three years later, Paul de Marky became his teacher, the same year that Oscar's older sister, Daisy, entered her shy kid brother in the "Ken Soble Amateur Hour" on CBC. Oscar won and soon had a weekly 15-minute broadcast on a local radio station and guest appearances on various CBC national shows such as "The Happy Gang." He also became pianist for the Johnny Holmes Orchestra while attending Montreal High School. By 1947 he was playing at a downtown club, the Alberta Lounge, and making his first recordings with RCA.

At the Alberta Lounge, Peterson met many of the top-name jazz stars visiting Montreal. Norman Granz, owner and manager of "Jazz at the Philharmonic" concerts, sought him out and quickly invited Oscar to make a guest appearance in New York. The Carnegie Hall appearance established Oscar as a permanent member of the Norman Granz group of musical artists. The following year the group, along with soloist performers such as Ella Fitzgerald, Coleman Hawkins, Buddy Rich, and Gene Krupa, went on a 52-city tour.

Within a few years Peterson was one of the group's highest-paid members and making numerous records for Granz. A *Time* magazine feature in 1953 opened, "At the age of 28, a Montreal Negro named Oscar Peterson is one of the world's finest jazz pianists." It pointed out that Mr. Peterson was returning to Montreal to be with his family as well as to spend four to six hours a day practising the classics. As Oscar explained, "I play Chopin because he gives you the reach. Scarlatti gives you the close fingering. Ravel and Debussy help you on those pretty, lush harmonics. Bach gives you counter-point."

The Oscar Peterson Trio included bassist Ray Brown and guitarist Herb Ellis. As owner of a recording company and Peterson's manager, Granz released dozens of their records on the Verve label. One of the most outstanding was recorded at the Stratford Festival in Ontario in 1956. In 1958, a drummer, Ed Thigpen, replaced Ellis. His arrival prompted more recordings. In 1959 during a six-day session, 124 tracks were made to produce eight new albums.

Critics claimed Granz was overrecording his most successful artist. There was also criticism of Petersons's playing. One critic said he was "too commercial," and another observed, "His improvisations often seemed haphazard structures." A French writer stated, "Peterson's metre and accent are far too mechanical to mean anything very positive," and an American wrote, "His melodic vocabulary is a stockpile of cliches."

Oscar and Granz tended to dismiss the critics as did some of the most schooled musicians. Lalo Schifrin, a composer who trained at the Paris Conservatory, wrote, "Oscar represents a tradition lost in this century — the virtuoso piano improviser, like Chopin, the tradition of bravura playing that started with Beethoven and reached its apotheosis with Franz Liszt."

In 1963, Oscar, with Ray and Ed, visited Villingen, Germany, to perform a private engagement at the home of Hans Georg Brunner-Schwer, who, passionately interested in jazz, had a nine-foot grand piano and the most modern recording equipment. Annual visits and recording sessions followed until

1968 when Brunner-Schwer arranged to release four albums from these sessions on an MPS label. Peterson and other musicians felt these were the best he had ever made. The critics agreed. One critic in London commented about the "My Favourite Instrument" album: "It is a luxury to be able to indulge in a categorical statement for once and assert that this is the best record that Peterson ever made."

In 11 years Peterson made 15 albums for MPS. In 1963 he also recorded his own composition, *Canadian Suite. African Suite* followed in 1979. In 1984 Peterson went on a tour of Russia that ended abruptly because of the poor treatment he and Granz received there.

In the 1980s Peterson became involved in an issue closer to home when he took exception to Canadian television commercials that ignored Blacks, Chinese, or Japanese. An article in *Toronto Life* by Gene Lees expressed Oscar's concern, and soon newspapers picked it up. The Attorney General for Ontario, the Honourable Roy McMurtry, co-hosted several low-key lunches for advertising firms and company executives with Peterson as the key speaker.

"Oscar played a very major role," McMurtry recalls. "I think it was a very important initiative. Oscar is somebody I am very proud to know." Oscar admits that "there was a certain amount of shock value when I spoke out on the subject because I think I have a fairly creditable record as a human being, and as a Canadian."

Canadians have agreed. Besides being named the best jazz player 14 times in the *Down Beat* Readers Poll as well as in numerous other polls in the United States, he has, in Canada, won three Grammy awards, been awarded honorary degrees by nine Canadian universities, been named in 1973 an Officer of the Order of Canada and elevated in 1984 to Companion of the Order. None of this has changed him from being friendly and approachable. Once, when his wife chided him about the Order of Canada, Peterson shot back, saying, "Hey, that means a lot to me. I can think back when I was a kid. I never dreamed my country would honour me."

The Toronto Star

"Oscar represents a tradition lost in this century — the virtuoso piano improvisor, like Chopin, the tradition of bravura playing that started with Beethoven and reached its apotheosis with Franz Liszt."
Lalo Schifrin

MVJ

Frederic Newton Gisborne

1824-1892

Linking Continents by Cable

NAC/C-59292

A NATIVE of Broughton in Lancashire, England, Frederic Newton Gisborne was one of the pioneering engineers who "wired the world" with submarine cables. He directed the laying of the first submarine cable on the floor of the Gulf of St. Lawrence and put into place the early arrangements for the first successful transatlantic cable. The record of his life and work provides clear evidence of the seemingly impossible problems and personal perils that Canada's telecommunications pioneers had to overcome.

Gisborne, educated privately in England, took a special interest in electricity, civil engineering, and related scientific subjects. At seventeen, he embarked on a world tour that gave him an appreciation of the great distances separating the world's continents. After coming to Canada in 1845, he quickly took an active interest in the rapidly developing field of telegraphy, realizing that this communication system provided a means of linking the continents.

In 1832 Samuel Morse, a graduate of Yale, had conceived the idea of transmitting messages, or signals, by means of electrical impulses transmitted by wire. Within a couple of years he had completed the first working model of his telegraph system.

After Morse's system had been put into commercial operation, courses in telegraphy were offered at various institutions. Gisborne enrolled in one of these courses in Montreal and ranked the highest in his class. In August 1847 he accepted a position as head of the Quebec office of the Montreal Telegraph Company.

Later that year he joined in the formation of the British North America Electric Telegraph Association (BNAETA) and became its superintendent. Acting on behalf of the Association, Gisborne visited New Brunswick and Nova Scotia, hoping to persuade the governments there to participate in the construction of a telegraph line from Halifax to Quebec. Despite his continuing efforts that included, on one occasion, snowshoeing more than one hundred miles to the St. Lawrence River dragging all his belongings behind him on a toboggan, he and his colleagues in the Association had, by 1849, completed only a single line from Quebec City to Rivière-du-Loup. That spring he became the superintendent and chief operator of the telegraph lines owned by the Nova Scotia government.

At that time Gisborne was aware of the difficulties that had been encountered in the laying of cable in salt water. He knew that Morse had laid an underwater cable in New York Harbour in 1842 and that Ezra Cornell had laid one under the Hudson River three years later. In both cases salt water had quickly corroded the underwater cables. Gisborne knew that this problem had to be solved, especially since Nova Scotia is almost entirely surrounded by salt water. Gisborne was convinced that, if a solution could be found, Newfoundland and Halifax could be linked by submarine cable. He was authorized by the Government of Nova Scotia to seek the support of Newfoundland for such a project.

In Newfoundland, Gisborne signed a contract to build a telegraph line from St. John's to Harbour Grace and Carbonear. On returning to Halifax, he proposed not only that a line be laid from Newfoundland to Nova Scotia but also that Newfoundland be linked with Ireland by transatlantic cable. Government leaders in Nova Scotia regarded Gisborne's idea of a transatlantic cable as impractical. Nonetheless in March 1851 they decided to form a private corporation, The Nova Scotia Electric Telegraph Company, to assume responsibility for all of the existing telegraph lines in Nova Scotia and to build additional lines.

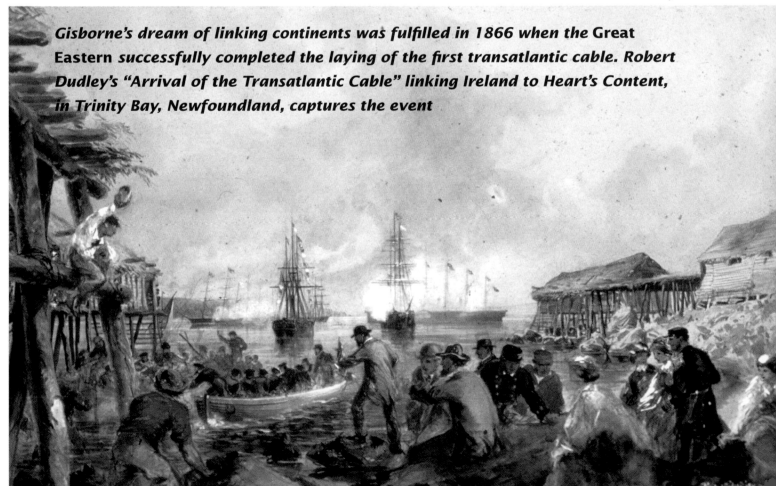

Gisborne's dream of linking continents was fulfilled in 1866 when the **Great Eastern** *successfully completed the laying of the first transatlantic cable. Robert Dudley's "Arrival of the Transatlantic Cable" linking Ireland to Heart's Content, in Trinity Bay, Newfoundland, captures the event*

Gisborne proceeded with the installation of telegraph lines in Newfoundland. By early September 1851, he and his colleagues had completed the line from St. John's to Cape Ray through more than three hundred miles of exceedingly difficult terrain, none of which had been previously explored.

Soon after he had embarked on this challenging project, he was abandoned by the six men who had initially worked with him. They were replaced by four Indians. One died and two deserted him. Finally in early December 1851 he and his exhausted companion returned to St. John's. But Gisborne's harrowing experience in Newfoundland had not discouraged him in the least. He was more than ever determined to link Newfoundland and Ireland by cable. Within a few weeks he went to New York and later to London to arrange the necessary financing for the transatlantic project.

In England Gisborne met a British engineer, John Watkins Brett, who was actively involved in experimentation and development of submarine telegraphy. Brett made an initial contribution to Gisborne's project as had several businessmen in New York City. Thus, when he returned to St. John's, he was able to persuade the Newfoundland legislature to grant exclusive rights to telegraph construction in Newfoundland for 30 years to his new company, financed through his business contacts in both New York and England.

By late November 1852, a submarine cable was laid on the floor of the St. Lawrence from Carleton Head, Prince Edward Island to Cape Tormentine, New Brunswick. Using machinery and installation methods developed largely by Gisborne himself, it was the first successful submarine cable in North America.

Having completed this project, Gisborne was convinced that he could now complete his great transatlantic submarine project. He organized a company in New York for this purpose, receiving confirmation that the necessary capital would be provided. With this assurance he went to Prince Edward Island, acquired all the cable rights there, and then proceeded to Newfoundland to superintend the completion of the telegraph line from St. John's to Cape Ray.

While involved in this difficult task, Gisborne learned that a disagreement had occurred in New York City and that the financing on which he had relied would not be provided. Despite major financial crises that almost destroyed him financially, Gisborne struggled on. Again he went to New York. Again he established new financial arrangements, this time with Cyrus West Field who, although he was in the paper business, became greatly interested in Gisborne's visionary transatlantic cable project.

Field organized a consortium and went to Newfoundland with Gisborne. In April 1854, the legislature of Newfoundland incorporated the New York, Newfoundland and London Telegraph Company. Gisborne arranged the transfer to this new company of telegraph rights in Newfoundland and Prince Edward Island and acquired similar rights in the state of Maine. It was agreed that Gisborne would be the chief engineer of the new company. He finally completed the laying of the cable from Cape Ray to Cape Breton in July 1856 and the line from Newfoundland to Nova Scotia by October of that same year.

Gisborne now had good reason to believe that the transatlantic cable project would finally be completed. Soon, however, when he came to the conclusion that his associates in the endeavour planned to cheat him, he removed himself completely from the project. Thus, when the first permanently successful transatlantic submarine cable was completed in 1866, Gisborne was not directly involved. But his ideas were, along with financier Cyrus Field, whom Gisborne had interested in this project in 1854.

When Gisborne returned to St. John's, Newfoundland, in May 1857, he was received triumphantly. There he returned to prospecting for minerals and explored Newfoundland's west coast from Cape Ray to the Strait of Belle Isle, securing financing for the development of two mineral projects. In the following decade he was involved in a variety of economic development efforts for Newfoundland. He engaged in similar activities in the 1870s in Nova Scotia, where he took a special interest in the development of coal deposits. Unfortunately, he again suffered major financial losses.

In 1879 Gisborne was appointed superintendent of the Telegraph and Signal Services for the Government of Canada. His first major undertaking was the reorganization of the telegraph system in British Columbia. When he had successfully completed this, he turned his attention to telegraph lines in Alberta and Saskatchewan. There he personally supervised the construction of new lines and the rebuilding of "pioneer" lines.

One of Gisborne's major achievements as superintendent of Canada's Telegraph and Signal Service was the installation of a cable along the Gulf of the Saint Lawrence for the transmission of information concerning fisheries, weather forecasting, and marine accidents. In the midst of all this work he participated in the founding in 1882 of the Royal Society of Canada.

When Gisborne died in 1892, he was planning yet another project. This time it was a transpacific cable. Death prevented him from contributing to its completion as he had to the successful transatlantic cable project.

Today, Frederic Newton Gisborne is remembered as a far-sighted, immensely creative, and courageous engineer and entrepreneur. He contributed not only to the advancement of telecommunications and the development of the coal industry in Cape Breton but also to the establishment of firm foundations for applied science and engineering in Canada. DMS

PAUL-ÉMILE CARDINAL LÉGER

1904 · 1991

Living the Servant Principle

FROM the day of his ordination as a member of the Sulpician Order in 1929, Paul-Émile Léger was a dedicated spiritual leader and counsellor. A key participant in the second Vatican Council of the Roman Catholic Church (1962-1965) called by Pope John XXIII to encourage spiritual renewal in the church, Léger shared valuable progressive insights with members of the Council during their deliberations. Throughout his long life of Christian service he contributed directly to the spiritual and physical well-being of many individuals in Canada, France, Japan, Italy, and Cameroon (West Central Africa).

Born in Valleyfield, Quebec, on the south shore of the St. Lawrence River on April 25, 1904, Léger, the son of a storekeeper, was educated in Montreal and Paris. Following his ordination, religious responsibilities took him to France in 1930. Three years later he went to Fukuoka, Japan, to establish a Sulpician seminary and to teach philosophy. On completion of this assignment, he returned to Valleyfield as vicar-general, to assist the Bishop of the diocese there.

In 1940, the same year that Paul-Émile Léger embarked upon his ecclesiastical work in Valleyfield, his brother Jules, who was nine years younger, began his career as a Canadian diplomat. Following ambassadorships in Mexico, Rome, Paris, and Brussels and a four-year appointment as Canada's Undersecretary of State for External Affairs, Jules Léger in 1974 became Canada's Governor-General.

During the entire period of his brother's career as a diplomat, Paul-Émile was serving with distinction in senior offices of the church. Following seven years in Valleyfield and three as Rector of the Pontifical Canadian College in Rome, Léger was appointed Archbishop of Montreal in 1950. Three years later he became a member of the Sacred College of Cardinals whose duties include electing the Pope and, as principal papal councillors, aiding in the worldwide government of the church.

In the early 1950s the Archdiocese of Montreal, for which Léger had responsibility, was in the

first stages of a major social revolution. Rapid urbanization and the audio-video "pop" culture, with its pervasive commercialism and contagious materialism, increasingly challenged Quebec's Catholic culture. Christianity in the Catholic tradition had been the primary influence in the lives of the vast majority of French-speaking Quebecers ever since their earliest ancestors had come from France centuries earlier. Profound changes were occurring when Léger became Archbishop of Montreal.

He had been nurtured in and was dedicated to all that was true and beautiful and lasting in Quebec's historic Catholic culture. But he sensed that a new, turbulent, increasingly difficult age was dawning. The church, he believed, must find new, compassionate ways to respond. Resolved to find appropriate answers, Léger began by listening to and caring for, all who were in need. Respect for the Cardinal widened as he worked on behalf of those who were chronically ill or otherwise handicapped or disadvantaged. Through his thoughtful yet stirring addresses, he stimulated religious, political, and social leaders to take essential action to deal with social inequities.

In a society where it was generally assumed that religious leaders were mindful of the sovereignty

Deciding that "it was time for deeds," Cardinal Léger left Canada in 1967 for Africa to work as a simple parish priest and to build a leprosarium

Jules and Paul-Émile Léger Foundation

and power of the state, Léger made it clear that the church was independent of the state. At the same time he took steps to overcome oligarchical traditions in the control of Catholic colleges and universities.

By 1962 Cardinal Léger could note that nearly three-quarters of the classroom teaching in the classical colleges in the archdiocese of Montreal was being done by lay teachers. Five years later he approved a non-denominational board and a lay president for the University of Montreal. These were only two of many positive steps he took to open traditional Catholic institutions more fully to the accumulated wisdom and good sense of non-clerical persons. He sought in other ways to ensure that the church drew upon that wisdom.

As Archbishop of Montreal, Cardinal Léger took a particular interest in the worldwide ecumenical movement and its efforts to bring Christians together in harmony. Thus as preparations were made for the Second Vatican Council, his gifts for reconciliation were called upon. He was invited to serve as a member of the preparatory commission for the Council from January 1959, when Pope John XXIII announced that the Council would be held, until October 1962 when deliberations began. He devoted much time to its work.

Léger made substantial contributions to the Council. As a result of his earlier work in Canada, France, Japan, and Italy and the many steps he had taken to help the church deal with problems and to rise to new challenges in his diocese, he foresaw many of the problems the Council would have to confront. He also anticipated many of the changes on practical issues set out in the documents on which the Council agreed and which were disseminated throughout the world. These changes, which reflected Léger's progressive spirit, were soon felt in many aspects of the life of the church.

When the Council completed its work, Léger took careful steps to effect further changes in the life of his diocese in keeping with the Council's decrees. Then in 1967 he retired as Archbishop of Montreal and went to the United Republic of Cameroon in West Central Africa as a missionary among handicapped children and lepers. This area of nearly 180,000 square miles, with a rapidly rising population of about five million when he went there, was in great need of the thoughtful humanitarian help he provided.

Léger's decision to go to Cameroon, in his retirement years, reflected the same ideals that had animated his entire adult life. As a deeply religious person he was contemplative. But he also embodied in his daily life the teaching of Saint James that if faith does not lead to helpful action it may, by itself, be a lifeless thing. Thus he was committed to vigorous action to make life better for ordinary people, particularly the less fortunate, wherever he went.

Many honours were conferred on him. Canadian universities granted him honorary degrees. In 1958 France awarded him the Grand Cross of the Legion of Honour. A decade later, soon after the government of Canada instituted the Canadian system of honours, he was made one of the earliest Companions of the Order of Canada, the highest honour his country bestows. DMS

WILLIAM EDMOND LOGAN

1798-1875

SIR WILLIAM LOGAN, founding director of the Geological Survey of Canada, increased the knowledge of the geological nature of Canada, contributed to the organized development of its mining industry, and made Canada's mineral resources known around the world. His insightful contributions to the development of geology as a science led to his induction, in March 1851, into the Royal Society of London, the first native-born Canadian so honoured. In 1855 he received the Cross of the Legion of Honour from the French government and the following year he was knighted by Queen Victoria.

"He formed a rock group and toured the country"

Logan was born in Montreal in 1798. After completion of his early education there, he entered the University of Edinburgh in 1816 where he developed an interest in geology. However, he left after a year of study to work in his uncle's accounting office in London. In 1831 his uncle sent him to Swansea, Wales, to manage the Forest Copper Works.

While fulfilling his management responsibilities, Logan devoted much time to stratigraphy — the study of the origin, composition, distribution, and succession of strata or layers of rocks. From 1831 to 1841, as an active member of the highly respected Geological Survey of London, Logan kept abreast of new insights that were modifying or sweeping away earlier ideas concerning the earth, its formation and structure.

When Logan began his studies of geology, there was much speculation concerning the origin of coal. Through his private study of coal deposits and their formation and through his collecting of fossils, he developed scientific data that greatly improved knowledge concerning the formation of coal. His ideas came to the attention of Charles Lyell (1797-1875), the leading British authority on geology. Lyell's high regard for Logan's work was a significant factor in the decision by the Canadian government to appoint Logan as its first geologist in the autumn of 1842.

Sir WILLIAM LOGAN
DIRECTOR 1842-1869

Logan was given the responsibility of undertaking an accurate and complete geological survey of Canada, in particular of the southern portion of the present provinces of Ontario and Quebec. He was asked to provide "a full and scientific description of its rocks, soil and minerals ... accompanied by proper maps, diagrams and drawings, together with a collection of specimens to illustrate the same." His initial appointment was for two years and the initial government appropriation for the survey was only 1,500 pounds sterling.

Surrounded by his rock collection in his spartan office, Sir William Logan was one of the world's greatest geologists when this William Notman photograph was taken in the early 1860s. Mt. Logan, named for Sir William Logan, is the highest mountain in Canada

When Logan embarked on his new assignment, he understood the scope of the task before him, but it seems that few Canadian political leaders did. However, because of the persuasive quality of his work and that of his colleagues, the mandate of the Survey was periodically renewed. Its funding, however, was occasionally in a perilous state. It was sustained only by the interim financing that Logan personally provided. For instance, when Parliament failed, as it did in 1863, to make the necessary financial appropriation, Logan himself paid the salaries of the staff. Thanks to Logan, the work of the Survey was sustained and ultimately gained international recognition.

Among Logan's primary interests was the development of a geological museum with a comprehensive collection of specimens of Canadian minerals. This strengthened and extended the work of the Survey. The exhibition of this collection in London in 1851 and in Paris in 1855 contributed to increased interest in Canada. In 1859 the Survey was credited with having done more for Canada's reputation abroad than anything else connected with the country.

Although he was a man of considerable wealth who earned and received recognition for his outstanding work, Logan was modest and unassuming. His spartan tastes were evident in his office which was also his mapping room and bedroom. His furniture was severely functional. In the corner of his office was an iron contraption that looked like a chair, but Logan never sat in it. At night it became his bed. He used the same rough blankets there as he did on his many, extensive field trips. When he was not away on a field trip or on other work on behalf of the Survey, Logan awakened at five a.m. to devote another long day to the work of the Survey and to his examination and preparation of geological data for presentation in map form. All this was done with infinite attention to detail.

In this thorough, disciplined manner, Logan, with the help of his assistants, completed his extensive field and laboratory work and his preparation of maps. In 1863 his masterly, 983-page volume, *Geology of Canada* was published. This was the summation of knowledge to that time concerning the geology of Canada. An atlas was published two years later and a larger geological map in 1869.

During his 27 years as Director of Canada's Geological Survey, Logan worked with great devotion and immense effectiveness in the establishment and development of the Survey as a combination of scientific precision and practical helpfulness. Upon his retirement on November 30, 1869, the Survey thus embodied the principles that had animated and given lasting significance to Logan's own life and work.

The highest of the St. Elias Mountains in the southwestern Yukon Territory of Canada is Mount Logan. It is named after Sir William Edmond Logan, the creator and inspirer of the Geological Survey of Canada.

D.M.S

BATTLE OF AMIENS & GENERAL A. W. CURRIE

A Greater Triumph...

ON APRIL 9, 1917, the Canadian Corps, consisting of four infantry divisions numbering almost one hundred thousand, captured an important tactical landmark in northern France known as Vimy Ridge. This was a great achievement as the Germans during the previous two years had already repulsed several Allied attempts to seize the ridge. Blood of troops from the British Isles had already permeated the ridge. But France had suffered the most. Fifty thousand Frenchmen had lost their lives in vain attempts to wrest the ridge from German forces. Ultimately the capture of Vimy Ridge cost Canada ten thousand casualties, 3,598 of them fatal, but it won the Canadian Corps a reputation as one of the hardest-hitting Allied formations on the Western Front. Because this was the first Allied victory since the beginning of the war almost three years earlier, Vimy Ridge is almost always regarded as the greatest Canadian triumph of the Great War, overshadowing what was actually a greater triumph — the Battle of Amiens.

The battle of Amiens began on August 8, 1918. This was the first day of what war historians call "The Last Hundred Days." The Canadian attack so surprised and disoriented the Germans that their commander-in-chief, General Ludendorff, said that August 8, 1918 was "the blackest day of the German Army in the history of the war." And Sir Julian Byng, the British general who had commanded the Canadian Corps at Vimy Ridge, told his successor, Ontario-born General Arthur Currie, that the Canadian performance at Amiens was "the finest operation of the war."

It is no wonder that Ludendorff and Byng made such statements. During the hundred days which followed the Canadian Corps' initial and speedy penetration of the German line, the Corps, under Currie's command, had liberated 500 square miles of territory containing 228 cities, towns, and villages and captured 31,000 prisoners, 590 heavy and field guns and thousands of machine guns and trench mortars. Fifty German divisions — approximately one-fourth of the total German forces on the Western Front — were defeated. By nightfall on the first day of the battle of Amiens, the Canadian Corps' penetration of the enemy line was unequalled: no other engagement on the Western Front up to that time had achieved this kind of success as the result of a single day's fighting.

General Arthur Currie's men broke the German line at Amiens on August 8, 1918. Currie, from Strathroy, Ontario, became a hero. In this view, October 1918, Currie is standing left, next to the Prince of Wales. To the Prince's right is Brig. Gen. Morrison and divisional commander, Major-General David Watson. This ceremony marked the freeing of Denan by the 4th Canadian Division

A year earlier, when the Canadian Corps had assaulted Vimy Ridge, Currie had been the general commanding the First Canadian Division. An unsuccessful real estate agent and former school teacher when war broke out, Currie was also a keen amateur soldier holding the rank of lieutenant colonel after fourteen years of militia service. As major general, less than three years later, he commanded his division so well at Vimy that, when Byng was promoted to command one of the five British armies on the Western Front, he strongly urged that Currie, instead of another British general, succeed him as commander of the Canadian Corps.

Currie fell heir not only to the four fighting divisions which constituted his corps but also to extra thousands of men who constituted the corps troops, lines-of-communication troops, and base troops all of whom backed the fighting formations. This meant he commanded, all in all, some 120,000 Canadian soldiers. He proved so successful in the ensuing months that the British prime minister, Lloyd George, toyed with the idea of sacking the British commander-in-chief, Field Marshal Sir Douglas Haig, and replacing him with Currie. This would have put Currie at the head of five British armies totalling about a million men and would have elevated him over the heads of five senior army commanders, and thirteen corps commanders, all professionals with one exception. This was General Monash, the Australian corps commander, who, like Currie, was an amateur. Quite obviously, the British government and the War Office would never have countenanced this. Besides, because Haig was on intimate terms with the King, the Prime Minister's rather wild idea never materialized. However, the idea certainly speaks well of Canada's Currie and the men he commanded.

Currie proved himself such a successful tactician and administrator that, when the Allies planned their 1918 campaign with a view to winning the war by the spring of 1919, Currie and his Corps were chosen to spearhead the Allied advance. As history tells us, Currie's attack on August 8, 1918, met with such success and penetrated the enemy's defences so quickly and so deeply that the Germans were thrown off balance. This helped the Allied troops on Currie's flanks follow; the attack developed into a pursuit battle along the entire vast front.

The entire operation ended three months later when the Armistice was signed on November 11, 1918, Germany having been defeated six months sooner than the Allies had anticipated. But on August 8, 1918, at Amiens, the Canadian Corps, almost 100 percent amateur soldiers, delivered the first of the knock-out blows that won the war. *SG*

Elizabeth Arden

1884 - 1966

Elizabeth Arden Canada Inc.

WHEN the Humber Valley Conservation Authority was about to open Dalziel Pioneer Park (now Black Creek Pioneer Village) near Woodbridge, Ontario, in 1954, a local notable was sought for the tree-planting ceremony.

Someone recalled that Florence Nightingale Graham had been born and had lived on the property until she was 24 years old. Not only was she invited but she came. But her name was different! It was now Elizabeth Arden, one of the most renowned names in the world of glamour.

Creator of Beauty

Born Florence Nightingale Graham near Woodbridge, Ontario, Elizabeth Arden, viewed here at the height of her career in 1947, often accompanied her farmer father to Toronto's St. Lawrence Market as a child. Here she learned the art of selling...

Elizabeth was then 75 but looked much younger — appropriate for the woman recognized as the creator of beauty since opening a salon on Fifth Avenue, New York City, in 1910. *Fortune* magazine exclaimed in 1938 that she, as the sole owner of the Elizabeth Arden Company, was probably earning more money than any other woman in U.S. history. She was a *Time* cover story in 1947; a 1990 issue of *Life* magazine included her in its special feature — "100 Most Important Americans of the 20th Century."

Her return to Woodbridge, in 1954, no doubt brought back memories. She was the third of five children born to a Scottish father and English mother. They had eloped in the early 1870s by sailing to Canada and settling as pioneers in the Woodbridge area where Mr. Graham eked out a living as a market gardener. Following her mother's death when Florence was only six, she often travelled with her father to the St. Lawrence Market, Toronto, where she learned the art of selling farm produce. At age 17 she went to work.

She took up nursing but found she disliked the profession. She became, in turn, a clerk, a stenographer and a dental assistant, eventually leaving that work in 1908 to move to New York where an older brother had gone to better himself.

At first a bookkeeper with the E.R. Squibb Company, she spent hours in the labs learning all she could about skin care, an interest of hers since her teens when women were at last allowing themselves (or being allowed) to aid nature with a few lotions and creams. When Florence, whose own complexion was superb, had a chance to become a cashier for Eleanor Adair, an early beauty culturist, she quickly left Squibb, successfully pestering Adair to make her a "treatment girl." Before long clients were asking for "that nice Canadian girl." In 1909 she went into partnership with another culturist, Elizabeth Hubbard.

Together they opened a salon on Fifth Avenue, but the partnership soon soured. Hubbard moved out leaving Florence to pay the rent. This she did as well as borrow $6,000 from her brother to remodel the salon. She kept the name Elizabeth, and chose "Arden" from Tennyson's famous poem, "Enoch Arden." She also called herself "Mrs." — a title more acceptable those days for females in business.

Each day she arrived early to clean the salon spotlessly before giving treatments from 9 a.m. until 6 p.m. At the end of the day, she worked elsewhere as a manicurist under the name Graham, toiled in her laboratory, or managed the accounts. Within six months she had repaid her brother.

When a 1912 edition of *Vogue* stated that the discreet application of a little paint would enhance a lady's appearance, Elizabeth concocted a series of rouges and tinted powders that reflected her genius for shades of colour and enhanced her growing reputation with an ever-increasing number of clients. In 1914 she went to Paris where she visited several salons a day to learn their methods. Sailing home on the *Lusitania*, she met Thomas J. Lewis, a banker she had once approached for a loan. In 1915 they were married.

Following her return, she approached a chemical company to develop a "face cream that was light and fluffy like whipped cream." A. Fabian Swanson, one of the chemists, succeeded. Elizabeth called it Venetian Cream Amoretta and asked him to develop a lotion to go with it. This success, named Ardena Skin Tonic, led to their enduring collaboration.

In 1918 Elizabeth ran afoul of the U.S. tax system as she had never distinguished between company money and her own income. As a result of this, she hired husband Tommy, an experienced banker and army veteran home from overseas, to handle the books. She also permitted a younger sister, Gladys, to wholesale her products through tours and treatment sessions in major stores — a function Tommy took over with enormous success when, in 1920, Gladys settled in France to promote Arden products there and open a salon in Paris.

Throughout the 1920s and '30s, Elizabeth furiously competed against Helena Rubinstein and Dorothy Gray, opening salons in the United States and in such European cities as Cannes, Rome and Berlin. Her products were also marketed worldwide. This allowed her to claim, with a degree of accuracy, that "There are only three American names that are known in every corner of the globe: Singer Sewing Machines, Coca Cola and Elizabeth Arden."

Success, however, did not soften her. She made it clear that she ran the company, hired and fired at will, and once admitted, "I don't want them to love me; I want them to fear me." She couldn't accept criticism of her ideas or products and railed against anyone who infringed on her right to run things her way. She once declared that "standards should be set by me and not imposed on me." Her restlessness and drive also led to a divorce in 1934. A second marriage to a Russian prince in 1942 lasted only 13 months.

As a young girl, Florence had been put in charge of the horses on the Graham's leased tenant farm. She fell in love with them. Therefore it was quite natural for her to take up horseracing, this time with the same zeal and intensity she had shown in business. Horses were treated like favourite clients: her "Eight Hour Cream" was used for bruises, and Ardena Skin Lotion replaced horse liniment. Trainers, jockeys, and stable hands suffered the same fate as company executives. One trainer put it succinctly: "My mother used to say only horses sweat, people perspire. But here, the horses perspire; it's the trainers who sweat."

By the time her racehorse "Jet Pilot" won the Kentucky Derby in 1947, Elizabeth had more than 100 salons across America and Europe and some 300 products on shelves around the world. Her advertising campaigns were famous for creating glamour with such headlines as "Every woman has a right to be beautiful." Clients at her Fifth Avenue salon included many of the best-known women of America: the Begum Aga Khan, Claire Booth Luce, Toronto-born Beatrice Lillie, and Mrs. Dwight D. Eisenhower.

For three decades Elizabeth lived on Fifth Avenue in a ten-room apartment, decorated almost entirely in what had become known as her signature colour — pink. She never retired. In her eighties she still approved advertisements, checked every new product and flew off to visit salons unannounced. She became the second woman member of the Distribution Hall of Fame, was given an honorary Doctor of Laws by Syracuse University, and was presented by France with the Legion of Honour for her contribution to the world of beauty.

Throughout her long career, Miss Arden was a pathfinder. She inspired new ideas and breakthroughs such as full service salons; products for different skin types; eye makeup in North America; exercise classes and records (in 1921); and, makeup to match skin tone just to name a few.

An active and generous supporter of many charities, Elizabeth Arden was a member of the National Board of Directors of the American Women's Voluntary Services and a founder of the American Symphony. The Lighthouse for the Blind, the March of Dimes and the Heart Fund are but a few of the many causes she enthusiastically supported.

"It was a long life and a beautiful one," observed *Women's Wear Daily* in an obituary on October 19, 1966, two days after Elizabeth suffered a heart attack and died overnight. Born New Year's Eve, 1884,

Born on a tenant farm near Woodbridge, Ontario, Elizabeth Arden returned to her roots, ceremonially planting a tree in 1954 at the Dalziel Pioneer Park, today part of the Metropolitan Toronto & Region Conservation Authority. As a girl, she fell in love with horses. Thus it was natural in her later years to own yearlings, stables, and a Kentucky Derby winner

Metro Toronto & Region Conservation Authority

she had, indeed, had a long life.

Although she left a will, the company's future was not spelled out. It was as if she intended always to be its sole owner, chairman, and president. Eventually in 1971, one of the world's most famous glamour industries was sold to the Eli Lilly Corporation and then resold in 1989 to Unilever, the consumer goods conglomerate. The dream of the "little Canadian woman with the magic hands" had grown to a reality that even she might not have imagined. MVJ

William Maxwell Aitken

1879-1964

"Lord Beaverbrook is at his very best when things are at their very worst"

Winston Churchill

TO attain high political office and to serve effectively as a senior minister of state in a democratic society where one was born is a considerable achievement. To attain such office and to serve effectively on two separate occasions during two world wars in a country in which one was not born and, in addition, to have gained international recognition as a financier, newspaper publisher and philanthropist is a record of achievement of the rarest order. Such is the legacy of Max Aitken, born in Maple, Ontario, in 1879.

Having been raised in New Brunswick, Aitken attended but never took his degree from its provincial university. Aitken realized early in life that he had a natural talent for making money. He began by selling insurance and bonds, soon becoming an investor and underwriter, initially in a small way, on his own account in Halifax, Nova Scotia. In 1906 he moved to Montreal and acquired a seat on the Stock Exchange a year later.

In Montreal he demonstrated unusual skill in amalgamating companies engaged in similar business activities. He effected the mergers which resulted in the creation of Canada Cement and of The Steel Company of Canada (Stelco). While he profited substantially through his creation of these integrated companies there was much criticism of his unorthodox activities and of the Canadian merger movement generally. Since he had found a ready market in England for the bonds of The Steel Company of Canada, he moved there and became active, almost immediately, in English politics.

In December 1910 he won a seat in the British House of Commons. There he became Private Secretary, and soon chief advisor to Bonar Law, a fellow New Brunswicker, who was elected leader of Britain's Conservative Party late in 1911 and served as Prime Minister from October 1922 until May 1923.

During World War I, Aitken became a representative of the Canadian government with the expeditionary force and later was given responsibility for Canadian war records. Instead of being made a

Born in Maple, Ontario, Max Aitken was selling bonds when he was 21. Within 10 years he was a multi-millionaire after creating companies like Stelco and Canada Cement through mergers. In 1910, he moved to England and within a year was elected to the House of Commons. When he was made a peer he chose the title Beaverbrook after a stream near his Canadian home. At the time of his death in 1964, Lord Beaverbrook controlled one of the largest publishing empires in the world

member of the British Cabinet — he had hoped to become President of the Board of Trade — he was persuaded to resign his Commons seat so that the person appointed to that position might be elected in his place. In return, Aitken became a member of the House of Lords and was given the title Beaverbrook in January 1918. A month later, and much against the wishes of King George V, he joined the Cabinet as Chancellor of the Duchy of Lancaster and Minister of Information with responsibility for propaganda.

Not long after he had moved to England, Aitken had bought and later sold control of the Rolls-Royce automobile company and gained additional wealth. In 1916 he bought an interest in the *Daily Express* and gained complete control in 1922. Determined to transform it into one of London's most influential newspapers, he invested heavily in it.

Under his dynamic leadership the *Daily Express*, reflecting his genius and originality, gradually became one of the most popular and commanding daily newspapers of all time. By the late 1950s it had a daily circulation of over four million and was being printed simultaneously in London, Manchester and Glasgow. In 1921 he launched the *Sunday Express* and again invested heavily to ensure its acceptance as a popular Sunday paper. The following year he acquired the *Evening Standard* and later absorbed the Liberal paper, the *Pall Mall Gazette* and the *Glasgow Evening Citizen*.

Beaverbrook published these papers for political influence as well as for profit. Thus the papers bore his imprint to a greater or lesser degree depending on his particular interests at the time. Throughout his career as a publisher, he was dedicated to Empire Free Trade. Between the First and Second Great Wars he promoted the establishment of an Imperial Preference trading arrangement within the British Commonwealth. But in the end his campaign was not successful.

With other prominent British conservatives, such as Joseph Chamberlain and Winston Churchill, he struggled with what he regarded as the self-satisfied complacency of the British aristocracy. He criticized severely the self-serving practices of political leaders and claimed that he had forced Lloyd George to resign. He was clearly unsuccessful, however, in his efforts in the early 1930s to have Stanley Baldwin removed as Leader of the Conservative Party.

During the abdication crisis of 1936, Beaverbrook supported King Edward VIII not because he approved of Kings and Queens but because he was committed to the British Empire of which the King was the titular head. Thus he supported him. Again Beaverbrook failed.

On his appointment as Prime Minister on May 10, 1940, Churchill turned to Beaverbrook as a close friend with whom he had served in the British cabinet during World War I. While King George VI was reluctant, Churchill persuaded the King with tact and argument that Beaverbrook could serve Britain admirably as Minister of Aircraft Production. And he did. He threw all of his energy into the production of aircraft just as he had thrown himself into the struggle to increase the circulation of the *Daily Express* and his other newspapers.

Through a variety of ingenious means Beaverbrook ensured that the aircraft Britain needed for its survival were produced. He was, however, a difficult colleague for Churchill during World War II.

While their friendship was severely tested, it remained until the end of their lives. Churchill never forgot the creative and desperately needed drive which Beaverbrook provided as Minister of Aircraft Production during 1940-41. Beaverbrook served in other ministerial capacities during World War II and for a time as the British-Lend-Lease Administrator in the United States.

During the last two decades of his life, Beaverbrook renewed his interest in Canada. Through his munificence, the University of New Brunswick was strengthened. The Beaverbrook Art Gallery was built in Fredericton, New Brunswick. On his death in 1964, much of his wealth was set aside for Canadian projects administered by the Beaverbrook Canadian Foundation which he created.

Throughout his career Beaverbrook was an enigmatic and controversial figure who brought, wherever he went, excitement and optimism, thus removing some of the dullness from an increasingly difficult and uncertain world. DMS

As Minister of Aircraft Production in Churchill's wartime government, Beaverbrook galvanized the aircraft industry. This view of Beaverbrook was taken in 1941 after disembarking from airtransport at Gander, Newfoundland, to brief Canadian officials on the war effort

GLENN GOULD

Keyboard Genius

"JANUARY 2 is early for predictions," wrote *Washington Post* critic Paul Hume, "but it is unlikely that the year 1955 will bring us a finer piano recital than that played yesterday afternoon in the Phillips Gallery. We will be lucky if it brings us others of equal beauty and significance."

Hume was writing about a 22-year-old Canadian with flair. When Hume visited Toronto in 1987 for the first presentation of the $50,000 Glenn Gould Prize, he reiterated, "Gould made some of the most glorious music I have ever heard from any piano."

Two years after the Washington concert, Gould became the first classical musician from North America to be invited behind what was then called the Iron Curtain. At Gould's initial performance, the director of the Moscow Philharmonic went backstage during the intermission and declared, "We have never heard fugues like this." After the performance, Gould took numerous curtain calls and later left his crowded dressing room to return to the stage to play an encore — five pieces from Bach's *Goldberg Variations*.

He was already famous for his *Goldberg Variations.* His rendition constituted his first long-playing record with Columbia Records. Following a single performance at New York's Town Hall, in 1955, Columbia had signed him to a contract. Their executives tried to dissuade him from his choice, but he insisted, and in 1956, the year of its release, it became the year's best-selling classical record.

In making that record, Glenn brought along his own sawed-off chair that enabled him to sit just 14 inches from the floor so that he could keep his wrist at or below the level of the keyboard. He also displayed other eccentricities for which he became almost as famous as for his ability as a pianist.

These included, wrote Jonathan Cott in 1974, "loping on stage like a misplaced eland with unpressed tails, sometimes wearing gloves ... and conducting, humming, singing, combating, and cajoling, and making love to his piano as if it were Lewis Carroll's Snark." Off stage he was known for his bizarre dress: "gloves, mittens, T-shirt, vest, sweater, coat, and scarf all in warm weather," wrote Cott, while others reported on his hypochondria, his excessive need for privacy, his telephone calls

In 1957
Glenn Gould
became the first
classical musician
from North America to
play in the Soviet Union

The Toronto Star

after midnight that went on for hours, and numerous other idiosyncrasies that were seen as the trappings of genius and relished by the media.

The media did not take him seriously when he announced his decision to leave the concert stage, but in 1964 he did, never to make another concert appearance. Instead, he concentrated on making records and radio and television programs, claiming that "the functions of concerts had been — or would be soon — taken over by the electronic media."

Gould continued making records for Columbia in New York or at the Eaton Auditorium in Toronto with nearly all the sessions taking place at night and consisting of three steps — recording a complete take of the movement (or a large section of a major work), listening to it for any finger slips or imperfect musical balances, and replaying small inserts to correct the errors. He made more than 75 records for Columbia in this manner, all but 19 of them featuring Bach, Beethoven, Mozart, and Schoenberg.

As a composer, Gould completed *String Quartet, Opus I* in 1955. Performed by the Montreal String Quartet, it won praise from the local newspaper, *La Presse*, and later from a New York critic attending Ontario's Stratford Festival musical concerts that Gould co-directed. Gould convinced Columbia to record it with the Symphonia Quartet of the Cleveland Symphony Orchestra. *The Christian Science Monitor* called it "an intensely beautiful work." *The Saturday Review* was equally complimentary.

Gould did not compose any other serious musical compositions though he discussed many ideas with friends and associates, stating he would return to composing and conducting when he stopped recording at age 50. Instead he concentrated on being a CBC radio and TV producer throughout the 1960s and 1970s. Some of his documentaries he believed to be compositions in their own right, particularly his 1967 program, "The Idea of North." "Chopping it (interviews) up and slicing here and there and pulling on this phrase and accentuating that one ... or adding a compressor here and a filter there" is composing, he claimed. This view was shared by Barbara Frum who wrote, "Gould used his interviews to create a sound composition about the loneliness, the idealism, and the letdowns of those who go north."

In all, Gould produced, was interviewed, or performed in more than 100 CBC Radio or TV programs over the next two decades. These ranged from radio discussions about the music of his personal favourite pop singers such as Petula Clark and Barbara Streisand to a TV production about his city, Toronto. Some of his work was praised and some condemned. "The Gould broadcast ... is likely to stand as a forerunner of a new radio art," wrote the *Montreal Star* about "The Idea of North," whereas *The Toronto Daily Star's* Roy Shields, commenting on Gould's "Richard Strauss, a Personal View" wrote, "It is difficult to understand why Mr. Gould was allowed to write his own script.... His use of language ... is quite unintelligible."

Gould, however, loved writing and did so for print as well as radio and TV. He wrote many of the liner notes for his recordings which won him his only Grammy Award — he never got one for his music — as well as articles for *The New York Times*, *The Globe and Mail*, and for magazines such as *High Fidelity* and the *Piano Quarterly* where he could write about anything he wanted and at any length but without remuneration. Much of his writing was pedantic and his attempts at witty elegance sounded artificial, but the publisher of the *Quarterly* admitted to a biographer, "It didn't matter — I was going to publish it.... I took everything as a gift."

A few months before Gould's untimely death he received a letter from a New York fan asking permission to use his recording of the *Bach C Major Prelude and Fugue* in a film to promote the welfare of animals. Gould responded that he would be delighted, adding, "As it happens, animal welfare is one of the great passions of my life, and if you'd asked to use my entire recorded output in support of such a cause, I couldn't possibly have refused."

This was his last letter (now on record at the National Library in Ottawa). Five weeks later — right after his 50th birthday — he recognized he was ill. He called a close CBC friend, John P.L. Roberts, who wanted to call an ambulance, but Gould insisted that he be driven to hospital where he suffered a second stroke. Shortly afterwards, he slipped into a coma and, on October 4, with no hope of his recovery, his family authorized that the life-support systems be removed. His will, written two years earlier, left a major portion of his estate to the welfare of animals through the Toronto Humane Society. *MVJ*

KENNETH COLIN IRVING

Industrial Caesar

THE ESTABLISHMENT, progress, and financial success of the Irving Group of Companies is one of the greatest, and perhaps the most unusual, of all corporate accomplishments in Canadian economic history. By the early 1990s this Group included thousands of Irving automobile service stations in eastern Canada and northeastern United States, transport companies, forest industry operations, pulp and paper mills, newspaper, radio, and TV companies, Canada's largest oil refinery, a modern shipyard, and the first deep-water terminal in the western hemisphere.

During his lifetime, K.C. Irving was quick to share credit with his sons and associates for the amazing development of his organization and its many companies. They, however, were equally quick to emphasize that K.C. Irving was the person primarily responsible for the remarkable growth of their corporate colossus. His father, J.D. Irving, a well-established businessman, may have been a role model but from earliest days K.C. Irving was fiercely independent, first as a young boy running small business ventures in his home town and from the mid-1920s onward, as the overall enterprise grew, as its dynamic force, its master strategist and guiding influence.

Early in his life, young K.C. Irving demonstrated that he liked a challenge as had his great-grandfather, George Irving, who had sailed from Scotland for Canada across the howling Atlantic in 1822. Settling in 1826 in the Eastern section of New Brunswick in the area that was organized as Kent County, George Irving built a home and cleared 200 acres of land. When he arrived, New Brunswick was still largely underdeveloped with a population of some 70,000 people of European descent in an area of 28,000 square miles. Life was difficult and only those with self-reliance and hardihood were able to get ahead. George Irving had these qualities and bequeathed them to his descendants.

By the beginning of the twentieth century, J.D. Irving was operating a sawmill in Buctouche, a village on Northumberland Strait, on New Brunswick's east coast north of Moncton. The main commercial activities there were fishing, lumbering, and ship building. J.D. Irving gradually extended his business activities in Buctouche to include a general store, grist and carding mills, and farm and fish products marketing. He became a well-respected member of the Buctouche community, particularly among his fellow Presbyterians whose disciplined religious values he shared.

K.C. Irving was born in Buctouche on March 14, 1899, into the business and Presbyterian traditions which were central in the lives of his father and ancestors. During young Irving's formative years, automobiles were gradually becoming more

Founder of an empire that encompassed pulp and paper, oil refining, publishing and broadcasting, K.C. Irving was New Brunswick's first modern-day entrepreneurial industrialist. Inducted into the Canadian Business Hall of Fame in 1979, Mr. Irving was not so much motivated by the making of money as he was in the creating of businesses

J.D. Irving, Limited

widely used. His interest in automobiles and in other mechanical devices grew as he matured and was heightened during the time he served in the Royal Flying Corps in World War I. Before he entered the military he had studied for a time in Nova Scotia's Dalhousie and Acadia universities. But practical business affairs were of primary interest to him, and after the war he gained a considerable reputation in Buctouche as an automobile mechanic.

By the early 1920s he was operating a profitable gas station and Ford dealership as an extension to the Irving General Store. Soon he established in Buctouche his own garage and service station, the first in town. He sold Imperial Oil products as its agent in Kent County. When Imperial withdrew his right to sell their products he began in July 1924 to import gasoline and lubricating oil from the United States. This was a key step in the development of the Irving Group of Companies.

In 1925 the Ford Motor Company granted Irving its dealership for the city of Saint John and the surrounding county. K.C. Irving Limited was incorporated that year and Irving Oil Company Limited four years later. Saint John became the centre of his developing business interests. Bus and truck companies were acquired and new routes were opened.

As his network of service stations and transportation routes developed, his company built its own stations and service depots. He acquired the Saint John Shipbuilding and Dry Dock Company and built his own oil tankers. Soon his company was assembling vessels for other oil companies including Exxon and Shell. In partnership with Standard Oil of California, K.C. Irving completed construction of an oil refinery in Saint John in 1960. His shipbuilding company subsequently secured the prime contract for the Canadian Patrol Frigate Program.

When his father died in 1933, K.C. Irving had acquired J.D. Irving, Limited, the family lumber company. Five years later he purchased Canada Veneers, another company in the wood products field. It manufactured fuselages for Mosquito fighter aircraft during World War II. At the end of the war Irving acquired the New Brunswick Railway Company which, although it had no rolling stock, held large stands of timber. Gradually his timber holdings were extended in North America. K.C. Irving took a personal interest in the establishment of the company's first reforestation in the province of New Brunswick. By the late 1970s millions of trees had been planted to reflect his growing environmental interest in the future of his home province.

One of the strategic decisions taken by K.C. Irving was to concentrate on the development of his business interests in New Brunswick and nearby jurisdictions. By the 1960s his companies gave employment to about eight percent of the entire labour force in New Brunswick and this figure continues to grow. His newspapers, radio, and TV stations were primary sources of news and information.

The Irving organization has been the subject of vigorous criticism for the extent of its economic influence in New Brunswick. But thoughtful analysts are keenly aware that the Irving Group of Companies has provided and continues to provide employment for thousands of individuals and, through them, financial support for their families in an area in which high unemployment has been and continues to be a profound problem. Through the widespread employment it provides, the Irving

Group of Companies helps to alleviate that primary problem. It has done and is doing more than this. K.C. Irving and his companies have stimulated many enterprising young men. Various senior executives who have moved to other organizations completed their business apprenticeships serving the Irving conglomerate.

Early in his life, K.C. Irving learned that, through rigorous personal discipline and continuing intelligent action to secure desirable goals, an individual can be successful and help others in the process. In the financial dimensions of business, he learned from his father and, through his own experience, that, to succeed financially, income must exceed expense month by month and year by year. When this occurs the surplus can then be carefully invested in the development of an enterprise or invested in a brand-new undertaking. In short, careful attention to financial details allows money to be used to make more money.

K.C. Irving's careful learning of these lessons and his application of them were key elements in the financial and corporate success he came to enjoy. In addition, of course, he knew that he must use every moment carefully. Time must not be wasted because time, in a money civilization, is a primary factor in achieving success. When time is invested carefully, new opportunities for the advancement of a business can likewise be seized to advantage. Thus K.C. Irving numbered his days and applied the wisdom he gained in the development of his business enterprise. He bequeathed a great heritage to those who have come after him just as his ancestors had left him a most valuable cultural and business inheritance.

The Irving Group of Companies is now in the capable hands of K.C. Irving's three sons: James K. Irving, Arthur L. Irving, and John E. Irving and their associates.   DMS

In the mid-1950s, K.C. Irving took a step that was to see him recognized as a reforestation leader in North America. He lived to see his own company plant over 300 million trees in New Brunswick in a program widely praised as pioneering reforestation and environmental progress

Marshall McLuhan

1911-1980

Oracle of the Electronic Age

HERBERT MARSHALL McLUHAN was the first person to systematically and methodically analyze the effects of mass media on human perceptions as well as on the human responses that followed. He was a global pathfinder.... This scholarly Canadian professor of English Literature emerged as the most widely hailed authority, whether in North America, Europe or Australasia, on communications technology and the impact of mass communications upon modern society and culture.

Born in Edmonton in 1911, Marshall McLuhan had graduated from the Universities of Manitoba and Cambridge before he came in 1946 to join the English department of St. Michael's College at the University of Toronto where, by 1962, he was a full professor. It was there that he made his world mark.

His first major publication examined the Elizabethan poet, Thomas Nash. This early work not only displayed the breadth of McLuhan's literary grasp, but also showed his ability to handle the structure of information as communicated through print. With *The Mechanical Bride* (1951), he continued in a new but still consistent vein. Here he demonstrated how advertising could spread and structure mass awareness. When *The Gutenberg Galaxy* was launched in 1962, McLuhan shared his findings with an audience wanting to learn what print technology can do in cultural transformation. In 1964 there followed a work of truly global impact, *Understanding the Media*, and in 1967, *The Medium is the Message*, another classic in his career. By now the world had become for him "a global village" and man was returning to some of his tribal ways with the immediacy of communications reducing the separation of thought and action. *The Interior Landscape* (1969) and other volumes often jointly authored with his disciples came out in the 1970s.

By this time McLuhan was seen broadly as a guru — a kind of mystic super-salesman — by big advertising agencies in Manhattan and public-relations czars in Hollywood. *The New York Herald Tribune* called him "the most important thinker since Newton, Darwin, Freud, Einstein and Pavlov." In truth, however, beyond tongue-in-cheek pronouncements for the publicity bosses and faddists of the so-called real world, Marshall McLuhan stayed firmly committed to his own research and to a devoted graduate seminar that regularly met in an old coach house at St. Michael's. Although he frequented the skyscraper domains of Madison Avenue and visited many universities around the globe, his fundamental interest was the influence of mass media upon the people themselves. Thus he drew his famous division between "hot" media — print or radio, where information would crowd in on the recipient — and "cool" media like telephone and television where the user was far more personally, sensorily involved. The form our information takes is basic to the way knowledge is perceived and interpreted. All this pointed to his famous dictum, "The Medium is the Message." This vital part of McLuhan's revelation of the power of communications, led onward into our world computer age.

McLuhan received numerous honours and awards including the Albert Schweitzer Chair for the Humanities (1967) which he spent at Fordham University, New York. He founded the Centre for Culture and Technology which still functions at the University of Toronto.

The message that "The medium is the message" and the name of Marshall McLuhan are inextricably linked in the minds of all twentieth century communicators.

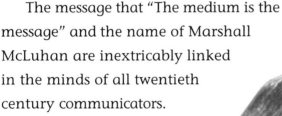

A communications guru from Toronto, Marshall McLuhan became a global figure with such publications as the Gutenberg Galaxy (1962) and Understanding Media (1964)

The Toronto Star

Merchant Prince of the Oceans

SAMUEL CUNARD, born in Halifax, Nova Scotia, the son of a master carpenter and timber merchant, became the world's foremost shipping magnate in the nineteenth century. The company he created not only operated the finest passenger liners of the times but also transformed navigation of the world's oceans.

Public Archives of Nova Scotia

Samuel Cunard

As a youth Cunard demonstrated remarkable business acumen. When only 17, he began managing his own general store. After joining his father, Abraham, in the timber business, he gradually expanded the family interests into coal, iron, shipping and whaling.

The Halifax Weekly Chronicle of July 2, 1813, contained an advertisement for a new company, A. Cunard and Son, agents for vessels loading for London and the West Indies. Thus began the

CUNARD LINE

IN UPPER NEW YORK BAY.

Born in Halifax, Samuel Cunard (1787-1865) amassed a large personal fortune by the 1830s. His shipping expertise led him to submit a successful bid to the British government in 1839 to undertake a regular mail service across the Atlantic from Liverpool to Halifax, Quebec, and Boston. At first his service was steamship, with iron ships being introduced in 1855. It is interesting to note that, in 1867, only two years after he died, Cunard liners ceased making regular Halifax stops, concentrating only on the prosperous New York-Liverpool route, reaching peak performance and profitability the decade before the outbreak of hostilities in 1914. Cunard dominated the Atlantic passenger trade with liners such as the **Lusitania**, **Mauretania** *and, later, the legendary* **Queen** *ships*

world-famous Cunard shipping line. Cunard developed efficient methods for loading and unloading cargo. By the time he was 27 years old, his ships were carrying the mail between Newfoundland, Bermuda, and Boston. Soon his fleet numbered 40 ships.

Early in his career Cunard recognized the economic disadvantages of ships entirely dependent on the movement of the winds. He began to think in terms of an "ocean railway" with passengers and cargo arriving by ship as punctually and as regularly as by railway trains. This idea was greeted with scorn. In 1833, however, *The Royal William* became the first "ocean railway" to cross the Atlantic entirely by steam. Cunard was one of the principal shareholders in that ship.

His experience with *The Royal William* led him to submit a bid to the British Government in 1839 to undertake a regular mail service by steamship from Liverpool to Halifax, Quebec, and Boston. Cunard agreed to sail at a time of the year when no other shipowner would: through the North Atlantic in winter! His bid was successful. With associates in Glasgow and Liverpool, he established the British and North American Royal Mail Steam Packet Company — the direct ancestor of the Cunard Line. The company built four steamships, and on July 4, 1840, the first of these mail steamers, the *Britannia*, sailed from Liverpool.

A paddle steamer, the *Britannia* crossed the Atlantic from Liverpool to Halifax and then on to Boston in 14 days and 8 hours. Cunard and 63 other passengers were on board. His experience persuaded him to have nothing but the best ships, the best officers, and the best men. He gave priority to safety over profits. This inviolate policy contributed to its success and the public esteem his company came to enjoy.

Other shipping lines sacrificed safety for speed, and lives were lost. Not a single life was lost on a Cunard ship in the first 65 years of the company's history — an incredible and unparalleled record. The first disaster his company experienced — the sinking of the *Lusitania* torpedoed by a German submarine on May 7, 1915 —occurred 50 years after Cunard's death.

Cunard initiated the system of sailing with green lights to starboard, red to port, and white on the masthead; this became the standard for the entire maritime world and is just one example of how well-managed his shipping operations were.

The innovative technologies his company adopted contributed to the improvement of international navigation generally. His ships were also the first to enjoy the marvels of electric lights and wireless.

In 1848 Cunard moved to London and, four years later, his company built the *Andes*. Made of iron and steel, it had propellers at the stern instead of the less efficient paddle wheels used on earlier steamships. Four years later the *Persia*, the largest ship of its time, was added to the company's fleet.

Early in his career Cunard learned that if he listened to advice from technical experts and welcomed bright ideas, selected employees carefully, paid and treated them well, his employees would reciprocate with loyalty and pride. And they did! His company prospered like none other.

In 1859 Cunard was honoured by Queen Victoria with a knighthood. By the time he died in 1865 his fleet dominated Atlantic shipping in the face of fierce competition.

The Cunard group became a public company in 1878, adopting the name Cunard Steamship Limited. It eventually absorbed Canadian Northern Steamships Limited and its principal competition, the White Star Line. Cunard dominated the Atlantic passenger trade to the end of the era of superliners.

DMS

PARTY OF SETTLERS BOUND FOR CANADA ON BOARD THE CUNARD LINER "CARONIA."

C.J. Humber Collection

Between 1891 and 1911 more than 1.8 million immigrants came to Canada to take up land. Many were transplanted across the Atlantic by the Caronia of the Cunard lines, as this illustration shows, circa 1910

Clifford Sifton
1861-1929

Opening Canada's Breadbasket to the World

PAC-PA 27943

A S FEDERAL MINISTER of the Interior from 1896 to 1905, Clifford Sifton was in charge of immigration during an era that basically saw Canada's vast western plains occupied and settled. Times were booming: western farms were in high demand and immigrants were pouring in. If any individual deserves credit for settling the prairies, it is Clifford Sifton whose energy, initiative, and leadership made this possible.

Born in 1861 in London, Ontario, he went with his parents in 1875 to the underpopulated province of Manitoba. There in 1882 he was admitted to the Manitoba bar, eventually entering politics for Brandon in 1888. By 1891 he had become Attorney General and Minister of Education in the provincial government of Thomas Greenway. In 1896 his stand on public education not only played a decisive part in the Laurier-Greenway schools compromise, which maintained some French and Catholic separate school rights in Manitoba, but also led Sifton on to Ottawa and into Laurier's Liberal Federal cabinet as Minister of the Interior.

The new minister took hold of a promising situation dynamically. Swelling industrialism in Britain and Europe required more food resources from overseas. The American West was all but full; attention therefore swung to Canada's "Last Best West" — an area masterfully promoted by Sifton. He sent agents and organized immigration campaigns not just to Britain and the United States but throughout central and eastern Europe too. Canadians and British newcomers flowed west to prairie grainlands; Americans were also attracted to the west, especially to the area that would become Alberta.

Sir Clifford Sifton introduced the world's first commercial film while Minister of the Interior in 1903. Financially backed by the CPR, the film's purpose was to attract European immigrants to settle as farmers in western Canada

GERMANS ICELANDERS SCOTCHMEN ENGLISHMEN AMERICANS FRENCHMEN SCANDINAVIANS
BELGIANS RUSSIANS AUSTRIANS IRISHMEN

THE MAPLE LEAF FOR EVER

"NOW THEN, ALL TOGETHER"!

Sir Clifford Sifton, Minister of the Interior, 1896-1905, was responsible for the settlement of the Canadian prairies. He is viewed here in this comic poster leading a gathering of multicultural settlers standing in a Canadian prairie wheatfield enthusiastically singing "The Maple Leaf Forever," Canada's patriotic anthem at the turn of the century

Non-English-speaking Europeans now arrived in ever-increasing numbers. Still the smallest element, they had a long future growth. When Sifton had to defend his freely open policies from popular prejudices against "foreigners," he urged that "stalwart peasants in sheepskin coats" made well-qualified settlers for the windswept but highly productive prairies. Thus Poles, Russians, Ukrainians, Hungarians, Austrians, Icelanders, and Jews took up lands. So did other ethnic elements. Many others found work in cities from Montreal to Toronto to Winnipeg or drifted north into lumbering and mining centres. The biggest impact, however, was on the Canadian prairies, where the brand-new provinces of Alberta and Saskatchewan were created in 1905.

Since he disagreed with Laurier's aim of providing Catholic separate school rights as previously legislated in Manitoba, Sifton resigned over the bills that created these provinces. In 1911 he even joined the Conservative side, because of the Liberals' push for reciprocal free trade with the United States: he saw this as a sellout to American big business. In any event, he headed Canada's first Conservation Commission from 1908-1918, was knighted in 1915, and also controlled the powerful *Winnipeg Free Press* until his death in 1929. His monumental work, however, was the settling of the West.

JMSC

HAROLD ELFORD JOHNS

Creating a Bomb of a Different Kind

K NOWN since ancient times, cancer has been and is one of mankind's most dreaded and deadly diseases. Fear of the disease has grown in the twentieth century as understanding of it has increased without adequate compensating knowledge of how to prevent and overcome it.

The incidence of cancer in the last quarter of the twentieth century has been estimated as 75 percent higher than it was in the second quarter. The search for means to treat the disease has attracted the attention of medical scientists throughout the world.

Shortly after radium was discovered in 1898, its potential was realized and it was given a key role in cancer therapy. Deep X-ray therapy was also developed. The cost of treatment using radium formed into thin needles and implanted near tumors was exceedingly expensive, given the high price radium commanded.

With the growing rate of occurrence, particularly of lung cancer which was relatively rare before 1900 but a major cause of death by the middle of the twentieth century, there was urgent need for new and more sophisticated systems of cancer therapy. Fortunately it had been learned, by that time, that a radioisotope, cobalt 60, might be used as an effective radioactive source for the treatment of cancer since it emitted strong penetrating rays spontaneously as it disintegrated. But a special machine was needed.

Cobalt 60 has a number of advantages. It is 6,000 times cheaper, much safer than the radium used in the conventional therapeutic x-rays in use since 1896, and 300 times more powerful. It can be used to produce a beam of high-energy rays capable of destroying deep-seated tumors. After World War II, physicist Dr. Harold Elford Johns, born of missionary parents in West China in 1915

Developed in 1951 and first used in Saskatchewan by Dr. Harold E. Johns and his colleagues, the "Cobalt Bomb," for many years, was a mainstay worldwide in treating patients with cancer

The treatment for cancer was revolutionized after Dr. Harold E. Johns developed medical equipment loosely nicknamed the "Cobalt Bomb." A bomb of a different kind, it would make Dr. Johns a global figure as he personally campaigned against cancer

and educated at McMaster University and the University of Toronto, took particular interest in the development of a cancer therapy machine using cobalt 60.

Devoting his career to the application of physics to medicine and biology, Johns secured a small quantity of intensely radioactive cobalt from the Canadian heavy-water reactor at Chalk River, Ontario, and studied it carefully. He published a series of papers in *Nature*, a scientific journal, and began to develop a cobalt radiation machine to administer radiation in carefully shaped and measured doses. His cobalt therapy unit, popularly and misleadingly known as the 'Cobalt Bomb,' revolutionized throughout the

Toronto General Hospital Association   world the radiation treatment of cancer.

The radiation machine that Johns and a machinist, John MacKay, developed, with great care and precision, used a cobalt 60 source in the form of a round cylinder about three centimetres by five and one-half centimetres inside a radiation-absorbing lead shield. The cobalt source was mounted on a wheel that could be turned to align it with an opening in the lead shield for the precise emission of the radiation beam aimed at the cancerous tumor. In due course this machine was manufactured by a company in the United States.

Work on cobalt radiation was also carried forward by Ivan Smith, a London, Ontario, physician, who used it in his treatment of cancer patients. In association with the Commercial Products Division of Atomic Energy of Canada Limited, the Eldorado A Cobalt 60 Therapy Unit was installed in the autumn of 1951 in the London Clinic of the Ontario Cancer Foundation. This was the first commercially produced equipment of its type in the world. In the years that followed, the machines developed initially by Johns and Smith became increasingly sophisticated.

A stimulating teacher and founder of Canada's first medical biophysics department, Dr. Johns wrote a variety of scientific papers and published a highly significant volume, *The Physics of Radiology*. For his outstanding scientific and humanitarian work, he has been honoured by scientific and professional societies throughout the world.

DMS

William Thornton Mustard

1914 - 1987

Giving Life to "Blue Babies"

During World War II, a Canadian army doctor attempted to prevent leg amputations by performing vein grafts. On returning home he overcame the problem of a baby being born to a mother with an Rh incompatibility factor. He also developed two procedures that bear his name, one to help polio victims and the other to save the lives of children whose major blood vessels to the heart were transposed. His name — Dr. William Thornton Mustard.

William T. Mustard was born in 1914 at Clinton, Ontario, to schoolteacher parents. He graduated from the University of Toronto Medical School in 1937 and, following postgraduate training at Toronto's Hospital For Sick Children (HSC) and the New York Orthopedic Hospital Associates, he joined the army in 1941. In 1944 at a casualty clearing station in Europe, he decided to insert a temporary glass tube to reconnect the severed main artery of a soldier's leg rather than amputate, later replacing the tube with a vein graft. While the success rate was disappointing, the technique was perfected by doctors in the Korean War of the 1950s.

In 1948 after a year at the New York Orthopedic Hospital Associates, Mustard, as one of seven surgeons on staff at Toronto's Sick Children's Hospital, solved the problem of a baby born to a mother

Following graduation from medical school in 1937, Ontario-born William T. Mustard became an orthopaedic surgeon. He developed an international reputation as a heart surgeon focusing his attention on blue babies after serving as a medical doctor during World War II. By 1957, his practice was limited to heart surgery and his operating procedures had become famous worldwide. Signed in 1976 to his colleague and good friend, Dr. Bill Bigelow, this photograph depicts the famous heart doctor at the prime of his life

To Bill
a great
future

Bill Mustard 1976

Courtesy, Dr. W.G. "Bill" Bigelow

with an Rh incompatibility factor (antibodies from the mother's blood attack the baby's blood and cause the child's death) when he and Dr. John Fraser replaced all of the baby's blood with a transfusion. In the first year, 21 of the 24 babies born with the problem were also saved by this process.

In 1952, five years after his return to HSC as one of its seven surgeons, he developed the first operating procedure that was to bear his name. The operation — an *ilopsoas transfer* — meant transferring the tendon of a healthy muscle to provide the motor action for one deformed by polio. For a leg deformity, for instance, he developed a technique in which he drilled a hole the length of the bone, put the tendon straight through the foot to the sole and fastened it with a button to prevent the tendon's pulling out. "If it isn't well fixed," he warned other surgeons, "it pulls out and the muscle atrophies and it doesn't do a damn bit of good."

He once told medical reporter Marilyn Dunlop of *The Toronto Daily Star*, "From my first year of internship right through the entire course of my life, I suppose, I seemed to be bubbling over with ideas," adding, "I was also looking for a simpler way to do things."

Although Mustard was primarily an orthopaedic surgeon at HSC, he was also establishing a reputation for heart surgery — particularly blue baby operations. In 1947, he spent a month observing the work of the influential Dr. Alfred Blalock and his team at Johns Hopkins University Hospital who were performing operations to correct what was called tetrology Fallot, a procedure performed on the major blood vessels around the heart to give blue babies a chance for survival.

With Dr. John Keith, the hospital's chief of cardiology he shared the conviction that tetrology Fallot could be performed on children under a year old (normal practice was to wait until the age of three, but many died before that). His persistence in carrying out such operations proved him right. He also simplified the Blalock operation by making the incision under the arm and operating from behind rather than in front.

His very first heart operation at HSC was so complex — a patent *ductus ateriosus* — that Mustard set up directly in front of him a sterilized copy of *Atlas of Anatomy*, written by his anatomy professor, J.C.B. Grant, and closed the ductus successfully.

In 1957, Dr. Mustard was asked to concentrate on heart surgery. He tried to develop a heart-and-lung machine and to carry out operations using the lungs of monkeys, but these experiments were failures. He also experimented on dogs to seek a solution to a second blue baby cause — the reversal of the great vessels of the heart where the aorta takes blood from the right lower chamber instead of the left, and the pulmonary artery carries red blood from the left ventricle to the lungs — a condition that killed nine out of ten patients in their first year.

Dr. Ake Senning of Sweden was the first to try to reverse the two arteries, but the operation was so complicated and so difficult that few surgeons tried it. Another doctor in the United States tried switching the veins rather than the arteries but the mortality rate was high. Mustard thought of an alternative: make the whole heart, instead of half of it, function backwards by using the pericardium — the lining around the heart — to function as a baffle that would create two upper altered chambers.

This solution led to a second operating procedure named after him and created a moving human interest story. His experiments with dogs had been unsuccessful, but he was given permission to attempt the operation on an 18-month-old child who had been given up for adoption when her parents separated before she was one. Maria was so ill that the agency allowed her to be cared for by Ben and Theresa Surnoski, an Ontario couple anxious to adopt her but not allowed to because she was not expected to live more than six months. The prognosis was right, for within that time period she became bluer and weaker and was obviously failing.

At HSC on May 16, 1963, Mustard carried out the operation with Dr. George Trusler assisting: within an hour Maria was transformed from blue to a healthy pink. Later adopted by the Surnoskis, she became one of Dr. Mustard's star exhibits at medical meetings before she married and had a healthy family of her own.

In the next five years, Dr. Mustard performed 26 more of these operations on children sent to him from as far away as California. Nineteen were successful. Other surgeons adopted the procedure. The Great Ormond Street Hospital of London sent him a Christmas card in 1966 displaying a photograph of 30 children with the caption "A Batch of English Mustards." It also became possible to perform the surgery on babies six months old, as was done until technology in the 1980s made possible the more complicated reversal of the giant vessels.

By then Dr. Mustard had retired with numerous honours, had written more than 60 published papers on a wide range of clinical and surgical subjects, and had edited a two-volume textbook on pediatric surgery that was translated into a number of languages. On retirement in 1977, he was awarded the Order of Canada in recognition of his achievements. One colleague recalled, "The way his residents felt about him was closer to adoration than admiration."

Ten years later, after having refused heart surgery for himself a year earlier, he suffered a massive heart attack while vacationing in Florida and died two days later on December 11, 1987. MVJ

Dr. William Mustard toasts Maria Surnoski celebrating her sixteenth birthday in 1977. She was the first blue baby to be saved with his pioneering surgical procedure in 1963

The Toronto Star

THOMAS "CARBIDE" WILLSON

1860-1915

Inventing the
Acetylene Torch

CANADIAN inventor, electrical engineer and entrepreneur, Thomas "Carbide" Willson in 1892 developed a calcium carbide process that could readily supply acetylene gas. And acetylene, which won wide use as an illuminating gas because of its strong white light, would, in the twentieth century, gain even wider value through the oxyacetylene torch employed in welding, steel-cutting, and bridge or building construction. Hence "Carbide" Willson pioneered a path in modern technology of truly global significance.

Born near Woodstock, Ontario, in 1860, Willson was educated at Hamilton Collegiate. By the time he was twenty, in 1880, he and a local blacksmith had built one of Canada's earliest dynamos which gave Hamilton its first electric arc light. This budding inventor took his growing electrical expertise to the United States where he worked with various companies such as Fuller Electric until, in 1891, he launched his own firm called the Willson Aluminium Company at Spray, North Carolina. He had also been experimenting with the electrical production of calcium carbide, and in 1892 he developed the process that made commercial production of acetylene feasible. This end product came from the simple addition of water to manufactured carbide. The result was bright bicycle lamps, adaptable lighting for areas where early equipment and wiring could not easily supply electricity, and, also invented by Willson, brilliant gas buoys and beacons for marine use.

By 1896 this pathfinder had sold his carbide patent in the United States to Union Carbide and had returned to Canada. At Merritton outside St. Catharines, he erected the Willson Carbide and Acetylene Works which harnessed water power from an old disused Welland canal to a big new hydroelectric plant; its electricity, in turn, then produced calcium carbide out of lime and coke. Willson flourished with his Canadian carbide industry that was based essentially on the water power of the Niagara region. Then in 1900 he also promoted the Ottawa Carbide Company and obtained the first power rights on the vast Saguenay River in Quebec.

In 1911 the all-but-tireless entrepreneur sold his entire Canadian manufacturing rights to Canada Carbide. He then moved to Ottawa to head his new International Marine Signal Company which was making the widely used Willson Buoys and Beacons. He was still moving and venturing when he died in New York in 1915. "A man with a very busy brain" was the apt term of the Woodstock *Review* for this Canadian harbinger of the twentieth century electro-chemical age. JMSC

A founder of the electro-chemical age, Thomas "Carbide" Willson, in 1896, sold his carbide patent in the United States to Union Carbide

PA/C-53499

RING CHAMPIONS

Dixon, Burns, McLarnin & Langford

To celebrate Mardi Gras week in September 1892, the New Orleans Olympic Club arranged a boxing extravaganza: champion John L. Sullivan would meet James J. Corbett for the world heavyweight crown. Two other title fights would take place that same week, one featuring the first black man to hold a world title. His name was George ("Little Chocolate") Dixon from Halifax, Nova Scotia.

Dixon had won the bantamweight crown in London, England, in 1890, when at age 20 he knocked out Nunc Wallace, considered unbeatable at that time. He added the featherweight title at Troy, New York, a year later when he stopped Cal McCarthy in 22 rounds, but he was not universally accepted as champion of that division until he beat Fred Johnson of England in June 1892. In New Orleans his title was on the line in the match against Frank Skelly. He won and went on to defend

the title a total of 23 times over the next three years, an achievement that ranked George Dixon as one of the greatest featherweight champions in the history of boxing.

While Dixon was boxing his way into history, another Canadian was on his way up to a championship. His name was Noah Brusso. Of Italian descent, he was born in 1881 in Hanover, Ontario. Starting as a welterweight fighting under the name of Tommy Burns, he gradually built up his body over 38 fights to clinch the heavyweight title in 1906. This occurred when the champion, Jim Jeffries, retired and selected Marvin Hart to replace him. Burns beat Hart seven months later in 20 rounds. A chunky, 175 pounder of 5 feet 7 inches, Burns was the shortest title holder in the history of the division. He also fought the shortest title defence in the history of heavyweights up to that time when he knocked out the Irish champion in 1.28 minutes of the first round. Described by one writer as gutsy and aggressive, Burns was also one of the few boxers of any era who fought without a manager.

Although Burns won a championship and defended it ten times before being beaten by Jack Johnson in 1908, he was not the choice of Canadian Press for the "Boxer of the Half Century." That honour went to Sam Langford, a native of Weymouth Falls, Nova Scotia, who began boxing professionally as a lightweight and ended his career ranked as one of the best heavyweight boxers in history. He was one of the few men to knock down the infamous Johnson as he did in 1906, before Johnson won the title from Burns. Langford never got a second

The first black boxer to win a world title in any division, George Dixon, according to Nat Fleischer, was the "greatest little fighter the black race has ever produced." Except for a brief spell, the Canadian was the world champion between 1890 and 1900 in either the bantamweight or featherweight divisions

FOLLOWING HIS FIRST FIGHT, CANADIAN NOAH BRUSSO, NOT YET CALLED TOMMY BURNS, IS IN DETROIT TRAINING TO BECOME A PRO.

8-3

NORMAN DREW
WALT McDAYTER

Toronto Telegram News Service

WITHIN FIVE FIGHTS, HE KNOCKS OUT ED SHOLTREAU IN THE FIRST ROUND TO BECOME MICHIGAN HEAVYWEIGHT BOXING CHAMPION.

SO POWERFUL WAS BRUSSO'S PUNCH, THAT DOCTORS CANNOT REVIVE SHOLTREAU. THE LITTLE BOXER IS CHARGED WITH ASSAULT AND BATTERY.

SHOLTREAU RECOVERS THE NEXT DAY, AND THE CHARGE IS DROPPED. BUT BRUSSO'S DISTRAUGHT MOTHER BEGS HIM TO MAKE A PROMISE...

ALL RIGHT, MOM... I SWEAR I'LL NEVER FIGHT AGAIN!

chance to meet Johnson as champion because, it was argued, people would not come to see two black men fight in the same ring at the same time.

Although born in Belfast, Ireland, in 1907 Jimmy McLarnin was the third world champion identified as a Canadian. His family farmed at Mortlack, Saskatchewan, for six years before moving on to Vancouver when Jimmy was nine years old. Dubbed "Baby Face," he was one of the most colourful and popular fighters of the mid-thirties, winning the welterweight crown by knocking out Young Corbett III in the first round and then losing, winning, and losing the title to Barney Ross in three 15-round battles over a one-year period. Describing the final bout on

Courtesy, Janet Butchart

C.J. Humber Collection

Agreeing to a showdown with the notorious Jack Johnson in Sydney, Australia, 1908, Tommy Burns lost his title to Johnson, the first black man ever to win the heavyweight championship of the world

C.J. Humber Collection

Vancouverite Jimmy McLarnin, welterweight champion of the world in 1933, lost and regained the title in 1934 with the renowned Barney Ross. He was one of the finest athletes ever produced in this country

May 28, 1935, one sportswriter wrote: "For 15 rounds at the Polo Grounds last night McLarnin, once again the baby-faced bomber, threw every punch he had, executed every wile learned in years of fighting the best of 'em. But it wasn't enough." He described how the scrappy McLarnin won the 15th and final round: "with as gallant a last stand as any champion ever made. For full three minutes he stood toe to toe, chin to chin, with Barney, and fired his last round of ammunition. He didn't save a bullet. When the bell rang, he didn't have a left hook or an uppercut or a right cross left in his body. If he had to lose — and he did — he certainly chose the magnificent way. He went down swinging."

The fortunes of these boxers are as varied as their weights and their careers. Dixon, described as a clever boxer and a devastating hitter for his size, boxed in both the USA and Britain, defending his title 23 times before being defeated by Terry McGovern in 1900. Despite excellent earnings from his ring career — his purse was $7,500 when he won the featherweight championship and he made another $5,000 on a side bet — Dixon kept fighting after losing the championship in order to cater to his weaknesses for gambling, alcohol, and the good life. In the next five years he won only 11 bouts and died in 1909 in New York City of consumption complicated by his heavy drinking.

Tommy Burns was one of the first heavyweight champions to travel extensively to meet challengers. After winning the title in 1906 in Los Angeles and defending it four times in California, he went to England, Ireland, and France for title matches before beating Bill Squires for the third time

Born in Weymouth, Nova Scotia, Sam Langford was the most feared fighter in the ring even though he fought constantly out of his division. Regarded by some authorities as the greatest boxer who ever lived, even Jack Johnson, after he won the heavyweight title from Tommy Burns, feared Langford, "the most talented fighter never to win a world championship"

in Sydney, Australia, in August 1908. Two weeks later he defended his title in Melbourne and then agreed to fight Jack Johnson in Sydney on Boxing Day, 1908.

Johnson, a huge black man from Galveston, Texas, knocked Burns down with his first punch and toyed with the Canadian for 14 rounds before police stopped the fight. According to boxing historian John Gromach it was a grudge match from the start filmed for silent pictures, "but no radio or talking picture could have used it since the contestants hurled insults and profanity at each other during the entire fight with even more abandon than their fists."

Burns, who was one of the first to fight for big purses (he got $30,000, Johnson got $5,000), fought ten more times in Canada and the United States, then gave up boxing to become a successful owner of a pub in London and a

C.J. Humber Collection

speakeasy in New York during the roaring twenties. Eventually settling in Bremerton, Washington State, he became known in the 1930s as a soft-spoken, likable, stately man who had "the respect of everyone," at least according to one local resident. Stricken in 1935 with an illness that nearly killed him, Burns turned to religion, was ordained a minister at his home city of Coalinga, California, in 1948, and served as an evangelist throughout the northwestern United States and Canada until he died of a heart attack while visiting Vancouver in 1955.

Sam Langford, known as the "Boston Tar Baby," challenged Johnson for a title fight repeatedly but was refused. By the time Jess Willard beat Johnson in 1915, Johnson's reputation as a womanizer — especially white women — angered the American public so badly that for the next two decades

there was no interest in seeing another black man win the heavyweight title. As a result, Langford had to settle for the heavyweight titles of Wales, England, Spain, and Mexico, the latter fought in 1923 when he was 37 years old and considered legally blind. He wound up angry, penniless, and stone blind sitting most of the time on the front stoop of an old tenement in Harlem. He died penniless in 1956 in Cambridge, Massachusetts, at age 70.

McLarnin was 12 years old and a Vancouver newsboy when he met 47-year-old Charles ("Pop") Foster. This meeting led to one of the most remarkable partnerships and legendary friendships of the fight world. "Pop" trained and managed Jimmy from then on and, with his parents' permission, Jimmy, at age 16, went with "Pop" to San Francisco in 1924 to fight as a 4 foot 10 inch 108 pound flyweight. He won ten bouts in four months and quickly became a mainliner. In 1925, he defeated the former flyweight champion, Pancho Villa, the first of 13 ex-champions, champions or future champions he was to fight in 77 bouts.

After the Villa fight he bought a house in Vancouver for his parents and eight of their twelve children still living at home. Between his 17th and 18th birthdays he grew six inches, lost a few fights, and was considered washed up at 19. In October 1927, however, he fought Kid Kaplan, former world featherweight champion with 11 fights as a lightweight. Although Kaplan broke Jimmy's jaw, McLarnin won by a knockout in round eight to reestablish his career.

In 1935 after losing the championship to Ross in their third match, McLarnin split decisions with Tony Canzoneri and defeated Lou Ambers in 1936, but his heart was no longer in the ring. He had married his childhood sweetheart from Vancouver and agreed with "Pop" who told him, "There are only two reasons to fight ... because you like it and you stopped liking it a long time ago ... and the other's for money and you know you don't need money."

Jimmy didn't. He had saved most of the more than a half million dollars he had made in the ring, went into business in a Los Angeles suburb, and took up golf, playing in various tournaments and with celebrities such as Bob Hope, Fred Astaire, and Joe Louis. When "Pop," known as his penny-pinching friend and manager, died at age 83, Jimmy was left his entire fortune as well. It amounted to $240,000.

MVJ

Written and illustrated by Walt McDayter and Norman Drew, this Tommy Burns comic strip was published in the Toronto Telegram during Canada's year of centennial celebrations (1967)

Women's Rights

Women Liberating Men

Women have always been primary influences in the private life of their families, organizations, and communities. They give birth to the children and attend to their early growth and development.

Much of the detailed work in every type of institutional endeavour in society at large is done by women. With a few notable exceptions, women had been excluded from the professions, other than nursing and teaching, and from the public life of organizations and communities as well as from the work of nations until the beginning of this century. Anticipating a worldwide movement for the wide sharing of human freedom, Canadian women had to engage in difficult legal proceedings in the 1920s in order to overcome oppression and exploitation and to gain legal status as "persons."

Early in the nineteenth century, thoughtful Canadian women created local organizations for charitable and religious purposes. They sought to help recently arrived immigrants and to assist needy women and children at local levels. Gradually, women began to establish organizations with broader regional and national objectives. Among these were the Woman's Christian Temperance Union (WCTU) and the Toronto Women's Literary Club, Canada's first suffrage group.

The WCTU, founded by Letitia Youmans, was organized in Owen Sound, Ontario, in 1874. Its influence quickly spread to other communities. The women who organized and carried forward its work

A widely known author and leader in the Canadian women's suffrage movement early in the twentieth century, Emily Murphy was the first woman in the British Empire to be appointed a magistrate. A pioneer in the struggle for women's rights in Canada, she led a decade-long campaign to have women declared legal "persons" in 1929

NAC/PA-138847

Women virtually had no public role in early 19th century Canada. Pioneering women writers of the time, however, afford us an opportunity to witness first hand what life then was like for them. Susanna Moodie, who witnessed the effects of the 1832 Montreal cholera epidemic, wrote three acclaimed volumes, all concerned with Canada: **Roughing it in the Bush** *(1852),* **Life in the Clearings** *(1853), and* **Flora Lindsay** *(1854). Her sister, Catharine Parr Traill, was also a writer of distinction.* **Backwoods of Canada** *(1836) gave an impressionistic account of settlers eking out an impoverished existence in the harsh hinterlands of Upper Canada. She also proved herself a gifted botanist and artist with* **Canadian Wildflowers** *(1868) and* **Studies of Plant Life in Canada** *(1885).*

Much of the writing by Canadian women in early 19th century Canada took the form of letters, especially to family members or friends. Some of these letters have been published this century, including those of Anne Langton who came to Canada in 1837. Her remark-able letters provide valuable information about the events surrounding the Rebellion of 1837 in Upper Canada. Similarly, Anna Jameson, travelling the same year in Upper Canada, chronicled her eight-month stay there in **Winter Studies and Summer Rambles in Canada.** *Readers on both sides of the Atlantic were attracted to this remarkable, independent woman's observation of pioneering Upper Canadian social life at an impor-tant time in Canadian history.*

Susanna Moodie

Masters and Fellows, Massey College

Catharine Parr Traill

J.M. Cole

Anna Jameson

Peterborough Centennial Museum

were deeply conscious of the profound problems that alcohol consumption — the demon rum — caused for wives and children for whom public agencies provided little if any assistance.

The organizers of the WCTU believed that alcohol was the primary source of many of the misfortunes that befell wives and children in the latter years of the nineteenth century. During that time primary industries such as agriculture, lumbering, and railway construction were major sources of employment, and manufacturing and mining were developing. Men employed in lumbering and mining camps were often away from their families for weeks, sometimes months at a time. After prolonged periods in the bush, many arrived home drunk and penniless. Their wives and children suffered. This was one of a variety of reasons members of the WCTU campaigned for prohibition of the production and sale of alcoholic beverages.

As the "White Ribbon Sisters" of the WCTU became more knowledgeable concerning the conditions that existed in many homes, their interest in reform widened. They began to campaign for mothers' allowances and women's suffrage. Leaders of the WCTU began to realize that, to effect the reforms they sought, women had to gain basic political rights.

During the last quarter of the nineteenth century small groups of women resolved to win for themselves and all Canadian women the right to vote in provincial and federal elections. To secure this right they embarked on what proved to be a long, difficult campaign. Historically men had argued that the primary responsibility of women centred in their homes. Many women agreed with them.

Politics, it was argued, was a man's game and was often dirty. Participants were bruised and hurt. To protect themselves, women should keep out of politics. And most of them did. Thus the separation continued between Canada's private life, in which women played primary roles, and Canada's public life from which women were largely excluded.

As democratic ideas such as "no taxation without representation" gained the attention of increasing numbers of women, those women who owned property began to press for women's right to vote. It should be noted that, for most of the first half of the nineteenth century, women property holders in Quebec had the right to vote in elections. But in 1849 they lost that right when the Quebec Franchise Act was passed. In what is now Ontario, the situation of women property owners at that time was the reverse of what it was in Quebec. In the first half of the nineteenth century women property owners in Ontario did not have provincial voting rights. After the middle of the nineteenth century, Ontario women owning property had the right to vote for educational officials at the local level. By the end of that century, women owning property could vote in most municipal elections in Canada.

Dr. Emily Howard Stowe

NAC/C-9480

By the end of the nineteenth century in Canada, women owning property could vote in municipal elections. The 1894 election, as indicated by these two posters, solicited both "ladies and gentle-men" to vote in the upcoming election being held on January 1 in the Ontario communities of Meadowvale, Peel County, and Goderich, Huron County

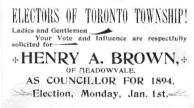

ELECTORS OF TORONTO TOWNSHIP!

Ladies and Gentlemen
Your Vote and Influence are respectfully solicited for

❖ HENRY A. BROWN, ❖
OF MEADOWVALE,
AS COUNCILLOR FOR 1894.
Election, Monday, Jan. 1st.

H. Alan Emerson

Municipal Elections 1894.

Ladies and Gentlemen :

At the request of several prominent ratepayers of our town to allow my name being brought before you as Mayor for the ensuing year, have given my consent and will, if elected, devote, to the best of my ability and judgment, the necessary time and attention pertaining to that office and would therefore respectfully solicit your vote and influence for me as Mayor for 1894.

Respectfully yours,

Goderich, December, 1893.   C. A. HUMBER.

C.J. Humber Collection

In 1876, Dr. Emily Howard Stowe founded the Toronto Women's Literary Club which became the first group in Canada committed to women's suffrage. She and her colleagues were aware that, in the late 1860s, John Stuart Mill, the English utilitarian philosopher and economist, had prepared the first legislative bill for women's suffrage in England.

Born in Norwich, in Upper Canada — now Ontario — on May 1, 1831, Emily Stowe became a school teacher, but, as a result of her husband's illness, resolved to become a medical doctor. Since Canadian medical colleges would not accept a woman as a student, she sought and gained admission to the New York Medical College for Women and graduated in 1867. She became the first English-speaking Canadian woman to practise medicine in Canada. At first she had to practise outside the law as she was not granted a professional licence to practise medicine until 1880.

Through her own personal experience in gaining acceptance as a medical doctor, she gained first-hand knowledge on which to draw as she and her daughter, Dr. Ann Augusta Stowe-Gullen, the first woman doctor trained in Canada, campaigned for voting rights for women. By 1883 the Toronto Women's Literary Club had become the Toronto Women's Suffrage Association. Then in 1889 it became the Dominion Women's Enfranchisement Association. Prejudice against the granting of the franchise to women was deeply rooted in the minds and traditions of members of provincial legislatures and members of the Parliament of Canada. Opposition to the granting of voting rights to women was also widespread in the general public until the first quarter of the twentieth century.

Dr. Ann Augusta Stowe-Gullen

During the last decade of the nineteenth century, the WCTU made one of its objectives the securing of basic political rights for women. These included the right to vote in provincial and federal elections and to stand for election to provincial legislatures and the House of Commons. Two decades of persistent efforts were required, however, before women began to enjoy these rights.

On January 28, 1916, women in the province of Manitoba were granted the right to vote in provincial elections and to hold office as members of the Manitoba Legislature. Women in Saskatchewan secured the same rights on March 14, 1916, and those in Alberta on April 19, 1916. British Columbia implemented the same policy on April 5, 1917 and a week later on April 12, women in Ontario were granted similar voting rights. Changes came more slowly in Eastern Canada.

Women in Nova Scotia were granted the right to vote provincially and to stand for election to the legislature on April 26, 1918. Similar laws were passed in Prince Edward Island on May 3, 1922 and in Newfoundland on April 13, 1925. Women were given the right to vote in provincial elections in New Brunswick on April 17, 1919, but it was not until March 9, 1934 that they gained the right to stand for provincial office.

Through the dedicated leadership of Thérèse Casgrain, who campaigned thoughtfully and ceaselessly on behalf of women, the Quebec Legislature finally gave women the right to vote in provincial elections on April 25, 1940.

By that time Canadian women had been exercising the right to vote in federal elections for more than twenty years. On May 24, 1918, all female citizens of Canada over the age of 21 were allowed to vote in federal elections whether or not they had the right to vote in provincial elections. Later, in July 1919, they were allowed to stand for election to the House of Commons but were denied the right to sit in the Canadian Senate until 1929.

One of the key leaders in the campaign to secure for Canadian women the legal right to sit in the Senate of Canada was Emily Murphy, a writer,

Thérèse Casgrain

journalist, and magistrate. She was supported, in her ten-year campaign to have women declared "persons" under the British North America Act (and thus eligible to sit in the Senate of Canada), by four other Alberta women. One of these was Nellie McClung, a highly effective advocate. Her career merits special attention.

By the 1920s, when she joined Emily Murphy in the struggle to ensure that women were declared "persons" under the British North America Act, Nellie McClung was widely known in Canada as an author, lecturer, and social reformer. She had grown up with the early movement for women's rights. Born Nellie Mooney on October 20, 1873, in Chatsworth, just south of Owen Sound, Ontario, where the WCTU had originated, she moved with her family when she was seven years old to a homestead in the Souris Valley, Brandon, Manitoba. Although she did not begin her formal schooling until she was ten years old, she made excellent progress and secured an elementary teaching certificate when she was 16.

In 1896 after teaching for six years, she married a Manitoba druggist, Robert Wesley McClung. Since her mother-in-law was the President of the WCTU in Manitoba, it was not long before Nellie became one of its key members. The WCTU had been brought into being by women whose religious convictions Nellie McClung shared. Thus she had a natural interest in its activities and dedicated herself to realizing its objectives.

A primary objective of the WCTU was the legal prohibition of the manufacture, sale, and distribution of alcoholic beverages on the grounds that such beverages were destructive of individual, family, and social life. Prohibition was finally approved in Canada during World War I. Since many women had suffered and were suffering grievously as a result of alcoholism and its concomitants, they were determined, against great odds, that prohibition should continue.

The work of the WCTU, while important to Nellie McClung, had not been her only interest. She and her husband were busy bringing up their children and Nellie devoted time to writing. Her first novel, *Sewing Seeds in Danny*, a witty description of a small town in Western Canada, was published in 1908. It quickly gained popular attention and soon became a best-seller. Three years after its appearance she and her husband moved to Winnipeg where she gave birth to her fifth child.

In Winnipeg Nellie was soon in demand as a speaker to women's rights groups and to reform organizations. Members of the Liberal Party persuaded her to share in their efforts to reform Manitoba's political life which was then dominated by the Conservative Government led by Sir Rodmond Roblin. In the midst of her reform efforts in Manitoba, however, she and her husband and family moved to Edmonton, Alberta. There she found many opportunities to continue her activities.

As her reputation as an author and lecturer spread, she received many invitations to speak publicly. In 1921 she lectured widely in England where she was enthusiastically received by her audiences. That same year she was elected as a

Nellie McClung

The Toronto Star

Liberal member of the Alberta Legislature for Edmonton and served there from 1921 until 1926. Later in the 1930s she served as a member of the first Board of Governors of the Canadian Broadcasting Corporation and was a delegate to the League of Nations in 1938.

Nellie McClung was, of course, only one of a considerable number of women who made important contributions to the winning of political rights for women and to the general improvement of the status of women. Her friend, Agnes McPhail, had a much longer career as an elected representatives of the people. She was a member of the House of Commons in Ottawa from 1921 until 1940 and was a member of the Ontario Legislature from 1943 until 1945 and again from 1948 until 1951. Nonetheless as a teacher, an advocate of women's rights, a reformer, an author, and member of the Alberta Legislature, Nellie McClung made a comprehensive contribution to the achievement of political rights for Canadian women.

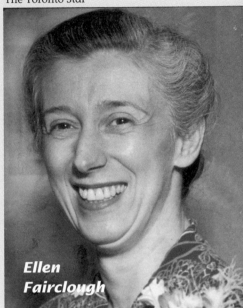

Ellen Fairclough

When Nellie McClung died in Victoria, British Columbia, on September 1, 1951, major advances had been made in the widening of political opportunities for women and the redefinition of their place in Canadian society. But much remained to be done.

Further progress was made in 1957 when Ellen Fairclough was appointed Secretary of State of Canada in the Cabinet of Prime Minister John Diefenbaker. As a member of the Federal Cabinet, Mrs. Fairclough shared in the executive authority that governs Canada at its highest levels. As Canada's first woman Cabinet Minister, Mrs. Fairclough was a key contributor in the winning of essential political rights for Canadian women.

Kim Campbell

Finally, in 1993, Canada's first female Prime Minister, Kim Campbell, received the seals of office. Her appointment came at a most difficult political and economic time and she and her government were soon defeated in the federal election of October 1993. But a woman had served in the highest political office in Canada. This was yet another key step in the winning of political rights for women in Canada, indeed in the world.

Reflecting a global trend since World War I, the traditional exclusion of women from political office has slowly come to an end not just in Canada but worldwide. The election of such world leaders as Margaret Thatcher, Golda Meir, Benazir Bhutto, Mary Robinson, Gor Harlem Brandtland, and Indira Ghandi clearly demonstrates this dramatic development.

But the need to strengthen the base and widen opportunities for women continues.   DMS

Pierre Beauchemin

1892-1968

Mining Quebec's Klondike

RENOWNED for his intuition, courage, and determination as a mining entrepreneur, Pierre Beauchemin, one of the foremost developers of Canadian mineral resources, provided the leadership which made the Sullivan group of mines in the Abitibi region of Quebec an extraordinarily profitable mining operation. By the 1930s, the frantic gold rush to Val d'Or, centre for the Sullivan mines, had become second in fame only to the celebrated Klondike Gold Rush of 1898. Beauchemin also established the Quebec Lithium Corporation which brought Canada's first lithium mine into production.

Raised in the St. Lawrence River Valley and the Abitibi region north of Noranda, Quebec, Beauchemin gained his initial business experience in the lumber industry in Amos, Quebec. Like many others, he and his brothers encountered financial problems in the 1920s. Convinced that the mining industry offered better long-term prospects than lumbering, he persuaded his brothers to invest in a particular mining venture.

Although geologists and mining engineers saw little possibility of its development, Beauchemin concluded that the Sullivan mine in the nearby Val d'Or (Valley of Gold) area had significant potential. Years earlier, a prospector, Jim Sullivan, had discovered and begun to develop a small gold-bearing vein. A number of people in Amos, Quebec, had purchased stock in the Sullivan company. In 1927 Beauchemin and his brothers took a major financial interest in it.

The Sullivan mine was brought into production in the spring of 1934. Soon the mill, which had been installed on the property south and east of Rouyn-Noranda, Quebec, was processing 500 tons of ore a day. Beauchemin's intuition had been correct. The Sullivan mine became a great success.

Beauchemin used some of the profits from the Sullivan to acquire properties in Bourlamaque Township east of Val d'Or. Extensive drilling on a site southeast of Val d'Or brought disappointing results but Beauchemin was persuaded to continue. A large orebody containing copper, zinc, silver, and some gold was discovered. The site was incorporated as East Sullivan Mines Limited in 1944 and financed primarily through Beauchemin's company, Sullivan Consolidated.

In addition to the East Sullivan Mine, Beauchemin also developed Quebec Copper in the Eastern Townships and contributed to the development of the Louvicourt Gold Fields. Sullivan Consolidated also began to develop the mineral potential of an area of more than ten thousand acres, 25 miles north of Val d'Or. The discovery and development of this property by the Quebec Lithium Corporation Limited led to Beauchemin's designation as "Canada's Mr. Lithium."

Lithium, a silvery-white metal, is one of the lightest of all the solids. It is used today to increase the tensile strength of aluminium, magnesium, and aluminum-zinc alloys. An alloy of lithium and lead is used to cover electric cables. In addition to lithium's industrial uses, a variety of lithium compounds are used for medical purposes.

The success Pierre Beauchemin gained through his perseverance and entrepreneurship established his reputation as one of Canada's most accomplished mine developers. He was honoured by Laval University and the University of Montreal. When the Canadian Mining Hall of Fame was established in 1988 he was elected, posthumously, as a charter member of this select company of individuals who have made Canada's mining industry known around the world.

DMS

When the dust settled and the frantic goldrush to the Val d'Or area of Quebec in the 1930s was completed, Pierre Beauchemin emerged as the foremost Quebec miner and one of Canada's leading mine developers

The Northern Miner

BERNARD LONERGAN

1904-1984

BERNARD LONERGAN was one of the leading thinkers of the twentieth century. Today, his published writings have earned him international recognition as a scholar of the highest standing.

Honoured Thinker

Regis College, University of Toronto

His most widely known work — *Insight: A Study of Human Understanding* (1957, 1992) — is a classic in its field, one of the great philosophical treatises of our time. It is ranked by experts in the field with two of the most influential English language contributions to literature concerning human understanding: John Locke's *Essay Concerning Human Understanding* (1690) and David Hume's *An Enquiry Concerning the Principles of Morals* (1751).

In his explanation of how human beings gain understanding, Lonergan analyzed not only historical and contemporary philosophical ideas but also recent developments in mathematics, both the natural and social sciences, as well as theology; he also made a thorough study of common sense. He examined in some depth the methods used by authorities in these areas of specialization. In his analyses, Lonergan sought to explain how scholars, scientists in different fields, and people of common sense, think and arrive at their conclusions, and how their methods of investigation are inextricably interrelated and interlinked by common denominators.

His aim in writing *Insight* was to offer a comprehensive explanation of knowledge in all spheres of thinking and to set out precisely and unequivocally how individuals are influenced by the complicated processes they employ in their efforts to acquire knowledge.

The ability of individuals to confront and understand themselves is, in Lonergan's view, the essential origin of more comprehensive knowledge. "The point," wrote Lonergan, "is to discover, to identify, to become familiar with the way in which we use our intelligence."

Given the requirement for rigorously tested knowledge in our so-called "information age," the prior need, as Lonergan suggests, is for each individual to become familiar with how we use our intelligence and how we can use it better. The profound difficulty, which he identified, is that many other existential concerns "invade and mix and blend with the operations of intellect to render it ambivalent and its pronouncements ambiguous." The issues raised and the desirable courses of action for their beneficial resolution proposed by Lonergan are crucially important in individual and social life and have major implications for the future of human civilizations.

Methods in Theology (1972) stands, with *Insight* (1957), as Bernard Lonergan's most important work. It is Lonergan's answer to those who argue that in this time of cultural change and dissolution the believer is afloat on a sea of multiplying theologies, without rudder or compass. Lonergan was resolute in his refusal to be defeatest on this point.

In his study of history, Arnold Toynbee analyzed the cyclical development and decline of civilizations. He suggested that a civilization, as a living organism, has the possibility of recovering its vitality. Contemporary civilization in the West clearly has grave and profound difficulties. Fortunately, the ideas that scholars such as Lonergan have developed are available as guides for intelligent individuals and for the collective action necessary to encourage cultural and social revitalization.

Lonergan taught seminarians at College de l'Immaculee-Conception, Montreal (1940-46), at Regis College, Toronto (1946-53), and at the Gregorian University, Rome (1953-65). Later he taught at Harvard University (1971-72) and Boston College (1975-83). His primary intellectual and spiritual home for many years was Regis College, Toronto. There, and at other Lonergan Research Institutes around the world, more and more scholars have discovered and devoted attention to Lonergan's writings .

While his published work is intellectually demanding and thus has had only a restricted readership, its exceptional value has been recognized widely. Lonergan was a Companion of the Order of Canada in 1970, the highest honour granted in Canada in recognition of exemplary merit and achievement. This honour is restricted to 150 at any one time. He was also a Corresponding Fellow of the British Academy.

Lonergan was born at Buckingham, Quebec, in 1904 and died in 1984 at the Jesuit Infirmary in Pickering, Ontario. DMS

Lonergan Institute, Regis College, University of Toronto/courtesy Mike Kerr Photography (Ottawa)

When Bernard Lonergan, S.J., was invested as Companion of the Order of Canada by Governor General Roland Michener in 1970, the world-renowned philosopher\theologian was honoured for devoting a lifetime to articulating a generalized method of inquiry. Lonergan Research Institutes are located in Manila, Sydney, Melbourne, Naples, Rome, Montreal, Boston, Santa Clara, Mexico City, Bogota, Twin Cities (Minnesota), and Cagliara (Sardinia)

ALEXANDER GRAHAM BELL

1847-1922

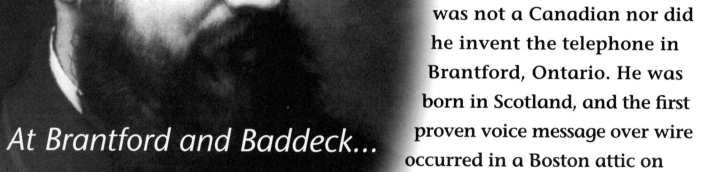

At Brantford and Baddeck...

This 1882 portrait of Alexander Graham Bell by Timolëon Marie Lobrichon hangs in the corporate board room of the National Geographic Society, Washington, D.C.

Department of Canadian Heritage, Parks Canada, Alexander Graham Bell National Historic Site

ALEXANDER GRAHAM BELL, the many-faceted genius, was not a Canadian nor did he invent the telephone in Brantford, Ontario. He was born in Scotland, and the first proven voice message over wire occurred in a Boston attic on March 10, 1876.

Brantford is, however, a vital part of the telephone story as, in 1874, Bell had there devised the principle of the telephone. And Canadians have another legitimate claim to Bell because, for 37 years, he visited or resided in Baddeck, Nova Scotia — sometimes for as much as six months of the year. There at his home in Cape Breton called Beinn Bhreagh (Gaelic for beautiful mountain), where he and his wife Mabel are buried, he invented and developed other projects benefiting flight, medical science, audiology, and genetics.

In Brantford Bell proved that voice could be carried over long distances. While visiting his parents at the Bell homestead in August 1876 he achieved this on three separate occasions: first, from their

Tutelo Heights home to the general store and telegraph office in Mount Pleasant, just south of Brantford; next evening from the telegraph office in Brantford to the family homestead where a party was being held for his uncle; third, on August 10, from the local boot and shoe shop in Paris, Ontario, that doubled as a telegraph office, to the family homestead some 13 kilometres (7 miles) away.

A reporter for the *Brantford Expositor* who was present at the second call listed 16 of the most prominent visitors before paying scant attention to the telephone demonstration. On the third occasion townspeople in Paris crowded into the shop and were thrilled and fascinated when, after some crackling and static, they heard singing and a recitation of Shakespearean verse from the Bell home. The young teacher of the deaf and "visible speech" had changed the world!

In 1885, Bell, with his wife, Mabel, visited the Bras d'Or Lakes region of Cape Breton where Mrs. Bell's father had mining interests. It reminded him of Scotland and he immediately arranged to buy a property that became not only the site of a sprawling mansion to accommodate numerous famous guests but also a centre for labs and workshops. There, hiring many local residents to work on his projects, Bell explored his eclectic interests. Some considered him a crackpot or cranky, but most admired him as a cheerful and beloved genius, an extraordinary eccentric humanitarian.

Bell was fascinated by the sheep that were included with the property he had bought. Observing that those with more than two nipples produced more twins, he believed this could be an important means of increasing wool and food production. Thus he launched enthusiastically into a study of sheep that continued for the rest of his life.

A note in Mabel's diary while they were visiting England in 1877 indicated Bell's early interest in flying. "Alec ... saw some seagulls flying and since then has been full of flying machines." A week later she added, "Flying machines to which telephones and torpedoes are to be attached occupy the first place just now from observations of the seagulls."

It was 1891, however, before Bell became committed to flight development. His friend, Samuel P. Langley, Secretary of the Smithsonian Institute in Washington, D.C., invited him to see his models. Bell enthusiastically noted, "I shall have to make experiments upon my own account in Cape Breton. Can't keep out of it."

But Bell did not pursue the idea to the exclusion of everything else. He continued his work with and for the deaf, made speeches, attended scientific events, developed a type of artificial respiration apparatus — forerunner of the artificial lung — and probed the distillation of fog to make fresh water, all the while making copious notes about flight. Late in 1894, he began tests on wings and propeller blades. When Langley invited him, in 1896, to witness the first trials of a steam-powered, propeller-driven

Bell with grandson hauling in the tetrahedral kite at Baddeck, Nova Scotia, 1908

Alexander
Graham Bell
National
Historic Site

aeroplane model, Bell photographed the event and wrote to Langley, "I shall count this day as one of the most memorable in my life."

That same year Bell launched into experiments with kites. This became his undoing as far as developing a successful flying machine but led to his discovery of the tetrahedron attributed to Buckminster Fuller decades later. Fuller agrees it was Bell's discovery! Invited to see Bell's notebooks at the National Geographic Society (Bell was a founder and, in 1898, its second president), Fuller describes Bell's notebooks as "almost like the Leonardo books," adding, "I was astonished to learn about his discovery of what I call "the octahedron-tetrahedron truss."

Bell's kites were the talk of Baddeck: dozens of local people were employed to build and test them. Helen Keller, whom Bell began to teach when she was only six, was among the Baddeck visitors to fly them, one of which, in December 1905, lifted a workman 30 feet off the ground.

Encouraged by his experiments, in 1907 Bell, with Mabel's financial support, formed the Aerial Experiment Association and hired some bright young men to assist him. J.A. Douglas McCurdy, a

Beinn Bhreagh, A.G. Bell's sprawling estate on Nova Scotia's Cape Breton Island, is surrounded by rugged headlands and salt lochs which reminded him of his native Scotland. The large house, styled after a French chateau, made Beinn Bhreagh a gathering place with a great outdoor laboratory for genetic, aviation and marine experiments

Alexander Graham Bell National Historic Site

Helen Keller was a favourite
friend of Dr. Bell. Here she is
viewed with her mentor and
Annie Sullivan (standing),
her teacher

Chris Haney, bottom left, and Scott Abbott, bottom right, conceptualized the world's No. 1 board game in Montreal in 1979. When their company, Horn Abbot, was incorporated in January 1980, it was agreed that each would receive 22 percent of the company. Ed Werner, top left, corporate lawyer, and John Haney, top right, brother of Chris, each agreed to receive 18 percent of the company. Time magazine has called Trivial Pursuit "the biggest phenomenon in game history"

Trivial Pursuit ®

"What mighty contests rise from trivial things"

Alexander Pope

O N DECEMBER 15, 1979, when Chris Haney and Scott Abbott got together in Montreal for a game of Scrabble and found pieces of the game missing, they wondered aloud why they shouldn't invent a game of their own. They did! **It was Trivial Pursuit!**

The concept was developed that afternoon, but it took them two years and two additional partners before the game was launched, at a loss to the inventors, in the fall of 1981.

They've since made up for it, many times over. All four are now millionaires and the initial 34 people who scraped together as little as $1,000 for five shares—or accepted shares instead of payment for services — have also realized fortunes as Trivial Pursuit has become the world's No. 1 board game.

Haney, photo editor at *The Gazette* in Montreal with an offbeat sense of humour, and Abbott, a sportswriter with The Canadian Press with a superb memory for detail, had been friends for four

It would take approximately 17.1 million Trivial Pursuit board games, placed end to end, to stretch from New York City to Los Angeles. Almost 25 million games were sold in North America in 1984 !

years when they created their brainchild that afternoon. They decided it would be an old-fashioned board game of questions and answers "all about the kind of things we knew from being in the news business," recalls Haney. He suggested the name "Trivia Pursuit," but his wife, Sarah, suggested adding the "l" because "it sounded better."

Unlike many ideas conceived over a beer, this one wasn't forgotten! Haney contacted his older brother, John, then working backstage at the Shaw Festival at Niagara-on-the-Lake. They knew they would need legal advice, preferably free, so John called Ed Werner, a former hockey teammate at Colgate University, then practising law at St. Catharines, Ontario.

By January 1980, a company, Horn Abbot Ltd., was formed to manufacture and sell the game. The name was derived from Chris's nickname "Horn" and Abbott with a "T" removed so that they could use a logo they dreamed up of an abbot blowing a horn under an archway. It was also agreed that Chris and Scott would each own 22 percent of the company; John and Ed, 18 percent each; and the remaining equity would be sold in minimum lots of five shares of $200 each. Werner also arranged to copyright and patent everything possible — the name, the trademark, and the design of the board.

By then they had developed six different categories for the game and settled on having 1,000 questions per category. They also decided to create two more editions a year for the first two years to keep the game upbeat and fresh.

True to their off-the-wall approach, Haney and Abbott used their press passes to interview executives attending the annual Canadian Toy Fair in Montreal that February, in 1980, where "we got a crash course in capitalism," recalls Chris.

Finding the much-needed investors was an equally unusual process. For the most part, they approached friends and acquaintances. Some turned them down, but among the 34 who put up $40,000 were a *Gazette* copyboy who cashed a savings bond and borrowed the rest from his mother, a few other media people, and some of Werner's lawyer friends who were cajoled into buying.

By the fall of 1980, Chris had quit his job and along with Sarah, John, and loads of reference books, sailed for Nerja, a popular Spanish vacation centre overlooking the Mediterranean. There they took a mock-up of the game to the beach and tested their questions on sunbathers. Scott kept his job but joined them on vacation to hone and polish the multitude of questions, all of which began with journalism's five W's: who, what, where, when, why?

On returning to Canada in the spring of 1981, the partners settled around Ed's diningroom table in St. Catharines to edit and organize the questions. They acquired an office in Niagara-on-the-Lake and arranged with an unemployed 18-year-old artist, Michael Wurstlin, to develop the final art work in exchange for five shares. By November 1981, when the first 1,100 sets were ready, they had cost Horn Abbot almost $75 each to manufacture, an outlandish price for a board game. They sold each game initially for $15 so that retailers could price the game at $29.95 — still considered exorbitant for a board game.

They sold out. But their enthusiasm crashed at the Montreal and New York toy fairs of early 1982 when fewer than 400 orders were taken and two major game companies turned them down. "At that point we could have been had for a song," Haney acknowledges. He had exhausted his savings, had sold everything but his cameras, and had driven himself to anxiety attacks that forced a recuperation at his father-in-law's farm. Still they soldiered on and, encouraged by the fact that Canadian stores that had sold the initial supply of games wanted more, they wrote a second edition, Silver Screen. After they secured a $75,000 line of credit against personal liability, they put another 20,000 games into stores. Production costs were still high, but they broke even. Then the head of Chieftain Products (a Canadian company and distributor for Selchow and Righter — a major games company in the United States) became interested. He sent a game to the United States company where three top executives played it, loved it, and thought it might be their answer to the video game challenge.

The U.S. company agreed to manufacture and sell Trivial Pursuit in the United States and hired a PR consultant who launched an unusual direct mail promotion to 1,800 of the top buyers attending the 1983 New York Toy Fair and to Hollywood stars. Both promotions were successful, and the game took off beyond anyone's wildest imagination.

By the end of 1983, even before the Christmas rush, 2.3 million games had been sold in Canada, and a million more in the United States. Selchow and Righter could not keep up with the demand as retail sales soared that year. In 1984, a record 20 million of the games were sold in the United States alone, contracts were signed for European and Australian distribution rights, and retail sales exceeded one billion dollars. The kitchen table capitalists were newsmakers all over North America. Becoming award winners, caused them to replace their customary T-shirts and jeans for tuxedos to attend a dinner in Toronto to receive an Ontario Business Achievement Award.

Today, multiple versions of Trivial Pursuit are sold. The questions have been adapted to challenge players of different ethnic backgrounds in 19 languages and 33 countries. Horn Abbot continues to turn out new additions of Trivial Pursuit under the direction of President Jim Ware, a tax lawyer lured from a leading law firm in Toronto in 1984. In December 1993, Games magazine named Trivial Pursuit to the Games Hall of Fame.

The partners are still friends, pursuing widespread interests including ownership of two golf courses outside Toronto, race horses, a junior hockey team, and numerous other pursuits besides the one that made it all possible.

MVJ

MAPLE SYRUP

Thousand-Year-Old Recipe

PRODUCTS of the sugar and black maple hardwood trees were well known to First Nations people of the St. Lawrence and Great Lakes areas long before Europeans arrived. Other maples also produced the basic sap that could be boiled into syrup, but, because the sugar content was much lower, they were used far less. Hence, maple syrup country was that where hard maples grew numerously: parts of the present Maritimes, Southern Quebec and Ontario, upstate New York, New England, Michigan, and Wisconsin. The making of the syrup and sugar was and is a North American activity based primarily on the native deciduous forests spread broadly throughout eastern Canada.

Early European venturers were delighted with the delicious, fragrant sweetness of maple syrup and sugar — for, until West Indian plantations made cane sugar widely available, they had mostly known only honey. In 1663 the English chemist, Robert Boyle, described sap collection as recorded in the accounts of Massachusetts settlers and, in 1673, French priests in New France similarly sent reports back home.

The people of the First Nations had an age-old collecting technique. As the warming days of early spring brought sap rising in the maple woods, they cut a diagonal slash in each lower trunk and inserted a hollow reed through which the sap dripped into a small bark container. These were subsequently taken to bigger bark or log containers where fire-heated stones were dropped into them until the sap had boiled down to a dark, sweet syrup often referred to as "sweet water," especially when

E.S.Shrapnel

Demonstrating a maple sugar bush and springtime sap gathering, this colourful lithograph, taken from Thomas Conant's Upper Canada Sketches *in the late 19th century, illustrates natives with local settlers from the back country gathering and preparing sap for maple sugar. Today the province of Quebec supplies more than 50 percent of the world's supply of maple sugar*

used in the cooking of venison. Further boiling produced maple sugar. European settlers basically kept to this pattern, merely replacing bark vessels with either wood or metal pails and large cast-iron kettles hung by chains over boiling fires.

Indeed, for many subsequent generations throughout both French and English Canada, the "maple moon" month or the "sugaring off" period would remain a special occasion on the country calendar. Then, in the melting days and freezing nights from March into April (depending on local weather), rural families would gather at their shanties in the sugar bush to collect and boil the sap — and to make maple taffy or maple candy for young and old alike by pouring syrup with the consistency of melted wax out onto a clean, white snowbank.

Only around the 1940s did methods change. A modernized maple syrup industry introduced networks of plastic pipes leading from the trees to a central evaporating plant. Despite this, market demands exceeded supply, and prices soared.

Today, especially in Southern Quebec and in eastern Ontario, maple syrup and maple sugar continue to add their flavour (literally) to a distinctive Canadian farm-and-bush industry.

JMSC

This 18th century engraving, one of the earliest known views depicting the making of maple sugar in Canada by aboriginals, is taken from Moeurs des Sauvages Ameriquains, compare'es aux moeurs des premier temps, *published in Paris in 1724 by P. Lafitau*

Hans Selye

1907-1982

Understanding Stress

ENDOCRINOLOGIST Dr. Hans Selye became internationally known for conceptualizing and proving through research that stress, for better or for worse, is a constant influence in our day-to-day existence.

His abiding interest in this subject began in his early years as a medical student in the University of Prague. Born into a wealthy and cultured family, Selye chose a career in medical research rather than taking over his father's lucrative surgical practice.

Writing many years later Selye reported that in his early, formative years he was "still capable of looking at patients without being biased by current medical thought." He wondered why physicians, since the dawn of medical history, had concentrated their efforts on the recognition of individual diseases and the discovery of specific remedies for those diseases "without giving any attention to the much more obvious 'syndrome of just being sick'." Undeterred when professors discouraged him, Selye, with great confidence in his own abilities, persevered.

Describing a syndrome as "a group of signs and symptoms that occur together and characterize a disease," Selye set out to analyze how the "general syndrome of being sick" characterized diseases generally. The search for understanding and application of knowledge concerning this syndrome became the central feature of Selye's entire academic and scientific career.

After completion of his academic and professional studies in Prague, Paris, and Rome, he received a Rockefeller Research Fellowship and accepted a position at Johns Hopkins University in Baltimore, Maryland. In 1932, he was appointed Associate Professor of Histology (the microscopic, scientific study of organic tissue) at Montreal's McGill University. By 1945 he had become the first Director of the Institute of Experimental Medicine and Surgery at the University of Montreal. He served in that position until his retirement in 1976. Subsequently he established the International Institute of Stress.

As he developed his theories and ideas on stress, Selye came to the conclusion that what he originally had described as "the General Adaptation Syndrome" (G.A.S.) should have been called the

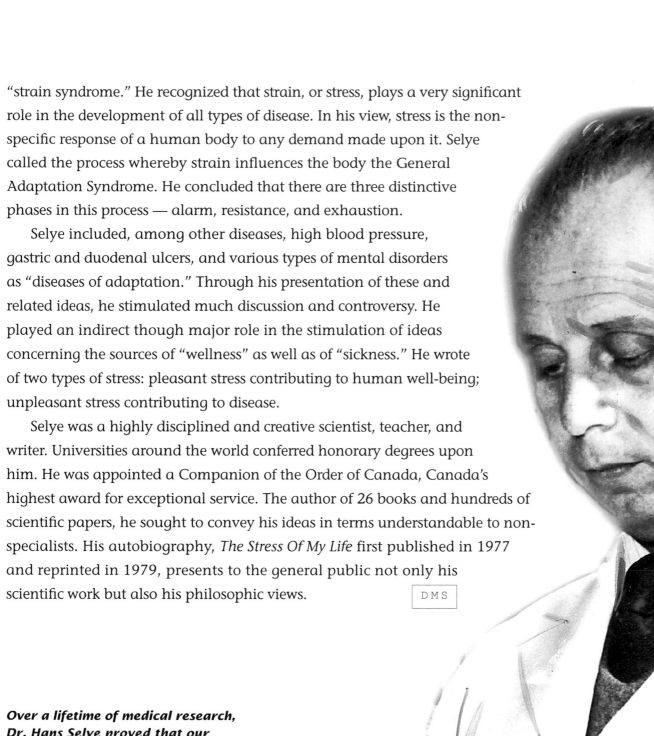

"strain syndrome." He recognized that strain, or stress, plays a very significant role in the development of all types of disease. In his view, stress is the non-specific response of a human body to any demand made upon it. Selye called the process whereby strain influences the body the General Adaptation Syndrome. He concluded that there are three distinctive phases in this process — alarm, resistance, and exhaustion.

Selye included, among other diseases, high blood pressure, gastric and duodenal ulcers, and various types of mental disorders as "diseases of adaptation." Through his presentation of these and related ideas, he stimulated much discussion and controversy. He played an indirect though major role in the stimulation of ideas concerning the sources of "wellness" as well as of "sickness." He wrote of two types of stress: pleasant stress contributing to human well-being; unpleasant stress contributing to disease.

Selye was a highly disciplined and creative scientist, teacher, and writer. Universities around the world conferred honorary degrees upon him. He was appointed a Companion of the Order of Canada, Canada's highest award for exceptional service. The author of 26 books and hundreds of scientific papers, he sought to convey his ideas in terms understandable to non-specialists. His autobiography, *The Stress Of My Life* first published in 1977 and reprinted in 1979, presents to the general public not only his scientific work but also his philosophic views. DMS

Over a lifetime of medical research, Dr. Hans Selye proved that our daily lives are influenced by two different kinds of stress: **pleasant stress** *contributing to "wellness"* **and** **unpleasant stress** *contributing to disease and sickness*

The Toronto Star

Joseph-Armand Bombardier

1907-1964

Creator of the Snowmobile

A VISIONARY GENIUS, Joseph-Armand Bombardier was one of Canada's most successful entrepreneurs as well as a gifted inventor. His best-known invention — the snowmobile — is a multipurpose, motorized vehicle that was designed to travel efficiently over most kinds of snow conditions.

Bombardier was not so much a tycoon as he was a thinker. Always mindful of snow, he plotted how to escape its confinements, how to accept the inevitable presence of winter conditions, and how best to travel in the midst of them. With his various winter vehicles — two of the major ones being the snowmobile and the Ski-Doo® — the incredible Bombardier unintentionally introduced a new winter sport, snowmobiling. It was Canada's first major contribution to the world of sport following the introduction of ice hockey in the late nineteenth century.

Today, in both Canada and the United States the Ski-Doo® is primarily used for recreation. In the Netherlands, however, the snowmobile is sometimes used in the construction of dikes; in Scotland in the laying of pipelines; in Peru in the handling of heavy logs; in Lapland it is used in the rounding up of reindeer.

Bombardier, born on April 16, 1907, was the son of a prosperous farmer from the small community of Valcourt, east of Montreal near Sherbrooke, Quebec. The severe Valcourt winters created snowdrifts so high that sometimes buildings almost disappeared during the rugged winter months. Roads plugged deep with snow prevented the use of vehicles and thus isolated many rural communities.

As a teenager, mechanically minded Bombardier spent the long winters thinking about a vehicle that could travel over snow and thereby ease the solitude imposed by winter. In 1922, when he was only 15, his father gave him an old Model T Ford. Bombardier removed the motor and attached it to the framework of a typical four-passenger sleigh — the usual mode of transportation for French-Canadian families during Quebec's severe winters. He installed a huge wooden aeroplane propeller on

Musée J.-Armand Bombardier

The birth of a new industry occurred when J.-Armand Bombardier introduced the Ski-Doo® in 1959

A mechanic by training, J.-Armand Bombardier proved to be a very perceptive and creative business-man. His invention of the snow-mobile became the foundation for a business empire that today includes the building of aircraft, subway cars, railway cars, and all-purpose vehicles

the drive shaft behind the transmission. Then, using four sleigh runners to glide across the snow, he drove this "strange mechanical animal" through the main street of his hometown village.

A self-taught man, by 1935 J.-Armand Bombardier had designed and built a rubber-cushioned, sprocket wheel-track system that made possible full-scale production of multipassenger snow vehicles. By 1937 he had introduced his principle of steering by skiis in front of a tracked drive. On June 29, 1937, he was granted his first patent. He quickly put up a sign on his garage — "L'Auto-Neige Bombardier" — and went into business. Success was inevitable and immediate.

During the war years, Bombardier succeeded in building a variety of snow vehicles including the Kaki, the B-1, and the Armoured Track, some of which were labelled "Penguins" by the armed forces. The famous B-12 snowmobile sold worldwide immediately after the war. For example, 1,000 B-12 vehicles were produced in each of the years 1947, '48, and '49. The B-12 was a very useful snow vehicle in that it could transport twelve enclosed passengers at one time in addition to various kinds of materials during severe winter conditions. By 1953, Bombardier had introduced the famous MUSKEG, an all-purpose vehicle with eight wheels and two tracks on each side. It was used primarily for oil exploration in Canada's northwest.

During the winter of 1959, Bombardier perfected a light, reliable, one- or two-passenger snow vehicle called the Ski-Doo®. Winter has never been the same since. Production that year was 225 machines; by 1994 over two million units of the Ski-Doo® had been manufactured.

Bombardier was an unusual man — a visionary with a big dream — who turned down repeated offers to sell his company to large American corporations. After ten years of trial and error on a succession of experimental models, Bombardier was not about to let his company slip through his fingers. Even though his big snowmobiles and muskeg tractors were shipped and used around the world from Japan to Antarctica, Bombardier was content to stay close to his roots — Valcourt, Quebec. In 1942, however, J.-Armand Bombardier went public and the company name became Bombardier Limited. But even as the company grew and expanded, Mr. Bombardier never lost the desire to drive his creations himself.

Bombardier had a simple philosophy of merchandising that today seems strange in the era of parts manufacturers and subcontractors. He wanted to make everything himself! He firmly believed that if a product was good it would sell without the offering of special incentives. He never gave credit or shipped on consignment. He believed that if the product was useful, well-made and met the needs of individual or corporate buyers, they would willingly pay for it. And they did!

Bombardier Inc. is now one of the world's largest manufacturers of transportation vehicles. Such well-known consumer products as Ski-Doo® and the just-as-popular watercraft Sea-Doo® have made the name Bombardier recognized worldwide.

The company created by Armand Bombardier has become one of the world's leading aircraft manufacturers operating Canadair (Canada), deHavilland Inc. (Canada), Learjet Inc. (the United States) as well as Short Brothers PLC (the United Kingdom).

The company is also a world leader in the manufacturing of subway and railway cars. In Europe it is engaged in making special-purpose rail vehicles for the English Channel tunnel in addition to high-speed trains for continental use. In Canada, the United States, and Mexico, Bombardier Inc. manufactures subway, light rail, monorail, commuter, intercity trains as well as freight-train cars.

A creative genius, inventor, and entrepreneur, J.-Armand Bombardier literally set out to revolutionize snow transportation. No one can question his success! His premature death in 1964 came when he was at the very height of his career. But the dreams he had in the 1920s continue to be fulfilled. He would no doubt be proud to learn that the dynamic business establishment he founded today employs some 36,500 people worldwide and has annual sales exceeding four billion dollars.

DMS

Musée J.-Armand Bombardier

One of the most important events in the life of J.-Armand Bombardier occurred when, as a teenager, his father gave him an old Ford. He converted it into his first snowmachine as photographed here in 1923

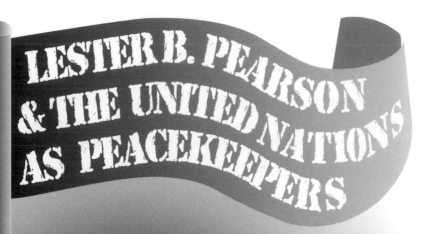

LESTER B. PEARSON & THE UNITED NATIONS AS PEACEKEEPERS

Planting Seeds For World Peace

FROM Cyprus or the Congo in the 1960s to Yugoslavia or Somalia or Rwanda in the 1990s, Canadians have shared widely in the peacekeeping work of the United Nations. In fact, UN peacekeeping forces are very much the product of a Canadian initiative taken by Lester B. Pearson, then Canada's Minister for External Affairs, during the Suez Canal crisis of 1956. Pearson had been president, in 1952, of the United Nations General Assembly and later became Canada's Prime Minister (1963-1968).

In October 1956, Israeli troops backed by Britain and France attacked the key Suez Canal area, which Egypt had earlier seized. Faced with a situation that threatened to disrupt the alliance of Western powers — or even lead to world war — Pearson proposed a United Nations Emergency Force to stabilize the danger zone and offered Canadian troops to serve in such a collective force. Working through its secretary-general, Dag Hammarskjold, he succeeded in getting the UN to adopt his bold proposal. The UNEF thus quickly came into being under the command of Canadian General Eedson L.M. Burns; a Canadian contingent was a permanent inclusion. Despite difficulties, this UN Force succeeded in restoring order. Pearson, for his efforts, received the Nobel Peace Prize in 1957. Above all, a major instrument had been added to the UN's global operations, one for which Canada, today, deserves a large portion of the credit.

Still, the Canadian idea for peacekeeping grew quite naturally out of Canada's own role in the United Nations established in 1945. This was a world body with which Pearson, as a top Canadian diplomat, had close links from the beginning. Neither a great nor a small power — it was small in population but large in size and production — Canada behaved as a responsible, influential middle power by actively supporting the UN in promoting collective security around the globe. Thus from the start Canada entered into joint efforts to calm world trouble spots. For example, it sent officers as part of military observer groups to supervise ceasefire lines in 1948 in both Kashmir and India, and from 1953 on, along the Arab-Israeli borders. But these were small observer groups, not substantial forces able to maintain order. Thus the real development of UN peacekeeping came after the sizable commitment made at Suez.

Canadian units, from 1964 on, would spend close to three decades in keeping the peace between Turkish and Greek Cypriots on a bitterly divided island. More recently they have faced bombardment and bloodshed in Bosnia or Somalia or Rwanda — and the widespread list goes on. Nonetheless, Canada can be proud of the idea put forward by Lester ("Mike") Pearson that has so clearly expressed Canada's commitment to the cause of peace.

JMSC

This historic view portrays Lester B. Pearson, Canada's Minister of External Affairs (and future Prime Minister, 1963-68), receiving the 1957 Nobel Peace Prize, in Norway, from Gunnar Jahn, Chairman, Nobel Committee (1942-66)

(NAC/PA 114544)

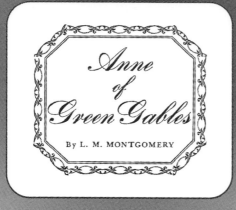

1874-1942

I N 1917 L.M. Montgomery published various autobiographical articles entitled "The Alpine Path." The image of life as a long climb to the ultimate peak of success came from a poem that she had discovered as a child that expressed well her own burning desire for literary success. "I cannot remember a time when I was not writing, or when I did not mean to be an author," she wrote. "To write has always been my central purpose around which every effort and hope and ambition of my life has grouped itself." Montgomery's life story is that of progress along this path.

Lucy Maud was born on November 30, 1874, into a family with deep roots in Prince Edward Island. Following her mother's death in 1876 and her father's moving to Saskatchewan, Maud was raised by maternal grandparents on a farm in Cavendish on the Island's north shore. Hers was a solitary childhood, enlivened by her active imagination, voracious reading, and great love of Nature's beauty. She later felt that her very isolation had shaped her destiny. "Were it not for those Cavendish years, I do not think that *Anne of Green Gables* would ever have been written."

When she was nine, Montgomery began to express herself in writing, first with poems and a diary. Attempts to publish finally met with success in 1890 when a long poem was accepted by a Charlottetown newspaper. To prepare for her chosen career as well to qualify to teach so as to earn immediate money, she took postsecondary education. She taught for one year, then studied more

English literature at Dalhousie College in Halifax, Nova Scotia. While a student, when she received her first payment for writing, she promptly invested this in five volumes of poetry.

Returning to teaching, Maud continued to write for publication, even rising early on cold mornings to work wrapped in a heavy coat. When her grandfather died in 1898, she returned to Cavendish to help her grandmother at home. Writing when time permitted, she was able to report in 1901 that she could now make a living by her pen. She worked from 1901 to 1902 on a Halifax newspaper but found that she could still produce fiction in spare moments in the office. Back in Cavendish, she kept up her household duties and writing along with regular diary entries and lengthy correspondence.

In 1904 Montgomery began her first book. About a girl sent to an elderly couple who had applied to an orphanage for a boy, *Anne of Green Gables* was written with enthusiasm but put away with disappointment after five publishers' rejections. Another try succeeded, and *Anne* was published in 1908. It sold quickly and far beyond its anticipated audience of teenage girls. Older readers, men and women, responded to Montgomery's believable characters, lively plots, sense of humour, sensitivity to natural beauty, and message of an underlying goodness in life despite its darkness. *Anne* eventually was translated into many languages including Braille. Her author could record: "The dream dreamed years ago at that old brown desk in school has come true at last after years of toil and struggle."

Public and publisher's demands led speedily to an *Anne* sequel. Three more

Shown here in 1884 as a 10-year-old budding author, Lucy Maud Montgomery began writing verses as a child

Always concerned with life on Prince Edward Island, Montgomery's books were published all over the world, translated into several languages and adapted to stage and film. In all, seven sequels to Anne would be written as well as an autobiographical Emily trilogy. Her legacy also includes hundreds of poems, many short stories, dozens of books of fiction, and personal diaries

University of Guelph

This photo of L. M. Montgomery was taken circa 1904-5 while she was writing Anne of Green Gables which was rejected by publishers five times before its publication in 1908

University of Guelph

books followed, and then Montgomery had to leave her beloved home and island. After her grandmother's death in 1911, Maud married her long-time fiancé, the Rev. Ewan Macdonald, and moved to the Presbyterian manse in Leaskdale, Ontario. She was soon the mother of two sons and busy with the many activities of a minister's wife. To these concerns were added worries: her husband's emotional ill health which must be kept secret, the agonies of World War I, the loss of special friends, and two drawn-out lawsuits. Yet she continued to write for an eager public and created more memorable characters and heroines to join Anne's company.

Of Montgomery's additional books written in Ontario, all but one were set in her much-missed province. Yet she benefited from living near Toronto, finding there a welcome intellectual environment. She met other Canadian authors, spoke to women's clubs and schools, and attended plays and movies. Her achievement was increasingly recognized in fan letters, the establishment of a National Park in Cavendish, and stage and film adaptations of her books. Internationally famous people sent praise and sought to meet her. She also received formal honours as the first Canadian woman Fellow of the Royal Society of Arts and Letters, Officer of the Order of the British Empire, and winner of a French medal for literary style. Not only would she become Canada's most enduring literary export, but red-haired Anne would become a world-famous character.

The Macdonalds moved to Norval, Ontario, in 1926, retiring to Toronto by 1935. Maud, who could experience great delights also knew great despair. By 1942 she was worn down by her husband's and her own illnesses, family problems, and the horrors of another war. She died on April 24 and was buried in Cavendish.

But her legacy continues. Her books, today, are widely read in many languages. Adaptations to other media take them to even larger audiences. Her works are especially valued in Poland and Japan. Thousands from there and elsewhere visit Montgomery-related sites including even a former tourist home in Muskoka, north of Toronto, where she stayed for only two weeks in 1922. Newsletters, souvenirs, plaques, a Canadian stamp, and even a ferry in her name all attest to her celebrity status.

Once neglected by academics, Montgomery's writings are now the subject of theses in North America and abroad and the focus of a recently established Institute at the University of P.E.I. As recent publishing has made her non-fiction writing more available, scholars have begun to give these as detailed attention as her stories. Her letters and journals are particularly rich sources on the social and cultural history of her times.

By 1917 L.M. Montgomery could realize that she had indeed climbed her Alpine path. Today she might be surprised and even taken aback to see the extent of her success worldwide. In 1901 she confided to her journal, "I never expect to be famous. I merely want to have a recognized place among good workers in my chosen profession." Now internationally famous, Lucy Maud Montgomery has far exceeded that modest goal.

VC

Wilfred G. Bigelow

From Cooling Hearts to Pacing Them

Medtronics Canada

HAVING to amputate a man's frostbitten fingers led Dr. Wilfred G. Bigelow to make two major medical discoveries — the use of hypothermia to allow the first open-heart surgery and the development of the pacemaker to enable people to live normal lives despite life-threatening heart deficiency.

It was 1941 when "Bill" Bigelow, a resident surgeon at the Toronto General Hospital, expressed concern at the lack of research on frostbite and was challenged by his professor to do something about it. The challenge was accepted and his early frostbite studies showed that lowering the temperature of an extremity (local hypothermia) reduced its metabolism or oxygen requirements. On his return from serving overseas as a front-line surgeon with the Canadian army in England and northwest Europe, Dr. Bigelow spent a year at Johns Hopkins University Hospital where pioneer heart surgery operations to ease the lives of blue babies were being performed. It was not possible, however, to do open-heart surgery and correct the condition under direct vision. This prompted Dr. Bigelow, as a result of his studies in local hypothermia, to investigate whether it might be possible to cool "the whole body, reduce the oxygen requirements, interrupt the circulation, and open the heart."

This is a small modern implantable pacemaker showing how the battery pack can be replaced without disturbing the conducting wire to the heart. The development of the heart pacemaker is one of the most extraordinary and rapid advances in global health care in medical history

Courtesy, Dr. W. G. Bigelow

The origins of the heart pacemaker are deeply rooted in Canada. The story is identified with three dedicated Canadians who reported from Toronto in 1950 a heart pacemaker that could start and maintain the function of a stopped heart. They had developed a pacemaker where the circuit produced an electrical discharge that simulated nature's gentle stimulus, with no heart muscle damage. An unexpected discovery with experiments demonstrated that their pacemaker, applied to a normal beating heart, could control the heartbeat at a slower or faster rate. It dominated nature's pacer.

This device was housed in a cabinet about a foot long, together with a long intravenous catheter that could conduct both stimulating wires with a bipolar electrode (as in use today) to stimulate the inside wall of the heart. This was duly reported to the scientific world in 1950.

The Toronto pacemaker was of very little use to patients because of its size. P.M. Zoll reported success using this circuit in a few hospital patients in Boston in 1952. It literally sat on the shelf for nine years until transistor circuitry caught up with invention and made possible a small unit implantable under the skin. In 1959 Åke Senning of Stockholm was first to accomplish this.

Since then a prodigious and brilliant evolution in biotechnology, mostly from the United States, has produced smaller and more durable units capable of incredibly complex functions. It has become a major factor in the management of literally millions of heart patients.

Gathered together 25 years later to celebrate the first Canadian production unit are, above: left, Dr. Bill Bigelow, the pioneering heart surgeon who conceptualized the modern day pacemaker; Dr. John Callaghan, standing behind the original unit and holding an implantable model; and right, Jack Hopps, who, as an electrical engineer from the National Research Council, joined forces with Bigelow and Callaghan to become the father of bioengineering in Canada.

The discovery of the pacemaker and the intravenous bipolar electrode was a serendipitous spinoff from the Bigelow team's long-term research in hypothermia

235

Actually, at that time (mid 1940s) any fall in body temperature was considered as dangerous or lethal with an increase in metabolism. Keeping an accident victim warm with many hot water bottles after surgery was mute evidence of this widely held belief.

Returning to the Toronto General Hospital in 1947, Dr. Bigelow obtained a small room in the basement of the Banting Institute to carry on his search with a team of researchers, in an atmosphere of scepticism. As a first step, they made the milestone basic discovery that with certain controlled anaesthesia, the metabolism fell steadily as the body temperature was lowered. Then in 1949 they made their first open heart attempt on a dog whose body temperature was lowered to 20° C, and the circulation was stopped for 15 minutes; this allowed Bigelow and an associate to see a heart beating without blood for the first time. The dog was rewarmed and survived.

In 1950, Dr. Bigelow and co-worker Dr. John Callaghan announced their hypothermia experiments at an American Surgical Association meeting in Denver. Their landmark presentation stimulated worldwide research. It opened the door to the whole burgeoning field of hypothermia and open heart surgery.

Two years later a successful operation using hypothermia was performed in the USA. Following this, "...a steady stream of surgeons and scientists from around the world came to see our first Canadian open-heart surgery and to visit our Banting and Best Institute laboratory," Dr. Bigelow reported.

The first successful open heart operation using the heart-lung pump followed a year later. Hypothermia was the most common form of open heart surgery for about five years while the pump technique was undergoing refinements. Finally, about 1960, the two techniques were combined and used by surgeons around the world on a daily basis.

Today very cold chemical solutions are injected into the coronary arteries during surgery to protect the heart further.

The invention of the heart pacemaker was the direct result of the hypothermia experiments. In 1949, during an experimental operation, a dog's heart suddenly stopped. Dr. Bigelow recalls: "Out of interest and in desperation, I gave the left ventricle a good poke with a probe I was holding." All four chambers of the heart responded. Further pokes clearly indicated that the heart was beating normally with good blood pressure. This led him to discover that an electric pacemaking device could enhance their hypothermia experiments. This is probably the first time that a fully oxygenated heart in arrest had been stimulated.

He discussed the concept with Dr. Callaghan "well into the night." They decided that Dr. Callaghan would review the literature while Dr. Bigelow sought expert help. This came from the National Research Council at Ottawa which provided the part-time services of an electrical engineer, Jack Hopps.

Research was launched on two fronts — one to enable them to lower the temperature below 20 C in hypothermia experiments; the other, to study the pacemaker at normal body temperatures. With the safety factor now improved in hypothermia operations, the normal temperature studies began to dominate their interest. Using dogs and rabbits, they again painstakingly collected data, studying the most effective and safe electric current, and made a movie of their key experiments before presenting their findings at the Annual Surgical Congress of the American College of Surgeons meeting at Boston in October 1950.

As Dr. Callaghan had done "the lion's share of the work, particularly in the normal body temperature studies," he made the ten-minute presentation which was "one of the scientific highlights of the day, with great interest from the news media," Dr. Bigelow recalls.

These experiments provided a triple discovery:

i Hopps and associates designed a pacemaker circuit that provided a gentle electric stimulus duplicating the normal body nerve stimulation with no damage to the heart muscle;

ii A cardiac catheter carried two wires with a "bipolar " electrode tip allowing insertion through a vein with no uncomfortable chest muscle contractions;

iii. The pacemaker not only started a stopped heart, it could effectively increase or decrease the heart rate.

Because of its size — roughly a foot long and several inches high and wide — there was limited interest in the pacemaker's initial use. A successful clinical experiment was carried out by a Boston doctor in 1952, but it was 1959 before a pacemaker, using transistor circuitry, enabled a Swedish doctor to implant the first unit under the skin.

Faulty batteries, body fluids leaking through the encasement, and broken wires caused numerous pacemaker failures that required emergency surgery, further delaying its widespread use for several years. Worldwide experiments by both medical people and manufacturers, however, ultimately made it possible to implant units to meet the needs of individual patients, such as a "demand" unit to perform only when required, and one with two electrodes to react to emotional and physical exertion. Finally, the invention of a lithium battery by a Buffalo electrical engineer in 1972 launched the pacemaker as a modern medical and technical miracle for countless thousands of people around the world.

Dr. Bigelow pioneered several cardiac surgical procedures and established the first complete three-to four-year training program for cardiac surgeons in 1956. Now retired, he has received 20 major honours and awards, including the Order of Canada; he has authored two books, *Cold Hearts* and *Mysterious Heparin*, and has written more than 100 medical papers. His pacemaker co-worker, Dr. Callaghan, became internationally known as professor of cardio-thoracic surgery at the University of Alberta. Jack Hopps, who established the biomedical engineering division at the National Research Council, is considered "the father of bioengineering in Canada." He also became Secretary General of the International Federation of Medical and Biological Engineering. He and a brother are pacemaker recipients. _MVJ_

Hugh MacLennan

JOHN HUGH MACLENNAN, a five-time winner of Canada's prestigious Governor General's Literary Award, contributed immensely to the creation of a distinct Canadian literature. His outstanding literary talents secured for him national and international acclaim before his death on November 9, 1990.

Although MacLennan regarded Halifax as his home town, he was born in Glace Bay, Nova Scotia, a Cape Breton coastal community dominated, for many years, by the coal-mining industry. When he was seven years old, MacLennan moved with his family to Halifax. On the morning of December 6, 1917 he witnessed, as a ten-year-old boy, the Halifax explosion caused by the collision of a Belgian relief ship and a French munitions vessel. This explosion, estimated to have been the world's worst before the dropping of the nuclear bomb on Hiroshima, Japan, in August 1945, left an indelible impression on young MacLennan. No wonder! Sixteen hundred Haligonians died in the explosion, nine thousand were injured, and more than 25,000 lost their homes or encountered major difficulties as a result of property damage.

Dramatizing Canadian Culture

The explosion occurred at 8.45 A.M. Since classes in Halifax schools did not begin in those days until 9.30 A.M., MacLennan, was still at home and thus escaped death or injuries he might have suffered had he been in school.

On completion of his secondary school studies, MacLennan enrolled at Dalhousie University. Following graduation in 1929 he accepted a Rhodes Scholarship to Oxford. Then, after completing his work at Oxford, MacLennan travelled across Europe. During this period, the emergence of Hitler and Mussolini was generating widespread, international anxiety. MacLennan next went to Princeton University, New Jersey, where he earned a doctorate in classics. While there he began to write about international problems, some of which he had personally encountered.

Returning to Canada in 1935, MacLennan began his teaching career at Lower Canada College. At the outbreak of the Second World War he was aware that weapons of increasingly destructive power would be used. He remembered his experiences during the Halifax explosion when two-and-a-quarter square miles of the industrial section of the city had been completely destroyed: a raging fire had been followed by an enormous tidal wave. These experiences had given him a sense of what might happen in the Second World War.

During the summer of 1940, MacLennan began writing his first novel. Published the following year, *Barometer Rising* became a landmark publication not only exploring the tragic events of the great Halifax explosion but also dramatizing a Canadian setting. Indeed, the publication of *Barometer Rising* marked the beginning of a distinct Canadian literature written to appeal to an international audience.

MacLennan's next work, *Two Solitudes*, published in 1945, examines the historic clash between the English and the French cultures of Canada. It was embraced both at home and abroad as a novel with international appeal. That same year he began teaching at McGill University where he continued as a member of the English department until 1981.

The Precipice, appearing in 1948, examines the strict Protestantism still prevailing in certain communities of Ontario in the 1940s. His exploration of the impact of Calvinism both on the individual and on social life stimulated widespread interest much beyond the Canadian border.

Each Man's Son (1951) describes the escape of a Cape Breton youth from a life in the mines and draws upon MacLennan's experience and knowledge of Nova Scotia. In that novel MacLennan provides fascinating portraits of the Highlanders from Scotland who settled in that magnificent but industrially troubled section of Canada. His careful description of the beauty of the Cape Breton landscape is in sharp contrast with the coarseness of the company town with its tenement houses, row on row, and the exploitive aspects and dangers of its labour-intensive collieries. It gained international appeal because its coal-mining town could be situated in England or Pennsylvania or any coal-mining region in the world. Such was the universality of MacLennan's novels.

By the early 1950s MacLennan had gained a permanent position as an outstanding contributor to Canadian literature. His later novels — *The Watch That Ends The Night* (1959), *Return of the Sphinx* (1967), and *Voice In Time* (1980) — further enhanced his outstanding reputation. MacLennan's essays also received enthusiastic response. *The Other Side of Hugh MacLennan*, published in 1978, is a collection of some of his widely admired essays.

The exceptional quality of MacLennan's writing brought him many honours. He received, for example, the Royal Bank Award for 1984, established to honour a Canadian citizen or a person living in Canada "whose outstanding accomplishment makes an important contribution to human welfare and the common good." In 1987 he was the first Canadian awarded the prestigious James Madison Medal which is granted each year to a Princeton University graduate who has earned outstanding distinction in his profession. This is particularly true of MacLennan, one of Canada's internationally acclaimed authors.

DMS

Gratien Gélinas

Actor, director, producer, and playwright, Gratien Gélinas, with puppet Fridolin, the soft-hearted but cynical young Montréaler who was the central character in the annual revue **Fridolinons**

In the Tradition of Chaplin and Molière

A MONTREAL critic, after the first performance of *Tit-Coq*, wrote, "Literary historians will no longer be able to say that dramatic literature does not exist in French Canada."

He was right. On opening night, May 22, 1948, Gratien Gélinas, as playwright and actor, went beyond his long-established *Fridolinons* revues to create a dramatic production that reflected and drew attention to a truly French-Canadian perspective.

Tit-Coq ran for almost a year, first in French, then English, and was lavishly praised by the critics and the public in both languages. It then ventured to stages in Chicago and New York where audiences at first had difficulty understanding a relatively simple plot. In the play, a French-Canadian orphan becomes a soldier, meets a young woman and her family before going overseas but, while he is serving overseas, she marries another man. On his return, both realize they still love each other but can do nothing about it, mainly because divorce is out of the question because of the religious convictions of her family and the doctrine of the Roman Catholic Church.

The play itself had evolved from an earlier successful revue called *Fridolinons* which Gélinas, as writer and actor, had created for radio in 1937. His first professional acting role, five years prior to this, had been a major part in a serialized radio program while he was, at the same time, working for an insurance company, a job he began in 1929 at age 20. He had loved performing since childhood but had never considered acting as a full-time occupation until, with his wife's encouragement, he quit his job in 1937 to launch the radio character Fridolin on a local French station.

Fridolin was an instant success in Quebec! Within months, Fridolin became a household surname with the station warning listeners against false productions. Gélinas then decided to stage the monologue as an annual revue. He continued with both radio and the revue until 1942 when he gave up radio to concentrate on the stage production that continued until 1946.

On stage, Gélinas took greater liberties in language than he could with radio and also moved from short sketches to complete plays, but the character remained the same. Fridolin was a puny young teenager from the slums of East Montreal who carried a sling shot and wore short pants held up with suspenders over a tricolour hockey sweater and knee socks that were always askew. Fridolin, played by Gélinas, spoke the language of the people, suffered their frustrations, cursed their curses, and commented candidly on authority, skillfully combining humour with pathos to attract audiences from every social and educational level of French-Canadian society. One reviewer in 1946 pronounced that Gélinas was doing for Canada "what the Abbey Theatre did for Ireland and the Moscow Art Theatre for Russia."

With the success of *Tit-Coq*, Gélinas received honorary doctorates from the universities of Montreal and Toronto. He made a film version of the play in 1953, and in 1956 starred in the Stratford Festival (Ontario) productions of *Henry V* and *The Merry Wives of Windsor*. In 1958 he founded La Comédie canadienne and wrote, directed, and starred in his second major play, *Bousille et les justes*, which was eventually staged more than 300 times in 26 different Canadian cities. That year he also became a member of the Royal Society of Canada, where he was introduced as belonging "to the tradition of Chaplin, Molière and those other moralists who have chosen to purge society of its follies by making it laugh at itself."

A year later he was a founding member of the National Theatre School of Canada and, in 1966, wrote what many consider his most sophisticated play, *Heir les enfants dansaient (Yesterday the Children Were Dancing)*.

This play was praised, particularly in English Canada, as a breakthrough in communication between the French and English communities of Canada. The late Nathan Cohen, entertainment critic of *The Toronto Daily Star* commented, "At last ... a play that deals directly and forthrightly with the central fact of Canadian conscience ... a play which disturbs, unsettles, and amuses, and vaults to an extraordinary level of political insight."

Working within a popular tradition, Gélinas brilliantly connected Canada's two distinct peoples by prodding cultural funny bones and generating intellectual laughter. 　MVJ

Charles Saunders

1867-1937

CHARLES E. SAUNDERS, a shy, quiet young man, was bullied by a dominating father into becoming a chemist instead of following his heart-felt wish to become a musician. As a result, he developed a grain that gave Canada the title of "granary of the world" and won him a knighthood. His discovery was Marquis wheat.

This photograph of Sir Charles Edward Saunders was taken in 1934, three years before his death

Canada Department of Agriculture

Born in London, Ontario, in 1867, as the youngest of six children Charles learned horticulture as a boy from his genius father, William, a druggist who owned a farm and put his children to work cross-breeding various berries and other products long before agricultural colleges had begun teaching such techniques. As a result, in 1886 William became the first director of Canada's five experimental farms with headquarters in Ottawa.

By then, Charles was a student at the University of Toronto, his wish to pursue music having been overruled by his father, and spending his summers working with a brother, Percy, on one of the experimental farm's major interests — development of a wheat strain that would mature in time to escape imminent frost. Following graduation in 1888, he attended Johns Hopkins University, receiving his Ph.D. in chemistry in 1891. He taught chemistry and geology at Central University in Kentucky before returning home in 1892 to marry Mary Blackwell who shared his love for music.

Together they opened a studio in Toronto, advertising that they were available for "concerts, recitals, etc.," adding that "Saunders also accepts pupils in singing and flute playing." Saunders also taught music at both Havergal and St. Margaret Ladies' colleges but conceded, years later, that his music career "was doomed to failure because my standards were too high.... I would not adopt popular music."

The need for an earlier-maturing wheat for the prairies (which were being populated as the result of cheap land and railroad development) prompted William Saunders in 1903 to appoint Charles, who had earlier left music and joined the Experimental Farms, to the position of Dominion Cerealist.

Charles attacked the problem with long hours of work and infinite patience. Beginning with a re-examination of all the hybrid strains left in dozens of musty bottles from previous experiments dating back to 1892, he grew new strains and made single-head selections of the most promising results. This led, in 1893, to the planting of a hybrid Red Fife Hard and Red Fife Calcutta seed grown at Agassiz, British Columbia. When this showed a good yield and good chewing qualities (Charles

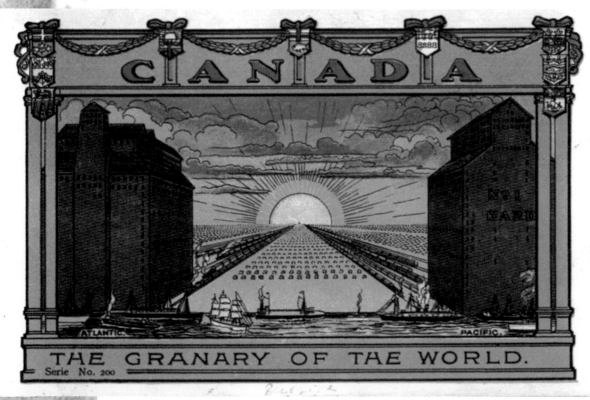

Canada became a great agricultural nation largely because of Charles Edward Saunders. His development of the Marquis strain became "the wheat that won the west," making Canada one of the great grain-producing nations of the world

had hit upon the shortcut of chewing seeds to determine their gluten quality) he grew more of this seed and sent 23 pounds to Angus McKay, head of the experimental farm at Indian Head, Saskatchewan.

The new seed matured three to ten days earlier than Red Fife. Harvest results over the next two years proved its superiority. In the meantime, not only making his own flour but also baking his own bread, Saunders continued to test it for milling and baking qualities and thereby confirmed its outstanding qualities. By 1909, McKay advised Saunders he had complete confidence in it. Named Marquis by Saunders, it was distributed to the farmers of the West for the spring planting of 1910.

One farmer who obtained five pounds of Marquis Wheat was so impressed with it that he entered the New York Land Show and won the $1,000 prize for the best hard spring wheat grown anywhere in the world. He won twice more with Marquis in 1914 and 1915, and with other varieties in 1916 and 1918. Marquis, however, continued to be the dominant variety grown on the prairies: in fact, 90 percent of the more than 17 million acres of prairie wheat grown in 1920 was Marquis.

Charles went on to develop a new hull-less oat that he called Liberty, to improve varieties of barley and corn, and to prepare many papers that were given to agricultural and scientific groups in Canada, the USA, Britain, and France until poor health forced him to resign in 1922 on a pension of $900 a year.

Charles and Mary moved to Paris, studied literature at the Sorbonne, and lived happily but frugally on his meagre pension until western farmers, as one journalist put it, "raised more than wheat" and his pension was confirmed at $5,000 annually in 1925. That year he returned to Ottawa and was awarded the first Flavelle Medal for Science by the Royal Society of Canada and an Honorary Doctor of Science Degree from the University of Toronto. In 1934, he was knighted.

By then Sir Charles had been recognized for an entirely new vocation. In 1928, a collection of his essays and poems printed in French won admiration in Quebec and France. The reviewer of *Le Devoir* wrote, "I was delighted to find humour rendered in French by a master of our tongue." The French government decorated him for the work.

His Marquis Wheat achievement, however, remained uppermost with the public. Invited to speak about it by the Royal Society in 1929, he humbly and humorously gave credit to "God Almighty" for the discovery and correctly predicted that if and when Marquis was replaced, it would likely be "a descendent who will be crowned."

He was right. As early as 1916 rust began causing serious losses and numerous new varieties were developed: Thatcher, Renown, Apex, Regent, and Redmen. All had Marquis somewhere in their pedigrees.

Sir Charles died on July 25, 1937, one year after his wife. Among the worldwide obituaries was that of the London *Daily Express* which ended succinctly with the observation, "He added more wealth to his country than any other man. Marconi gave power. Saunders gave abundance. Great lives, these."

MVJ

David Fife and Red Fife Wheat

The most popular wheat grown in nineteenth century Manitoba was Red Fife, named after David Fife, a farmer who had settled near Peterborough, Ontario. In 1841 this pioneer asked a friend in Scotland to find some seed from a ship carrying wheat from a northern European country. The friend sent a tiny amount in time for spring planting. Fife's planting resulted in five healthy stools that were quickly reduced to one when an ox ate four of them.

Nevertheless, in the spring of 1842 Fife carefully planted the seed from the salvaged stool to produce a pint of plump red seed. Another planting yielded bushels and soon neighbours, along with farmers in Michigan, Illinois, Wisconsin, and Minnesota, were sowing Red Fife.

Between 1867 and the mid-1870s, a grasshopper plague destroyed the wheat crops that had been harvested in the Red River area of Manitoba ever since the arrival of the Selkirk settlers in 1811. New seed was bought in the USA. It was Red Fife! It flourished in the Manitoba soil rendering a grain far superior to any available up to that time. But early frost always remained a threat.

More than a quarter century would pass before Red Fife was superceded by the famous hybrid – Marquis Wheat. MVJ

Lang Pioneer Village, Ontario

David Fife, viewed in this early photograph with his wife Jane Beckett, introduced "Red Fife Wheat" in 1842. By 1851, its popularity had spread throughout the province of Ontario and into Wisconsin. For over 60 years it was "spring wheat" in Canada. It was the parent of the famous Marquis Wheat

JEAN VANIER

Changing the World One Heart at a Time

JEAN VANIER is a widely respected spiritual leader and an advocate of mentally handicapped adults. His public lectures, television presentations, and books have gained a world-wide audience. He is particularly well known in French- and English-speaking countries for his seminars and writings on the application of Christian principles in daily life.

Born on September 10, 1928, in Geneva, Switzerland, he is the son of the late Pauline and Georges-Philéas Vanier who was appointed Governor-General of Canada in 1959, following a distinguished career as both military officer and diplomat. At the time of his son's birth, Georges was the Canadian representative to the League of Nations in Geneva.

Following military service in the British and Canadian navies, young Vanier resigned his commission in 1950 determined to find a more direct way to work for peace in human life. He went to France and became a member of a community of lay people who lived and worked together while studying philosophy and theology. Upon completion of his doctoral thesis on Aristotle's ethics, he began teaching in St. Michael's College, in the University of Toronto.

His studies and his work as a teacher made him deeply aware of the profound complexity and widespread confusion in the modern world. He became convinced that new Christian initiatives were urgently required.

In 1963 he returned to France to visit Father Thomas Philippe, his spiritual father and teacher who was then Chaplain for a residence of 30 mentally handicapped men. Vanier believed that Christians have a special responsibility to help each individual find and enjoy a meaningful place in the life of a family. One of the practical ways he found to accomplish this was to invite the less fortunate to live with him in his home and to encourage them in every way possible to feel that his home was their home. Thus, in 1964 he bought, in Trosly-Breuil, a small house to which he gave the

Jean Vanier believes that the deepest need of an individual human being is to love and be loved. L'Arche, a community of loving relationships founded by Vanier in 1964, fosters the needs of the developmentally handicapped to be nourished in a religious tradition

name *L'Arche* (the Ark) and, as a practical application of his belief, invited to it two men from an asylum to live with him. By 1966 a total of eight men had been welcomed into his home.

Gradually other homes for mentally handicapped adults were established in France, Canada, the United States, and other countries. Some were for men, some for women, and others were integrated. By 1993 there were 105 *L'Arche* communities in 26 countries.

In addition to providing special care for mentally handicapped adults, Vanier has taken a personal interest in young people. Convinced that the interests and activities of young people function as a barometer of the quality, the heights and depths of human aspirations and experience, Vanier is concerned that a considerable percentage of young people today are "touching the things of death."

Jean Vanier visits** **L'Arche** **Daybreak** **in Richmond Hill, Ontario, one of the more than 100** **L'Arche** **communities worldwide. The aim of** **L'Arche** **is to offer not a solution but a sign, a sign that a society, to be truly human, must be founded on welcome and respect for the weak and downtrodden

The Toronto Star

At the same time he is aware that others are touching matters of central importance that have continued largely unaltered, or altered only marginally, throughout human history.

Among these are the idea of authority and attitudes to established traditions. Vanier senses that traditional attitudes toward material possessions are beginning to change. This reflects a yearning among many, the young included, for improved personal relations, for new supportive attitudes, and for the elimination of exploitation in human affairs, particularly in the relations between men and women.

Vanier believes that, if mankind's ideas about authority and possessions are to change, if there is to be a new meeting of people, the fundamental prerequisite is a new and more enduring commitment to the establishment of proper relationships between individuals and among humanity in general. This would require a true renaissance in religious understanding and practice. The religious life of individuals, families, communities and nations must be transformed. This transformation must begin, as far as Christians are concerned, in the lives of individuals.

For Vanier, the Western world in particular must come to a fuller understanding of what religion actually is. Whatever form it takes — and it takes many strange as well as creative forms — religion is what binds together individual lives. Unfortunately, the lives of many individuals, families and communities are falling apart because people have been holding onto the practice of fundamentally flawed beliefs that promote fear, or greed, or the manipulative and/or exploitive use of power.

In his every-day life, Vanier practices a wholesome, life-enhancing Christianity based on pure relationships with his fellow human beings and with God — the Creator, Redeemer, and Sustainer of life in all its dynamic forms. In his public addresses, television appearances, and writings, Vanier emphasizes that Christians have a special responsibility to be caring, sensitive individuals, attentive to God and to their fellow human beings. Each person must seek integrity and wholeness in his or her own life and nourish these qualities in others. The gift of life is precious: those who enjoy its advantages fully have a responsibility to share that fullness with the disadvantaged.

In 1987 Vanier received a most appropriate honour. He was made a Companion of the Order of Canada. Engraved on the medal presented to each recipient is *Desiderantes Meliorem Patriam* ("They desire a better country"). Jean Vanier is deeply committed to extending that principle to encompass the whole of humanity and he quietly seeks its realization through his day by day work.

DMS

Adelaide Hunter Hoodless

1857-1910

Visionary Social Reformer

ADELAIDE HUNTER HOODLESS, one of Canada's most creative social reformers at the turn of the century, was a primary participant in the establishment of the Women's Institutes, the National Council of Women of Canada, the National Council of the YWCA, the Macdonald Institute in Ontario, Macdonald College in Quebec, and the Victorian Order of Nurses.

At the annual meeting of a farmers' organization in 1893, she startled those in attendance by stating forcefully that the health of their wives and children "which you are neglecting is far more important than that of your animals."

She spoke with the conviction born of a tragic personal experience. One of her children, an infant son, had died in 1889 after drinking infected milk. This tragic event motivated her for the rest of her life.

She endeavoured, by various means, to assist women throughout Canada to provide more intelligent care for their children, their families, and themselves.

Born in 1857, on a farm near St. George, north of Brantford, Ontario, young Adelaide was the youngest of 13 children. Her father died before she was born. As she matured she became aware of the difficulties her widowed mother faced in raising her large family alone.

When Adelaide married John Hoodless, a successful manufacturer, she moved to Hamilton, Ontario. There, after the death of her infant son, she led a campaign for the pasteurization of milk. She became the president of the Hamilton branch of the Young Women's Christian Association when it was organized in that city. Her experience in the YWCA strengthened her beliefs that girls, and through them their families, would benefit greatly if they were trained in homemaking.

This 1909 portrait of reformer Adelaide Hunter Hoodless by John W.L. Foster was painted shortly before her untimely death which occurred while she was giving a public address in Toronto

Classes she initiated in domestic science at the Hamilton YWCA received a most enthusiastic response. In 1893, after serving as a delegate to the World Congress of Women in Chicago, she proposed the establishment of a National Association of the YWCA to assist underprivileged girls. This was founded the following year and she became its president in 1895.

Through various activities, Mrs. Hoodless became a recognized authority on domestic science education and child welfare. As treasurer and home economics convener of the Hamilton Local Council of Women, she organized the second branch of the Victorian Order of Nurses, today a national, non-profit organization providing home nursing care, particularly for the elderly and chronically ill.

At the end of the nineteenth century, as a result of Hoodless' efforts, courses in domestic science for girls and manual training for boys were added to the Ontario school curriculum. Ontario's Minister of Education, the Hon. G.W. Ross, asked her to travel across the province to inform the public about domestic science and to write a book on the subject. She thus became one of the first women on the province's payroll. Her book, *Public School Domestic Science*, was published in 1898.

Her crowning achievement was founding the Women's Institutes. On February 19, 1897, she spoke to a meeting of farmers' wives in Stoney Creek, Ontario. Out of that meeting came the first Women's Institute. The inaugural meeting was held shortly afterward at the home of Mrs. E.D. Smith in Winona, Ontario.

Adelaide Hoodless was eager to initiate resources for the development of the abilities, confidence, and prospects of women living in rural communities. Her aim was to establish and develop what might be described as a rural university for women and, within ten years, more than 500 Institutes had been organized across Canada.

Through the efforts of Mrs. Hoodless, her associates, and supporters such as Senator E.D. Smith, the Institutes became widely influential: increased attention was paid to child welfare and women's interests; medical care and child dental care were more frequently provided; recreational and additional library facilities were established; services for helping immigrants to preserve their own cultures and customs were improved.

In 1903, through a grant secured by Mrs. Hoodless from tobacco magnate Sir William Macdonald of Montreal, the Macdonald Institute was established in the Ontario Agricultural College in Guelph (and later, Macdonald College in Quebec) to train Canadian women in the teaching of domestic science.

Adelaide Hoodless died suddenly on the eve of her 53rd birthday in 1910. Her vision and determination, however, continue to stimulate women in Canada and around the world. During World War I, Women's Institutes were introduced into England and Scotland. In 1919 the Government of Canada granted the Institutes a federal charter and provincial representatives met that same year in Winnipeg to form the Federated Women's Institutes of Canada. Their membership today is 30,000.

DMS

NORTHROP FRYE

1912-1991

World-Leading Literary Theorist

INTERNATIONALLY renowned literary critic, celebrated Canadian author, and inspirational teacher to thousands, Northrop Frye spent most of his highly productive academic career at Victoria College, University of Toronto. Born at Sherbrooke, Quebec, in 1912, raised in Moncton, New Brunswick, in an evangelical Methodist environment, Frye, a student at Victoria College in the early 1930s, joined the staff of its English department in 1939 following two years of graduate work at Merton College, Oxford. Much later, in 1978, Frye was named Chancellor of Victoria. Although his links to Victoria stayed close virtually to his death in 1991, he was anything but local in his work and interests. Indeed, his influential scholarship earned him global accolades and a worldwide reputation verging on reverence. This led to numerous honours, ties with and lecture tours to many centres of learning in other lands. Overall, his scholarship includes some 25 books of profoundly critical analysis of English literature that focuses primarily on symbolism and on the Bible as the very foundation for Western world literature.

His first key work, *Fearful Symmetry* (1947), studied the deliberate symbolic patterns used in the prophetic poems of William Blake, religious romantic and visionary artist of England's late eighteenth century. Next — in point of significance — came *Anatomy of Criticism* (1957) wherein Frye set forth a whole universe of verbal symbolism shared by all of Western literature. He sought, in fact, to provide a unified pattern for literary studies beyond the merely personal outbursts of the would-be great. For that effort he gained worldwide supporters and some opposition. Yet he went on further with his

Great Code (1982) which analyzed the writings and rhetoric of the classic English Bible. This was followed by his last major work, a second grand biblical study, *Words with Power,* published in 1990. Frye made literary criticism a discipline itself. This had global impact. Those students, both undergraduate and graduate who attempted to follow his footsteps, were affectionately called "small Fryes."

He also produced *Northrop Frye on Shakespeare* in 1986, edited the *Canadian Forum* in younger years (1948-52), and wrote about the Canadian identity with sensitive, compelling penetration of Canada's character and image. He was, besides, a stimulating member of Massey College, a renowned graduate and research institution of the University of Toronto. But first and foremost, Frye was a brilliant teacher. In social conversation he might often have seemed withdrawn, though always he was both kind and sensitive. In lecture performances he was totally committed, glowing, and inspiring while his smaller, advanced seminars were no less a challenging experience of wit and insight. Consequently, he drew students from across the country, from the United States, and from around the world. From England to Australia and back to Canada he left an indelible mark. Just as there are courses offered on Milton or Keats or Shakespeare, there are today educational institutes offering courses on Frye.

Genius and a warm heart can sometimes go together. They clearly co-existed in this very special, Canadian intellectual.

JMSC

One of the 20th century's most esteemed and respected interpreters of western literature, Northrop Frye, mythologist and cultural intellect, generated a global following that today is reflected in the world's great institutions of higher learning

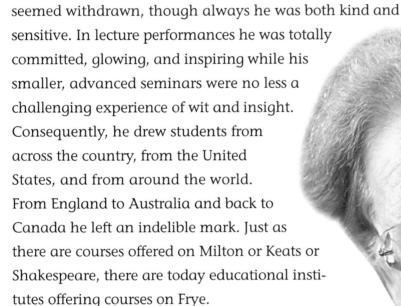

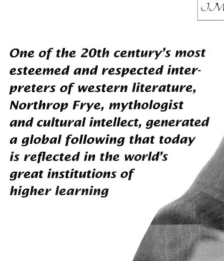

The Toronto Star

Franc R. Joubin

Finding New Wealth for Nations

FRANC JOUBIN is a legend in mining circles around the world. During an amazing career that began in gold mining, he supervised the development of Canada's last hand-hewn mine in British Columbia, searched for strategic minerals during World War II, and engaged in uranium exploration and mining in Northern Saskatchewan, British Columbia, and Ontario. Then he did what few people in human history have ever done: he returned to the place where he had completed his mining apprenticeship, purchased the mine and its nearby competitor, and merged them into a single corporation. Later, for nearly twenty years he worked, on a volunteer basis, for the United Nations providing "on the spot" assistance in the preparation of inventories of mineral potential for developing countries on five continents.

Born, 1911, in San Francisco of French parents (a father from Brittany and a mother from Normandy), Joubin was endowed at birth with the strength and resilience of the Bretons and the intelligence and elegance of the Normans. These qualities, combined with his own creative attitude, enabled him to develop as a helpful and joyful human being despite many adversities in his formative years — his father's death from war wounds, his mother's hospitalization, and his own life in orphanages. Reunited with his mother and brother when he was about ten years old, he began working to support them.

Throughout the 1930s, he worked continuously and studied, when he had saved enough money, at Victoria College on Vancouver Island, and later at the University of British Columbia (UBC) where he specialized in both chemistry and geology. During his undergraduate years at UBC, in the great Depression of the 1930s, he got a summer job with Pioneer Gold Mines, then one of Canada's leading gold mines, with operations in the Bridge River valley in British Columbia.

Painting (1990) of Dr. Franc R. Joubin, one of the world's most successful and respected prospectors and geologists. According to Peter C. Newman, Joubin "brought Canada into the nuclear age"; Pierre Berton has called Joubin "a legend in mining circles around the world"; Former Lt.-Gov. of Ontario, the Hon. John Black Aird, has called this Canadian mine hunter a "visionary," one who "made a great difference to many people" (painting by C. Finn)

Stimulated greatly by the pioneering work of Pierre and Marie Curie on the use of radioactive materials for medical purposes, he devoted careful attention, as an undergraduate, to the study of uranium and scientific and technical means for its location. Upon graduation from UBC in the late 1930s, he began to work full-time for Pioneer Gold Mines as a geologist.

Following World War II and his completion of his Master of Arts degree in geology, he moved to Toronto as the Eastern Canada representative of Pioneer and mastered the secrets of the speculative penny stock jungle in Canada's investment capital. When the wartime ban on prospecting for uranium was lifted, he acquired one of the first portable Geiger counters for the identification of radioactive minerals and began his careful search for uranium.

He directed a small group of geologists, engineers, and metallurgists that discovered, developed, and prepared for production ten uranium mines across Canada: in the Beaverlodge district of

Saskatchewan, in British Columbia, and north of Lake Huron in Ontario. Since he knew that uranium is typically associated with nickel and cobalt, he and members of his group studied with particular care geological maps of the region west of Sudbury, Ontario, and southwest of Cobalt to the north.

He soon determined that uranium might be found on the north shore of Lake Huron. To test his theory he sought financial support from major mining corporations, but none would provide him with the necessary funding. However, Joseph Hirshhorn, a mining promoter well-known in both New York and Toronto, agreed to provide $35,000 for preliminary testing. Working together they developed what became known as the Pronto Mine. When assay tests confirmed Joubin's theory, the value of units in their Pronto Syndicate rose dramatically.

After the success of the Pronto venture, Joubin and his colleagues also discovered and developed most of the major mines that came into production in the Elliot Lake region north of Lake Huron. The development of these mines established Canada as the world leader in the production of uranium. During this same period, Joubin and his colleagues also discovered and developed two successful copper mines, one in Saskatchewan and one in Ontario, and a large iron ore deposit in Labrador.

Within five years of the initial development of their first mine on the north shore of Lake Huron, Joubin and Hirshorn sold the major portion of their mining interests, gaining a thousandfold return on the original investment. This enabled Hirshorn to develop his remarkable art collection for which the museum and sculpture garden, which bear his name, were subsequently created on The Mall in Washington, D.C. That magnificent building and garden are as much a silent monument to Franc Joubin's skills as a prospector and geologist as they are a widely acclaimed monument to Joe Hirshorn's shrewdness in art collecting.

By the mid-1950s Franc Joubin had become widely known and celebrated. A world-famous movie producer wanted to film his life and accomplishments, and leading publishers urged him to let them publish his life story. But Joubin had other ideas. He became an independent global mining consultant and increased his efforts to promote international peace.

Joubin had first become interested in pitchblende, a form of uranium, because of its role in x-ray and cancer therapy. The later use of uranium for destructive military purposes appalled him. Consequently he devoted much time to the early development of the Canadian Peace Research Institute and the use of uranium for nuclear power generation. Later he was one of the founders of the Canadian Institute for Radiation Safety (CAIRS).

In the early 1960s he became directly involved in the Technical Assistance Program of the United Nations assisting developing countries to prepare inventories of their own mineral resources. Geological and mining officials in more than 30 countries benefited through his analyses and counsel. During his years with the UN he made a variety of mineral discoveries. Some were of the same order as his uranium discovery that had resulted in the development of the community of Elliot Lake. The value of the ore located there was estimated, in the early 1980s, to be about $30 billion.

While he was with the UN, he discovered natural gas in the Caribbean, uranium in Somalia, potash in Poland, rock phosphate in central India, and copper on the old Marco Polo silk trail in Iran. In identifying this last find, Joubin recognized ancient slag, in the desert sand, from a mine he judged was operating more than 500 years ago. He also discovered in Panama, Mexico, and Columbia, porphyry copper deposits that had been largely buried beneath younger rock.

In the midst of his many activities overseas Joubin had not forgotten Canada. He had become greatly intrigued by the discovery of oil in the North Sea and wondered whether oil might also be discovered beneath Canada's Hudson Bay. He organized an international company, SOGEPET. After much careful planning and the securing of large sums of money, drilling was commenced. While oil and gas have yet to be found in adequate economic form or quantity, he remains confident that both are present in the northern region of the Hudson Bay Basin. He and his associates realized, however, that because of the sub-Arctic location the development of the oil and gas potential there is still in the distant future.

Unlike many other prospectors and geologists who have vast treasures of great stories but rarely write them down, he has published his memoirs in a fascinating volume, *Not For Gold Alone*. He hopes this volume will encourage others to search for the wealth that lies at their feet.   D.M.S

World-renowned geologist, Franc Joubin, at a gala with the late Viola MacMillan who helped transform the Prospectors and Developers Association from a small, regional group into a highly respected, educational association of professionals engaged in mining exploration. Called "Queen Bee" by associates, she was President of the Prospectors and Developers Association for twenty years and is an elected member of the Canadian Mining Hall of Fame (courtesy /Franc Joubin)

THE ELECTRON MICROSCOPE

W hile there is little doubt that a German physicist developed the basic principles of the electron microscope, both Canada and the United States claim to be first in making it practical. The evidence, however, clearly favours Canada as two postgraduate students working in the Physics Department of the University of Toronto with their physics professor, between 1937 and 1939, developed the first ever transmission electron microscope.

The reason for the dual claim is straightforward. Following graduation with a Ph.D. in 1940, one of the students, James Hillier, joined Radio Corporation of America (RCA) at Camden, New Jersey. Here he reaped recognition for adopting the design of the University of Toronto microscope and developing it into the prototype for the RCA production model. The commercial electron microscope for RCA was supervised under the watchful eye of a Russian-born scientist, vice president of the corporation.

The original electron microscope as developed in 1938 in McLennan Laboratories of the University of Toronto is now on permanent exhibition at the Ontario Science Centre, Toronto, Ontario

Hillier, a native of Brantford, Ontario, was doing postgraduate work at the University of Toronto, under Professor Eli Burton, a native of Green River, Ontario, when he was commissioned along with Albert F. Prebus of Edmonton, Alberta, another University of Toronto postgraduate student, to work on the electron microscope project in the fall of 1937. A physics professor at the University of Toronto since 1922, Burton was head of the department when he visited Ernst Ruska at the Berlin Technische Hochschule in 1935 where he saw first hand the pioneer two-stage transmission model achieving image resolutions beyond that of the light microscope.

As one of Burton's major interests was colloids — substances such as smoke composed of particles, some of which were invisible even under the best of optical

"Travelling the Unknown World of Inner Space"

Dr. John H.L. Watson

Albert Prebus, left, had just received his M.Sc. from the University of Alberta and James Hillier was a graduate student in mathematics and physics at the University of Toronto when they were asked by Professor E.F. Burton, Director of the Physics Department, the University of Toronto, to undertake the construction of a high-voltage magnetic compound electron microscope with the aim of applying it to the investigation of biological specimens. When the electronic microscope was completed in 1938 by the budding spectroscopists, it was the first of its kind in North America. Both the National Research Council and the Banting Institute funded employment for the two workers during the summer of 1938

microscopes — he decided upon returning home to try improving on the microscope he had seen in Germany. He selected two of his brightest students to undertake the job.

They both knew that, in principle, a microscope using electrons had the potential of surpassing optical models since the wavelengths of speeding electrons is much smaller than the wavelengths of light which meant an electron microscope would have the ability to reveal much smaller objects than could be observed through optical units which, in the late '30s, could magnify particles up to 2,000 times their size.

In early 1938 — a mere four months later — the University of Toronto team of Hillier and Prebus, under Burton's supervision, proved them right when they tested their machine using a simple razor blade edge. Viewed through an optical microscope the edge looked relatively sharp; under their electron microscope, the same edge looked like a jagged mountain range as the microscope showed the razor's edge 7,000 times its size. Another year was spent on further refinements to the unit before both students completed their postgraduate studies and took jobs in the United States.

Hillier went to RCA where he developed electron microscopes for commercial use under Vladamir K. Zworykin, a Russian-born scientist who, according to the *World's Who's Who of Science* is credited with several inventions leading to television as well as the electron microscope. In the *Who's Who of Science*, however, Hillier is identified as the "builder of the first successful high resolution electron microscope in the Western Hemisphere, 1939-40," a statement supported by the late Issac Asimov, one of America's most respected authors on science, who wrote in his *Guide to Science*, "... the first really usable one was

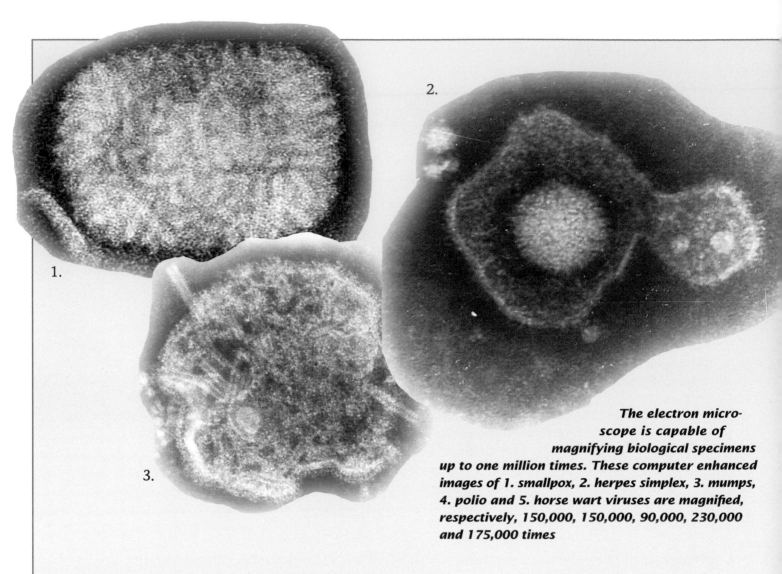

The electron microscope is capable of magnifying biological specimens up to one million times. These computer enhanced images of 1. smallpox, 2. herpes simplex, 3. mumps, 4. polio and 5. horse wart viruses are magnified, respectively, 150,000, 150,000, 90,000, 230,000 and 175,000 times

built in 1937 at the University of Toronto."

Hillier also wrote a number of papers about the development of the electron microscope while at RCA, and later became president of the Electron Microscope Society of America as well as the National Society of Engineers in the United States. He was also the recipient of the Albert Lasker Award, the David Sarnoff Founders Medal and is a member of the National Inventors Hall of Fame.

Prebus, for many years a professor of Physics at Ohio State University, proceeded in 1940 to design and construct an electron microscope shortly after receiving a post-doctoral position there. He played a major role in the incorporation of the Electron Microscope Society of America in 1942.

Professor Burton, whose entire career was spent at the University of Toronto, served as a member of the National Research Council from 1937 to 1946, and was involved in secret research on radar during World War II. Shortly after his death at age 69 in 1948, the Electron Microscope Society of America held a special meeting in Toronto dedicated to the memory of Professor Burton — in recognition of his pioneering work "in introducing the art and instrumentation of electron microscopy to the western hemisphere." In 1973, the same society introduced an award in his name — the Burton Medal — to be awarded annually to a promising young scientist in the field of electron microscopy. MVJ

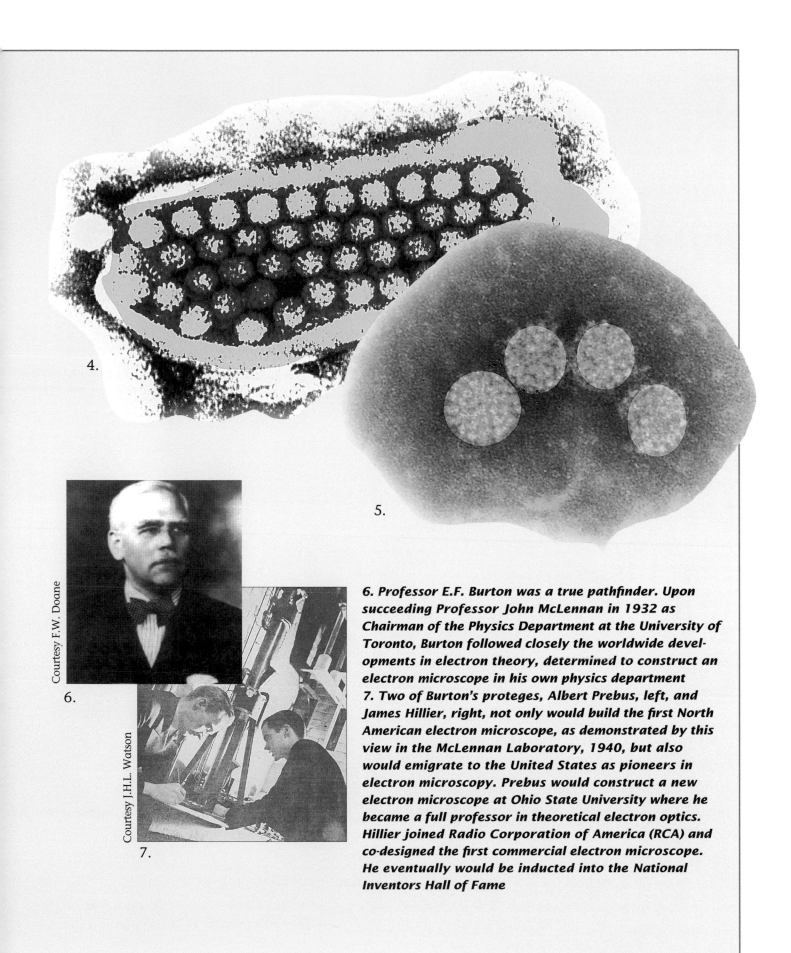

4.

5.

Courtesy F.W. Doane

6.

Courtesy J.H.L. Watson

7.

6. Professor E.F. Burton was a true pathfinder. Upon succeeding Professor John McLennan in 1932 as Chairman of the Physics Department at the University of Toronto, Burton followed closely the worldwide developments in electron theory, determined to construct an electron microscope in his own physics department

7. Two of Burton's proteges, Albert Prebus, left, and James Hillier, right, not only would build the first North American electron microscope, as demonstrated by this view in the McLennan Laboratory, 1940, but also would emigrate to the United States as pioneers in electron microscopy. Prebus would construct a new electron microscope at Ohio State University where he became a full professor in theoretical electron optics. Hillier joined Radio Corporation of America (RCA) and co-designed the first commercial electron microscope. He eventually would be inducted into the National Inventors Hall of Fame

The Story of Heparin

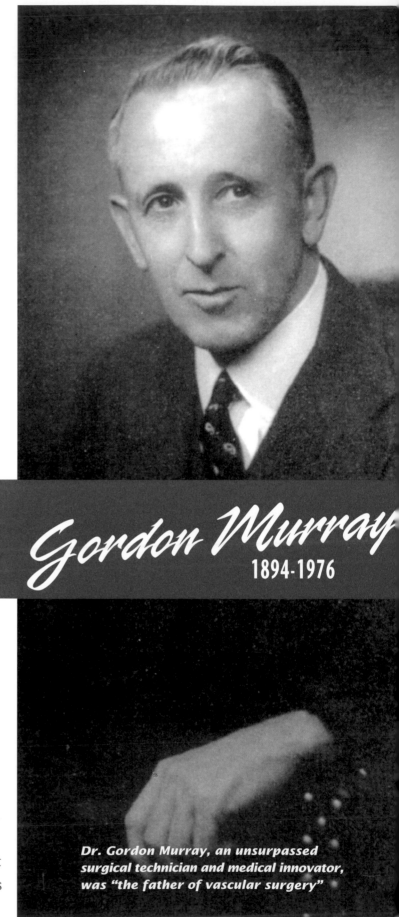

Gordon Murray
1894-1976

Dr. Gordon Murray, an unsurpassed surgical technician and medical innovator, was "the father of vascular surgery"

D R. GORDON MURRAY was the first Canadian surgeon to operate on disorders of the arteries and heart. In the 1930s he introduced the anticoagulant "heparin" to world clinical practice; in the 1940s he developed the first artificial kidney in North America; and in the 1950s was the first surgeon to transplant a human heart valve.

Murray was born in Western Ontario and died in 1976 in Toronto at age 82. By mid-century his surgical innovations at Toronto General Hospital had led to international recognition: in his time he was the most famous surgeon in Canada. In 1967 he was the first physician to be named a Companion of the Order Of Canada.

He contributed in several fields of medicine but is best remembered for his pioneering achievements in surgery of the arteries and the heart. He was the first to recognize that heparin, which stops blood from clotting, was the key to these new fields of surgery.

Heparin is derived from mammalian tissue and was first extracted from dog liver in Baltimore in 1916. The American discoverers, Jay McLean and William Howell, were unable to obtain a product pure enough for human use. Almost two decades later, the University of Toronto team of Charles Best, Arthur Charles, and David Scott was successful in preparing a pure product, first from beef liver and later from beef lung. Murray had shown interest in surgical correction of blocked arteries and thus was chosen to evaluate the potential of the new drug.

His initial animal experiments clearly demonstrated that, when heparin was present, the flow through blood vessels could be completely stopped and yet the blood would not clot. Operations on blood vessels were possible.

In 1935 he began treating patients with the new drug. Its remarkable power of preventing blood clots allowed success in hitherto impossible operations on arteries and veins. Murray educated the international medical community in this field of surgical endeavour and was honoured in many countries as "the father of vascular surgery."

Kidneys from cadavers were attached to groin vessels to achieve survival in short-term renal failure. Control of clotting made an artificial kidney possible; he built and first used one successfully in 1946. Patients who were referred to him with acute kidney failure were the first in North America to be treated with renal dialysis.

In 1955, the 61-year-old surgeon performed the first successful transplant of a human heart valve. Contrary to predictions, the valve was not rejected by the recipient but worked well for many years. This led to the development of biological heart valves which are in common use today. Although the heart-lung pump which allowed open-heart surgery was a later development, it was also dependent on heparin.

Murray was a pathfinding surgeon, not overly tolerant of criticism from less visionary colleagues. His compulsion to search for better methods of treatment continued, and in the final years of his career he reached beyond his grasp. Convinced that some forms of cancer would respond better to enhancement of the immune system rather than to surgery, he embarked on a trial of an anti-cancer serum derived from horses injected with human cancer cells. Also, believing that the crushed or severed spinal cord would heal if it could be joined with precision and without tension, he developed a complex operation for traumatic paraplegia. His last years were shadowed by criticism of these controversial activities.

Dr. Gordon Murray was a charismatic teacher of surgeons, a brilliant innovator, and an unsurpassed surgical technician. Vascular and open-heart surgery, renal dialysis, and organ transplants are now commonplace. Heparin is routine treatment for venous thrombosis and blocked coronary arteries. The initial breakthrough is our legacy from Gordon Murray. RJB

The Underground Railroad

A CITY OF REFUGE IN CANADA, FOR AMERICAN SLAVES.

A PUBLIC MEETING Will be held THIS EVENING (D.V.), at Seven o'Clock, in the TONTINE,

To receive a Deputation—the Rev. WM. KING, and Mr. WM. DAY, a gentleman of Colour—who will give information regarding the Slave Population of America, and the Elgin Settlement in Canada—a city of refuge for the Negro Race.

You are earnestly requested to attend.

Armagh, Saturday, 8th Oct., 1859.   PRINTED AT THE ARMAGH GUARDIAN OFFICE.

Rev. William King, a former slave owner from Louisiana, canvassed as far away as Ireland in 1859 to raise money for the Elgin Settlement in southwestern Ontario. American slaves by the hundreds were drawn by the underground railway to this "city of refuge"

NAC/MG24J14, p.857

The Hidden Road to Freedom

"WHEN my feet first touched the Canada shore, I threw myself on the ground, rolled in the sand, seized handfulls of it and kissed them and danced around, till, in the eyes of several who were present, I passed for a madman."

Josiah Henson

Underground Railroad was the widely popular term for the network of paths of flight, safe houses, and willing guides — men and women, white and black, Canadian and American — that helped slaves escape northwest from the American South to freedom before the American Civil War (1860-65) ended slavery in the United States. Dr. Martin Luther King referred to nineteenth century Canada as the "North Star" in the history of Black America. The old spiritual, "Follow the Drinking Gourd," reminded slaves to keep their eyes on the Gourd, the Big Dipper, which pointed the way north to Heaven. Heaven was freedom and this was particularly true in Canada.

The Underground Railroad had a definite Canadian component because its final, most secure terminus lay directly across the American boundary in Upper Canada, today called Ontario. That became especially evident after the American Fugitive Slave Law of 1850 made clear that "runaway" Black slaves from the South could be taken and returned even from the so-called Free States of the North. As a result, a much larger flow of refugees came over the Niagara and Detroit borders into a Canada where there was security and safety for Blacks of all ages, without chance of their seizure by well-paid slave-hunters ranging the Northern States for their bounty.

From its earliest years Upper Canada had actually been a haven for enslaved Blacks. It was the leglislation of 1793 of Upper Canada's first governor, John Graves Simcoe, that prohibited any future importation of slaves and further ensured that slavery would no longer exist following the death of

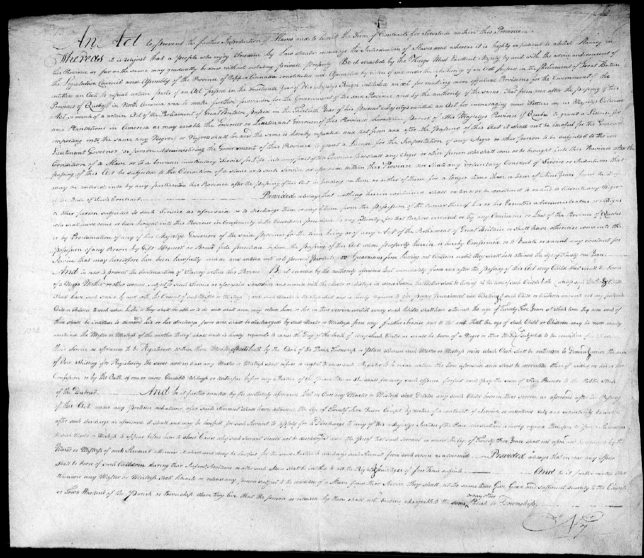

Nearly seven decades before Abraham Lincoln was confronted by the slavery issue, John Graves Simcoe, Upper Canada's first Lieutenant Governor, proposed legislation to abolish slavery in the British Colony. The text of the Act as passed by the Second Session of the Parliament of Upper Canada (future Ontario) and signed into law by Simcoe in 1793 is illustrated here

existing victims. This farsighted legislation was enacted some seventy years before Abraham Lincoln's abolition legislation.

This notably liberal stand by a Tory governor made Upper Canada a favoured arrival point for Blacks of all ages fleeing the democratic American republic to the south. In fact, some 30,000 courageous adventurers found their way to the province. They included such memorable figures as Josiah Henson, who made his way to Upper Canada in 1830. Eleven years later, on 80 hectares (200 acres) of land he had bought with Quaker and Abolitionist support, Henson founded the British American Institute for Fugitive Slaves, the first educational system in Canada in which skills such as blacksmithing and carpentry were taught primarily to former slaves. By 1842 he had founded the Dawn Settlement of

The underground railway was a busy operation. "Depots" were points of destination; "agents" hid runaway slaves in their homes; "conductors" transported slaves to freedom; "stations" dotted the length of the "railway line." Fast-tracking to freedom meant late night meetings and careful planning. Even though the journey was treacherous, nearly 30,000 slaves found freedom at Canadian "terminals"

Black farmers in southwestern Kent County. Henson not only became the patriarch of this settlement, but published his autobiography in 1849. It led Harriet Beecher Stowe, the powerful antislavery American author, to interview him and it thus inspired the title character of her celebrated *Uncle Tom's Cabin*, published in 1852.

In Kent was also the Buxton Settlement organized in 1849 by the Elgin Association to help ex-slaves take up land. This charitable body was strongly based on Anglo-Presbyterian support and soon backed as well by the Anti-Slavery Society of Toronto which had been formed in strong Canadian response to the American Fugitive Slave Law. It heard eloquent speeches from visiting British and American foes of slavery, but also from George Brown, Presbyterian owner of the influential Toronto *Globe*. Brown worked ardently with the Society to assist suffering Black fugitives who found a path to Canada in the worst years before President Lincoln abolished American slavery in 1863. All in all, Canada, with long ties with North American Black history, shared significantly in this heroic epic of the Underground Railroad.

JMSC

1. Provincial Freeman.

DEVOTED TO ANTI-SLAVERY, TEMPERANCE, AND GENERAL LITERATURE.

SAMUEL R. WARD, Editor | TORONTO, CANADA WEST, SATURDAY, AUGUST 12, 1854. | VOL. I.—NO. 21.
ALICE M. SHADD, Cor. Editor |

2. VOICE OF THE FUGITIVE.

RY BIBB, EDITOR. SANDWICH, C. W., MARCH 12, 1851,

3. *The old Matthew Elliott home in Amherstburg, Ontario, where Eliza of* Uncle Tom's Cabin *fame took refuge during the days of slavery in the United States*

4. *Original home of "Uncle Tom" (Josiah Henson), born into slavery in Maryland, 1789, died near Dresden, Ontario,1883*

5. *The most famous slave to ride the underground railway to Upper Canada was Josiah Henson, the alleged model for Tom in Harriet Beecher Stowe's* Uncle Tom's Cabin. *After reaching his freedom depot in 1830, Henson assisted more than 100 slaves in their journey following the "drinking gourd" — the North Star — to Canada*

1. The Provincial Freeman *and* 2. the Voice of the Fugitive *were two anti-slavery newspapers founded by Black abolitionists who settled in the British colony (present-day Ontario) in the mid-19th century. The former paper was founded in 1853 by Mary Ann Shadd, the first Black woman in North America to publish and edit a newspaper. She encouraged Black fugitives to integrate and become self-supportive within the British colony. The latter paper, founded in 1851 by Henry Bibb, a former slave from New Orleans who had been "educated in the school of adversity, whips and chains," supported the development of self-sustaining Black communities in the province of Upper Canada*

3.

The Old Eliott Home Eliza Cottage Where Eliza of Uncle Toms Cabin Fame took Refuge in Slavery Days, Amherstberg, Ont.

Original home of "Uncle Tom" Born in slavery 1789–died near Dresden–1883.

4.

5. 3-5,C.J. Humber Collection

NICKEL

Serving the World

INCO Limited

I N THE LATE nineteenth and early twentieth centuries vast deposits of nickel ore were discovered in Northern Ontario. Through the careful application of entrepreneurial, scientific, and technical skills in the development of these deposits, Canada emerged as the world's leading nickel producer.

Unrefined nickel had been used for millennia. But miners of copper and silver in Saxony regarded nickel ores as troublesome and called them "Kupfernickel" — "Old Nick's (The Devil's) Copper." In 1781, when Axel Fredrik Cronstedt, a Swedish mineralogist and chemist, isolated nickel he retained that name.

To develop a mineral deposit discovered near Sherbrooke, Quebec, a Boston entrepreneur, W. E. C. Eustis, organized the Orford Nickel and Copper Company in 1865 and established a refinery in New Jersey to process the ore. Later, in August 1883, near the site of present-day Sudbury, Ontario, Tom Flanagan, a blacksmith working on the construction of the Canadian Pacific Railway took samples of rust-coloured material later identified as containing copper sulphide.

Thomas and William Murray, merchants from Pembroke, Ontario, registered a claim in February 1884 on the site where Flanagan had found his specimens. The Murray Mine subsequently became a steady producer of nickel. Other discoveries made nearby led to the development of the Worthington, Frood, Stobie, Creighton, Evans, Levack, and Copper Cliff mines.

Among the many prospectors and developers who came to the region was Samuel J. Ritchie, an Ohio factory owner. Ritchie and business associates acquired the Copper Cliff, Creighton, Evans, Frood and Stobie mining claims for the Canadian Copper Company which had its head office in Cleveland, and authorized to operate in Canada.

Open-pit mining commenced in May 1886 on the Copper Cliff site. Robert Thompson of the Orford Company signed a contract for the smelting of 100,000 tons of 7 percent copper ore at the Orford refinery in New Jersey. When tested, however, the ore from the Canadian Copper Company

ABOVE: *Nickel is corrosion and heat resistant and it adds strength when alloyed with other metals*

mine at Copper Cliff was found to contain only 4.5 percent copper. It also contained 2.5 percent nickel. This was not what had been expected nor what was wanted. Since Thompson and Ritchie were primarily interested in copper they had to solve three problems: copper and nickel had to be separated and refined; a nickle market had to be developed; a profit had to be made.

Initially, difficulties were encountered in separating the copper from the nickel. Fortunately, when a workman hit a fragment of the cooled molten mixture with a sledge-hammer the nickel and copper broke apart. Experimentation established that if sodium sulphide was added during the refining process, and the molten mixture was cooled slowly, two layers formed which could be separated. Most of the sodium and copper sulphides were in the top layer while the bottom was largely nickel sulphide. Through repetition of this process and the careful use of additives and roasting, the sulphur could be removed and commercial quality nickel would result. The "Orford tops and bottoms process" was patented in 1890. With refinements, it was widely used until the middle of the 20th century. While Thompson and his colleagues were patenting the Orford process, Ludwig Mond, a chemical manufacturer in England, patented the nickel carbonyl process, using carbon monoxide as his refining agent.

With the refining problem solved, the question of a market for nickel remained. The total world production of nickel in 1886 had been less than one thousand tons with a selling price of a $1.00 per pound. Ritchie and his colleagues in the Canadian Copper Company might be able to

INCO Limited

Nickel stainless steel is preferred to meet architectural demands for precision, beauty, durability, and economy. The metal sculpture Pas de Trois is located at the corner of University and Wellington Street in downtown Toronto

INCO Limited

Nickel is found just about everywhere including the kitchen sink. In fact, the manufacture of stainless steel kitchen sinks consumes more than 55 million pounds of nickel per year

recover their investment and even enjoy a profit from the copper in the Sudbury deposits, but what was to be done with the nickel? Happily, an English inventor and metallurgist, John Gamgee, provided the solution to that problem. The US Navy had approved the use of nickel steel plate which Gamgee had developed and the US Congress voted $1 million for the purchase of the new metal. Other countries followed. Additional uses for nickel were gradually developed.

Canadian Copper considered buying the Mond process, but could not agree on a price. As a result of an internal disagreement, Samuel Ritchie was ousted, but this company which he had created dominated nickel production in the 1890s.

When Mond could not sell his nickel carbonyl refining process, he incorporated the Mond Nickel Company in 1900, acquired nickel properties in the Sudbury area, processing the ore in Wales.

In 1901 Thomas Edison, requiring nickel for a storage battery, acquired mining rights in the Sudbury region. When quicksand was encountered Edison abandoned his Sudbury project. Had Edison continued drilling deeper a body of nickel-copper ore would have been reached. In the late 1920s the Edison site was acquired by Falconbridge Nickel Mines. The successful development of that company by Thayer Lindsley is one of the great sagas of the nickel industry throughout the world.

In 1902 the International Nickel Company was incorporated in the State of New Jersey through the amalgamation of Canadian Copper, the Orford Copper Company, the Société Minière Caledonienne and others. When it was created, the International Nickel Company was the world's dominant nickel producer and refiner. It became the primary catalyst in the expanding use of nickel.

Alloys of nickel and steel, which possess special properties of strength and toughness, were gradually used in the manufacture of automobiles, buses, railway locomotives, trucks, and agricultural, mining, and construction equipment. Earlier, of course, nickel was used for coinage. Initially, however, when International Nickel came into being the use of nickel alloys for military purposes provided the primary market.

In September 1915, the Government of Ontario appointed a Commission to inquire into the "resources, industries and capacities, both present and future ... in connection with nickel and its ores." In its report the Commission noted that, given the extent of Ontario's nickel deposits, Ontario possessed the most extensive, high quality nickel deposits known to exist anywhere in the world. It also noted that the refining of nickel could be successfully carried out in Ontario. The International Nickel Company had indicated a year earlier that this would be done.

In July 1916, The International Nickel Company of Canada Limited (INCO) was incorporated. Control of all mining, smelting and refining processes of The International Nickel Company registered in New Jersey, were transferred to the new Canadian company.

Following World War I there were two major nickel producing companies in Canada — INCO and the Mond Nickel Company. In 1928 the two companies merged. By that time Falconbridge Nickel Mines had been incorporated.

In his early efforts to develop Falconbridge, Thayer Lindsley relied on several of INCO's experts, whom he persuaded to join his new company. Lindsley knew that INCO was the primary custodian of scientific and technical information concerning the production, refining and uses of nickel. A key contributor, over many years, to INCO's success was Robert C. Stanley.

In 1901 Stanley joined the Orford Company as a metallurgist. Three years later, he devised the method for producing a new nickel alloy. Stronger than pure nickel it resisted the severely corrosive effects of rapidly flowing seawater. This remarkable quality resulted in this new metal, named Monel, being used in a variety of domestic and industrial applications. Shortly after Stanley became President of INCO in 1922, a new INCO rolling mill was built in Huntington, West Virginia. Subsequently INCO's international operations in the production of nickel alloys were based there.

The leadership which Stanley provided came at a critical time in INCO's history. During World War I the production of the company had been geared almost entirely to military needs. When the war ended the nickel industry was largely without markets. New uses for nickel had to be found to ensure INCO's long-term development and financial viability. Under Robert Stanley's direction continuous, high quality research was given priority. Nickel alloys were used in the manufacture of aircraft, electrical, energy and marine equipment and parts and many other products.

As soon as airborne magnetometers were available, INCO's exploration experts used them in their search for nickel deposits. Canada's second largest nickel deposit was discovered in northern Manitoba in 1956 by this means. An entirely new community named Thompson, Manitoba, came into being as a result. It was named in honour of John Fairfield Thompson, INCO's former chairman and chief executive officer.

INCO's emphasis on research and innovation, which Robert Stanley initiated and emphasized, has been, perhaps, the single most significant factor in INCO's continuance as the world's leading nickel company. Early in the 1990s, additional large nickel deposits identified on the western edge of the Sudbury Basin were confirmed as the largest known, undeveloped nickel-copper deposits in that basin. Other advanced technologies have enabled INCO to re-open and to operate safely older mines closed earlier for safety reasons.

A century after nickel was discovered and began to be mined in Canada, two Canadian mining companies — INCO and Falconbridge — continue as leading international nickel producers. Major competition from Russia, however, has reduced Canada's share of the world nickel market. Ironically, Russia gained control after World War II of the Petsamo district of northern Finland where, in 1935, an INCO exploration team had discovered a rich nickel orebody which INCO developed, financed and supervised until late 1939. By that time thoroughly modern mining and smelting facilities had been installed. These fell under German control during the war and later under Russian.

INCO was compensated later for its loss, but it is one of the strange ironies of twentieth century history that INCO, by providing foundations for the modern Soviet nickel industry, was the early creator of its own competition. This is a further, though ironic, indication of the extent to which Canadian companies have taught the world how to discover, develop, process and use nickel. *DMS*

THAYER LINDSLEY

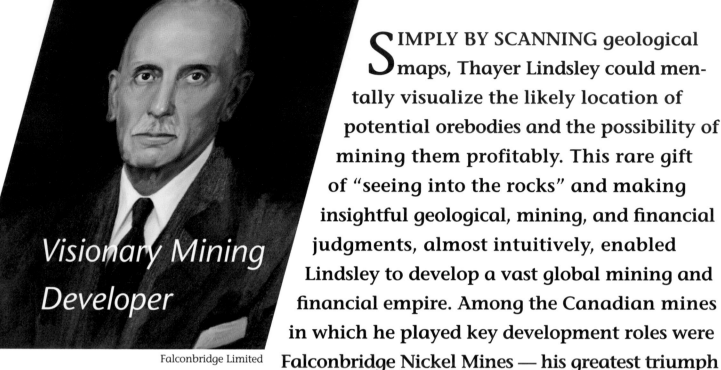

Falconbridge Limited

Visionary Mining Developer

1882-1976

SIMPLY BY SCANNING geological maps, Thayer Lindsley could mentally visualize the likely location of potential orebodies and the possibility of mining them profitably. This rare gift of "seeing into the rocks" and making insightful geological, mining, and financial judgments, almost intuitively, enabled Lindsley to develop a vast global mining and financial empire. Among the Canadian mines in which he played key development roles were **Falconbridge Nickel Mines — his greatest triumph — Frobisher, Sherritt-Gordon, Canadian Malartic, Beatty, and Giant Yellowknife.**

Born in 1882 in Yokohama, Japan, where his father, a member of a wealthy Boston family, was a manager with Canadian Pacific Railways, Lindsley enrolled in civil engineering at Harvard. Upon graduation he took up postgraduate studies in geology and mining engineering at Columbia University.

By 1911, having ventured to the Porcupine gold-mining camp in Northern Ontario, he wrote an account of what he had seen there. Failing in his efforts to interest American mining companies in Canadian opportunities, he became involved in the resolution of mining problems in the western United States. After serving in the First World War as an artillery officer in the U.S. Army, he took over an iron mine in Oregon and returned it to profitable operation.

Quick to respond to new opportunities, he returned to Canada and accepted, in 1924, a position as a geologist with Ontario's McIntyre Porcupine Mines. Soon, he teamed up with Joseph Errington, also a mining engineer, to stake claims in the Sudbury Basin. By 1926 they had incorporated Sudbury Mines Limited. Two years later Lindsley, his brother, Halstead, and Errington, together with Gen. Donald Hogarth and Lt.-Col. C.D.H. MacAlpine, formed Ventures Limited, a holding company for mining properties in which they each took an interest.

After careful study of the Sudbury Basin, Lindsley decided that he and his colleagues together should purchase a group of claims in Falconbridge Township that had been acquired earlier by Thomas A. Edison as a potential source of nickel for a storage battery he had invented. Unfortunately for Edison, the terrain was difficult to drill, and quicksand was encountered at a depth of 80 feet. Discouraged, Edison abandoned his Sudbury project. Had he continued drilling 20 more feet, he would have discovered one of the world's most lucrative nickel-copper deposits.

The Edison claims reverted to the Crown and were subsequently restaked and drilled by a Minneapolis group. There were indications of an ore body estimated at 5.7 million tons of nickel-copper ore above the 500-foot level.

Lindsley's study of the claims convinced him of their potential value. Agreeing to buy them for $2.5 million, he made a $500,000 down payment. On August 28, 1928, Falconbridge Nickel Mines Limited was incorporated and acquired all the Edison claims.

It was then assumed that an independent nickel company could not compete successfully with International Nickel Company since it was thought that all of the patents for nickel refining were under its strict control. Lindsley, however, knew that a nickel refinery in Kristiansand, Norway, owned the rights to an electrolytic nickel-refining process. Falconbridge Nickel Mines bought control of the Kristiansand refinery. With the completion of a sales agreement with London metal agents, Falconbridge gained the advantage in the sale of nickel and copper to European clients.

Despite the severe economic problems of the 1930s, and the price of Falconbridge shares falling from a high of $14.85 to a low of 16 cents, the company still showed a net profit of over one million dollars in 1933 and paid its first dividend of 25 cents a share. Falconbridge was on the way to success.

Overcoming many difficulties during the Second World War, including the loss of the refinery in Norway, Falconbridge progressed steadily. At this time five mines were in operation and several more were in the process of development. Ore reserves of nickel and copper stood at nearly 40 million tons. Gold, silver, platinum, and cobalt were also being produced. The iron and selenium in the ores were both being utilized.

In 1955, Lindsley retired as President of Ventures Limited. Falconbridge absorbed Ventures the next year. But Lindsley kept several of the companies which had been under the Ventures umbrella and quickly began a new chapter in his life with offices in Toronto, New York, Paris, Casablanca, and Perth, Australia.

In the early 1970s, when petroleum shortages threatened, Lindsley argued that solutions were close at hand. He had patented a system for the release of additional oil from partially tapped sources and, in the case of tar sands and heavy oil deposits, from sources that had scarcely begun to be tapped.

His amazing combination of modesty, intuitive sense, and visionary capability as a mine finder and developer has few if any equals. Throughout his long career Lindsley gave credit and constant encouragement to his associates whose personal success brought him great satisfaction.　DMS

James Y. Murdoch

1890-1962

Creative Mining Executive

Noranda Inc.

IN THE SPRING OF 1922, James Murdoch, a thirty-two-year-old Toronto lawyer, incorporated Noranda Mines Limited at the request of Humphrey Chadbourne, an American mining engineer. Earlier, Chadbourne had formed a syndicate with another mining engineer, Samuel C. Thomson, to search for the best mineral prospects in Northern Ontario. They hoped that Murdoch would help them find and develop a big, highly successful mine. Murdoch did that and much more: he created one of Canada's most successful mining and industrial corporations.

Several months after the incorporation of Noranda, the Thomson-Chadbourne syndicate took an option on a mineral prospect that had been staked by Ed Horne, an experienced prospector. Situated east of Kirkland Lake, Ontario, it was thirty miles into Quebec, near the shore of Lake Tremoy, subsequently called Lake Osisko. A year or so later, when it was established that the Horne property could be mined profitably, Noranda mines was expected to employ as many as 500 men. By the early 1990s, however, the company employed about 30,000 people in North and South America, Africa, Europe and elsewhere around the world! J.Y. Murdoch, more than any other single person, had created and established the bases for the amazing success of this company. As its first president, he was its guiding genius for thirty-five years.

Murdoch had graduated from Osgoode Hall Law School in Toronto, his hometown, only nine years before he was appointed president of Noranda, but, at the time of his appointment, he was already respected for his work as a mining lawyer.

Within a year of Murdoch's appointment as head of Noranda, the value of the Horne property was becoming clearer but primarily as a copper mine, not the gold mine Horne had sought. By late 1926 a rail line had been built to the area. Several years later it became obvious that Noranda, with estimated ore reserves of more than 50 billion tons, could become one of the world's great mines. By that time Murdoch and his colleagues had demonstrated that they had the financial and technical expertise and management ability to ensure that it would.

As president of Noranda, Murdoch was determined to develop a profitable group of related companies that would mine and refine minerals and process them into finished goods such as wire, cable, and other industrial products. He knew that to achieve this objective Noranda needed the strong

As a young lawyer, J.Y. Murdoch not only drafted the incorporation of Noranda Mines Ltd. but served as its president from 1923-1956. Called Noranda Minerals today, the multinational, multi-product company owes a great deal of its huge international success to this visionary mining executive born in Toronto in 1890

OPPOSITE
J.Y. Murdoch, left, and Humphrey Chadbourne (with camera), 1926, at the Noranda site in Quebec

financial backing which the Thomson-Chadbourne syndicate provided. The syndicate included 14 United States executives of great experience, wealth, and influence. One was a former president of the United States Steel Corporation, another was a senior executive of E.I. Dupont de Nemours, another was a former United States ambassador to France, still another was an outstanding New York lawyer. That men of such influence and wide experience relied on Murdoch and allowed him to develop a distinctively Canadian company, not merely a mining company controlled by United States investors, was a clear indication of the extent to which he had quickly earned their trust.

Murdoch also realized, however, that, if Noranda was to develop as a Canadian company, influential Canadians had to be persuaded to invest in it. Murdoch secured this necessary investment.

Before the Thomson-Chadbourne syndicate had been formed, Murdoch had gained the confidence of mining executives in Canada. Among these was Noah Timmins, President of Hollinger Consolidated Gold Mines, one of Canada's most successful mining corporations. Through conversations Murdoch had with Timmins, an agreement was reached in the mid-1920s whereby Hollinger would advance Noranda $3 million on a short-term basis to finance the construction of the buildings and to acquire the machinery and provide the working capital needed for Noranda's early development as a mining and smelting company.

By the end of 1927, five years after Murdoch and members of the Thomson-Chadbourne syndicate had begun their partnership, the HORNE mine was in production. The previous year a civil engineer had been engaged to develop a new town named, like the company itself, Noranda, a contraction of the words "Northern" and "Canada." Murdoch was aware of the urgent need for a carefully planned community to overcome the difficulties encountered in Rouyn, the rough-and-tumble town which had grown up in the area surrounding the mine. Thus he arranged for the incorporation of Noranda and served as its first Mayor until 1929.

To carry forward his plan for Noranda, Murdoch decided to build an electrolytic copper refinery in Montreal East to process raw materials into finished products. An operating company, Canadian Copper Refiners Limited, was organized in 1929 and given the responsibility of processing the raw sulphide rock from Noranda's properties in Rouyn township into marketable shapes of refined copper.

In August 1930 Murdoch completed an agreement between Noranda Mines and Canada Wire and Cable Limited, Canada's leading manufacturer of wire and cable. The agreement provided that Canada Wire would purchase its copper requirements from Canadian Copper Refiners. In turn, Noranda would purchase shares in Canada Wire. The proceeds from the purchase were to be used by Canada Wire to construct and operate a copper rod rolling mill and wire plant next to the Canadian Copper Refiners' plant in Montreal East. This agreement was mutually beneficial. It gave Noranda a major purchaser for its copper and, at the same time, gave Canada Wire a base for the production of rod for its own operations as well as for domestic and export sales to other wire manufacturers. In due course Noranda acquired a controlling interest in Canada Wire and Cable which it sold many years later to a major French corporation.

In 1937 Murdoch secured an undertaking from mining officials of the Province of Quebec that the Quebec government would build an access road to an isolated region of the Gaspé, if the results of exploration by Noranda's prospecting crews were sufficiently encouraging.This area had been explored for minerals as early as Champlain's time in the early seventeenth century. By late 1939 Murdoch concluded that work should continue in the Gaspé but that it would have to be delayed until the necessary roads were built and World War II had ended.

By the outbreak of that war, Noranda was Canada's second largest producer of copper. When the war ended, the company had produced, from its inception, over 1.6 billion pounds of copper and more than 4 million ounces of gold. The total value of this production was $258 million of which over $107 million had been paid in dividends to shareholders. Murdoch had led Noranda to prosperity!

During World War II Murdoch's administrative and financial skills were constantly in demand in the wider public community as well as in Noranda. He served in senior positions in two wartime corporations and was president of the National War Services Funds Advisory Board. He also served as chairman of the National War Services Committee of the YMCA.

As soon as men and supplies became available at the end of the war, work was resumed on Noranda's property in the Gaspé. In 1952 the mine was brought into production by Gaspé Copper Mines, a Noranda subsidiary. The development of this new mine had a major impact on the entire Gaspé peninsula. Cables carrying electricity were laid on the floor of the St. Lawrence River to supply electric power to the new mining operation. Significant improvements came to the Gaspé with the establishment of Noranda's operations there. The mining community which developed there was named Murdochville to honour Murdoch.

J.Y. Murdoch's management of the risks in the development of the Horne Mine, and the later Noranda mines and other ventures, brought outstanding financial benefits to those who had invested in Noranda. Murdoch, however, did more than merely make money for investors, important though that was. Through his insightful management of Noranda's affairs, he made an outstanding contribution to the development of Canada's mining and industrial capabilities. His significant contributions and powerful talents were widely recognized and honoured.

In recognition of his contribution to Canada's war efforts from 1939-1945 he received the Order of the British Empire. Laval University in Quebec conferred on him an honorary degree of Doctor of Laws. When he died in 1962, Murdoch was a director of more than 30 companies, many within the Noranda group, still others in banking, insurance, paper, oil, railways and other industries.

Nearly 30 years after his death he was elected a charter member of the Canadian Mining Hall of Fame. His colleagues in the mining industry honoured him as a great mining executive and as a primary contributor to the development of Canada. Murdoch had described his native land as "a great and rich young nation whose frontiers beckon the man in whom the spirit of high adventure is strong."

DMS

JOHN PATCH

1781 - 1861

I N 1858 a petition signed by more than 100 prominent citizens of Yarmouth was submitted to the Nova Scotia Legislature asking that a pension be granted John Patch who "conceives he has rendered essential service to the world at large."

Propeller of Ships

The "essential service" that was referred to was the invention of the screw propeller, recognized by then as one of the major inventions of the nineteenth century for steamships of all description. As further evidence that Patch was the inventor, the petition enclosed a declaration from the Butler brothers of Yarmouth who wrote, "We assisted him in making the machinery for the first trial, which took place in 1833. We accompanied him in a small boat to which the propeller was attached and crossed the harbour several times."

The reason for the petition was that John Patch was now a lame, sick, 77-year-old living in a Yarmouth poorhouse.

Patch was born in 1781 — the same year his sea captain father died in a shipwreck off Seal Island — but little is known of his early years in Nova Scotia. It is believed he worked as a fisherman and sailor for many years before getting the idea for a screw propeller while watching a small boat being sculled by a single oar moved in a particular pattern over its stern. According to a half brother writing in the *Yarmouth Herald* in 1875, Patch had been considering a screw propeller for almost 30 years, but scientific gentlemen to whom he showed his plan "laughed at him, telling him it was just as impractical as perpetual motion."

Despite such discouragement, in the winter of 1832-33 Patch worked in a shed at nearby Kelley's Cove on what was described as "two twisting fans appended to a shaft" two and a half feet in diameter, while the Butler brothers, Robert and Nathan, developed a hand crank and wooden gears. That summer Patch carefully tried out his invention alone on a small boat after dark in Yarmouth Harbour, the first tests being made after dark. Later, however, the Butlers were passengers and many other residents saw him hand-propel the boat around the harbour.

The following year Patch got the opportunity to try out his propeller on a larger vessel when his friend, Captain Robert Kelley, installed the propeller with its hand crank and wooden gears on board his 25-ton sailing ship, *Royal George*. Shortly afterwards, on a trip to Saint John, the invention was put to the test. The wind died, becalming all the other sailing ships, but the *Royal George*, which utilized the hand-cranked propeller, continued its trip to Saint John.

Kelley wanted Patch to go to England and patent the invention, but Patch, whose favourite expression was "time enough yet," eventually decided to go to Washington instead. There are several versions of what happened next. One, told by a descendant as late as 1947, contends that he was "fleeced" when he befriended two fortune seekers while sailing from Yarmouth to Boston on his way to Washington and that, under the influence of alcohol, he signed over all of the rights to the invention for a bottle of liquor and a barrel of flour. Another account maintains that he reached the patent office in Washington where he became discouraged when told not to waste his money patenting such an impractical invention. A third version suggests that he may have been the victim of a swindling patent office lawyer who talked him out of making the application and later sold the invention to a British peer.

What is known is that Patch never made a penny from his invention (or received the barrel of flour) and never received recognition for his invention apart from that accorded by the people of Yarmouth. This was partly because, since paddle wheels were still considered the prime means of propelling large ships, little interest was shown in any other form of propulsion at that time. In 1837, however, a screw propeller was installed in the 3,700-ton British steamship *Archimedes* and in the 1840s the British navy also turned to this form of propulsion for its fleet.

Patch also made improvements to steam engines and improved the dip of the paddle wheels for steamers. But he never relinquished his interest in propellers. In October 1848, while working at Boston, he was the subject of an article in the *Scientific American* that published an illustration of what he now called the "Double Action Propeller." The story accompanying it told how a Mr. John Patch, "a very ingenious mechanic of Boston," had developed the unit and continued "… it is different from other propellers that have been used and it is exceedingly simple."

The article also reported that "the inventor would like it if some of our enterprising ship owners would try one on a large scale and he would be perfectly willing to superintend its erection, at a fair mechanic's wage — a very small consideration indeed." The new unit, however, was never developed and Patch later returned to Yarmouth.

By 1858 Patch was without money and unable to work. This prompted his fellow citizens to sign the petition that was drafted by one of the city's best-known lawyers and orators, C.B. Owen. At the Legislature in Halifax, it was referred for study to the committee on trade and manufacture. Six weeks later the committee tabled its recommendation: "Beg leave to report that they do not recommend the prayers of these several petitions to the favourable consideration of the house."

Patch, therefore, remained in the poorhouse where, three years later, he died penniless and bitter.

MVJ

DR. JAMES

1861-1939

The Inventor of Basketball

Dr. James Naismith described the dribble as *"one of the finest plays, one of the sweetest, prettiest plays"* in all of basketball. When Naismith applied to be the Director of Physical Education at the University of Kansas, A.A. Stagg, *"the Dean of American Football,"* recommended his good friend for the position, stating that Naismith was the *"inventor of basketball, a medical doctor, a Presbyterian minister, a teetotaller, an all-around athlete, a non-smoker and the owner of a vocabulary without cuss words"*

NAISMITH

IN THE AUTUMN OF 1891, Luther Gulick, head of the Physical Education Department at the International Training School of the Young Men's Christian Association (YMCA) in Springfield, Massachusetts, asked James Naismith and the other physical education instructors to develop new games that could be played indoors during the winter. Gulick knew that the students, who were YMCA physical education directors from various cities throughout the United States and Canada, found the traditional drills and exercises monotonous. He needed games that the students could learn readily and would enjoy playing.

The instructors experimented with combinations and variations of existing games but none were satisfactory. Naismith remembered rock-throwing games he had played with boyhood friends in the farming and lumbering community where he had been born near Almonte, about thirty miles south-west of Ottawa, Ontario. From analysis of the advantages and disadvantages of these and other games he had enjoyed in his youth, he created a new game that today is the world's most popular team sport.

The basic rules, generally speaking, still apply. Five central principles were to be carefully observed:

i) A ball — preferably large and light in weight and handled with open hands rather than stick or bat — was to be used.

ii) Running with the ball was prohibited, but it could be passed in any direction among the players and/or could be rolled or dribbled by any player possessing it.

iii) No member of either team was to be restricted from receiving, passing, dribbling, or shooting the ball toward the goal at any time the ball was in play.

iv) Horizontal goals, in the form of baskets elevated higher than any player's reach, were to be placed in the centre of each of the opposite ends of the play area to encourage accurate rather than forceful shooting or throwing of the ball.

v) Both teams were to occupy the same play area, each team having its own end. No rough play or harsh bodily contact — holding, pushing, shouldering, striking, tackling, or tripping — was to be permitted. If such occurred, penalties as set out in the rules were to be imposed.

For the goals, Naismith nailed a wooden half-bushel peach basket at each of the two opposite ends of the balcony that surrounded the floor of the gymnasium in the Springfield school. It was quickly realized that the game would be more enjoyable if the bottoms of the baskets were removed. Soon the baskets were replaced by metal rings with cord nets suspended from them. It was also recognized that each of the two baskets had to be placed a short distance in front of backboards.

During the first two years in which the game was played, a soccer ball was used. Later, a ball four inches larger in circumference became the standard.

Initially, since Naismith was anxious to ensure that all of the students in his group, then numbering 18, might participate in the game, each of the two opposing teams consisted of nine players. Experience soon made it clear that only five players from each of the two opposing teams should play on the court at any one time.

The Springfield team, which included five Canadians, won the first competitive game. During the Christmas holidays following that first game in 1891, those who had played in or witnessed it told others about Naismith's new game. It was suggested that the game should be called "Naismith Ball" but he insisted that it be called "basketball."

Soon Naismith began receiving requests for copies of the rules he had devised. On January 15, 1892, they were published in the Triangle, the paper of the YMCA International Training School. Interest in the game spread quickly in both the United States and Canada.

Canadians took a particular interest in the game since Naismith was a Canadian and five Canadians had participated in the first match. Lyman Archibald, one of the Canadian participants in that early match, introduced the new sport in 1892 at the YMCA in St. Stephen, New Brunswick. That same year it was played at the YMCA in Montreal. When Archibald moved to Hamilton, Ontario, in 1893, he introduced it there. That same year it became popular at the University of Toronto. In 1894, the Graduates Society of McGill University provided a basketball trophy for faculty and student competition.

Interest in the game spread rapidly, especially in the United States, and the growth of this new team sport dramatically increased the membership of local YMCAs. Within five years, however, several YMCAs prohibited basketball because ill feelings developed from time to time among supporters of opposing teams and because small groups of basketball players often dominated the local YMCA gymnasia, squeezing out members accustomed to participating in other sporting activities in the same gyms. Ironically, basketball's very popularity contributed to its banishment from some local YMCAs.

Some YMCA members terminated their memberships and rented halls in order to play the exciting new game. This rental of facilities other than local YMCAs contributed in 1898 to the organization of professional basketball in the United States. The National Basketball League came into being that year.

Basketball eventually achieved international recognition: in 1893, it was introduced in France; In June 1894, a demonstration of the game took place in London, England; In 1896, it was played in Sao Paulo, Brazil. Soon Australia, China and India were playing the game; Japan was playing in 1900 and Iran by 1901. Gradually basketball became a global sport attracting both men and women and enthusiastic spectators. In 1936 it became a regular event at the Olympics.

Dr. James Naismith Basketball Foundation

When this 1928 picture of Dr. Naismith and his wife was taken, basketball had evolved from peach baskets to netted hoops and an estimated 15 million worldwide were playing the game. The sport's popularity was in fact so great that the 1936 Berlin Olympic Committee invited Dr. Naismith to address the basketball teams participating for the first time in a team sport in any Olympics.

Who was this man who, through his new game of basketball, brought entertainment to countless millions of spectators worldwide and exhilaration and well-being to the many tens of thousands who played it? Life had not been easy. Orphaned by the time he was nine years old, Naismith had had to struggle to gain his education. He worked for a time as a lumberjack, before returning to Almonte, Ontario, at age 20, to complete his high school education.

Upon completion of his secondary education, he was admitted to McGill University and studied to become a Presbyterian minister. At McGill he played football. In 1887 he became an instructor in physical education there and continued in that position until he went to Springfield in 1890 to study psychology. The following year he was given an appointment as a physical education instructor. It was at Springfield that he introduced the new game of basketball.

From 1895 until 1898 Naismith was the Director of Physical Education at the YMCA college in Denver, Colorado. During that period he also studied medicine and graduated in 1898 from the Gross Medical School of the University of Colorado. That same year he was appointed chairman of the Physical Education Department at the University of Kansas, a position he held until his retirement in 1937.

Naismith was a true sportsman in the fullest sense. The essence of his idea of sportsmanship is clear: "Let us be able to lose gracefully and to win courteously; to accept criticism as well as praise; and to appreciate the attitude of the other fellow at all times."

During his professional career, Naismith published several volumes focusing on athletics and was credited with the invention of the protective helmet for football players.

In 1941, on basketball's fiftieth anniversary, two years after his death (he had died in Lawrence, Kansas, on November 28, 1939), the Naismith Memorial Basketball Hall of Fame was organized as an honorary society. The museum, completed in 1968 on the campus of Springfield College, honours his creation there of the game that is now played and watched with great enthusiasm in most countries around the world and acknowledged as the most popular team sport in the world. DMS

Born in Almonte, near Ottawa, Dr. James Naismith invented basketball while attending school and acting as a physical education instructor at the international YMCA training college in Springfield, Massachusetts. He is viewed (centre, right) here with his first team in 1891. Basketball today is the world's most popular indoor sport, rivaling only soccer for its universality

Dr. James Naismith Basketball Foundation

Margaret MacBurney
FORWARD

EDMONTON
COMMERCIAL
GRADUATES
BASKETBALL
CLUB
▼
WORLD'S
CHAMPIONS

Gladys Fry
CENTRE

J. Percy Page
COACH

Mildred McCormack
FORWARD

Kate Macrae
GUARD

Mae Brown
UTILITY

CAPTAIN
Elsie Bennie
GUARD

The Edmonton Grads

"The Grads have the greatest team that ever stepped out on a basketball floor."
Dr. James Naismith's observation was based on the following facts:
In the 25-year period, 1915-1940, the Canadian women's team won 96.2 percent of their games with an average score of 48 to 20. Of the 522 games played, 502 were won by the official World's Basketball Champion Grads.
In all, 125,000 miles were logged, including 3 trips to Europe, in defence of their many titles, by the 38 players, all but two of whom were graduates of McDougall Commercial High School in Edmonton, Alberta. "Ladies first and athletes second," the Grads had only one coach, J. Percy Page (inducted into Canada's Sports Hall of Fame in 1955), whom Naismith described as the "greatest coach and the most superb sportsman it has ever been my good fortune to meet."

Stephen Leacock

1869-1944

Monarch of Wit

CONSIDERED one of the greatest humorists of the English-speaking world, Stephen Leacock, a half century after his death, still ranks among Canada's most popular writers. His ability to stimulate spontaneous laughter continues to endear him in Canada and abroad, his works having been translated into many languages, including both Chinese and Japanese.

Born in Swanmore, England, on December 30, 1869, Leacock came to Canada with his parents when he was six years old. Third of a family of eleven, he was educated at Upper Canada College where he later taught for nine years the modern

Now a tourist attraction and museum, Leacock's summer home outside Orillia, Ontario, became a retreat for the world-famous humorist who has more books in print than any other Canadian author, living or dead

hes © Stephen Leacock

Y BAY, LAKE COUCHICHING, 1928

languages he had studied as an undergraduate at the University of Toronto.

At the University of Chicago, he specialized in economics and political science, receiving the degree of Doctor of Philosophy in 1903. That same year he became a lecturer in economics and political science at Montreal's McGill University.

As he had already gained experience as a teacher and, additionally, had a great sense of humour, it is not surprising to learn that Leacock became one of the most popular faculty members at McGill. Within five years of his initial appointment he became a full professor and was the head of the economic and political science department until his retirement in 1936.

Leacock's first book, *Elements of Political Science*, appeared in 1906. It quickly gained attention as a serious text book. During Leacock's lifetime, it was his best-selling volume, having been translated into 18 languages and designated as required reading in many American universities.

The following year, Leacock went to England under the auspices of the Rhodes Trust to lecture on "Imperial Organization." This was the first in a long series of public lectures delivered by Leacock. Through his exuberant lectures and humorous publications, Leacock gained widespread renown that brought credit both to himself and to McGill University. In 1912 he made his first professional tour of England during which he delivered fifty lectures. This tour contributed to his growing reputation and to his annual income, which soared that year to more than $20,000, an astronomically high income for a university professor at that time.

Leacock was the author of more than 60 books, half were works of humour. Among his best-known are his *Nonsense Novels* (1911), *Sunshine Sketches of a Little Town* (1912), *Arcadian Adventures with the Idle Rich* (1914), *Moonbeams From The Larger Lunacy* (1915), *Further Foolishness* (1916), *The Unsolved Riddle of Social Justice* (1920), *My Discovery of England* (1922), *The Garden of Folly* (1914), *Short Circuits* (1928), *Humour: In Theory and Technique* (1935), *Humour and Humanity* (1937), *My Remarkable Uncle* (1942), *Our Heritage of Liberty* (1942), *How to Write* (1943), and his posthumously published autobiography, *The Boy I Left Behind Me* (1946). Articles he wrote appeared year after year in a great number of American publications such as *Vanity Fair* and *Life* as well as in many Canadian and British periodicals.

His genius as a humorist was first fully appreciated in the United States. The recognition he gained there was the major factor in persuading Canadians that Leacock was not only an outstanding literary figure but also one of the world's greatest humorists. He proved that at least one Canadian with a great sense of humour was able to make money by generating laughter! His books were often sold out within the year; multitudes flocked to his public lectures and readings.

Leacock valued the community over the individual, and the middle road over extreme deviation. His satirical writings attacked rampant individualism, materialism, and the worship of technology. Politically active, with his speeches and writings he helped defeat the Liberal government in the 1911 Canadian general election. He also joyfully satirized the literary fashions of his time.

In practically all of Leacock's writings he attacks, in one way or another, illusions, prejudices, and selfishness. His best-known work, *Sunshine Sketches of a Little Town*, provides subtle insights into Leacock's delightful character and interests. The fictional town of Mariposa was modelled on the real Ontario town of Orillia. When Leacock defined humour as "the kindly contemplation of the incongruities of life," he obviously had *Sunshine Sketches* in mind.

But there is a deeper, more serious side to some of Leacock's humour. Apart from *Sunshine Sketches*, his best-known work is, perhaps, *Arcadian Adventures with the Idle Rich*. In *Arcadian Adventures* Leacock aggressively satirizes the life of the wealthy ruling class in Montreal. There is no doubt that, at times, his "kindly contemplation" gives way to profound indignation, if not anger, at the selfishness that isolates the rich from the rest of humanity. In that work Leacock resorts to satire with the hope that it will contribute to the improvement of the behaviour of the wealthy by exposing their traits to ridicule.

Leacock continued to write until almost the end of his life and to share his exuberant sense of humour wherever he went. During his lifetime he received many honorary degrees and the Governor-General's Award. He died on March 28, 1944. A Canadian postage stamp acknowledged Canada's affection for him; the Leacock Medal for Humour, awarded annually to a Canadian for the best book of humour, honours and commemorates this monarch of wit.   *DMS*

Stephen Leacock received his Ph.D. from the University of Chicago. For 33 years he taught economics and political science at McGill University

Charles Fenerty

1821 - 1892

Paper Maker

ON OCTOBER 26, 1844, Nova Scotia's *Acadian Recorder* published a letter from Charles Fenerty claiming that the small piece of paper he enclosed "is as firm in its texture, as white, and to all appearance as durable as the common wrapping paper, made from hemp, cotton, or the ordinary materials of manufacture." The difference, he pointed out, is that it was "actually composed of spruce wood reduced to pulp." He added, "I entertain an opinion that our forest trees, either hard or soft wood, but more especially the fir, spruce, or poplar, on account of the fibrous quality of these woods, might be easily reduced by a chafing, and manufactured into paper of the finest kind."

When he wrote the letter, several years after he had begun his experiments to develop paper from wood pulp, Fenerty was only 23. A bright and observant teenager with a better-than-average education, Charles was born and worked on the family's ancestral property of 500 acres on the Windsor Road of Lower Sackville. Called Springfield Lake, it had been a grant to his Irish grandfather, William, in 1874. There William and his descendants worked primarily as lumbermen, supplying the Halifax dockyard with spruce, pine, and hardwoods from the three sawmills on their property that had, with further grants and purchases, grown to 2,000 acres.

On his trips to Halifax, Charles often visited a paper mill at the head of the Bedford Basin. There, his awareness of the difficulty the mill had in obtaining enough rags — then the chief raw material in the manufacture of paper — prompted him to experiment with the product he knew best, wood.

There are three versions of how he developed the idea. One suggests that he purposely set out to produce paper from wood because he knew, from his studies, that wood was a vegetable fibre, and vegetable fibre was also used in the composition of cotton rags. A second version was advanced by a local citizen who recalled years later that Charles developed the idea from observing how heavy timbers chafing against each other at the family sawmill produced a small amount of fuzzy material and it was this that prompted him to produce paper from wood. The third belief is that Charles got the idea from observing wasps building their nests, a theory that had been advanced by a French scientist, who had done nothing to prove his concept.

While some researchers still debate the three versions, others argue about the year Fenerty produced his paper from wood pulp because Friedrich Keller of Saxony filed a patent for the process in 1840. John Booth Jr., writing in the *Canadian Pulp and Paper* magazine in November 1920, stated that a local citizen recalled seeing Fenerty in 1838 reduce spruce wood to a pulp and make a crude piece of paper using a crude iron spoon to press out the moisture. In the same article, Booth also wrote that he interviewed a 90-year-old Sackville woman who could trace back, through a series of events, that her father first inspected paper Fenerty made from spruce in 1839. Another writer suggested that Fenerty was experimenting from 1839 onwards.

Regardless of date, Fenerty's invention was of little interest to paper manufacturers in North America until the outbreak of the American Civil War caused a severe shortage of cloth and woven by-products. As a result, John Thompson of Napanee, Ontario, began producing paper from wood pulp in the early 1860s. By then, the Keller patent in Germany had led to further inventions: the development of paper from wood pulp with rag fibres added strengthened the product. And in the late 1860s a Montreal manufacturer built a wood-grinding mill at Valleyfield, Quebec, based on the German patents. It was not until 1875 that a wood pulp mill was established in Fenerty's native province of Nova Scotia.

By then Fenerty had travelled extensively. His wanderlust began after his proposal of marriage to a young woman was turned down. He also wrote poetry: one poem, "Betula Nigra," inspired by a giant black birch on the family farm, won first prize in 1854 at the Halifax Exhibition. He left home again, eventually arriving in Australia where he worked in a gold mine. There he also wrote *Essay on Progress* which, originally intended for publication in Melbourne, was published in Halifax in 1866. By then he had returned to Sackville to marry the sister of the woman who had spurned his proposal. He spent the rest of his life farming, lumbering, writing, tending his berry and currant gardens, and eventually served the community as a health warden, wood measurer, and an Overseer of the Poor from 1870 to 1881. He was also tax collector for the district from 1883 to 1890.

In the winter of 1890-91, his health broke down and he was no longer able to walk the mile and a half to the Anglican church where he was a lay reader. When he died in he left no posterity but his poetry.

In 1926 the Nova Scotia Historical Society unveiled a tablet at his birthplace that read:

> Here in January, 1821, was born Charles Fenerty, who after experimenting from about 1839, produced
> paper from spruce wood pulp, which invention he made public in 1844. He died at Lower Sackville, June 1892.

In 1955 the tablet was mounted on a more permanent stone cairn, and in 1987 Canada Post produced, for its Canada Day issue, four stamps to honour science and technology. They included Fenerty with three other pioneer inventors: R.A. Fessenden for radio, F.N. Gisborne for undersea cable, and G.E. Desbarats with William Leggo for half-tone engraving. MVJ

WALLACE RUPERT TURNBULL

1870 - 1954

A Most Prolific Genius

ALTHOUGH BUSH PILOTS during the 1920s flew thousands of miles and performed incredible feats of bravery and entrepreneurship to serve the remote areas of Canada's north, Wallace R. Turnbull, working in his own laboratory at Rothesay, New Brunswick, was, in fact, Canada's first aviation pioneer. His interest began even before the end of the nineteenth century and his invention of the variable pitch propeller in 1927 revolutionized the aircraft industry.

Born at Rothesay in Saint John, New Brunswick, in 1870, the son of a wealthy businessman and banker, Turnbull attended school there before going to Cornell University where he received a master's degree in electrical engineering. He then went with his bride to Germany where he undertook post-graduate work in physics, returning in 1895 to study further at Cornell and join the Edison Light Company (General Electric Company), at Harrison, New Jersey, as an experimental engineer.

By 1900 he believed that the airplane was imminent. He shared his interest in aviation with such pioneers as Dr. Samuel Langley, who advanced the theory of flight; Otto Lillenthal, who experimented with gliders; and Gustave Eiffel, who built the world's first wind tunnel. He was reluctant to admit his conviction, however, for fear of being considered a "crank."

In 1902 he left General Electric to return to Rothesay where he established himself as a consulting engineer and built a laboratory. There he built Canada's first wind tunnel out of an old packing case and experimented with lift devices, internal combustion as well as turbine engines and propellers, the latter taking him, in 1906, to visit Alexander Graham Bell at Baddeck, Nova Scotia. He thought Bell's belief in kites was wrong because of the excessive drift factor. That same year he applied for his first of what would eventually number 17 patents. Most of these dealt with aeronautics; the first was broadly titled "Improvements in Aeroplanes and Hydroplanes."

In 1909, for his study published in *Scientific American* on power absorbed by the airscrew, he won a bronze medal. Two years later he wrote the *Laws of Airscrews* that scientifically identified today's well-known laws of air propellers. By then he had also filed a broad patent on a double curvature aerofoil to be executed by a British company, but the deal fell through and the patent lapsed.

When World War I began, he closed his lab and went to Britain to volunteer his services to several aircraft manufacturers without remuneration, but also without success. Later, he joined Sage and Company which the Admiralty had commissioned to manufacture aircraft.

For the duration of the war Turnbull remained with Sage. Initially he was an aircraft inspector but later was given a free hand to work on various wartime devices including air propellers, bomb sights, and torpedo screens.

Returning to Canada at war's end, he concentrated his interest in the variable pitch propeller which he had considered originally in 1916. His first model, developed partly in England, was brought back to Canada to be completed at Rothesay, December 1922. In the same year Turnbull obtained a Canadian patent for it and interested the R.C.A.F. in testing it in an Avro trainer.

In February 1923, the propeller won a silver medal at the Inventions Show in New York City, but later that year, when it was tested with a mechanical brake control, it proved impractical. In October the propeller was destroyed in a hangar fire at Camp Borden.

By then Turnbull was already working on a new design with alternative control mechanisms. One design retained brake shoes; the other was an experimental model using an electrical motor drive. The R.C.A.F., through its research committee, selected the second unit. Canadian Vickers Limited made the blades, and Turnbull developed the electrical control unit at Rothesay. The results at Camp Borden in 1927, of a test that included an assessment of takeoff, cruising speed, and fuel consumption were "remarkably good" wrote J.H. Parkin in the *Canadian Aeronautical Journal* in 1956.

Changing the angle of a propeller in flight, in relation to the air, had a profound effect on air transport and completely changed the face of aviation history. Ability to adjust propeller pitch allowed greater payloads to be carried efficiently and safely in the skies.

Within months of the test Turnbull applied for patents in Canada, the US, and Great Britain and began negotiations with firms for the rights to his invention. He sold the patent in December 1929 to the Reed Propeller Company, a subsidiary of the Curtis Aeroplane and Motor Company which was, in turn, a division of the Curtis-Wright Corporation of the United States. In 1935 the export division of that company reached an agreement with the Bristol Aeroplane Company of England and royalties were paid until the US Government purchased the patents outright in 1944.

Turnbull, meanwhile, pursued other interests. As early as 1919, he had proposed a scheme to utilize tidal power at the confluence of the Petitcodiac and Memramcook Rivers of his home province and, while further studies proved his idea had merit, the availability of cheap coal won out. He was, however, invited to be a director of the Petitcodiac Tidal Power Company when it was organized in 1928, and his interest in tidal power remained throughout the rest of his life. He also served on the board of the Turnbull Real Estate Company as well as the Turnbull Home for Incurables.

In 1936, when the Associate Committee on Aeronautical Research announced plans for a museum at Ottawa, Turnbull donated some of his early and priceless inventions and memorabilia including his model of the variable pitch propeller which was brought back from a museum in England.

Although Turnbull was better known and respected outside Canada as one of the world's outstanding pioneer scientists in aeronautics, his own country finally honoured him as an achiever when the University of New Brunswick conferred an Honorary Doctor of Science upon him in 1942. As well, the Engineering Institute of Canada named him an honorary member in 1951, three years before his death at the General Hospital in Saint John, New Brunswick. *MVJ*

The greatest contribution that Wallace Rupert Turnbull, opposite right, made as an aeronautical engineer was his invention of the variable-pitch propeller, tested in flight in 1927. This achievement permits angular adjustment of the propeller blade while cutting air in flight. It made flying safe and efficient at all spans, especially at take off and landing. Its invention is as essential to aviation as the gearbox is to the automobile or the screw propeller to boats. Better known and respected outside his own country, Turnbull was finally honoured by Canada when the Engineering Institute of Canada named him an honorary member, in 1951, three years before his death

National Research Council Canada

Harry Botterell, John Counsell, & Al Jousse

Revolutionaries in Spinal Cord Injury Management

BEFORE World War II, few individuals survived a spinal cord injury and physicians generally believed that there were no effective treatments. During the 1930s a small number of physicians began to question this belief. In Canada, Dr. Harry Botterell, a neurosurgeon at the Toronto General Hospital, chose to treat three men with incomplete lesions of the spinal cord. Despite his colleagues' arguments that treatment was fruitless, Botterell developed a team approach that emphasized active medical and nursing care and physical retraining. All three patients survived and — amazingly — returned to live and work in their communities.

In 1939 Botterell joined the Royal Canadian Army Medical Corps and became the chief neurosurgical officer at the Canadian Military Hospital in Basingstoke, England, where he developed a specialized unit for soldiers with spinal cord injury. This unit demonstrated that bed sores, respiratory and urinary infections (the common causes of death following spinal cord injury) could be prevented. During this period Botterell argued that a veteran with spinal cord injury should return "to the main stream of life rather than be set aside as a hermit."

At Basingstoke, Botterell treated Lieutenant-Colonel John Counsell who had received a spinal cord injury during the ill-fated Dieppe landing in 1942. Botterell urged Counsell to consider returning to Canada to argue for treatment in Canada for veterans with spinal cord injury.

In January 1945, Botterell was appointed director of neurosurgical services at the Christie Street

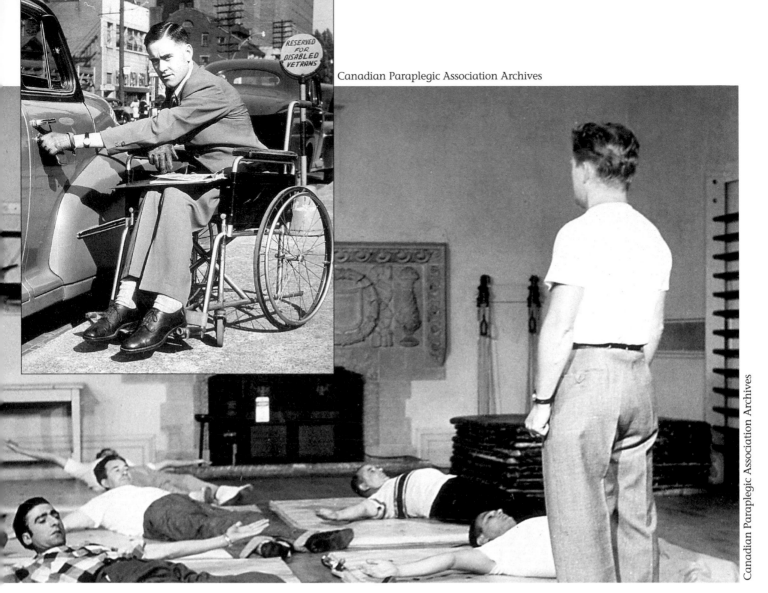

TOP
An injured veteran, Andy Clarke returned to an independent life beyond the confines of "paraplegic colonies" as this 1946 Toronto view demonstrates. Mr. Clarke prepares to get out of his wheelchair and into a car equipped with special hand controls and standing in a designated parking zone for disabled veterans

Canada's first rehabilitation centre for spinal cord injury is Lyndhurst Lodge, established by Dr. Botterell in 1945 in Toronto. This Lyndhurst Lodge view depicts a retraining class, circa 1946

Military Hospital in Toronto. On his arrival, he found veterans confined to their beds with little hope of leaving the hospital. Once again he developed a specialized unit for spinal cord injury and established the first rehabilitation unit for spinal cord injury in Canada at the newly acquired Lyndhurst Lodge in Toronto. In March 1945 he appointed Dr. Al Jousse as Lyndhurst Lodge's medical director responsible for the coordination of all aspects of treatment. Jousse was well aware of the impact of a physical disability since he himself used canes for walking.

In a landmark article in 1946, Botterell and Jousse wrote that "the primary purpose of treatment at every stage from bed to brace-walking is, to return the patient to independent life beyond the confines of hospital or paraplegic colonies." They went on to argue that depression was not always a direct result of paraplegia but often the result of the loss of independence and meaningful participation in community life. Not everyone agreed. Jousse later described the common response from medical colleagues: "We were told we would fall flat on our faces; it was a futile endeavour. But Harry Botterell ... didn't allow anything to discourage him. He would say: 'Let's get going, get these people up and going,' which we did!"

By May 1945 John Counsell had drawn together a coalition of veterans with spinal cord injury, physicians, and prominent Canadian civilian and military figures to establish the Canadian Paraplegic Association, the first association in the world for individuals with spinal cord injury. The central philosophy of the Association was the belief that "paraplegics could lead useful, reasonably normal lives." Under Counsell's leadership the Association helped veterans establish their place in society and business and then, unlike many other veterans' organizations, provided assistance to civilian paraplegics.

Over half of the 200 Canadian veterans with spinal cord injury went to Lyndhurst. They took part in physical retraining programs, learned to manage activities of daily living, and to manoeuvre the new collapsible, self-propelled wheelchairs that Counsell had convinced the Department of Veterans Affairs to provide. By 1946 many of the veterans had cars with newly designed hand controls that gave them the mobility to travel independently in the community. Veterans were encouraged to use the stores of the neighbouring community and encouraged to attend the same university and vocational training programs as their non-disabled peers. They were able to go out in the evening and go home on weekends. One veteran described the benefits of this experience: "Once you get out into the community, you learn more on the weekends out or weeks at home, than in hospital."

By 1946, survival rates had changed from below ten percent during World War I to over 92 percent. Most veterans were also living in the community and over half were employed or attending university or training programs. These veterans were among the first Canadians to demonstrate that it was possible to live and work in the community using a wheelchair.

Other physicians around the world also developed programs for spinal cord injury during the post World War II period. However, the Canadian programs were the first to argue for and demonstrate that full, meaningful participation in all aspects of community life was possible.

After discharge from the army, Botterell developed a special unit at the Toronto General Hospital for civilians with spinal cord injury. During the 1960s and 1970s, he served first as Dean of Medicine at Queen's University and later Vice Principal, Health Sciences. Counsell continued to lead the Canadian Paraplegic Association and saw it established as a national association serving all Canadians with spinal cord injuries. He retired from the position of president in 1967 and died in Toronto in 1977 at the age of 66. Jousse was one of the first Canadians to propose the integration of individuals with disabilities into all aspects of society. A pioneer in the development of rehabilitation in Canada, he was a professor of Rehabilitation Medicine and Director of the School of Rehabilitation Medicine at the University of Toronto until 1972. Jousse continued as the medical director of Lyndhurst until his retirement in 1975. He died in Toronto in 1993.

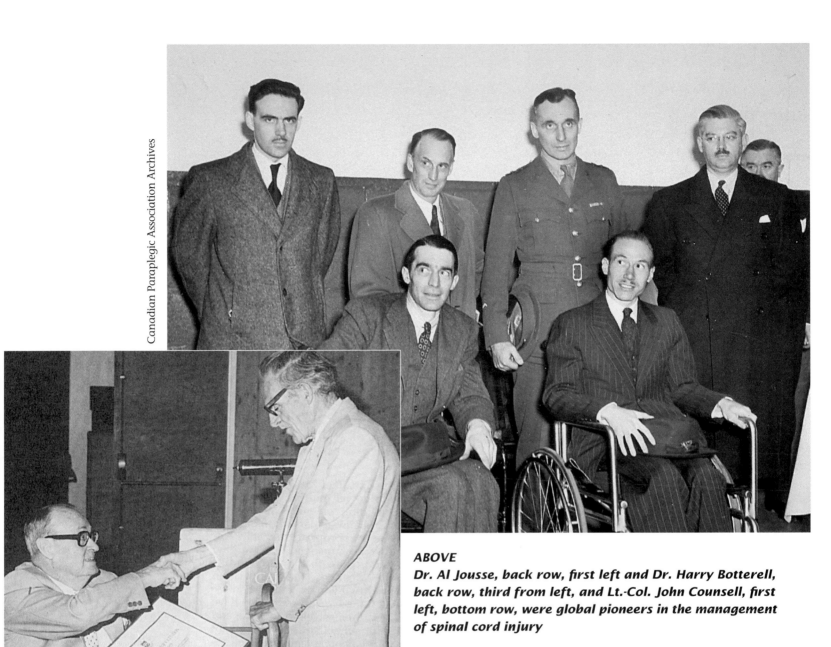

ABOVE

Dr. Al Jousse, back row, first left and Dr. Harry Botterell, back row, third from left, and Lt.-Col. John Counsell, first left, bottom row, were global pioneers in the management of spinal cord injury

Mr. Ken Langford, left, congratulates Dr. Al Jousse, O.C., on being awarded the Distinguished Service Citation. For 20 years, Dr. Al Jousse was the man in charge of the University of Toronto's Division of Rehabilation Medicine

The Canadian revolution in spinal cord injury was the result of a unique partnership between Dr. Harry Botterell, an articulate, visionary neurosurgeon; Lieutenant-Colonel John Counsell, a quiet, effective political leader; and Dr. Al Jousse, a compassionate, dedicated physician. Together these three men provided the leadership that resulted in a revolution in Canada in the management of spinal cord injuries and the life experience of individuals with spinal cord injury.   *M.T*

OMOND SOLANDT

Insightful Interpreter of Scientific Research

BROOKE CLAXTON, Canada's Minister of Defence after World War II, said that Omond Solandt, as head of Canada's Defence Research Board, knew "more British secrets than any American and more American secrets than anyone from the British Isles."

Solandt, one of Canada's most distinguished scientific executives, was born in Winnipeg, Manitoba, on September 25, 1909. Upon graduating in medicine from the University of Toronto, he embarked on research in physiology with Charles Best, co-discoverer of insulin. Pursuing advanced studies in physiology, Solandt, in 1939, was appointed lecturer in Mammalian Physiology at the University of Cambridge.

Early in World War II, Solandt was made responsible for the Southwest London Blood Supply Depot. He was asked to determine why army tank personnel fainted when their guns were fired. His conclusion — that fumes from the firing of the guns were sucked into the tanks and caused the tank crews to faint — led to his appointment as Director of the Physiological Laboratory at the British Medical Research Council.

Promoted to the rank of colonel in the Canadian Army in 1944, Solandt had contact with many British scientists in addition to senior military officials during the war. This enabled him to learn in some detail how British military policy was made and what roles scientists played in its development.

After the bombing of Hiroshima and Nagasaki, Solandt was made a member of a British War Office task force commissioned to examine the effects of the bombing in Japan. With Jacob Bronowski, a mathematician who later became widely known for his television series "The Ascent of Man," Solandt completed a careful analysis of the casualties of the atomic bombing.

Solandt and Bronowski worked together for two weeks in each of Hiroshima and Nagasaki. Visiting hospitals, they met and conversed, through interpreters, with victims, their relatives, and others who could provide first-hand accounts of what had happened during the bombing. Solandt and Bronowski sincerely wished to learn what the victims of the nuclear bombing had experienced. Much to their surprise, they encountered no hostility.

Their on-site studies in Japan led to the publication of the first-known report on the deaths and injuries caused by the bombing of the Japanese cities. They provided detailed maps showing ground zero — the centre point of the atomic explosion in each of the two cities — and the various zones of injury.

After the war, Canada's military and political leaders agreed to consolidate the nation's defence research programs. Solandt was made Director General of Defence Research, 1946-47, and was invited to prepare plans for future military research. From 1947 until 1956, he was Founding Chairman of Canada's Defence Research Board. Working closely with Canada's National Defence Department, the Board had liaison officers in London, Washington, and, eventually, in Paris.

Far-removed from public view, Omond Solandt was a dedicated medical scientist and distinguished scientific research executive. He contributed in many ways to the resolution of problems that imperil the lives of human beings throughout the world

Toronto Star

From the outset Solandt was determined to ensure that the Defence Research Board would stress applied research. He was fully conscious of the need for pure research, but he was absolutely convinced that in defence matters Canada had to give priority to applied research.

In addition to work on traditional military interests such as explosives and propellants and, to a limited extent, missile development, the Board encouraged research, in particular, on Arctic atmospheric conditions. The region 50 miles above the earth's surface is designated the ionosphere. Here electrically charged particles called "ions" are produced through the effects of radiation from the sun and other extraterrestrial bodies on the neutral atoms and molecules of the air. In the ionosphere, the number of ions is sufficient to influence the natural reproduction of radio waves.

The interest of Canada's Defence Board in the ionosphere was pertinent to the siting and installation of the DEW line (the distant, early-warning radar system) installed across Canada's northern region in the 1950s. This was one of a variety of applied research activities in which the board took a special interest during this "cold war" period.

When his responsibilities with the Defence Research Board ended in 1956, Solandt worked for nearly a decade as a senior corporate executive. From 1956-63, he was Canadian National Railway's senior officer responsible for research and development. He assumed similar responsibilities upon becoming director of DeHavilland Aircraft and Hawker-Siddeley Canada. He then returned to work at the federal level as Founding Chairman of the Science Council of Canada. This council, established by an Act of Parliament in 1966, was established by the Federal government to advise on policy matters concerning science and technology.

Initially it was assumed that the Council would act on ministerial requests. However, experience indicated that the best approach for the Council was to operate without ministerial direction. Since the 25-30 members of the Council were essentially representative Canadian scientists, this approach seemed desirable.

During Solandt's chairmanship, the Council gained widespread respect, particularly after its fourth report, "Towards a National Science Policy in Canada," was published in 1968.

In this report the Council explored the desirability of encouraging personnel from private industry, universities, and government research agencies to work together on major mission-oriented projects. The council believed that, in the best interest of Canada and the world, such projects should involve the study of the atmosphere, diminishing water resources, the development of the Canadian north, transportation, the urban environment, and new energy sources.

The idea of a series of mission-oriented projects as a means of assisting Canada in overcoming fundamental problems was never implemented. Many of the problems identified by the Council under Solandt's far-sighted leadership continue to plague the daily lives of Canadians. The validity of the proposals he and his colleagues made is confirmed daily.

After completing his work with the Science Council, Solandt assumed chairmanship of an Ontario Government Commission created to deal with a multifaceted problem: the transmission of electric power. Often called "The Solandt Commission," it was established to advise the Ontario Government of any potential problems associated with the transmission of power to certain areas of the province. Many potential ecological, political, scientific, social, and technical problems, as well as financial issues, required thoughtful resolution. He and his colleagues submitted carefully reasoned recommendations for action to resolve these concerns.

During the last 20 years of his life, Solandt made many significant contributions through his efforts to make the world a better place. He served, for example, as a consultant to the International Development Research Centre in Ottawa on the establishment of a centre for agricultural research in the dry areas of Lebanon, Syria, and Iran. During the same period he became a trustee and chairman of the Executive and Finance Committee of the International Maize and Wheat Improvement Centre in Mexico City. He was also a member of the Board of Governors and the executive committee of the International Centre for Insect Physiology and Ecology in Nairobi, Kenya. Similarly he advised the International Livestock Centre for Africa in Addis Ababa, Ethiopia, and the International Institute for Tropical Agriculture in Ibadan, Nigeria.

In 1982, the *Ocean Ranger,* the world's largest semisubmersible drill rig, capsized and sank off Newfoundland when it was hit by 90 mph winds and 50-foot waves. The entire crew of 84 lost their lives. The government of Canada asked Solandt to investigate the disaster. Again he brought to bear the intellectual and creative gifts, knowledge, and insight he had drawn upon some 40 years earlier when asked to advise the British Army why tank personnel fainted after firing their guns. Solandt and the members of the Canada/Newfoundland Royal Commission on the *Ocean Ranger* marine disaster found that the rig had capsized as a result of concurrent effects: the raging storm, inadequate rig design, and lack of informed action by those involved. Serving in 1984 as the chairman of the conference on offshore safety in Eastern Canada sponsored by the Royal Commission, he recommended sweeping changes in government regulations for training, safety practice, and procedures in offshore activities in Canada.

In the last years of his life, Solandt was a valued board member of the Canadian Institute for Radiation Safety (CAIRS). With a Board of Governors representing industry, labour, government, scientific and educational agencies, the Institute, unique in the world, is dedicated to resolving and preventing problems faced by individuals engaged in ionizing radiation-risk activities.

Throughout his long and distinguished career as a medical scientist and scientific research executive, Omond Solandt was far-removed from public view. Through his careful application of knowledge in war and in peace, however, he contributed in many ways to the resolution of problems that imperil the lives of human beings throughout the world. His many contributions in Canada and abroad, while not widely known, were outstanding.

DMS

Before Edison

Two Canucks beat Edison to light bulb

THE INVENTION in 1879 of the incandescent electric light is credited to the American genius Thomas Alva Edison — but two Canadians beat him to it.

They produced light in a bulb by heating a carbon filament using its resistance to electricity, six years before Edison announced discovery. Their invention was, in at least that respect, more advanced than Edison's, using nitrogen in the bulb as is done today.

But Edison bought the rights to their patent while he was conducting his own experiments to perfect a bulb to light the world.

The names of the two Canadians — Henry Woodward, a medical student at the University of Toronto, and Matthew Evans, a Toronto hotel keeper — were lost to history because investors backed down from the enormous costs of exploiting their invention.

Prophetically, Evans had lamented, "The inventor never gets the reward of his labour." They never even got the credit.

Woodward and Evans were neighbours who frequently got together to experiment with Woodward's large battery and induction coil. At dusk on a late winter day in 1873, they noticed the light from the spark at the contact post. According to the report in the *Canadian Electrical News and Engineering Journal* (Feb. 1990), Evans drew out his watch and exclaimed: "Look at the light from the spark! Why you can even see the time!"

"My!" said Woodward, "if one could only confine that in a globe of some sort, what an invention we would have! It would revolutionize the world!"

The first incandescent lamp was constructed at Morrison's Brass Foundry on Adelaide St. West in

ABOVE: Henry Woodward's original arc lamp, backed by a reflector, gave out such strong light in 1874 that work horses along Toronto's King Street West halted opposite the building in which the experiment was taking place. People from the surrounding neighbourhood ran over to see the factory, next to the Gurney Foundry premises, thinking the bright illumination was a fire

Toronto. Documents describe it as "consisting of a water gauge glass with a piece of carbon filed by hand and drilled at each end for the electrodes and hermetically sealed at both ends."

After exhausting the air in it, Woodward filled the bulb with nitrogen. The Canadians' patent suggests that, "... after the air is extracted, the bulb be filled with rarefied gas that will not unite chemically with the carbon when hot."

In his patent, Edison would later call for a nearly perfect vacuum "to prevent oxidation and injury to the conductor by the atmosphere."

After Edison's discovery, a Professor Thomas proclaimed that if Woodward had not filled the bulb with nitrogen after exhausting the air, "He would have had the honor of being the inventor of the incandescent light as used for commercial purposes."

But in fact, the Woodward and Evans lamp was years ahead of Edison's in this! Bulbs today of more than 40 watts contain a mixture of gases, usually argon and nitrogen, instead of air. "The gases help lengthen the life of the filament and prevent electricity from jumping inside the lamp," explains the *World Book Encyclopedia*.

The Woodward and Evans invention worked in the same way lamps work today, connected in a circuit similar to one Edison devised. In the mid-1870s, six of their lamps were connected in a series to demonstrate their incandescence to promoters who had come together to finance the discovery's commercial applications.

Here's how Evans later described the bulbs coming to incandescence though only a weak battery was at their disposal as an electrical source.

"There were four or five of us sitting around a large table. Woodward closed the switch and gradually we saw the carbon become first red and gradually lighter and lighter in colour until it beamed forth in beautiful light. This was the most exciting moment of my experience."

A Russian applied for a patent for an incandescent bulb in Washington at the same time as Woodward and Evans. Patent authorities declared the two inventions in "interference" but later awarded the patent to the Canadians, declaring they had proved "priority of invention."

But by this time, the financiers balked at putting more money into the development of the invention. In disgust, Woodward sailed to England and abandoned his efforts. Evans, who had already spent $20,000 of his own money in perfecting the incandescent light, apparently did not have the resources to carry on alone.

RIGHT: On August 3, 1874, the Dominion of Canada granted medical student, Henry Woodward, and Toronto hotel keeper, Matthew Evans, letters patent (no. 3738) "for inventing a new and improved method of obtaining light by electricity." Credited with discovering the principle of the incandescent light, Matthew Evans, viewed here, died in 1899. Henry Woodward left Canada for England, circa 1877

original curator of the lamp section of its Museum of Electrical Progress.

Edison, already a wealthy and famous inventor, had the resources at his discovery factory in Menlo Park, N.J., where he'd invented the phonograph. A syndicate of industrialists advanced him $50,000 and formed Edison Electric Light Co. after he announced, in September 1878, that he planned to invent a safe and inexpensive electric light to replace gaslight.

Meanwhile, one of the promoters in the moribund Canadian syndicate, A.M. Sutherland, moved to New York and in a letter written in 1896 described how Edison acquired the rights to the Canadian invention: "In the course of business I was thrown into more or less intimate relationship with the now famous electrician, Thomas A. Edison, who was at that time experimenting with the electric incandescent lamp at Menlo Park, New Jersey. In talking about it one day, I chaffingly said: *Why, Edison, you are nowhere! I am part owner of a patent several years older than yours on about the same thing you claim.*

"He asked what patent I referred to and I told him, he remarking: *O, I know that patent. It is no good.*

"The next day one of Mr. Edison's men, whom I knew very well, asked me how much I would take for my claim in the Woodward Patent, and that day I sold it to this gentleman, who in turn made over the papers to Mr. Edison. This is all."

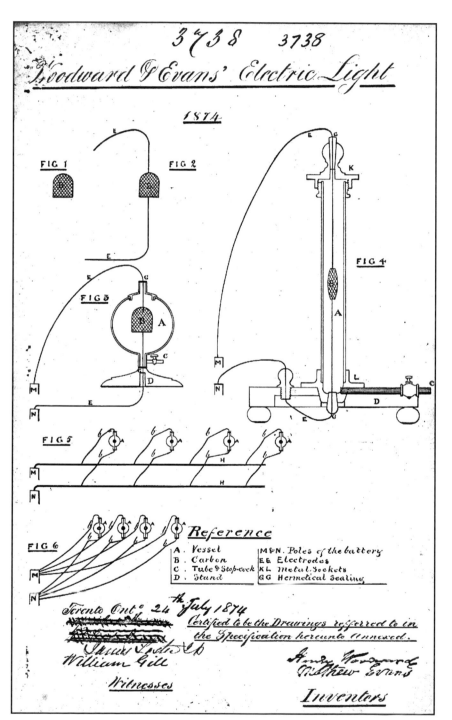

Filed with Henry Woodward's Canadian patent application for "inventing new and useful improvements in the art or process of obtaining light by means of electricity" are these graphic illustrations demonstrating the procedure to the state of incandescence using hermitically sealed globe or glass vessels. This patent was granted by the Dominion of Canada on August 3, 1874. On August 29, 1876, Woodward was granted U.S. patent no. 181,613. This was some 38 months before Thomas Alva Edison received a similar patent for an "improvement" in his electric lamps

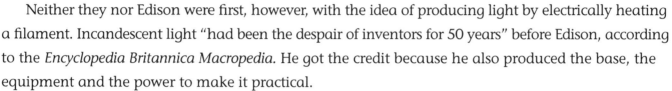

View of Thomas Alva Edison, circa 1879, the year he patented the electric light bulb — five years after two Canucks had beat him to it! Edison's grandfather was a Loyalist who had settled in Nova Scotia in 1783, moving to southwestern Ontario by 1811 where he served in the 1st Middlesex Militia as a captain during the War of 1812. His father fled to the U.S. as a Mackenzie sympathizer during the Rebellion of 1837, settling in Milan, Ohio. Thomas A. Edison, as a boy, during the summers used to visit his aging grandfather at Vienna, Ontario

Sutherland does not make clear whether the sale occurred while Edison was working on the invention or attempting to improve it.

Many of the world's greatest inventions have evolved from previous pioneering work. So it is with the incandescent electric light bulb. Woodward and Evans didn't get the credit for inventing it. They never even got credit for helping to light the way for the discovery!

Neither they nor Edison were first, however, with the idea of producing light by electrically heating a filament. Incandescent light "had been the despair of inventors for 50 years" before Edison, according to the *Encyclopedia Britannica Macropedia.* He got the credit because he also produced the base, the equipment and the power to make it practical.

The search for practical electric light had begun in earnest in 1802 when English chemist, Sir Humphry Davy, demonstrated the incandescence of platinum strips heated by electricity. Inventors in Italy, Germany, Russia and around the world were in the race.

Before the discovery by the two Canadians and almost 20 years before Edison's successful demonstration in 1879, English physicist Sir Joseph Wilson Swan had produced an electric light using a filament of carbonized paper in an evacuated glass bulb.

For various reasons, including air in the bulb, it was inefficient and quickly burned out. But the successful Canadian design was similar.

And Edison's successful carbon filament lamp, which he developed after 14 months of trial and error in search of a successful filament, was similar to the Canadians' invention.

Swan's pioneering work — he produced a working electric light in 1878 but apparently failed to patent it in time — is omitted in most general references to the invention, at least in the United States.

Similarly Woodward and Evans' contribution to the invention of the incandescent light bulb is all but forgotten, even in Canada.

WS

Excerpted and published with permission from Walter Stefaniuk, courtesy The Toronto Star, *August 29th, 1991.*

H.R. MacMillan

1885 - 1976

C.J. Humber Collection

MAZO DE LA ROCHE, already famous for her all-Canadian Jalna and Whiteoaks family novels, wrote *Growth of a Man* in 1938. She sought permission to dedicate her new novel to her famous cousin because the story was basically a romanticized account of his youth. But he demurred.

"I think I would find it impossible to read any intimate biographical publication relating to me — if I were important enough to justify its production," Harvey Reginald MacMillan replied. He said this the same year a leading financial publication described him as the "No. 1 industrialist and business leader of British Columbia."

MacMillan in 1938 was chairman of the H.R. MacMillan Export Company started in 1919. It had grown from a small timber brokerage firm of only three people into several separate but integrated companies known around the world for sales in logging, lumber, plywood and door manufacturing, railway tie production, and shipping.

His early years are revealed in his cousin's novel. Born in 1885 in a Quaker community near Newmarket, Ontario, he was two years old when his father died. Because his mother worked as a housekeeper, he was brought up on the nearby farm of his Scottish grandfather. Only 16 when he graduated from high school, he subsequently attended the Ontario Agricultural College at Guelph "because it was the cheapest education I could get."

Recognized as a voracious reader, he played hockey and football and was editor of the college magazine. Through one of his teachers, he also earned nine cents an hour at the school's experimental forestry plot. In 1906 he graduated with honours in biology.

Two years later, following stints with a survey party in Manitoba, a logging camp in Maine, a

Born of United Empire Loyalist stock in 1885 in Newmarket, Ontario, Harvey Reginald MacMillan became one of the largest exporters of forest-products in the world. By the time he retired as chairman of MacMillan and Bloedel Ltd., in 1951, this "emperor of wood" had generously endowed forest and fisheries research at the University of British Columbia

forestry crew in British Columbia, he graduated with a Master's degree from Yale University. A Yale professor described him as one of the most brilliant forestry students he had ever encountered.

"H.R.," as he was to be known, joined the forestry department of the Canadian government and, as assistant inspector of forest reserves, "set aside tracts unsuitable for farm settlement and began the development of a national parks system." While inspecting Glacier National Park in the United States, he caught a cold that developed into tuberculosis. It took him more than two years to overcome this illness, most of his rehabilitation spent at Ste. Agathe-des-Monts, Quebec. There his mother "set up housekeeping in a small flat and ... devoted her whole time to looking after me," he wrote to his cousin Mazo.

Returning to the forestry department in 1911, he was hired as chief forester a year later by the British Columbia government which had enacted new forest legislation. Because of his youthful appearance "they thought they had hired the wrong fellow," MacMillan later recalled, but within months he had a staff of foresters conducting surveys and making inventories of standing timber until World War I interrupted their work. Unable to enlist because of his earlier bout with TB, he returned to the Federal government as a special trade commissioner to seek world markets for Canadian lumber.Over an 18-month period, MacMillan visited Britain, Holland, France, South Africa, and India. This tour made him realize Canada had raw material "but sadly lacked the organization to sell it to the world." In 1916 he joined a British Columbia lumber firm but a year later was back in government with the Imperial Munitions Board to obtain Sitka spruce — the best wood for aircraft manufacturing.

By 1919, with the backing of a British lumber importer he had met on his tour, "H.R." decided to establish his own export lumber business with both men putting up $10,000 to launch it. He recalled later, "I had so little money and so little knowledge, and the job was so great, that I didn't know it couldn't be done. So I went ahead and did it."

A year later he hired one of his former B.C. government foresters, the quiet and industrious William J. Van Dusen, and they remained a successful team for more than half a century. Convinced

P.R.Co's Mills
Powell River, B.C.

that only personal visits would generate sales, he and Van Dusen took turns travelling extensively.

Orders came from Britain, Australia, New Zealand, Japan, and California and in 1921 he made a major sale to India. Getting lumber to these countries motivated him, by 1924, to move into the shipping business. In 1927 there were 30 ships. This prompted the *Canadian Lumberman* to observe in 1929 that "MacMillan would be selling to the moon, if he could get delivery."

By the mid-thirties, MacMillan represented roughly 40 percent of British Columbia's lumber export sales — a fact that its B.C. competitors tried to change. MacMillan met the challenge, filling every contract despite some slow deliveries. "MacMillan was obsessed with the sanctity of a contract," an executive of Mac-Blo later recalled.

"H.R." became lumber controller for the Federal government in 1940, but red tape caused him to quit five months later. C.D. Howe then appointed him president of Wartime Merchant Shipping Ltd. in Montreal, a crown corporation that had built 200 cargo vessels by the end of 1943. He worked without salary, paid his own expenses, and even though his own company, run by Van Dusen, had expanded, he made a point of telling B.C. lumbermen, "We must kill off that hangover from the last war — great profits. There can be no profits in this war to capitalists, labour, or anyone else. Instead there will be a sharing of losses."

Returning to MacMillan Export in 1944, he expanded its ownership of timber stands by buying other companies. In 1945 he made the company public. Rapid growth continued throughout the 40s and lead to the 1951 merger with Bloedel. Five years later, at 71, he stepped down as chairman. He then became chairman of the board's powerful finance and policy committee until it was replaced by an executive committee in 1959.

Despite suffering a stroke in 1966 at age 80, H.R. continued on that committee until 1970 when he and Van Dusen retired and became honorary board members. They did not attend any further board meetings but, when it was announced in 1975 that the company was getting out of the shipping business, he wrote to a "MacBlo" executive requesting that "he would please come up (he was confined to his home by then) and explain it to me."

When he died the next year, editorials in Canada and around the world praised his business acumen, his genius with a dollar and a piece of timber, and his dynamic entrepreneurship. His famous cousin Mazo had summed up his complexity, some years earlier, by describing him as "tender and hard, imaginative and stolid, pugnacious and yielding, lovable and cold." His will left almost half of his estate to the H.R. MacMillan Forestry Building at the University of British Columbia. Other grants included $3 million for a city planetarium, a donation for the native peoples of northern Canada, and funding for 48 PhD Fellowships. *MVJ*

OPPOSITE: The roots of MacMillan Bloedel Limited, Canada's largest exporters of forest-products company, can be traced to the Powell River Paper Company Limited which began in 1909. In 1959, MacMillan Bloedel merged with Powell River becoming the world's most integrated forest-products firms. This view is of the Powell River Company, circa 1915

HOLLYWOOD

The Original Canadian 3-peat

©A.M.P.A.S. ®/Academy of Motion Picture Arts and Sciences

Two Canadian-born movie stars share the limelight in 1931. Marie Dressler, left, is honoured by the Academy of Motion Pictures and Arts as Best Actress of the Year and Norma Shearer, who had won the same award in 1930, presents her Canadian confrere with the most famous of all mantlepiece artifacts

WHEN Marie Dressler won the academy award for best actress in 1931, she was the third consecutive Canadian-born actress to win the coveted statuette. She was 61. A large-framed, squared jawed woman, she had left her Cobourg, Ontario, home nearly 50 years earlier to become one of Hollywood's most loved comic actresses. A year before her, Norma Shearer, born in Westmount, Quebec, won the same award as the star of *The Divorcee*, and in 1929, Toronto-born Mary Pickford won an Oscar for *Coquette*, the first talking picture she made.

Pickford was born Gladys Louise Smith in 1893 in a house where Toronto's Hospital For Sick Children now stands. She and her mother Charlotte, three-year-old sister Lottie and a younger brother Jack were left impoverished on the death of her father in 1898. Charlotte, a one-time actress, became an active stage mother and, before she was six, Mary was playing six evenings and two matinees for $8 a week at Toronto's Princess Theatre.

Mary loved the stage. By 1901, she was well known in Toronto and a hit in many provincial small towns. Two years later, she played the lead of a little mother in a production that included her sister and brother. It also toured in the United States, and this led the family to settle in New York where young Mary made a point of meeting David Belasco, a prominent producer.

He suggested a name change. After she chose her paternal grandmother's name of Pickford and he added Mary, he gave her a role in *The Warrens of Virginia* where she quickly established a reputation as a "very creative and highly imaginative little body."

Mary also approached D.W. Griffiths who was experimenting with film production at New York's Biograph. At 17 she made her initial film appearance in *Her First Biscuits*. Other films followed and

STARS

MISS MARY PICKFORD.

S.62-2.

As Mary Pickford, the Toronto-born actress would become known as "America's Sweetheart" but prominently showed her Canadian heritage by having a maple leaf insignia displayed in her bedroom at Pickfair. When her old home on University Avenue in Toronto was torn down to make way for the Hospital for Sick Children, she arranged to have 20 bricks sent to her as souvenirs

soon one critic wrote, "This delicious little comedy, *They Would Elope*, introduced again an ingenue whose work in Biograph pictures is attracting attention." In 1910, she went to Hollywood and a year later, she actually did elope with actor Owen Moore.

Mary alternated between movies and stage for a few years, but by 1914 she was committed to films, making seven that year, eight the next. In 1917, she signed a $10,000 a week contract with certain controls including the selection of productions and the roles she played.

She starred in *Pollyanna* and *Suds* in 1920. That same year, she became a partner in United Artists Studios with Chaplin, Griffiths, and Douglas Fairbanks Sr., whom she later married. Anxious to change her image, she asked fans, through *Photoplay* magazine, to suggest roles she should play. She was disappointed when they proposed *Cinderella*, *Heidi*, and *Anne of Green Gables*.

As a result, she made fewer movies in the 1920s. Despite an early belief that talkies would be like "putting lipstick on the Venus de Milo," Mary won an Oscar, only the second Oscar ever presented to a female, for her role in the 1929 production *Coquette*.

After two productions were essentially failures, in 1933 Mary turned, not very successfully, to producing. Her personal life was troubled. Her mother died in 1928, brother Jack in 1932, and Lottie four years later, the same year she and Fairbanks were divorced. She married actor Buddy Rogers the following year.

On a 1948 visit to Toronto for the world premier of her production, *Sleep my Love*, she told reporters that it "made her utterly sad to drive down University Avenue and see her old home gone."

Mary talked of returning to the screen and was approached for *Sunset Boulevard* but wanted script changes that director Billy Wilder refused to consider. Later, she tested for *Storm Centre* but withdrew, saying that she wanted her comeback to be in a technicolour film. She then retired from public life. One public appearance occurred in 1965 when the Cinematheque Français in Paris screened more than 50 of her films over a month-long period. On opening night she asked in fluent French for a little understanding because "the films had been made so long ago." The audience gave more than that — they cheered heartily — the last time Mary accepted any audience applause.

Too ill to attend the ceremony for her honorary Oscar in 1977, she accepted it at her home, the theatre audience witnessing on screen a woman, brittle with age, with bright shiny eyes, and an ill-fitting blonde wig lying uneasily on her head. She died two years later, her death certificate indicating she was only 85 instead of the factual 87.

Norma Shearer's career also started in the silent movie era. Born in 1900 to a wealthy construction owner, Norma showed promise as a pianist, and enjoyed a happy childhood until her father's business failed in her teenage years. Forced to live in more humble circumstances, Norma played the piano in a sheet music store before her ambitious mother decided to leave her husband and take Norma and a younger sister to New York. A brother, Douglas, stayed behind.

Before the end of 1920, Norma, despite being just five feet two and with indifferent legs, was modelling for a tire company as Miss Lotta Miles. She met the editor of *Photoplay* magazine who admired her spunk. He introduced her to a number of people. Soon she was being paid $5 a day as an extra in a two-reel film.

In 1923, she got a Hollywood contract with MGM for $150 a week. There, she met 24-year-old Irving Thalberg, considered the boy genius of MGM. Thalberg loaned her to various studios to gain experience before making *Pleasure Mad* at MGM. One of the cast later recalled her as "a little thing, but she did have big ideas, a big ego, and even then, obviously a big talent."

Soon she was starring in movies with such established stars as Adolphe Menjou, Lon Chaney, and Conrad Nagel. She married Thalberg in 1927, and he carefully guided her film career until his death from heart trouble in 1936. A perfectionist, she took voice lessons from several coaches before making her first talkie in 1929. Her haunting, well-pitched voice prompted another co-star, Basil Rathbone, to comment that her discipline and distinctive voice would have made her a fine stage actress.

In 1930, she made *The Divorcee* while pregnant, carefully hiding her figure behind tables, chairs, and drapes rather than take time off in case her fans might forget her. Her Oscar performance as best actress enhanced her studio-promoted title as "The First Lady of the Screen."

In 1931, she was again nominated for an Oscar, but lost out to another Canadian-born actress, 61-year-old Marie Dressler.

Shearer continued to be a major film star throughout the 1930s, playing the leading roles in Noel Coward's *Private Lives* with Robert Montgomery, Eugene O'Neil's *Strange Interlude* with Clark Gable, and *Smilin' Through* with Leslie Howard and Frederic March. "She had a wonderful sincerity and poise," March recalled.

National Film Archives

Born in Montreal, and a graduate of Westmount High School, Norma Shearer became a popular Hollywood actress, winning Best Actress in 1930 for her role as a liberated woman in The Divorcee. *This clip from* The Divorcee *shows her dancing with Theodore von Eltz. She would receive five more nominations as Best Actress before she retired from movies in 1942. Following the 1936 death of her MGM movie mogul husband, Irving Thalberg, Shearer's movie appearances became more infrequent. She might have captured more recognition as Best Actress had she not turned down the roles of both Scarlett O'Hara in* Gone With The Wind *and Mrs. Miniver*

He also co-starred with her in *The Barretts of Wimpole Street* while Howard played opposite her in the 1936 production of *Romeo and Juliet*.

In 1938 she performed in a lavish production of *Marie Antoinette* with Tyrone Power and John Barrymore to earn another Oscar nomination and was touted for the role of Scarlett O'Hara in *Gone With the Wind*. Fans, however, objected to her playing such a perverse role causing her to withdraw her name. She also refused the role of *Mrs. Miniver*, preferring instead to maintain a more youthful image. She made *Escape* with Robert Taylor, who, like most of her co-stars, found her charming but fussy about lighting and camera angles.

In 1942 she married Martin Arronge, a well-known promoter of Squaw Valley, and retired from the screen.

A multi-millionaire still holding considerable stock in MGM, she and her husband travelled extensively and enjoyed a quiet social life with close Hollywood friends before her health deteriorated in 1976.

Four years later she moved to the famous retirement hospital, The Motion Picture Country House and Lodge. By 1982 she was unable to recognize either her children or husband. A few months before her 83rd birthday America's first lady of the screen died of bronchial pneumonia.

It was Norma Shearer who presented the best actress award to Marie Dressler in 1931. Having been nominated herself, she was gracious in defeat, describing Marie as "the grandest trouper of them all."

Marie had first appeared on stage almost 50 years earlier at age 14 after she had left her Cobourg, Ontario, home with an older sister because she couldn't tolerate her German father's volatile temper and his inability to provide for her Canadian-born mother. Christened Leila Marie Koerber, she adopted the name of an aunt, got a job with a stock company, and later held chorus jobs with touring light opera companies. She played Katisha in *The Mikado* and for more than a year learned a new comic opera every week.

Marie reached New York in 1892, performing in *The Robber of the Rhine*. At the same time she sang in a Bowery beer hall and a music hall to help support her sister and brother-in-law Richard Ganthony, who later became a successful playwright. In 1893/94, she was Lillian Russell's supporting actress in two productions before becoming a star as a music hall singer in *The Lady Slavey*. Numerous musicals followed for the remainder of the century and into the twentieth. She was a big hit in a successful 1907 vaudeville tour in London, England, titled *Oh Mr. Belasco*, but two other musicals in England failed and she returned to America in 1909.

A year later, she had her greatest stage success as Tillie Blobbs, making popular the song "Heaven will Protect the Working Girl." This success led, in 1914, to her first movie with the Canadian-born producer Mack Sennett. Her co-star was Charlie Chaplin, making his first movie for Sennett. Over the next three years she made other Tillie movies without Chaplin.

Throughout World War I, Marie toured, at her own expense, to sell millions in Liberty Bonds and

Will Rogers called Cobourg, Ontario-born Marie Dressler "... a sensational musical-comedy star." In 1931, she won tinseltown's premier award as Best Actress of the year. Her role as Min (right) in Min and Bill *is captured in this clip with her opposite, Wallace Beery, who would win the Best Actor award the next year*

entertain troops. But, the flapper image of the 1920s was disastrous for her: it suited neither her brand of humour nor her age (she was now in her fifties). As a result, she was virtually out of work for several years until Frances Marion, a personal friend and screenwriter, learned of her plight and fought to have her play the part of the waterfront soak Marty in Eugene O'Neil's *Anna Christie* featuring Greta Garbo.

Marie's performance rivalled that of Garbo and led to a series of comedy hits with MGM studios including one with Jack Benny and another with Norma Shearer in 1930. In 1931, her Oscar performance was in *Min and Bell* when she teamed up with bulky comic actor Wallace Beery. A year later, she was again nominated for her role in *Emma*. She played *Tug-Boat Annie* with Beery in 1933, and this was followed by *Dinner at Eight* — a totally different role described as "splendid" by a *New York Times* critic.

By then, however, Marie was ill, and after one more film she died of cancer, leaving, as one reviewer wrote years later, "a void in the field of character acting that has never been filled."

When they received their Oscars, Mary Pickford was at the height of her fame, Norma Shearer was near the beginning of a brilliant career (She went on to win five more academy award nominations during the 1930s and to be called "The First Lady of the Screen.") and Dressler was nearing the end of a long career. Indeed, these three Oscar-winning actresses collectively provided countless hours of viewing pleasure in the early days of film. *MVJ*

ADAM BECK

1857-1925

The Power Behind Electrical Power

ON THE NIGHT of October 11, 1910, more than 8,000 people crowded into Berlin's (now Kitchener) largest ice rink to see their city, through the publicly owned Ontario Hydro Commission, become the first in Ontario to get electricity.

When the moment came in the darkened arena for Premier Sir James Whitney to push the button, he grasped the hand of the man beside him and said, "With this hand which has made this project complete, I now turn on the power." It was a gracious tribute to Adam Beck.

Interest in publicly owned power took root in Berlin, Ontario; meetings about it were held in both 1902 and 1903. Beck, the new mayor of London, attended the second one along with 66 other representatives of municipalities, boards of trade, and manufacturing associations. Later Beck was one of seven officials named to determine which municipalities were interested in a revolutionary concept for hydro-electric power. In December 1903, as London's MLA as well as mayor, Beck was appointed to the newly created Ontario Hydro-Electric Power Commission.

When the Conservatives, led by Whitney, won the 1905 election, Beck became minister without portfolio and was appointed to chair a new commission of inquiry into public power. The original municipal group was still active, but Beck now considered it a "dead duck" and soon released, in his name, many of that group's findings and recommended that seven municipalities proceed "with a 60,000 horsepower development unless the other municipalities mentioned, joined them, in which case a 100,000 horsepower development was favoured."

This was the first of many aggressive acts Beck perpetrated over the next two decades in his zeal for public power. At the same time, he was vilified by private power interests of both Canada and the United States who relentlessly tried to discredit him. They failed. The Hydro movement had caught the imagination of the public, and Beck cleverly manipulated a largely supportive press to play the role of an unsullied knight championing the cause of cheap power for the people.

As the system expanded (London and Hamilton followed Berlin in 1910, Toronto in 1911) Beck made enemies within his own party by disregarding government red tape and rules of procedure. He could

Chairman of the Ontario Hydro-Electric Power Commission (now Ontario Hydro) from 1909-1925, Adam Beck built and expanded this public utility into the largest publicity-owned power authority in the world

not tolerate anyone around him who questioned his vision for a new Ontario. To be against him was to be against "Hydro," an attitude that backfired in 1912 when he rudely refused to see an investigating New York Senate Commission. Consequently, the Commission's report condemned the Hydro project as a failure.

The 1913 annual report, however, stressed otherwise. Hydro was now operating in 56 communities, had bought out all the private power companies except those in Toronto, Hamilton, London and Ottawa, and showed revenues of $2.6 million which yielded a surplus of $620,000.

In 1914 Beck received a knighthood. An expert horseman (he had a stable in London), during World War 1 he served as an honourary colonel in charge of procuring horses for the army in Eastern Canada. He also made available to soldiers with TB, a sanatorium he had built in Byron. His dictatorial methods in continuing to run the facility, however, caused complaints from both the troops and staff.

Petulant even with his own party whenever he didn't get his own way, he deliberated, in 1919, about replacing Sir William Hearst as its leader or about becoming leader of a Hydro non-partisan government. Instead, he ran as an independent, claiming this was the best way for him to "look after the interests of Hydro." He lost, partly because of his arrogance and defection from the Conservative Party which

When Premier Whitney and Ontario Hydro Chairman Adam Beck pushed "the button" in Berlin, Ontario, in 1910, to unleash the hydroelectric power generated by Niagara Falls, it made available cheap electricity across southern Ontario and stimulated industrial growth throughout Ontario's business community

also lost that election to the United Farmers of Ontario. The UFO then approached Sir Adam to become its leader, but his insistence that he must have an absolutely free hand with regard to Hydro made them choose another. The municipalities, on the other hand, quickly passed a resolution demanding he continue as chairman.

In 1920, Sir William MacKenzie, his archenemy in Ontario, agreed to sell out to Hydro, making it, in Sir Adam's words, "the largest organized power system in the world." His sparring with government, however, continued. He promoted electric railways (radials) between communities despite evidence that they wouldn't pay and insisted on the completion of the Queenston/Chippawa canal power project in 1921, where costs ballooned in two years from an estimated $14.5 million to $50 million. This caused the UFO government to launch the Gregory Inquiry and stimulated new attacks by American private power interests.

On January 1, 1923, Sir Adam lost a bitter campaign to have Hydro radials on the Toronto waterfront. In June, however, he handily won the provincial election in London — his "home" city since the 1880s when he moved his successful cigar box company there from Galt and, following his marriage, built a mansion. In 1924 he attended the World Power Conference in London, England, and met British government officials. The result was an announcement in the House of Commons that "one of the greatest authorities is available to manage the project."

Back home, Sir Adam denied press speculation about his leaving Hydro, and in October faced new problems when his long-time private secretary was arrested and charged with stealing $29,990 from the Commission. The secretary then registered 39 charges against Beck and other senior officers. These included excessive expense accounts, personal use of company cars, conflict of interest charges, "fixing" the books to make the radial systems look viable, and, in 1912, of sending lamps costing $22.48, and paid for by Hydro, to Sir Adam's home in London.

Within months, a commission dismissed all charges and the press applauded. One paper wrote, "Another attempt 'to get' Sir Adam Beck has failed miserably," and a Buffalo journal, describing him as "perhaps the most successful exponent of public ownership on this continent," suggested the uproar was partly due to his battle with private power interests.

The press support, however, didn't end the attacks. When the Gregory Inquiry was released in 1924, private power interests in the United States sponsored new attacks by known Hydro critics on both sides of the border, despite the report's finding that the engineering department was "made up of men of high professional qualifications ... serving the Commission zealously and efficiently," and that Hydro was "fundamentally sound and should be maintained ... in its full integrity."

Sir Adam was pleased. Now a widower and in poor health, he returned from a Baltimore hospital early in 1925, aware that time was running out. True to the Gregory Inquiry's description of Hydro engineers, however, he remained the ever-zealous chairman until his death, at 68, in mid-August. As a tribute to him on the day of his funeral, every factory wheel in Ontario was stopped at a given moment as the power of the Hydro over a range of 400 miles was suspended. MVJ

ICE HOCKEY

Creating Canada's Game

Canada is widely known as the home of ice hockey. Millions of Canadians have enjoyed the game since it was first played in an organized way in the last half of the nineteenth century. The game gradually developed into its present form through the activities and interest of many individuals and groups.

Hockey has been described as a game in which two opposing groups of players attempt to drive a ball, puck, or other small object through the goal of their opponents by means of sticks. In Ireland a game of this type called "hurley" was played before 1300 A.D. In Scotland the game was called "shinty" or "shinny." In England it was called "bandy" and in France "hocquet" from the old French word for a shepherd's crook.

Early in the seventeenth century the metal skate was invented in the Netherlands and later brought to England. During the severe winter of 1813-14 in England, a game of "bandy" is known to have been played on the ice of Bury Fen in Huntingdonshire. Within a few years definite rules had been developed for playing "bandy" on ice.

When and where ice hockey began in Canada is uncertain. There are accounts of games being played early in nineteenth century Halifax, Montreal, and elsewhere. In the centennial edition of the Picton (Ontario) *Gazette* (1831-1931), there is an interesting account of his early acquaintance with ice hockey by Archibald MacMechan, who graduated from University College in Toronto in 1884 and taught at Dalhousie University, in Halifax, from 1889 until he died in 1933.

In 1871 we never heard of ground hockey or hockey sticks and we should not have known the meaning of the word "puck." All those new-fangled things came long afterwards, things to be bought in stores. We made our own shinnies (sticks). We went to the woods with our little hatchet and cut a sapling with a crooked root. This was trimmed, the bark pealed off and seasoned, and lo! there was your shinny. The name of the game was also that of the implement with which it was played. Instead of a rubber puck, which was not then invented, we used the kneecap or knuckle bone of a cow or ox. It was a solid oblong, measuring perhaps two and a half inches long by one inch wide and three-quarters of an inch thick. It could stand any amount of hammering from any number of shinnies. Any number could play as the leaders chose sides, and there were the fewest rules. You learned what to do in a minute. It was a game without subtlety or fine points. We played a simple game in a howling mob on a short, icy street. It seemed utterly unreasonable to us that the peaceful residents should object to our noise. Our skates were steel blades in a wooden body, with a hole bored in the boot heel to take a screw; and then all was strapped on.

MacMechan's account of hockey as he knew it in 1871 is a good description of the game played by many young Canadians in the less affluent, less urbanized years before World War I. There are other accounts, however, which indicate that ice hockey was taking on a more organized form earlier in the nineteenth century.

Games are reported to have been played in a Montreal rink near the intersection of Bleury and Dorchester Streets in February and March, 1837, between a team of French Canadians who called themselves "Les Canadiens" and a team called "Dorchesters." There were eight players: goal, point, cover-point, centre, rover, home, right side and left side.

In his volume *Halifax, Warden of the North,* for which he received the 1948 Governor General's Award, Thomas H. Raddall stated that ice hockey in Canada actually began in Nova Scotia in the eighteenth century when it was played on the Dartmouth Lakes by members of the military garrison in that area. The soldiers, who had seen Indians playing a primitive form of "hurley" on the ice, developed their own version of the game and played it on skates. Raddall also reported that when the soldiers went to other military posts along the St. Lawrence River and the Great Lakes Basin, they played the same game there and secured their sticks from the Indians of Nova Scotia.

Capturing the essence of ice hockey in rural Quebec, this exuberant John Little painting of 1957 hangs in the Montreal executive offices of The Molson Companies. The farmhouse backyard has been converted into a hockey rink; the referee here does not wear a striped shirt because he is the parish priest; the fans are not corporate executives but family who keep warm by standing near the outdoor stove. There are no Toronto Maple Leaf team sweaters on these budding habitant *players!*

"Fast skating, sharp passing, smart, clean defensive play — that's hockey!"
Jean Beliveau, 1970

"I predict that the boys from old Quebec will always excel in hockey. There is something about their zeal and their temperament which makes hockey their natural game"
Frank Selke Jr., 1962

Confirmation that garrison teams played their particular form of ice hockey comes from a diary of 1846-47 kept by a man named Edwin Horsey. He noted in his diary that soldiers greatly enjoyed playing "shinny." Groups of fifty or more players on each side participated in games played on the ice on Kingston harbour. Some who have studied the history of ice hockey in Canada argue that the first Canadian game of ice hockey was played in Kingston in the winter of 1855. Others maintain that it was in Montreal that ice hockey, in its present form, was first played in Canada.

Members of a Montreal football club played an ice hockey game at the Victoria Skating Rink in Montreal on March 3, 1875. The game that day, advertised in the *Montreal Gazette*, appears to have been novel in at least one particular way. In earlier references to ice hockey it is clear that the game was played with a hard rubber ball. The advertisement for this game stated, however, that the game would be played "with a flat, circular piece of wood." Soon, it appears, the centre portion of a lacrosse ball, with upper and lower rounded parts cut off evenly, was used as a puck.

These early games were played on a sheet of ice at least one hundred and fifty feet long and sixty feet wide. Goalposts, later frozen into the ice, were six feet high and about nine feet wide, and centred in both ends of the ice surface. In 1899 W.A. Hewitt, subsequently the secretary of the Ontario Hockey Association for many years, introduced goal nets at a game in Montreal. This was a valuable step in the evolution of the goal.

A small group of students at McGill University began to play ice hockey in the mid-1870s. J.G.A. Creighton is credited with having brought the game from Halifax to McGill. There, three students — W.L. Murray, W.F. Robertson and R.F. Smith — recognized the need for a standard set of rules. They studied carefully the rules for English rugby and field hockey. Then they prepared a set of rules that,

McGill University Hockey Club, viewed here, emerged in the late 1870s and is believed to have been the first organized ice hockey team in Canada

Goal nets were added to the game of hockey by 1899 and became standard equipment for all hockey games by the turn of the century

in their judgment, would be appropriate for ice hockey. To that point there was little uniformity in the rules for ice hockey. If the game was to attract wider interest and participation, agreement was needed on readily understandable rules that could be applied easily without much wrangling.

The rules devised at McGill by Murray, Robertson and Smith were of great help in the organization and conduct of the game there and elsewhere. The McGill University Hockey Club, which emerged in the late 1870s, is believed to have been the first organized hockey team in Canada.

Many years later, in 1936, Murray told the *McGill News* that he and other students at McGill rented the Crystal Skating Rink on Dorchester Street near Dominion Square for Saturday mornings. Initially, there were fifteen men on each side, as in rugby. They soon found that there were too many players on the ice and they reduced the number to seven: three forwards, one centre, two guards, and a goalkeeper.

Murray reported that he suggested in 1883 that "it would be a great thing for hockey if a series of matches could be played during Montreal's Ice Carnival Week." The Carnival committee agreed with Murray's proposal and offered a $750 silver cup, emblematic of the hockey championship of the world, to the team winning most matches during the week. Six teams entered the contest and played each other twice. The McGill team won the championship.

In the last half of the nineteenth century ice-skating rinks appeared in many communities in Canada. The world's first covered rink was built in Quebec City in 1852. Ten years later the Victoria

STORMING OF THE NEW ICE PALACE.

"Canada is the birthplace of this tremendous game. You invented it and you always want to be the best. Prove it!" Anatoly Tarasov, former U.S.S.R. head hockey coach, 1969, three years before the first Canada Cup, 1972

The committee organizing Montreal's Ice Carnival Week, in 1883, agreed that staging ice hockey tournaments simultaneous would help popularize the game. They also provided trophies forerunners of the Stanley Cup introduced in 1893

Skating Rink in Montreal opened. (This large rink provided the standard size for ice hockey.) These and other early rinks were intended for skating, not for ice hockey. Those who wanted to play hockey usually had to wait until the leisure skating was over. Nonetheless, enthusiasm for ice hockey spread quickly in Canada.

A hockey league developed in Kingston, Ontario, and operated during the winter of 1885-86 with four teams competing. About the same time the Amateur Hockey Association of Canada was organized. Then in 1890 the Ontario Hockey League, later the Ontario Hockey Association, was formed through a merger with other leagues such as the one in Kingston.

Interest in ice hockey was destined to spread beyond Canada. Some Canadians, studying at the Universities of Cambridge and Oxford, organized teams in their respective universities. The first Cambridge-Oxford ice hockey match was played at St. Moritz, Switzerland, in 1885. Each year since then, save for wartime and several other years, Oxford and Cambridge ice hockey teams, usually composed mainly of Canadians, have met for their friendly annual encounters. These two ice hockey teams, like their counterparts at several Canadian universities, are among the most historic and continuous hockey teams in the world.

In March 1892 the Governor General of Canada, Lord Stanley, arranged for a challenge cup to be presented annually to the champion hockey team in the Dominion of Canada. The Stanley Cup, as it became known, was awarded in 1893 to the Montreal Amateur Athletic Association team. The introduction of this trophy marked the beginning of a new era in the history of ice hockey.

CANADA'S FAVORITE WINTER SPORT—HOCKEY

Dear Dana.
Visited a game here, the other Eve...

The Victoria Skating Rink opened in Montreal in 1862. It was Montreal's most popular winter gathering place. Note the unprotected spectators standing at the sides. At the time, the rink had the best facilities in the world to stage ice hockey

One month before he died, former Canadian Prime Minister Lester B. Pearson enlarged one portion of a hockey team photograph of himself and former Governor General Roland Michener, taken while both attended Oxford University as students in the early 1920s, and presented it to his friend of 50 years. Often, young men who came to know one another through hockey established lifelong friendships

Hockey had emerged first as a friendly sporting encounter. Young men who came to know one another through hockey sometimes established enduring friendships. One of the most remarkable of these was that of Lester Pearson, Canada's Prime Minister from 1963 until 1968, and Roland Michener, Governor General of Canada from 1967 until 1974.

In the early 1920s Pearson and Michener played together for the Oxford University Ice Hockey Club. Their participation in ice hockey at Oxford and their mutual enjoyment of the game strengthened their friendship.

Before Christmas 1972 when he knew that he was dying, Pearson came across a photograph of the Oxford ice hockey team taken at the time of the annual game with Cambridge a half century earlier. In the photograph Pearson and Michener are sitting side by side. Pearson had that portion of the photograph enlarged and framed and gave it to the Governor General.

The role of ice hockey in the genesis of enduring friendships is a rarely mentioned aspect of this great sport. It was, however, a primary feature of ice hockey in its earliest years in Canada. DMS

John E. (Jack) Hammell

1876-1958

Giving Wings to Prospectors

Throughout recorded history various individuals have searched for minerals and precious stones in the earth's crust. It was not, however, until gold was discovered at Sutter's Mill in California that prospecting began to emerge as a full-time activity for venturesome individuals.

Since that famous California goldrush of 1849, an unending number of prospectors in search of undiscovered mineral treasure have roamed countless miles on foot, often with heavy packsacks on their backs. Some of this wearisome work began to be eliminated by the late 1920s when Jack Hammell and two other knowledgeable Canadians organized the world's first aerial prospecting company, Northern Aerial Mineral Exploration (N.A.M.E.) Limited. Its creation would change forever the hunt for mineral resources.

Born north of Toronto in Beeton, Ontario, in 1876, Jack Hammell went to the United States as a youth. There he ventured into the boxing ring as a prize fighter, and later tried his hand as a newspaper reporter as well. However, news of the great silver discoveries in Northern Ontario at the turn of the century drew him back to Canada.

Gradually Hammell became a skilled prospector and mining promoter. While prospecting the Cobalt, Porcupine, and Kirkland Lake regions of Northern Ontario, he became widely known as a forceful, determined character who got things done his way and delivered on his promises. Other prospectors sought his advice and help in securing needed money to develop their mineral finds.

His first major success as a promoter followed his decision, in 1915, to seek financing for prospectors who had staked claims on the northern section of the Manitoba-Saskatchewan boundary. The site was given the flamboyant name of Flin Flon, the name of a fictional prospector.

More than a decade passed before production began at Flin Flon. Eventually Hammell's determination, energy, and enthusiasm produced dramatic results despite adversities. Through his efforts and those of his loyal supporters, the zinc-copper deposits developed at Flin Flon made it one of Canada's largest mining operations.

A major opportunity came to Hammell in 1925, the year prospectors Lorne and Ray Howey discovered gold at Red Lake in Northwestern Ontario. The Howeys asked Hammell to look at their findings. Exuberant over what he saw, he made a deal. To bring essential supplies to Red Lake before winter set in, Hammell arranged with the Ontario Department of Forestry for the use of five of its aircraft. By this means, he shortened a prospector's journey from ten days by dog team to an hour-and-a-half by aircraft. Hammell quickly learned, through his own experience, the many advantages as well as the dangers in using aircraft in prospecting and mining activities. But for him the advantages clearly outweighed the dangers.

Thus he responded with great enthusiasm in 1927 when Harold A. ("Doc") Oaks suggested that together they join with James A. Richardson Sr. of Winnipeg in the formation of the aerial mineral exploration company, which would become widely known as N.A.M.E. Bush flying was not new. But the creation of N.A.M.E., combining the knowledge, experience, and vision of Hammell as a prospector and developer, of Oaks as a flyer and mining engineer, and of Richardson as financier, marked the beginning of a brave new era in Canadian mineral exploration and development.

Within a relatively short period, N.A.M.E. was operating 10 aircraft from 34 bases in Northern Canada and meeting the transportation needs of some 200 prospectors. Hammell had predicted that, if Canadian prospectors, engineers, and geologists were given "wings," they would "find more mineral deposits in the next five years than had been discovered in the last half-century."

Unfortunately, the collapse of the stock market in 1929 interrupted fulfilment of Hammell's prediction. But President Franklin Roosevelt's action which led to the price of gold rising to $35 an ounce in 1934 gave great impetus to gold mining in Canada. Hammell's prediction was going to be realized!

By the mid-1930s, 11 Canadian aerial transportation companies were operating. N.A.M.E. was no longer among them, but a gold deposit discovered in 1928 by two prospectors at Pickle Lake, about 200 miles due north of the present city of Thunder Bay, was coming into production. Those prospectors had been served by N.A.M.E. The Pickle Crow venture, financed by Hammell, had begun to reward him handsomely.

During his long career as a mining promoter, Jack Hammell worked vigorously to develop many mineral deposits. Eight of them became profitable mining operations. By the time of his death in 1958, they had provided their shareholders with about $200 million in dividends. Hammell's contribution, however, must be measured in more than material terms.

The "wings" Hammell gave to prospectors, mining engineers, and geologists took top-heavy burdens off their backs. Gradually those "wings" became flying workhorses serving not only the Canadian mining industry but Canadians generally. And the principles of bush flying, in its origins a distinctively Canadian art, were refined, elaborated, and exported around the world, thanks initially to Jack Hammell.

WILDER GRAVES PENFIELD

Mapping the Brain

ALTHOUGH Wilder Penfield was born in the United States, completed his under-graduate education there and in England, served during World War I in France, qualified as a medical doctor and practised in the United States and did not come to Canada until he was 37 years old, he was later cele-brated as "the greatest living Canadian." The unprecedented esteem he enjoyed in Canada resulted both from his renown as a brain surgeon of unsurpassed skill and from recognition of his unique contributions to Canadian life as founder and director of the world-famous Montreal Neurological Institute.

Penfield was born in Spokane, Washington, on January 26, 1891, the son of a medical doctor. He moved with his mother to Hudson, Wisconsin, when she and his father separated in 1899. There he graduated, at the head of his class, from Galahad School, a private institution which his mother and three young teachers had organized. Upon graduation he went to Princeton University and completed his bachelor's degree in philosophy in 1913. He was chosen "Best All-round Man" by his classmates and later won a Rhodes Scholarship.

In January 1915, as a member of Merton College, Oxford, he enrolled in courses that would assist in his completion of a medical degree at Johns Hopkins University which he planned to enter on his return to the United States. He was assisted in arranging this by Sir William Osler, Oxford's Regius Professor of Medicine who had concluded that Penfield could become a good doctor. Anxious to help, Osler invited the young American to accompany him on medical consultations around England from one hospital to another. Through his association with Osler, Penfield came to regard medicine as mankind's most noble calling.

Sir Charles Sherrington, the distinguished English physiologist, noted for his experiments that established modern understanding of integrated nervous functions, also became a primary influence

Founder and first director of the world-famous Montreal Neurological Institute, Dr. Wilder G. Penfield believed that the brain represented the most important unexplored field in the whole of science

on Penfield. Through Sherrington's lectures Penfield was introduced to the study of the brain. He also completed courses in histology, pharmacology, bacteriology, and chemistry.

During the Christmas break from studies at Oxford, in late 1915, Penfield worked briefly as a volunteer in a Red Cross hospital. When he was returning to this Red Cross work in late March 1916, after the winter term at Oxford, the ship on which he was travelling was torpedoed in the English Channel. Although he was erroneously reported dead and his obituary was published in an American newspaper, he survived the torpedo attack but spent three weeks in a hospital in Dover, England, and several weeks recuperating at Sir William Osler's residence in Oxford.

On his return to the United States, Penfield was given academic credit for his science studies at Oxford and embarked upon his final years of medical study at Johns Hopkins. In April 1917, however, the United States declared war on Germany and began to enter fully into the First World War. The following June, Penfield married Helen Kermott. Several weeks later he and his wife took a ship to France where they both worked in an American Red Cross hospital in Paris.

In late 1917 they returned to the United States. Penfield completed his medical studies at Johns Hopkins and received his medical degree. After having served his internship in Boston and later having assisted Dr. Harvey Cushing, one of the most gifted brain surgeons in the United States, he returned to Oxford for advanced studies in clinical neurology and neurosurgery. While in England he developed a special interest in epilepsy. When this period of his advanced research was finished successfully, Penfield and his family, which by this time included two children, returned to the U.S.

He accepted a position at New York's Presbyterian Hospital. Through his work there and at the New York Neurological Institute, his interest in epilepsy was deepened. In his effort to advance his knowledge and ability in his areas of specialization, Penfield studied firsthand the methods used by specialists in Spain, Germany, and elsewhere.

In 1928, with William Vernon Cone, his primary associate in neurosurgery, Penfield accepted an appointment at the Royal Victoria Hospital in Montreal. There he developed a good working relationship with Dr. Colin K. Russel, a well-established neurologist who supported Penfield in his surgical treatment of epilepsy. Penfield began to make plans for an institute for the study and, he hoped, the eventual cure of epilepsy and other brain diseases.

Although his initial application to the Rockefeller Foundation was not successful, by 1934 the Foundation finally agreed to join with the Province of Quebec, the City of Montreal, and private donors to help financially in the implementation of Penfield's plan to establish the Montreal Neurological Institute. Gradually the Institute, the first of its kind in the world, emerged as a centre of outstanding research, teaching, and treatment. Surgeons and scientists worked closely together, drawing on new research findings to improve methods of diagnosis and surgical treatment. Like his celebrated mentor, Osler, Penfield worked with great skill and concentration as he constantly sought to find new means to cure epilepsy and related dysfunctions.

In collaboration with his colleagues, Penfield developed a new surgical approach that became known as the "Montreal Procedure."

Relying on a local anaesthetic, Penfield carefully examined the exposed brain tissue of an aware patient. As the patient described what he or she was feeling, Penfield probed sections of the brain. Using this method, he was able to identify, in many cases, the precise location of the damaged brain tissues that were causing epileptic seizures. As he did this he was able to map areas of the brain in terms of their respective functions.

Through his research Penfield developed an interest in the connection between the brain and the human mind. His research concerning epilepsy led him to study the cerebral cortex, that part of the brain in which are centred all motor, sensory functions and impulses that give rise to our variety of thoughts and feelings. As he carefully probed the brain, he found that careful administration of a mild electric shock to one of the temporal lobes could, miraculously it seemed, cause the patient to recall precise personal experiences that had long been forgotten. By this means he was able to locate the accumulated store of memory of past events and the emotions, sensations, and thoughts to which the events had given rise. Penfield's research into the structure and function of the brain, it might be added, was guided by his desire to discover a physical basis for the philosophical belief in the human soul.

Penfield performed more operations for epilepsy than any other surgeon in the world to that time. Unprecedented success attended his efforts. Half his patients were cured of seizures. His outstanding record of accomplishments as a neurologist and neurosurgeon later brought him many of the world's highest honours. His many scientific writings were accepted as definitive statements in their field. During the Second World War he was a member of a surgical mission in Moscow. Subsequently he went on a similar mission to China.

Like Osler, he devoted much time during the last two decades of his life to writing and publication of his work. His writings on the relationship between science and religion reflected his insight as a renowned scientist and dedicated humanitarian with a sincere belief in God. He served as the first president of the Vanier Institute of the Family. He vigorously advocated early second language training for children and argued convincingly that "the child who hears a second language very early has a great advantage in many aspects of education and life."

Penfield was particularly concerned about the future of Canada. In an address, delivered in French to L'Institut Canadien du Quebec on November 27, 1967, he stated: "There is a background of change that threatens us in Quebec and in Canada.... Straight ahead along the great highroad of cooperation, destiny and greatness beckon. This is the road that we should choose."

As his life neared its end, Penfield returned to the deepest subjects that had exercised his mind in all his endeavours. In 1975, in *The Mystery of the Mind*, he set out his final views on the relationship between the human brain and the human mind. *No Man Alone*, his autobiography covering the period 1891 to 1934, was published in 1971.

Penfield died on April 5, 1976, revered by the nation he had served for nearly fifty years. DMS

Edward Samuel Rogers

1900-1939

EDWARD ("TED") ROGERS launched Canada into the age of electronic information and entertainment after he perfected an alternating current radio tube in 1925. That same year he began manufacturing the "Majestic" five-tube batteryless radio just in time to demonstrate his product at Toronto's Canadian National Exhibition. Each radio sold for $260 and, despite the high cost per unit, the "plug in, tune in" was an immediate success.

Plugging in the World

His elimination of the earlier need for an array of dry- and wet-cell batteries was a major advancement in both the improvement of radio reception and in the development of the entire radio-manufacturing industry.

The family had wanted "Ted" to become a business executive, but early in his life he had become enthralled by radio as he transmitted radio signals by key from his family's garage. At 13 he won a prize for the best amateur-built radio in Ontario. When his Morse code signals were received in Scotland in 1921, he became the first Canadian amateur to send a radio message across the Atlantic.

Rogers was born in Toronto on June 21, 1900, into a highly respected and wealthy family descended from Quakers. He graduated from Pickering College, a Quaker secondary school, and for a time studied practical science at the University of Toronto. Developing his own laboratory in the family garage and working on his own projects, this amateur engineer was soon transmitting radio signals to the Pacific Coast.

By 1921 "Ted" came to the conclusion that battery-operated radios were too expensive, too bulky and too heavy. He consciously decided to develop a radio that would run on alternating current and eliminate, among other problems, the constant hum present in battery-operated reception. Working day and night for over a year, he perfected an alternating radio tube and filed a patent application. It was granted as number 269205 in March 1927.

Simultaneously, to enlarge the market for radios, the Rogers family founded Toronto's radio station CFRB in February 1927. It immediately became one of Canada's most influential and successful broadcasting companies. The call letters of Canada's most listened to radio station CFRB, stand for "Canada's First Rogers Batteryless."

Rogers was issued an experimental television broadcasting licence and was working on the development of radar at the time of his death in May 1939. His son, Edward Samuel — born in Toronto on May 27, 1933, and also called "Ted" — took over the family business which he has developed into an international communications network — Rogers Communications Inc.

DMS

Courtesy, Edward ("Ted") Rogers

When Edward ("Ted") Rogers (1900-1939) perfected the alternating current (A/C) radio tube in 1925, he launched Canada into the age of electronic entertainment. Today, his son and namesake guides Rogers Communications, a world leader in communications technology

Patrons...
Generating Heritage Awareness

AMJ Campbell Van Lines	348	KPMG	412
American Express	383	Kodak Canada Inc.	397
Arbor Memorial Services Inc.	361	Kraft General Foods Canada Inc.	350
Ashland Chemical Canada Ltd	355	MacMillan Bloedel Limited	390
Babcock & Wilcox Industries Ltd.	353	Magna International Inc.	367
Bridgestone/Firestone Canada Inc.	384	Mentholatum Co. of Canada, The	404
Brookfield Development Corporation	363	Merck Frosst Canada Inc.	396
Burroughs Wellcome Inc.	388	Microsoft Canada Inc.	370
Canadian Association for Community Living	374	Midland Walwyn Capital Inc.	380
Catelli Pasta	409	Molson Companies, The	338
Choice Hotels Canada Inc.	366	Morguard Investments Limited	395
Chrysler Canada Ltd.	369	Municipal Trust	365
CIBA Vision	354	North West Company, The	400
Color Your World Inc.	399	Ontario Hydro	352
Connaught Laboratories Limited	387	Philip Environmental Inc.	386
Country Style Donuts	358	Power Corporation of Canada	342
Dominion of Canada		Procter & Gamble Inc.	376
General Insurance, The	360	Prudential Insurance Company	
Digital Equipment of Canada Ltd.	362	of America, The	391
Eli Lilly Canada Inc.	349	Radio Shack	382
Elizabeth Arden Canada Inc.	394	Royal Bank of Canada	343
Ford Motor Company of Canada, Limited	346	Royal Doulton Canada Limited	385
Golden Griddle Corporation, The	411	S.C. Johnson and Son, Limited	356
Hiram Walker	359	St. Lawrence Cement	378
Home Hardware Stores Limited	398	Sifto Canada Inc.	340
Human Resources Technologies Inc.	410	Specialty Brands	389
IMASCO	372	Syncrude Canada Ltd.	368
Inco Limited	364	Unisource Canada Inc.	408
Integral Consulting Inc.	406	United Parcel Services Canada Ltd.	375
Interforest Ltd.	344	Vestcap Investment Management Inc.	371
International Verifact	407	W.C. Wood Company Limited	392
Knob Hill Farms Limited	402	Ward Associates	401

Canadian Corporate Achievers

A Special Introductory Message...
Maurice Strong

The Honourable Maurice F. Strong, P.C., O.C., LL.D.

We Canadians are a modest people whose entrepreneurial spirit is very high in proportion to our relatively small population. Because our country is so vast, so resource-rich and sometimes so formidable, our business and industrial giants have become world leaders in the new eco-industrial revolution which has emerged in an effort to reverse the earth-depleting practises of the past.

What you will find in the following pages celebrating corporate achievements are inspiring stories of Canadian companies whose commitment to business and industry excellence is matched by their concern not only for the country in which they do business but also for the "Whole Earth" and all world citizens.

As we approach the new century, we can anticipate a change in consciousness world-wide. For Canadians, long recognized as innovators and humanitarians, the change has already begun. We present these profiles to you as celebrations of our visionary national character.

Chairman and CEO, Ontario Hydro, (1992-); Secretary-General of the 1992 UN Conference on Environment and Development (the Earth Summit) and Under-Secretary-General of the UN; during 1985 and 1986, Under-Secretary-General of the UN and Executive Coordinator of the UN Office for Emergency Operations in Africa;

Secretary-General of the UN Conference on Human Environment, November 1970 to December 1972; first Executive Director of the UN Environment Program (UNEP), Nairobi, Kenya (January 1973-December 1975); subsequently, President, Chairman, and CEO, Petro-Canada (1976-78);

Formerly, President, Power Corporation of Canada (1963-66); first President, Canadian International Development Agency, CIDA (1966-70); Chairman, Canada Development Investment Corporation (1981-84); Chairman, Board of Governors, International Development Research Centre (IDRC) in Canada; advisor to the UN and Chairman of the Earth Council;

Born and educated, Manitoba; recipient, honorary doctorates from 34 universities; Fellow of the Royal Society (U.K.), the Royal Society of Canada and the Royal Architectural Society of Canada.

The Molson Companies

Strength Through Diversity — for over 200 years

JOHN MOLSON opened his brewery to the public on July 28, 1786, and began The Molson Companies' proud heritage. Six generations of the Molson family have contributed to the company and Eric Molson is its Chairman today.

But success is not assured by being a long-established company, or a company that has made astute decisions in the past. The business world is dynamic, and in this context, the story of the company has many themes: business strategies honed by the needs of the time, diversification, and concern for the community — to cite three of the most important. The company's history is not just a list of the dates, times and places of The Molson Companies' milestones. Rather, it is a two-hundred-year demonstration of these business traditions.

 Today, **The Molson Companies Limited** is a Canadian public corporation with interests in over forty countries. There are four principal businesses — Molson Breweries, Diversey Corporation, Beaver Lumber Company and Club de Hockey Canadien.

The Molson Companies also has a 25 percent interest in The Home Depot Canada and a 44.5 percent indirect investment in Groupe Val Royal.

 Molson Breweries is the leading brewer in Canada, the leading exporter of beer to the United States. The strategic alliance of Molson Breweries with the Miller Brewing Company of Milwaukee has contributed to this success. This alliance allows Molson to become a major brand in the U.S. market in co-operation with Miller. At the same time, it provides opportunities for cost reductions and operating synergies that would not be available through a simple licensing arrangement.

While Molson is synonymous with Canadian beer in North America and the United Kingdom, Molson Breweries also has a global business perspective and

John Molson: Founder
The Molson Companies, 1786

licensing agreements with some of the world's best-known brands.

 Diversey Corporation, with operating companies in over forty countries, serves customers in more than one hundred countries around the world. Diversey is the prime global supplier of cleaning, sanitizing, metal surface treatment and water management products and systems. It is a good example of how a Canadian-based company can dominate a market segment worldwide.

 Beaver Lumber Company is the leading retailer of building supplies and do-it-yourself products in smaller Canadian cities, towns and rural areas. Complementing this business, The Molson Companies formed a partnership in Canada with The Home Depot, an Atlanta-based chain of warehouse stores widely regarded as the leading retailer in the home improvement industry. This partnership will build on the success of The Molson Companies' Aikenhead's Home Improvement Warehouse and expand this concept into Canada's major urban centres.

Club de Hockey Canadien is the fourth principal business of The Molson Companies. While venturing into international markets, The Molson Companies remain strongly rooted in Canada as a longstanding owner of the National Hockey League's premier franchise, the Montreal Canadiens.

The strategy of diversification continues the entrepreneurial legacy of John Molson. After John Molson established his brewery in 1786, he continually improved and expanded his brewing business. But he also did something more common in business two hundred years later: he began to diversify.

In 1797, John Molson opened a lumber yard. He went on to launch *The Accommodation*, the first of a fleet of steamships that served as commercial transport on the St. Lawrence River in 1809. Then came boat terminals, a foundry and the British American Hotel, in Montreal, in 1816, and the Theatre Royale in 1825. In the year he died, 1836, John Molson made one of his most significant contributions to the business life of his time by helping to create Canada's first railway line.

Diversification, coupled with a keen appreciation for the most timely investments, guided business development after John Molson's death: Molson's early participation in a "gas-light" company, distilleries, flour and saw mills and — a crowning achievement in 1855 — the granting of a Parliamentary Charter for the Molson's Bank. In 1925, its 125 branches became part of Canada's oldest chartered bank, the Bank of Montreal.

Paralleling these accomplishments, The Molson Companies' belief in social responsibility and community involvement has long been in evidence. John Molson was a

significant benefactor of the Montreal General Hospital, in 1822, Thomas Molson College was founded in 1857, and William Molson Hall, at McGill University, opened in 1862.

Building on this tradition, The Molson Companies Donations Fund was incorporated in 1973 as a non-profit organization. Its motto, "Partners in our Community's Future." The Fund provides support for initiatives addressing national and local needs in health, social welfare, education, and the environment.

Strategic agility. Diversification. A concern for community. These have been some of the key aspects of The Molson Companies' tradition for over two hundred years. A tradition, moreover, which continues to fuel the growth of this Canadian company around the world today.

1.

2.

3.

4.

1. Molson, highly respected throughout the brewing world, continues to produce and market the best quality beer as efficiently as possible
2. Diversey's worldwide resources, combined with dedicated customer service, give life to the company's commitment to "Global Strength — Local Care"
3. From coast-to-coast, Beaver Lumber offers customers value, assortment and service
4. Montreal Canadiens — winners of more Stanley Cups than any other National Hockey League team — are an internationally recognized symbol of excellence in sport

Sifto Canada Inc. *A Major Factor in the Health of our Nation*

ALTHOUGH he was prospecting for oil in 1866, Mr. Sam Platt's drilling rig hit paydirt of a different kind when it struck rock salt almost 1,000 feet beneath Goderich Harbour. The claim that he was only mildly surprised at the discovery is probably correct as native peoples of the area had earlier told him of the evidence of salt deposits throughout the region. His findings became the first recorded discovery of a salt bed in North America. By year's end, rock salt was being used as a source of brine for salt production.

Sam Platt proved to be a successful businessman when his company declared a 51 percent dividend the next year, the same year Canada became a nation.

Little did he realize, moreover, that his salt discovery was near the edge of a huge geological formation called the Michigan Salt Basin. His discovery initiated a salt rush. By late 1867, 12 independent salt wells were dotting the Maitland River valley down to its confluence with Goderich Harbour and Lake Huron. Salt fever had hit the area! Sam Platt had made salt, for centuries one of the world's most sought after commodities, synonymous with "the prettiest town in Canada."

His 1866 discovery, furthermore, distributed the seeds for the eventual creation of a major North American company destined to become, by the 1990s, one of the world's largest suppliers of salt.

Although dazzling-white salt from Goderich outclassed the more famous English salt by winning first prize at the 1867 Paris Exhibition, mass production of salt was not actually begun at Goderich until 1880 while the site was being operated by a chemist, George Rice. The site became known as the "Rice Block."

The production process was simple. Rows of some 100 heavy, open, cast iron kettles of 120 to 140 gallons each, of pumped brine, were set on furnaces dependent on wood for fire. This evaporation process produced a fine flake salt

1.

which was air-dried and then shipped in barrels made by coopers who worked on the site. As wood fuel in the area was consumed the cost escalated. The process was expensive.

Streamlining salt production was inevitable. Kettles were replaced by shallow steel pans 30 feet wide and 100 feet long. The final product was still coarse and the process was still expensive as imported coal for furnace heating replaced depleted wood sources.

By 1910, modernization at the Goderich solution mine turned to a vacuum pan process consisting of one vertical steel tank with internal heating tubes conducting steam. This operation produced granular salt crystals widely used for table salt. It was also cost-effective.

In 1919 the operation was purchased by banker, Charles Wurtele. The company was now called the Goderich Salt Company and under Wurtele's direction it became the largest industry in Huron County. It attracted the attention of E.P. Taylor who took control of the company and eventually it became a wholly owned subsidiary of Domtar Limited. The name Sifto was introduced in 1955.

Only since the late 1950s has salt actually been mined in the Goderich area. When it became apparent that rock salt was in a growth market, Sifto took action. A mining shaft was commenced in 1957 and completed in 1959. To meet the needs of municipalities requiring crushed rock salt for winter roads, in addition to domestic need for rock salt for water softeners, a second shaft became operational in 1968. A further increase in production was achieved when a third shaft

was added in 1983. Today the mine complex employs more than 300 workers.

In 1990, Domtar's Canadian salt-producing operations were sold to North American Salt Company of Kansas. At present, Sifto Canada employs over 500 workers. In addition to its Goderich facilities, it operates Saskatchewan's Unity plant employing 80 workers. Its high-grade products service markets from northwestern Ontario to the Pacific coast. Sifto's production process in eastern Canada is at the Amherst, Nova Scotia plant employing 70 workers. Its vapour recompression process produces an unequalled salt purity in North America.

According to Mark Demetree, President of North American Salt Company, Sifto Canada's success is the result of a unique employee diversity where "everyone is working together for a common purpose."

1. A common sight on any grocery store shelf is the Sifto salt box; 2. The Goderich Salt Company was a household name from 1919 to 1955 when Domtar introduced Sifto; 3. At a depth of 1,750 feet, the Sifto underworld, about one and one half miles wide, extends 2 miles into Lake Huron. The ceilings of the huge beehive complex average 45 feet in height. Thick pillars give the appearance of rooms that trucks travel through to carry rock salt to crushing and screening operations before it is hoisted to the surface in customized skips

Power Corporation of Canada

Proud Canadian-based International Corporation

POWER CORPORATION OF CANADA, today a major international holding and management corporation, was formed in 1925, in Montreal.

The purpose of the corporation was to acquire and develop steam and hydro plants serving industrial development and various Canadian communities.

Companies in which Power Corporation had substantial interest included: Canada Northern Power Corporation Limited, serving parts of Northern Ontario; the Ottawa and Hull Power Company Limited, serving the capital region and the Ottawa Valley; Southern Canada Power Company Limited, serving the industrial region of Quebec's Eastern Townships; the Dominion Power and Transmission Company Limited and its subsidiaries serving the golden horseshoe, including Hamilton, instrumental in developing the industrial potential of the entire area; Winnipeg Electric Company and its subsidiary Manitoba Power Company Limited supplying electric light, power gas and traction (street railway) to greater Winnipeg; and East Kootenay Power Company Limited servicing a territory from Cranbrook, B.C. to Blairmore, Alberta.

The Manitoba Hydro-Electric Commission acquired in 1953 the Winnipeg Electric Company, one of the original companies acquired by Power Corporation of Canada in 1925. This was the first of a series of acquisitions of the Corporation's investments in hydroelectric companies by various governments or agencies. In 1961 the government of British Columbia expropriated the assets of British Columbia Power Corporation, one of the company's west coast investments. This was followed by Quebec Hydro-Electric Commission's takeover of the company's interest in Quebec utility companies.

These nationalizations left Power with a substantial amount of cash and enabled the Corporation to redirect its activities and diversify. In 1968 Mr. Paul Desmarais, the new Chairman, provided new focus for the company. The strategy turned to developing substantial interests in fewer companies. Major interests were developed in the pulp, paper, and packaging industry — Consolidated-Bathurst Inc.; the international financial services industry, through The Great-West Life Assurance Company, Investors Group Inc., and Montreal Trustco; and the communications industry — *La Presse* and a number of regional newspapers in Quebec and several radio and television stations in Quebec and Ontario.

Paul G. Desmarais, P.C., C.C., Chairman, Power Corporation

During the period from 1984 to 1986, the financial services group was reorganized and renamed Power Financial Corporation. New investments included several European financial, energy, and communications companies. Pargesa Holding S.A., Geneva, in which Power Financial and the Frère Group of Brussels have equal interests, today holds substantial interests in companies including Compagnie Financière de Paribas, Imetal S.A. and CarnaudMetalbox of Paris; Petrofina S.A., Tractebel S.A., and Banque Bruxelles Lambert of Brussels, as well as Compagnie Luxembourgeoise de Télédiffusion, and Orior Holding S.A. of Switzerland.

In 1989 Power Financial accepted the offer of another Canadian holding company and sold its controlling interest in Montreal Trustco. As well, Power Corporation accepted an offer for its interest in Consolidated-Bathurst. A portion of the resulting liquidity was redeployed by Power in the communications industry to acquire a significant position in Southam Inc. of Toronto and an interest in Time Warner Inc. of New York.

Power Corporation has a valued, long-standing business relationship with China International Trust and Investment Corporation and with other entities in the People's Republic of China. In 1986, Power and CITIC co-invested in a British Columbia pulp mill. Recently, Power has developed interests in China in real estate development, electric power generation, gold mining — in partnership with American Barrick Inc. — and transportation.

For seventy years, Power Corporation has been a major contributor to the development of Canada and has established an important Canadian presence in the United States, Europe, and Asia.

THE ROYAL BANK story begins in 1869, a signal year in the annals of human progress. It was a time when our forebears were laying the foundations of the modern world with new ideas, new inventions and new enterprises.

In Halifax, the founders of the bank got their charter in the name of the Merchants Bank of Halifax. It had evolved out of the "upstart" unincorporated Merchants Bank, which had opened in 1864 as a private partnership offering short-term credit to traders in the bustling international port. Its seven promoters included a member of the Cunard family whose graceful new steamships originated there.

The vessels of Cunard and other lines opened up frontiers for the young bank east across the Atlantic and deep into the Caribbean. To the west, the emerging railways

Royal Bank of Canada

Serving Canadians Since 1869

Vancouver Branch: Circa 1910

Lobby, 360 Rue St. Jacques, Montreal

rapidly opened the seemingly endless frontiers of the new nation called Canada.

Almost from day one, the bank struck out boldly, and sometimes at great risk, into the hinterland, to beat the competition in pursuing opportunities along the arteries of developing trade. Its daring vault across the continent to British Columbia as the century closed is an example of this powerful drive to develop new areas.

In this spirit of reaching for new horizons, in 1907, chief executive Edson Pease, the visionary titan of Royal

Bank's history, orchestrated the move of the bank's head office from Halifax to Montreal's bustling Rue St. Jacques, then Canada's undisputed financial capital.

By 1910 the bank had conquered many geographical frontiers. It had grown with Canada into a national institution, the Royal Bank of Canada. It had branches from coast to coast and was starting to build a foreign reach that would give it global distinction.

What lay ahead was a different frontier — a frontier opened by the necessary restructuring of the Canadian banking system. While many banks were unequal to this task, Royal Bank was a winner. Through a series of insightful mergers, culminating with the Union Bank of Canada in 1925, it became the industry leader. This strategy of building its business is still firmly in place. Most recently, the acquisitions of Dominion Securities and Royal Trust have added enormous strength to the Royal Bank group by expanding and diversifying its reach and revenue at home and abroad.

To have prospered, and to have been Canada's leading financial institution for so long, is quite an achievement. But the challenge that lies ahead, says Royal Bank Chairman and CEO Allan Taylor, is to maintain this envied status as the bank reaches for new frontiers.

As Dr. Duncan McDowell says in his recent history of the Royal Bank called *Quick to the Frontier*, if there are heroes in the chronicles of Royal Bank, they are the men and women who mastered the art of what one turn-of-the-century banker called "cautionary boldness." It is a quality that has long been a hallmark of Royal Bank people and one that will serve the bank well as it prepares for the 21st Century.

Interforest Ltd.

Canada's Pre-eminent Producer of Hardwood Veneer and Lumber

Karl Heinz Danzer, Chairman

WOOD is so much a part of the products that shape our homes, offices, furnishings, and architectural styles. Those who desire fine veneers in the design and manufacture of furniture, panelling, cabinetry, or decorative woods look to Interforest Ltd. and its U.S. subsidiaries.

Durham — in the heartland of Ontario's agricultural and woodworking country — is home to Interforest Ltd., one of North America's largest producers and marketers of veneers. The peaceful rural setting belies the fact that customers from around the world come to Durham to inspect and purchase some of the choicest veneers available anywhere on the continent.

It is not by chance that Interforest settled in Canada in the early 1970s. The Danzer Group saw great potential in establishing a base in North America — in a sub-continent with vast natural resources and a venerable history in forestry. Based in Reutlingen, Germany, the Group is headed by Karl Heinz Danzer, the chairman and son of the company's founder.

The Group strongly adheres to a multi-domestic approach of conducting business. That means Interforest and other Danzer companies have a great deal of local autonomy in the way they manage their businesses and market their products. Corporate independence helps drive each company and contributes to the worldwide organization's growth and success.

Interforest is an integral part of the Danzer Group that now operates 11 veneer plants on three continents and also has worldwide lumber interests.

The company has grown dramatically and expanded rapidly over the last two decades. It currently exports to customers in 35 countries. From its ambitious start in 1973, Interforest employs 400 people in Canada and 200 in the United States. From modest revenues of about $6 million in 1976, the company earned in excess of $100 million in consolidated sales for 1993.

Southwestern Ontario has traditionally been one of Canada's most important centres for the woodworking and furniture industries. It also made good sense to take advantage of local traditions, skills, and facilities. To establish its North American base for veneer production, the Danzer Group entered into a two-year partnership with Abitibi-Price Ltd. to purchase an existing mill. In 1975, Danzer took over the entire operation that became headquarters for Interforest.

The challenge was to transform an industrious but local plant into a worldwide operation capable of turning out the fine veneers demanded by customers in the furniture and woodworking industries.

To accomplish its goals, Interforest would invest in quality — starting with buying the best hardwood logs available and introducing production

Sliced veneer set up in log form

processes designed to turn out veneers for the most discriminating customers.

The final arbiters in the selection of Interforest's products are its customers. They include furniture, door and plywood manufacturers; veneer resellers; splicing plants; and architectural millworks.

Visitors to Interforest's showrooms will often see the dynamic interaction that takes place between global customers who carefully scrutinize the veneers on display and the company's sales representatives. Purchases could be a modest buy of 100 square meters by a domestic furniture manufacturer or up to one half million square meters for an European customer. To meet customer requirements, the company also produces a range of thicknesses — from 0.2 to 2.5 millimetres.

Transforming logs into fine veneers is both a science and an art, using new technologies and a skilled workforce. But the whole process starts with the logs.

Interforest's buyers shop North America for the finest hardwood logs: red and white oaks, cherry, ash, maple, and walnut. In total, the company maintains a constant inventory of about 10,000 logs to ensure it can meet all customer requirements. Interforest also stocks large quantities of imported veneers to fulfil any demand.

Product quality and reliability extend to the company's lumber business. Interforest buys only the choicest lumber that it kiln dries, grades and distributes to markets around the world. The distinctive "brown bear" logo assures customers they are buying the best lumber available.

Durham is an immaculate operation that has set the highest of standards in veneer production, using the latest technology and equipment. It is also headquarters for Interforest's diverse interests in Canada and the United States.

In the Montreal region, Boucherville, Quebec, is the eastern veneer distribution facility and the company's Canadian centre for hardwood lumber sales. Here, lumber is kiln-dried, graded and exported to world markets. Another strategic location for the company's lumber interests is Shade Gap, Pennsylvania. Customers recognize Shade Gap as a main source for quality hardwood logs and lumber drawn from Pennslyvania's abundant woodlands.

Customers throughout the United States eastern seaboard rely on Interforest's operation in Greensboro, North Carolina. This location has established its reputation as a full-service veneer distribution centre for the company. In Newburg, New York, major office furniture manufacturers and decorative woodworking companies shop for choice veneers at the company's showroom and sales centre.

The company also owns Penn Beaver Veneer Corporation, an established manufacturer of sliced hardwood veneers in Darlington, Pennsylvania.

Interforest's values derive from a strong sense of ethics that emphasize the company's responsibility and commitment to customers, employees, and the environment. The company regards wood as one of the world's most precious, renewable resources that must be protected.

The partnership between people and technology ensures Interforest and Penn Beaver make the most of a hardwood log. One average veneer log yields enough to manufacture 25 desks or 25 cabinets.

Responsibility means nothing goes to waste. Large pieces left over from a log may be sold to woodworking companies. As for the remainder, Interforest and Penn Beaver recycle waste pieces as fuel to create steam for the Durham and Darlington plants.

Commitment to product quality, business integrity, customer service, employees, and conservation of a renewable resource creates responsibilities that Interforest has fully honoured since its inception in 1973. Such principles have assured this leading veneer producer of an excellent reputation among customers, employees, business associates, suppliers and the communities supported by Interforest Ltd.

Ford Canada

90 Model Years in Canada

The 1995 Windstar

FORD Motor Company of Canada, Limited, with headquarters in Oakville, Ontario, is the longest-established automobile company in Canada, producing a full line of quality cars and trucks.

Ford Motor Company was started in Detroit, Michigan, in 1903. A year later, in 1904, the Canadian automobile industry was established by a group of young Canadian entrepreneurs who founded Ford of Canada in what is now Windsor, Ontario. Gordon McGregor, the 31-year-old general manager, had just 17 employees in that first year.

The company is still a subsidiary of Ford Motor Company in Dearborn, Michigan, although its shares are traded on the Toronto Stock Exchange. Ford of Canada is a Canadian public corporation. Wholly-owned subsidiaries of Ford of Canada include operations in Australia and New Zealand.

Ford is in the process of investing more than two billion dollars in Canada by 1995. More than one billion dollars was spent at the Oakville Assembly plant in Ontario to re-tool and re-equip the plant as the sole source for a new multi-purpose mini-van, the Windstar, which competes in the fastest-growing segment of the North American automobile market. An additional

$400 million will be spent to expand the Ontario Truck Plant in Oakville by 44 percent.

In addition, in Windsor, Ontario, Ford is spending an additional one billion dollars to rebuild and equip Windsor Engine Plant Two, closed in December, 1990, to produce a new family of truck engines beginning in 1995. These investments, the largest in Ford of Canada's 90-year history, are providing Ford with the technologically-advanced, world-mandate products that will strengthen Ford of Canada's competitive position through the 1990s and into the next century.

As a result of such a vote of confidence in the Canadian work force, Ford of Canada believes it can provide stability of employment at its Canadian plants, even at a time when the global automobile industry is undergoing major restructuring.

Ford of Canada employs over 13,000 people. The company has its national parts distribution centre in Brampton, Ontario, with five other distribution centres and six regional sales offices across the country.

Ford of Canada is investing more than $3 billion at its plants in Oakville and Windsor, Ont. This is an aerial view of its plants in Oakville, with a new paint facility in the foreground

There are 650 automotive dealers in Canada who sell Ford, Lincoln and Mercury cars and Ford trucks.

Ford assembles cars and trucks at two plants in Oakville and one in St. Thomas, Ontario. The Oakville Assembly Plant produces the new Windstar minivan;

The 1994 Ford Mustang

the Ontario Truck Plant, also in Oakville, builds F-series pickups — the most popular vehicle, car or truck in North America. Another car plant in St. Thomas, Ontario, produces the Ford Crown Victoria and Mercury Grand Marquis — voted the "Best Vehicle Built in Canada" in 1992.

In Windsor, Ontario, Ford produces engines at the Essex Engine plant, aluminum engine parts at the Essex Aluminum plant and Windsor Aluminum Plant and iron castings at the Windsor Casting plant.

Affiliated Canadian companies of Ford of Canada include: Ensite Limited, which is a partner with the company in the Essex plants and operates an engine plant in Windsor producing engines and engine parts; Ford Credit Canada Limited which provides retail and wholesale financing to Ford automotive dealers; Ford Electronics Manufacturing Corporation which produces automotive electric components in Markham, Ontario.

Ford of Canada believes its commitment to Canada and

Canadians extends beyond economics or products. In Canada and the United States, Ford has conducted research on alternative fuel vehicles for more than 20 years and is now the recognized leader in testing those vehicles on roads throughout North America. Ford's alternative-fuel research effort has included methanol, ethanol, compressed natural gas, liquefied petroleum gas and electric vehicles.

Alternative fuels are fuels other than conventional gasoline and diesel fuel. Different approaches include the replacement of a significant portion or all of the conventional fuel used by a vehicle with gaseous fuels, electricity, or some other liquid such as alcohol (e.g. methanol or ethanol).

Ingenuity, entrepreneurship, enthusiasm and plain hard work, the blend of human traits upon which the company was founded, are as evident at Ford of Canada today as they were in 1904, when those seventeen employees in Windsor set out to build a better motorcar and, in the process, changed the world. Their resourcefulness lives on today in a company whose goal is stated in simple terms: To be a low-cost producer of the highest-quality products and services that offer the customers the best value.

Ford of Canada believes the future holds great promise for the company and for Canada as well. Ford Canada's mission is to better meet the needs of the customers by continually improving products and services. Ford believes that these values have been and will continue to be instrumental in achieving corporate success. The people and the quality of the products are first priorities at Ford, and customers are the main focus.

The Ford Ecostar Electric Vehicle

AMJ Campbell Van Lines

1977 IS A YEAR ETCHED in the memory of Thomas (Tim) C. Moore, now president and COO of AMJ Campbell Van Lines, Canada's largest, most successful moving company. It was the year that the young teacher walked away from the security of a teaching career to try and turn a small part-time business into a major corporation.

He purchased a 50-year-old local moving company with three trucks and $250,000 in business.

Like all true entrepreneurs Moore put all of his energy and effort into building his little company. The company was innovative and market driven. It concentrated on providing service not previously seen in this industry. The customer was "king." Moore aggressively recruited the best people to work in his ever-growing empire. Sales people, managers, drivers, packers — everyone was the cream of the crop. Not all came from inside the industry, particularly in the managerial ranks, but all were achievers, hard workers, entrepreneurs, and people with vision.

AMJ Campbell brought a new professionalism to the industry. Drivers and packers were placed on contract and were made accountable for their performance. A system of penalties and rewards was put into place. Employees at all levels could purchase shares.

Marketing efforts concentrated on the burgeoning corporate sector. In the late 1970s and early 1980s, corporations were moving thousands of employees across Canada. AMJ Campbell positioned itself as the expert in this area, designing special programs to assist employee relocations. AMJ was the first company to offer seminars to relocating employees.

As a member of North American Van Lines, AMJ was thwarted in its efforts to expand. Moore consequently affiliated his company with Atlas Van Lines when his contract with North American expired. Such a change was risky but AMJ Campbell clients were so loyal to the organization that the transition was made without loss of any customer base.

The company understood the importance of Value Added Benefits. Forming strategic partnerships with the likes of Canadian Airlines and Swiss Chalet, AMJ Campbell earned endorsements from such reputable organizations as the Ontario Medical Association and Canadian Olympic Association. AMJ has been the official mover of the Canadian Olympic team since 1984.

By 1986 the company had grown to 29 offices. A few of the smaller centres had been franchised. The company was now ready to diversify into other areas such as office moving, trade shows and displays.

In 1988, 70 percent of the company was sold to an investment group comprised of major business leaders. In 1989, AMJ purchased a key competitor making the company fully national with 35 offices from coast to coast.

Quick to forecast the downturn in the economy, AMJ Campbell moved to reduce overhead, eliminate inefficiencies and to franchise additional branch operations. By 1992 the parent company, CamVec Corporation, took the company public on the Toronto Stock Exchange. The strength of the partnerships, relationships and sensible management has made AMJ Campbell a financially stable company, open to new opportunities and yet true to its tradition of superior customer service.

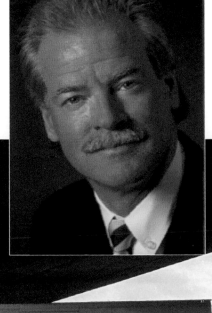

Tim Moore, president & COO of AMJ Campbell Van Lines, recruited only the "cream of the crop" to provide its customers with a level of service not previously seen in the moving industry

AMJ Campbell is Canada's largest moving company, and Atlas Van Lines' largest agent, with 36 offices coast-to-coast

Atlas Van Lines

World-Class Moving.

AMJ CAMPBELL VAN LINES

Eli Lilly Canada Inc. *Prescription For Quality*

IN a University of Toronto research laboratory, in 1922, two Canadian scientists made a discovery that changed medical science. And Eli Lilly and Company was there. Over the next several years, Lilly worked with Drs. Banting and Best to bring the life-saving miracle of insulin to the world. It was Lilly's first involvement with Canadian health care, but it provided only the merest hint of a bright future of innovation and excellence.

For over half a century now, Eli Lilly Canada has been a leader in Canadian health care. From the establishment of its first small operation, in 1938, Lilly Canada has been committed to turning research into medicine. Today it is one of the top research-based pharmaceutical companies in the country, producing prescription medicines for Canadians from its Scarborough, Ontario, facility.

Eli Lilly and Co. worked with Banting and Best to bring the miracle of insulin to the world

Each decade has brought new growth and innovation to Lilly. The 1950s saw the introduction of Salk Poliomyelitis, the first commercially available polio vaccine. In the 1960s, Lilly launched the first in a new class of antibiotics, called cephalosporins. During that same period, the company expanded into the sphere of veterinary medicine, with the Elanco Animal Health division. The diversification continued into the 1970s, as Lilly entered the medical devices and diagnostics field.

In the 1980s, Eli Lilly Canada moved to the forefront of the Canadian pharmaceutical industry, with the launches of several key products. These included human insulin, the world's first product of recombinant DNA, along with advanced antibiotics, and innovative new treatments for growth deficiency, ulcers and depression. And to ensure that the future holds just as much promise, scientists at the Lilly Analytical Research Laboratory continue to evaluate and test new medicines, seeking cures to infectious diseases, cancer, cardiovascular conditions, central nervous system disorders and endocrine diseases.

As an industry leader, Lilly has always been committed to turning out products of the highest quality

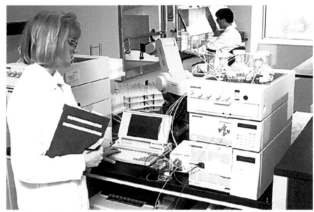

Today's Eli Lilly Canada is built upon its skilled employees, innovation, and advanced technology

and focusing on customer satisfaction. That approach to business was recognized in early 1993 when Eli Lilly Canada was cited as having achieved the criteria for "Class A" Manufacturing status, a level of excellence attained by fewer than two percent of North American companies. Moreover, since quality improvement must be ongoing, in 1993 Lilly also launched its Prescription for Quality process, designed to streamline the work of every employee and enhance the satisfaction of every customer.

Eli Lilly Canada recognizes that business has both an opportunity and a responsibility to be a constructive force within the community. The company is proud of its long commitment to good corporate citizenship, and its support of a number of local and national charitable initiatives.

For five years in a row, Lilly has received the United Way Platinum Award for achieving over 90 percent employee participation in the annual fundraising campaign. The company provides significant assistance to the Children's Aid Society, and Junior Achievement, and funds scholarships and co-op placements with Centennial College in Scarborough. Furthermore, Eli Lilly Canada is proud to sponsor several fellowships in medical science, and to provide funding for a number of Canadian researchers and research institutions.

A leader in business, and a leader in the community, Lilly is built upon a rare and special combination of committed employees, innovation, and state of the art technology. With lessons learned over its half-century history, Eli Lilly Canada is taking ever-greater strides in the effort to turn science into solutions.

Kraft General Foods Canada Inc.

A Tradition of Innovation

KRAFT GENERAL FOODS CANADA INC. came into being in 1989 when Philip Morris Companies Inc. bought Kraft Limited and amalgamated it with General Foods Inc., which it had acquired in 1985. The history of this relatively new company is rich and proud — one that brings together the legacies of two great food companies, globally recognized for their continual innovation in new product development, food technology, manufacturing processes, marketing programs and consumer response. Canadians have known Kraft General Foods products all their lives. They grew up eating JELL-O, KRAFT DINNER, MIRACLE WHIP, and CRACKER BARREL Cheese, and drinking MAXWELL HOUSE coffee, SANKA, TANG and KOOL-AID. Brand names like these which have earned consumer loyalty over a lifetime, have literally become household words.

Paddy and the J.L. Kraft wagon

When James Lewis Kraft was born in 1875 in Stevensville, Ontario, near Fort Erie, one did not anticipate that he would drastically change the manufacture of cheese. The second of eleven children, he helped on his father's dairy farm. By 1903 he had entered the wholesale cheese business in Chicago with $65.00 in capital. With a rented wagon and a horse named Paddy, Mr. Kraft bought cheeses daily from Chicago's warehouse district and resold them to local merchants. While his business prospered, he expanded it to include manufacturing.

However, Mr. Kraft never lost track of his main objective — to make cheese a more dependable and more marketable commodity that would keep better, cook better and could be packaged without waste and sold in convenient sizes. His determination was finally rewarded when, in 1916, Kraft was granted a patent for what became known as process cheese.

In 1920, Kraft entered the Canadian market by purchasing MacLaren's Imperial Cheese Co. Ltd. It began selling in Canada, on a national scale, process cheese in tins as well as loaves. One year later a factory

"La Belle Chocolatière" is one of Kraft General Foods oldest trademark symbols. She first appeared in BAKER'S advertising in the late 1800s and she is still on the package of the nation's leading baking chocolate

was opened in downtown Montreal. The Canadian company proceeded to open operations in Britain and Germany.

During the 1920s, Mr. Kraft also hired a home economist and opened the celebrated Kraft Kitchens. Two new products that continue to be true success stories within the grocery industry were introduced during the depression: MIRACLE WHIP salad dressing was launched in 1933 as an economic alternative to mayonnaise; KRAFT DINNER macaroni and cheese followed in 1937.

Like Kraft, the roots of General Foods run deep. They spring from many small businesses. Each was started by a food industry pioneer who worked with a passion to bring a better food or beverage to market. Those original risk-takers and entrepreneurs include:

Joel Cheek, who spent years developing a superior blend of coffee which made the MAXWELL HOUSE hotel in Nashville a landmark. "It is good to the last drop!" is how President Theodore Roosevelt described MAXWELL HOUSE coffee when visiting Nashville in 1907;

C.W. Post, founder of General Foods

Inventor Charles William Post, who, in 1895, paid $68.76 for second-hand equipment that he set up in a barn and produced a coffee substitute called POSTUM. Two years later he introduced POST GRAPE-NUTS cereal, one of the world's first pre-cooked breakfast cereals;

Food processor Orator Francis Woodward, who bought a gelatin business in 1897 for $450.00, improved the product and the package and worked hard to build a market which, ten years later, would make JELL-O jelly powder North America's most famous dessert with annual sales of $1 million;

German coffee merchant Dr. Ludwig Roselius, who, in 1903, gave a shipment of green coffee ruined by seawater, to his research lab. The brine-soaked beans led to discovering a way to remove caffeine. Roselius introduced his new coffee in France calling it SANKA because it was "sans caffeine";

Edwin Perkins, who had a problem with his mail-order business shipping "Fruit Smack," a bottled syrup. Glass containers were difficult and costly to mail. So he dehydrated the drink and sold it in paper packets and renamed it KOOL-AID.

In Canada the first General Foods company was Walter Baker Limited. A sales office opened in Montreal during the 1880s and in 1911 a chocolate mill was built there producing BAKER'S products. POST cereals were sold in Canada by 1903 and processed in Windsor, Ontario, after 1908 as a branch of the Postum Company. JELL-O jelly powder was made at Fort Erie from 1906. In 1919 the Douglas Pectin Co. of Fairport, New York, took over a steel plant in Cobourg, Ontario, and made it the first pectin plant in the British Empire to manufacture CERTO.

However, not until 1929 did a company called General Foods emerge as an important new force in the food industry. It was the result of a bold series of acquisitions by the Postum Corporation, the business started by Charles William Post. General Foods Sales Company Limited was formed in Canada in 1939.

The momentum for product innovation, inspired by the founders of Kraft and General Foods, continued after World War II. Both companies grew rapidly. The frontiers of processed food manufacturing were extended to include packaged dinners and entrees, calorie-reduced and fat-free salad dressings, sugar-free, light, and cholesterol-free products that have changed and enhanced the way Canadians eat.

Since the amalgamation of both companies in 1989, Kraft General Foods Canada Inc. has continued to grow through acquisition. Today, with its head office in Toronto and operations overseen from Montreal, Kraft General Foods Canada has a workforce of 4,500 employees across the country. With over 1,000 products, it is one of Canada's largest manufacturers and distributors of processed food products.

Just as the legacies of the founding fathers that came to make up Kraft General Foods have nourished and nurtured generations, Kraft General Foods Canada is committed more than ever to upholding their traditions with quality products representing exceptional value and continuing to meet the needs of consumers with "good food, good food ideas."

IN 1906 Ontario Premier Sir Joseph P. Whitney heeded the call from business, industry and citizens for public power and created the Ontario Hydro-Electric Commission with former London mayor Adam Beck as its chairman. In those days Hydro was solely a distribution system, purchasing power from its municipal partners. Its first power station was built on the Severn River in 1914.

Over the next four decades Hydro developed the Queenston-Chippawa project on the Niagara River (later named Sir Adam Beck Niagara Generating Station No. 1), Beck 2, the St. Lawrence Power Project

Ontario Hydro

The mission of Ontario Hydro is to help Ontario become the most energy efficient and competitive economy in the world and a leading example of sustainable development

and numerous other hydraulic power stations throughout the province. By the end of the 1950s, Hydro turned to coal-fired thermal stations to meet the continually expanding demand for electricity. Since 1971, when the first Pickering reactor came into service, nuclear plants have become the workhorses of the system.

For most of this century Hydro has been one of the foundations of the Ontario economy, providing reliable, low cost electricity to the province. As we prepare for the next century, the new challenges of a rapidly changing world confront both the province and the utility.

1992 marked the beginning of a new era for Ontario

Hydro. The corporation had already created an Environment Division and set itself a corporate goal of being in the vanguard of environmental protection. It had embarked on an extensive energy efficiency program. And it had established an Aboriginal and Northern Affairs Branch to address long-standing issues.

But these improvements had been grafted onto a corporate structure whose foundation was laid in a less complicated, more predictable and distant past. The corporation is being fundamentally re-fashioned to meet the dramatically different needs of the 21st century: to make it more business-like, more open, more flexible, more sensitive to customer expectations and more competitive.

As an energy service company Ontario Hydro is expanding and diversifying programs to help customers in all sectors get more value for their energy dollar. Ontario Hydro is building new partnerships with industry, government and customers to help Ontario benefit from energy efficiency and renewable technologies. Hydro is also committed to helping Ontario become a world leader in energy efficiency, competitiveness and sustainable development.

In June 1992, the United Nations Earth Summit in Rio de Janeiro produced a historic international accord called Agenda 21 — an action plan that recognises the right of human beings and nations to pursue economic development while respecting the environmental needs of present and future generations. It is a blueprint for sustainable development.

The challenge the Earth Summit set before the world is to transform Agenda 21 into reality in the years and century ahead. If future generations are to have opportunity and fulfilment, it is the responsibility of organizations like Ontario Hydro to lead the way by becoming models of efficiency and environmental preservation to the world.

The people of Ontario Hydro accept that challenge.

Babcock & Wilcox

BASED in Cambridge, Ontario, Babcock & Wilcox (B&W) is Canada's largest supplier of steam generation products and services. Steam generators, or boilers, use heat to convert water into steam, primarily for electric power generation and industrial process heating.

Babcock & Wilcox designs and manufactures steam generators for a wide range of applications for electric power generation and industry. In addition to boilers

A Firetube boiler on its way from the Goldie & McCulloch Company to Thessalon Pulp and Paper Company in Thessalon, Ontario, on September 18, 1901

This 1991 nuclear steam generator, bound for Northeast Utilities in Waterford, Connecticut, shows significant advances in technology and transportation methods

that run on conventional fuels such as coal, oil and gas, Babcock & Wilcox also specializes in nuclear steam generators. They supplied a unit for Ontario's first nuclear power facility in the 1950s, and have since manufactured the steam generators for every nuclear power plant in Canada and many more worldwide.

Babcock & Wilcox is extremely proud of its Canadian heritage. The company's roots in Canada reach back to 1844, when the Dumfries Foundry was established in what is now Cambridge, Ontario. Fifteen years later two employees, John Goldie and Hugh McCulloch, purchased the foundry, and in 1891 they incorporated and began to attract interest internationally. An 1889 newspaper article in the Babcock & Wilcox archives notes Goldie & McCulloch's expanding international portfolio:

> The Goldie & McCulloch Co. have just been given an order for $4,000 worth of machinery by a company doing business in the city of Mexico. The Goldie & McCulloch Co. have frequently made small shipments of machinery to Mexico, but this will be the largest consignment of all. They are to be congratulated on their expanding reputation. (*The Galt Reporter*, Aug. 3, 1889)

This expanding reputation attracted the interest of Babcock & Wilcox of New York, who were impressed with Goldie & McCulloch's international business experience and high-quality manufacturing expertise. In 1923 Goldie & McCulloch amalgamated with Babcock & Wilcox Limited of New York and London and became Babcock-Wilcox & Goldie-McCulloch Limited. Although the Goldie and McCulloch families no longer hold interests in Babcock & Wilcox, many local Cambridge residents still fondly refer to the company as "Goldie's."

Babcock & Wilcox's corporate achievement has much to do with their business strength internationally, a strength which has remained since the days of Goldie & McCulloch. In fact, the Canadian operation was given the responsibility for all international sales and service for the entire Babcock & Wilcox organization in 1982 because of their international success. Since then, the International Division of Babcock & Wilcox has sold to more than 35 countries and has established joint venture companies in Indonesia, China, India, Turkey and Mexico. Babcock & Wilcox was also one of the first two-time recipients of the Canada Export Award.

Long-standing Canadian ties and a strong international business base combine to make Babcock & Wilcox a true Canadian corporate achiever.

SINCE 1981, when CIBA Vision Canada Inc. was founded to serve the Canadian eye-care market, the company has grown to become a world leader, and Canada's leading manufacturer of contact lenses and lens-care solutions. CIBA Vision Canada reached market leadership in its optics business in only seven years. Since 1991, the company has been making rapid progress toward leadership in eye medicines.

For CIBA Vision, market leadership has always been a key goal, but a goal to be attained through leadership in areas such as research and development, environmentally responsible manufacturing, advanced information systems and logistics, product support —

CIBA Vision

Looking to the World

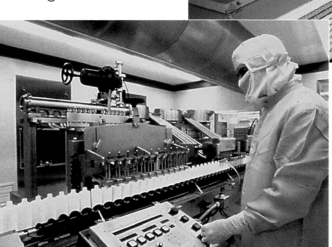

It was this pursuit of total quality which led CIBA Vision, in 1987, to purchase one of its prime suppliers, already a world leader in sterile manufacturing.

Sterile Pharmaceuticals Ltd. had built its own leadership in sterile manufacturing into an international success story. Founded in 1968 as a contract manufacturer of glass vials, ampoules, and injectables for the pharmaceuticals industry, the company pursued technical leadership from the outset.

Sterile manufacturing involves making and packaging products in an aseptic environment — the alliance of myriad technologies, immense training and human skill to pursue absolute purity in a manufacturing process. It is a high-risk, high-tech business in which microbiologists wage constant war against contamination of any kind, but no CIBA Vision product has ever been recalled. In 1993 CIBA Vision Sterile Manufacturing achieved registration to the ISO 9002 international quality standard.

Not content with leadership, CIBA Vision Sterile Manufacturing has always invested heavily in research and development to create ever more advanced processes. It has extended its leadership with unique achievements like aseptic blow-molding of plastic bottles and ampoules.

Such innovation depends

CIBA Vision leads the industry in customer satisfaction — staff are the key to this success

CIBA Vision staff work with state-of-the art "clean room" technology to ensure products remain pure throughout the manufacturing process

the systematic pursuit of total quality through team building.

CIBA Vision has always focused on providing real value and support to the eye-care professionals who are its clients. Advanced robotics and sophisticated telecommunications and computer systems have enabled CIBA Vision teams to provide just-in-time processing and 24-hour delivery of orders to major Canadian cities (same-day in the Toronto vicinity). CIBA Vision also supports the broadest range of contact lens products in the industry — over 250,000 different lens products and parameters — and the most common in stock, ready to be shipped. These are just some of the reasons why CIBA Vision continues to lead the eye care industry in customer satisfaction.

on the teamwork of skilled people working within the stringent constraints of the pharmaceuticals industry.

CIBA Vision Sterile Manufacturing occupies a 140,000 square foot manufacturing facility in Streetsville, and has grown from a staff of only seven, in 1975, to a still-lean 210 at present. As CIBA Vision sets new goals for continued leadership in the Canadian marketplace, the company keeps moving toward leadership in international markets, also. Already 90 percent of CIBA Vision's products are manufactured for markets around the world. With both capacity and skills to spare, CIBA Vision is looking out from Canada to the world, a Canadian success story.

Ashland Chemical Canada Ltd.

The Ashland Chemical plant is situated in Mississauga, Ontario

ASHLAND CHEMICAL is a specialty chemical company which manufactures and markets chemicals for Canadian industry and global export. Manufacturing and distribution facilities are located in Mississauga, Ontario, and Boucherville, Quebec.

Early operations date to the 1930s, through a chemical manufacturing plant originally built for processing vegetable oils, and a chemical and solvent distribution facility, both located in Toronto. These were replaced in 1975 with a modern chemical complex now located on a 34-acre site in Mississauga, Ontario. The manufacturing operation produces a wide variety of polymers, resins, and chemicals to serve ever-increasing national and worldwide markets. Ashland Chemical produces alkyd and latex resins for paint and coatings customers, polyester resin for fabricated plastics manufacturers, and sand binding polymers and chemicals for foundries.

Ashland's distribution divisions consist of several facilities including blending and bulk storage complexes – opened in 1981 in Mississauga and, in 1983, in Boucherville – supplying customers with industrial chemicals and solvents. In 1988, specialty chemicals for the pharmaceutical, cosmetic, and food industries were added and the General Polymer division also began distributing thermoplastic resins. Both these groups serve customers through separate distribution facilities in Mississauga and Boucherville.

Local research and development capabilities enable Ashland to develop products for specific Canadian customer needs through access to worldwide technology from associated companies.

Quality and consistency of product performance are the outstanding features of Ashland's reliable products, earning the company numerous product quality accreditations since the early 1980s. Today, continuous improvement has become the driving force behind Quality Plus, Ashland's commitment to quality and productivity. ISO-9002 certification for Ashland's manufacturing facilities ensures worldwide recognition of the company's quality standards.

Ashland's concern for environmental issues is reflected in commitment to the industry's Responsible Care process. A modern incinerator eliminates odours and the need to transport hazardous waste through the community. It also provides energy from waste to power the plant, decreasing energy consumption and CO_2 emissions. Emergency preparedness is part of Ashland's product stewardship responsibility. Waste reduction achievements have won community recognition through the Region of Peel's Waste Reduction Award.

A safe operation is essential for the well-being of Ashland's employees and part of the Total Quality Management process. Ashland's manufacturing facility has achieved 12 years without lost time injury, a truly world-class performance.

People are the key to Ashland's success. It is an organization of approximately 140 employees with a common goal of pursuing excellence in product and service to all inside and outside customers. Innovation is an essential part of the company's culture, technology, and products. Computers are a normal tool used by every employee. Productivity, quality improvement, waste reduction and emission controls are all dependant on the innovations of employees to ensure the continuous improvement required to lead the industry.

Ashland's employees view the future with confidence. Their skills, pride, dedication to the pursuit of excellence in product and service, along with modern operations, serve Ashland's customers now and in the future.

S.C. Johnson & Son, Limited

THE beginnings of S.C. Johnson & Son Limited, familiarly known as Johnson's Wax, were modest. In 1882, when Sam Johnson came to Racine, Wisconsin, to accept a position as a salesman for the Racine Hardware Company, his job was to sell parquet flooring manufactured by his firm. Four years later, Sam Johnson, at the age of 53, bought the flooring business from the hardware firm and with a workforce of two men and two boys he founded the company that bears his name today. Five days a week, Sam Johnson toured the countryside in his buggy selling flooring to contractors for fine homes, churches, hotels and public buildings. After the first year's operation, his ledger showed gross earnings of $3,148.27 and a net profit of $268.27. Under an account headed "Tithes" were his gifts to religious organizations that equalled a tenth of his income, a practice he followed throughout his life.

Original can of Johnson's Paste Wax

In the ensuing years, the entries in the ledger became larger and sales to customers as far west as Colorado, east to New England and south as far as Mississippi were recorded. In 1888 a new name appeared on the payroll account, that of Herbert F. Johnson who joined the company at the age of 20 at a salary of $40.00 per month.

Customers who had purchased Johnson flooring began to write asking for the best way to take care of their new floors. Sensing an opportunity to provide an additional service to his customers and to diversify his business, Mr. Johnson experimented with preparations of paste wax and soon cans of Johnson's Prepared Paste Wax were being sent along with each new floor he sold and were being advertised in the national periodicals of the day. A new industry had been launched.

By 1898, the income from the sale of wax, wood fillers and finishes exceeded that from flooring. The words "Johnson's Wax" were already becoming established as household words.

During the early 1900s the company flourished, new buildings were added to the facility in Racine and by 1910 the payroll grew to 92 people. In 1914, the first subsidiary was established in England followed by the establishment of an Australian subsidiary. In 1920, S.C. Johnson and Son, Limited was established in Canada.

This occurred when Herbert F. Johnson, then president of the company, set out by train to Toronto from Chicago to scout a location for the Canadian manufacturing facility. Coincidentally the Mayor of Brantford was also travelling on the same train. The two gentlemen met in the bar car and the Mayor convinced Mr. Johnson that the ideal location for his new factory was Brantford. Mr. Johnson never reached Toronto.

The Canadian operation started with 12 employees and manufactured four floor care products. Through aggressive research and product development, a firm understanding of consumer needs, a commitment to marketing investment and a close partnership with their customers, S.C. Johnson's

People have trusted the PLEDGE line of wood care products since 1959

Samuel Curtis Johnson

Herbert F. Johnson Sr.

Herbert F. Johnson

Samuel C. Johnson

product base has grown to include some 400 products for both consumer and industrial markets. Today, the company manufactures and markets some of Canada's best known household products such as PLEDGE, SHOUT, EDGE, RAID, OFF!, WINDEX and GLADE.

Throughout its 74-year history in Canada, the company has sought opportunities and innovations that have helped keep its products in the forefront of the marketplace. One such initiative was announced in December of 1992 when the Brantford headquarters assumed manufacturing responsibilities for a number of large volume specialty products including SHOUT Stick, GLADE Carpet and Room Deodorizer and SKIN-TASTIC Lotion tubes for the entire North American marketplace. This single move is expected to triple the company's forecasted factory volume.

S.C. Johnson is still a family-owned and family-run company. Mr. Samuel Johnson, the company's chairman, is the fourth generation of the Johnson family to run the company and his four children are all active in the business. This long history of family ownership has created a strong continuity of business philosophy

within the corporation. The company has long been committed to helping protect the environment while successfully manufacturing and marketing its products. S.C. Johnson's contributions to the global environment demonstrates that their commitment goes beyond rhetoric to action and results.

In 1935, the then president, H.F. Johnson Jr., flew to the Brazilian rain forest with a team of scientists to determine the ecological impact of harvesting Carnuba palm leaves for use in their wax products. To his relief, he discovered that the harvesting had a harmless effect on the rain forest. This expedition set the example that S.C. Johnson employees have followed ever since. Perhaps most notably, that tradition was demonstrated in 1975 when S.C. Johnson independently and voluntarily removed chloroflurocarbons (CFC's) from all of their aerosol products, a full 12 years before legislation.

S.C. Johnson has an exemplary reputation for being committed to the environment both locally and globally. In August 1991, the company was presented with the Ontario Lieutenant Governor's Conservation Award and in May of 1992 was the recipient of Environment Canada's Corporate Environmental Achievement Award.

The company and its employees, not content to rest on their laurels, have established specific and aggressive goals for further reducing their impact on the environment and will continue to play an important part in the growth of Brantford as well as the Canadian community at large.

GLADE continues as Canada's favourite household air freshener brand

Country style unveiled their award winning new store design during the summer of 1993

Country Style Donuts

IN March of 1963, the first Country Style Donuts store opened in the heart of Toronto. The concept was surprisingly simple: offer the customer a freshly brewed cup of premium coffee along with a large selection of donuts baked fresh daily; keep the store spotless at all times and provide fast and friendly service 24 hours a day, seven days a week. It was exactly what Toronto was looking for in the early '60s.

However, customers' needs have changed over the years, and their expectations for a coffee and donut shop have also changed. Today more than half of Canada's adult women work outside of the home; families are smaller; people are more mobile; leisure time has become a precious commodity and competition is fierce on all fronts. Country Style no longer positions stores on the "going home" side of the road in order for Dad to drop in on his way home from work for a treat of a dozen donuts for his family. Now Country Style is on the "way to work" side of the road — and in shopping centres, office complexes, and industrial parks — all to meet today's customers' requirements.

Over three decades, Country Style has grown with the market. The product line has been expanded from a single size of coffee and 56 varieties of donuts to such savoury items as thick homestyle soup, fresh green salads, hearty sandwiches, and rich chili. Today, select Country Style locations also feature specialty coffees, retail gift centres, and Yogen Früz brand frozen yogurt.

Over three decades of business, Country Style has been careful not to allow their store decor to become dated or suggest a dingy feeling, keeping pace, instead, with ever-changing fashions and designs. New sites have grown gradually in square footage from an average of 1,200 square feet in the early sixties to a standard 2,400 square feet in today's market. Country Style is also currently embarking upon a very innovative and aggressive redesign program to see all stores, both new and established, feature a bright new look which will carry them well into the next century.

In order to serve fully their franchisees, Country Style's head office grew as well. The staff has grown from one man's dream to over 70 people responsible for all the areas of running a franchise-based business, including the traditional areas of site selection, franchising, training, store development, operations, marketing, finance, supply and product development as well as overseeing central warehousing and distribution, equipment and a commissary facility.

Country Style Donuts will continue to build on their strengths. Their 30 years in business is testimony to a strong and dedicated group of owner/operators and staff who meet the needs of their customers 24 hours a day, in some 200 locations throughout Canada.

Interiors were redesigned after extensive research studies, giving stores a cleaner, brighter look

Package changes of Canadian Club over the years have maintained the identity of the brand which dates back to 1879

Hiram Walker & Sons Limited

One of the World's Largest Distillers

HIRAM WALKER was born in East Douglas, Massachusetts on July 4, 1816. At the age of 20 he joined the westward march and settled in Detroit where he gained experience as a grocer and grain merchant. By 1856, he had $40,000 to invest and a desire to go into milling and distilling. However, unstable temperance laws at the time encouraged him to look across the Detroit River to Canada to set up his business.

Canada offered a steady supply of quality grains, land, materials and labour cheaper than at home, and a more tolerant attitude towards the distilling of spirit beverages. Walker purchased a 468 acre tract of land and built a mill and distillery. By 1858, he was selling feed, flour and whisky. He made good, distinctively light-bodied whisky and its popularity increased.

Walker was a benevolent entrepreneur, who through his Walkerville Land & Building Company built and leased homes to his employees, both managers and workers. He provided amenities which many larger communities lacked, such as street lamps, plumbing, a fire brigade and free police protection, as well as financing for schools and churches. In 1885, Walker incorporated his own railway, which in four years enlarged his one industry village into a town supporting many diversified companies. In 1890, Walkerville was officially incorporated as a town and remained so until it was amalgamated with the City of Windsor in 1935.

Hiram Walker, a benevolent entrepreneur

Walker was the first in the industry to brand his whisky and the first distiller to put his whisky into individually sealed bottles — a step ahead of the usual practice of selling it in bulk from wooden barrels. He called it "Club" whisky as the uniquely smooth, mellow taste was enjoyed by gentlemen of the finer clubs of the day.

The success of "Club" whisky in North America alarmed U.S. distillers. They felt that consumers were not aware they were drinking a "product of Canada" and petitioned Washington for a law requiring Walker to clearly state his whisky as "Canadian." Walker complied, "Canadian Club" was born, and contrary to the predictions of the American distillers, this new brand did not falter. Rather it " ... hastened its growth and was firmly placed on the road to fame and fortune."

This success however spawned yet another problem for the company and the brand. Due to the unregulated nature of the marketplace, a number of fraudulent imitators tried to copy the trademark label. In defence of his reputation for quality, Walker lashed back with an advertising campaign exposing the "rascality" of the named men trying to sell "bogus liquors" and boldly challenging them to sue for slander.

Today, Canadian Club is the world's leading, premium Canadian Whisky and is available in 150 countries.

The Dominion of Canada General Insurance Company

This bust of Sir John A. Macdonald is proudly displayed in the office of the President and CEO at The Dominion's Head Office in Toronto

THE year was 1887. Canada was young and strong, the great railway spanned the country and enterprise flourished. George Gooderham, president of Gooderham & Worts Distillery, the Bank of Toronto, and the Canada Permanent Mortgage Corporation, surmised that the robust economy might be an excellent environment in which to start a wholly Canadian casualty insurance company. Believing in George Gooderham's new business venture, Sir John A. Macdonald, Canada's first Prime Minister and one of Confederation's signatories, agreed to serve as The Dominion's first President.

The company opened in November, 1887 at 38 King Street East in Toronto. Four short years later, the nation mourned the passing of Sir John A. Macdonald. In a speech in the House of Commons, Sir Wilfred Laurier remarked, "To his statesmanship, it is written in the history of Canada."

At the turn of the century, the company was growing rapidly, expanding both geographically and in the range of products that it offered. George Gooderham, the company's second president who died in 1905, believed that the development of the company should always be along sound and conservative lines. His son, Albert

The Dominion's logo, which is also the Canadian Coat of Arms, reflects how the history of the company is closely integrated with the history of Canada

Gooderham, articulated this management philosophy when he said, "We are building for the future, not the immediate present." To this principle of building slowly but surely, the company owes much of its growth and success. Successive generations of the Gooderham's

have continued their involvement in the company, with Peter Gooderham, George's great-grandson, currently serving as Chairman of the Board.

In 1969, the Board of Directors voted to join with The Empire Life Insurance Company as wholly-owned subsidiaries of E-L Financial Corporation, a move that formalized the close relationship between the Gooderhams and the Jackmans who controlled Empire Life. On December 11, 1991, Henry N.R. Jackman, then Chairman and President of E-L Financial Corporation Limited and Vice Chairman of The Dominion of Canada General Insurance Company Limited, was appointed Ontario's 25th Lieutenant Governor.

Today, The Dominion of Canada General Insurance Company is one of Canada's largest general insurance companies. With regional centres across Canada, supported by independent insurance brokers, The Dominion provides Canadians with a full range of personal property and business insurance services. Thousands of Canadians have been employed by The Dominion since its founding and events such as the employee 25-Year Club help to keep the tradition strong. The Dominion Group Foundation, established in 1978, coordinates the company's long-standing support of non-profit projects in education, medicine, research, social services and the arts.

The future offers many challenges for the financial services sector, as government policy alters the competitive arena. George L. Cooke, The Dominion's current President, notes that "With our proud heri-tage as the foundation, we are building a strong and promising future, one that would make George Gooderham and Sir John A. Macdonald proud and one that recognizes that insurance is first and foremost a service industry in which our people will always make the difference."

FROM its inception in 1947, with a single cemetery in London, Ontario, Arbor has developed a system of cemeteries and funeral homes across Canada and is now, in terms of the numbers of funerals, burials and cremations performed annually, the nation's principal supplier of funerary services.

Arbor's development reflects both the expansion of Canada in the last half century and the soundness

Arbor's second guiding principle is a concern to provide services that match closely the desires of consumers in each community. Though adherence to tradition runs strong in funerary matters, marked changes have occurred since 1947. Thus the incidence of cremation has risen from a nominal proportion of all deaths to about 35 percent nationally and much higher in many communities. To accommodate this trend, Arbor established

Arbor Memorial Services Inc.

Lamb's Funeral Chapel, Thorold, Ontario

of two principles which have governed the company's direction.

The first principle is that it is better for the consumer to determine funerary arrangements in advance than to wait until death occurs. Pre-arrangement gives the purchaser the opportunity to learn what services are available and to make informed choices free from the pressures of time and grief. The manifest advantages of pre-arrangement were little thought of fifty years ago and it is due in no small part to Arbor's missionary efforts in fostering pre-arrangement that the concept is now accepted and endorsed by all qualified commentators. Consistent with its belief that consumer education is of paramount importance, Arbor sponsors a series of articles about funerary topics which are supplied monthly to over 1,000 newspapers. The series, entitled "All Things Considered," is written by Joan Watson, an authority on consumer matters, and is not attributed publicly to Arbor.

22 crematoria between 1978 and 1990. Again, the practice of entombment in mausoleums had largely disappeared from Canada by 1939. After World War II, demand for entombment was revived by immigrants from Europe and was satisfied by the construction of mausoleums in major cemeteries. Over the years there has been a dramatic evolution in the design of mausoleums. The typical early structure might accommodate some 60 individual crypts; Arbor's latest building will contain over 5,000. The growing diversity of consumers' backgrounds has stimulated change in many other aspects of cemetery and funeral home operations. Hours of service have been extended to meet the needs of religious groups and shift workers. Memorials have become more imaginative. The forms of funeral service have been expanded and refined to suite a broadening range of individual preferences.

Commitment to these principles should help both consumers and Arbor as much in the future as they have in the past.

CANADIANS have always been visionaries, ready to blaze trails across uncharted territories, and it was in this great tradition that two entrepreneurs set up shop in Ottawa in May 1963, to sell computer technology to the scientific and defense groups in the national capital region, as the first subsidiary of a young New England-based firm called Digital Equipment Corporation (founded but seven years earlier).

The Canadian company, Digital Equipment of Canada Limited, sold a respectable half-million dollars worth of computer boards during its first year and the

including the world's fastest PC — the DECpc AXP/150 — based on the 64-bit Alpha AXP reduced instruction set computer (RISC) chip.

This PC runs at 150 Megahertz and established Digital Canada as a leading manufacturer and exporter of high-technology equipment. The firm's revenues in 1993 topped the billion dollar mark for the second consecutive year, of which approximately $700 million were for systems exported worldwide, aiding Canada's balance of payments. Included in these products were the VRL01 Medical Terminal, developed by Gibson Product

Digital Equipment of Canada Ltd.

parent corporation, recognizing the manufacturing prowess and expertise of its Canadian employees, began manufacturing its first mid-range, or minicomputers, in 1964, at the Canadian facility — the former Bates and Innes Felt Mill, located west of Ottawa in Carleton Place.

In 1971, the firm purchased 56 acres of land for a combination head office and manufacturing site in Kanata, Ontario, and in 1972 the troops moved in (the same year the firm recorded its 1,000th computer sale with revenues exceeding $22 million).

Since then the Kanata site has expanded five times to the point where today it covers half a million square feet and employs nearly 1,000 workers in various aspects of sales consulting, manufacturing, research & development and distribution. In fact, the plant now produces personal computers as well as computer boards and Digital's VAX systems, the ideal "server" for the many tasks which Digital's networking expertise connects to its workstations, personal computers and those of other vendors. By the summer of 1993, nearly 1,200 PCs a day were rolling off the assembly lines in Kanata,

Design and Digital in Ottawa, which won the Industrial Design Award for the Canadian Awards for Business Excellence (CABE) in 1992.

Across Canada Digital employs nearly 3,000 permanent employees and provides jobs for thousands of Canadians in related industries.

Although best known for its hardware and software products, Digital Equipment of Canada Limited is also one of Canada's top service companies offering 24-hour, 365-day telephone support on all its products and thousands of competitors' products from its national Canadian Technology Support Centre in Hull, Quebec. Here more than 250 experts, linked globally with comrades in 91 countries, keep Canada's business computers working, day in and day out. The firm recorded more than $250 million in services revenues in 1993, which went from simple break-and-fix services to running the computer data centres and networks of renowned firms such as Imperial Oil Resources, TransAlta Utilities and RBC Dominion Securities. The future looks bright for this IT star.

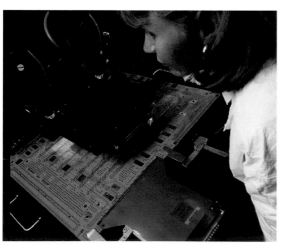

At Digital Canada's R&D lab, a Canadian scientist examines "interconnect" board, the electronic nervous system of computers

Kanata, employing 800 manufacturing staff, exports tens of thousands of personal computers worldwide, as well as VAX and Alpha AXP departmental and small business systems

Brookfield Development Corporation

Committed to Excellence in Real Estate Development & Customer Service

BROOKFIELD DEVELOPMENT CORPORATION strives to achieve a level of excellence in the quality of the projects it brings to the marketplace as well as the level of service it provides its customers. With quality assets in such major urban markets as Toronto, Denver, Chicago, Minneapolis/St. Paul, and Orange County, California, Brookfield today is widely recognized as a major North American real estate company centred in select, dynamic markets.

headquarters for doing business in Canada.

Also forming part of the Brookfield Canada Portfolio of quality projects are 320 Bay Street, and the head office of Northern Telecom Canada Limited, located in Mississauga, Ontario.

320 Bay Street provides a unique example of how the best of the past can successfully be combined with the most modern systems and design. The result is a thoroughly modern building restored to its 1930 art deco beauty.

The Northern Telecom Building situated along the 401 Highway has become a landmark for Metropolitan Toronto commuters. The design and location of the project provides Northern Telecom with a head office that performs to their high standards and complements their image of excellence in the market place.

The 320 Bay Street lobby, restored to its 1930 Art Deco design. Preserving achievements of the past enhances our future

The BCE Place Galleria, a pedestrian avenue of glass and light. A remarkable achievement

The Canadian operation, centred in downtown Toronto, makes up three million of the ten-million-square-foot, company-wide portfolio.

When discussing Canadian achievement, one need look no further than BCE Place, Brookfield's 2.6-million-square-foot project located in Toronto's financial core. It represents the very best in design and quality and Brookfield is proud to say that some of the world's most successful corporations have recognized this achievement and have selected BCE Place as their

The Brookfield focus is not only on developing the very best in commercial projects throughout North America, but also on providing outstanding service to our customers who require performance 24 hours a day, 7 days a week in their pursuit of excellence.

Around the world, achievement and quality are synonymous with the word Canadian. Brookfield Development Corporation salutes all those Canadians who strive to excel in their daily lives and contribute to their communities.

NICKEL. It is woven into the fabric of our everyday life — from stainless steel kitchen sinks and cutlery to dairy product tankers and computer housings. For over 90 years, Inco Limited has continued to be a world leader in turning mineral exploration and development into metals designed to enhance our standard and quality of life. "Stronger for our Experience" reflects the organizational philosophy of the company and its employees.

Inco Limited

Fabric of Life

Inco Limited is a major story of Canadian achievement. From its roots in the rough and ready mining environment of the 1880s, the company has grown to be one of the world's premier mining and metals companies. In addition to nickel, Inco processes 13 other elements including copper, cobalt, gold and platinum.

Laboratory research has created proprietary value-added products such as specialty metal powders used in the advanced batteries and electronic applications. Research and development have created new products such as high-nickel alloys for tubing, plate, sheet, bar, strip and engineered products used by customers in the energy, marine, aerospace, electrical and engineering industries.

Inco's research facilities worldwide continue to foster innovative new applications to increase metals recovery, improve processing capabilities, and develop new exploration methods and equipment. These initiatives help improve health and safety for employees and reduce the impact on the environment.

As early as 1917, the company established its first environmental project with the development of Nickel Park in Copper Cliff, Ontario. Annually up to 250,000 pine seedlings, grown in a company-operated nursery in a mine thousands of feet underground, are planted in Spring. In recent years, more than 1,800 acres at the tailings basin have been reforested. The concept of sustainable development is an essential part of the company's policy throughout its operations.

In 1988 Inco initiated the largest environmental

project undertaken by any mining company. Some $600 million has been invested in the Sulphur Dioxide Abatement Project to improve the process at the Sudbury operations to reduce emissions. When the project is completed in 1994, 90 percent of the sulphur in the Sudbury ore will be removed during processing. In recognition of its overall efforts throughout the years, Inco received the Corporate Environmental

At some of Inco's operations in Sudbury, Ontario, mining has continued for over 90 years. Over that time these operations have seen the full range of technical advances — from the pick and shovel in the early years to the computer - controlled drill today. And tomorrow technology will advance to the point where underground vehicles will travel and work, guided by a control centre on the surface

Leadership Award in 1991 from Environment Canada.

Since its creation in 1902, Inco has continued to broaden its scope of operations. It currently employs 9,600 in Canada and a further 8,100 in 19 other countries. The company is strongly committed to its communities through an active program of donations focused primarily on higher education and health. As part of its support for scientific research, Inco has provided facilities at its Creighton Mine in Sudbury for the Sudbury Neutrino Observatory, which, when completed in 1995, will enable the international scientific community to study these elusive sub-atomic particles.

With all successful ventures, the past is the benchmark and guide to the future. Inco's employees continue to strive towards new frontiers and accomplishments. Canadians, and people through-out the world, will continue to reap the benefits of this ongoing dedication to excellence.

The Municipal Trust Company

*The Best Little Trust
Company in Canada*

First branch of Municipal Trust, Barrie Main, opened its doors in the summer of 1971

THE pathfinder symbolizes the pursuit of previously unexplored opportunities. The essence of this spirit, in 1791, contributed to the founding of what is now the province of Ontario.

Exactly 200 years later, an Ontario-based financial institution dedicated to the same innovative pursuit of new opportunities, celebrated its 20th anniversary as, according to the *Report on Business* magazine, "the best little trust company in Canada."

The Municipal Trust Company is a retail subsidiary of Municipal Financial Corporation, a management holding company headquartered in Barrie, Ontario. The company was founded in 1971 by lawyer-businessman Maxwell L. Rotstein and lawyer-author Nancy-Gay Rotstein.

Municipal Trust completed its first year of operations with one branch, a half-dozen employees and $3.5 million in assets. Twenty years later, it operates 27 branches in 25 communities, employs nearly 600 people, enjoys a record of consistently positive earnings and manages assets of $1.3 billion.

Like the pathfinder of old, Municipal Trust identified and pursued previously unexplored opportunities, this time in the field of financial services. These opportunities have taken three forms: geographic; demographic; and quality customer service.

The geographic opportunity presented itself in Ontario's smaller cities and towns. In 1971, the Board of Directors recognized a number of these stable and prosperous communities were bypassed by larger and urban-centred banks and trust companies. Accordingly, there was little alternative to — and little competition for — the existing financial institutions in those markets.

Municipal Trust was launched in order to fill this vacuum. In fact, Municipal was the first to establish a trust industry presence in a number of the smaller yet fast-growing centres of south-central, eastern and southwestern Ontario.

Municipal Trust also discovered and pursued a demographic opportunity in the financial services marketplace. The company realized years ago that the customer base was undergoing profound change. In particular, opportunity existed to provide the increasing number of senior customers in the company's target communities with specialized financial products and services. Municipal Trust thus became one of the first financial institutions in Ontario to cater specifically to this growing and important segment of the market.

A third unique business opportunity lay in the area of customer service. It was clear even in 1971 that many customers were unhappy with the service provided by other financial institutions. Municipal Trust was founded on the belief that quality customer service is essential to marketing financial services and to customer loyalty. The company, since then, has become known for providing the high level of personalized service and community involvement necessary to attract and maintain discerning customers. As a result, Municipal Trust established the strong and lasting customer relationships which have earned it a reputation as "the hometown alternative" to other financial institutions.

The right markets, the right products and the right service. These factors have enabled Municipal Trust to prosper in a short period of time. The company's future innovations will be shaped by the qualities responsible for its record of success. Chief among these is the commitment to identify and pursue new opportunities...to continue as a pathfinder in the financial services industry.

Choice Hotels Canada Inc.

An Entrepreneur's Successful Journey to Canada's Largest Hotel Company

FROM the construction of his first family home to Canada's largest lodging chain, Maurice H. Rollins has been putting roofs over people's heads for over four decades. As visionary, Chairman and Chief Executive Officer of Journey's End Corpor-ation and Chairman of Choice Hotels Canada, Rollins is an inspiration to all Canadians.

As a young boy growing up in his native Belleville, Ontario, Rollins was always the first out to shovel a neighbour's driveway in winter or mow lawns in summer. His first break came when he ran into a former teacher who was working for an engineering firm. Although Rollins had pharmacist training only, he was hired and was quickly promoted to a Resident Engineer before the age of twenty. At the same time, he continued to operate a successful hamburger stand with a partner on nights and weekends.

In the 50s, Rollins purchased a lot for $200 and built his first home. Ten years later, Rollins Group of Companies were one of the largest fully integrated businesses in central and eastern Ontario, combining residential and commercial developers including lumber, construction, real estate, and management companies. He also developed properties in England, France, Switzerland and Frobisher Bay, NWT.

Through these businesses, Rollins began to observe that Canadian travellers had only two lodging choices: sive, full service hotels. Rollins reasoned that a market existed for a limited service lodging product which

Maurice H. Rollins, Chairman, CEO, Journey's End Corporation; Chairman, Choice Hotels Canada

offered clean, comfortable accommodation at a reasonable price.

The first 60-unit Journey's End Motel opened in Belleville in 1978. A second location opened in Kingston in 1979 and by 1980, the original location expanded to keep pace with demand. Rollins sold his lucrative group of companies to devote his energies full time to developing the Journey's End chain.

Several significant milestones followed: a provincial Outstanding Business Achievement Award; public issue with shares trading on the Toronto and Montreal stock exchanges; the silver medal for Entrepreneurship in the prestigious Canada Awards for Business Excellence; opening the 100th Journey's End property in downtown Montreal in 1989; and, a 29-storey Journey's End Hotel in midtown Manhattan at 5th Avenue and 40th Street in 1991 — with inventory peaking at 137 locations.

In July 1993, Rollins led Journey's End Corporation into a 50/50 joint venture partnership with Choice Hotels International ... a global industry leader with 3,000 hotels in 32 countries. Choice Hotels Canada was launched with seven brands ... Clarion, Quality, Comfort, Sleep, EconoLodge, Rodeway and Friendship Inns. With "Something For Everyone, Practically Everywhere" at over 175 hotels across Canada, and an ambitious growth strategy of 400 hotels in five years, Maurice Rollins' impressive journey continues.

MAGNA International Inc., headquartered in Markham, Ontario, is one of the largest and most diversified manufacturers of automotive components and systems in the world. The company has annual sales approaching $4 billion and employs approximately 17,500 people in more than 80 manufacturing and product development centres throughout North America and Europe.

Magna was founded in 1957 by Frank Stronach who was trained as a tool and die maker. The company quickly grew from a one-man tool and die shop and

operations, with each factory as a separate profit centre.

In order to attract and maintain top-notch managers, Mr. Stronach created a special arrangement in which managers received a predetermined portion of the factory's profits. Initially, only managers participated in the profit-sharing plan. But when Magna eventually became a public company, with Mr. Stronach as the controlling shareholder, the principle of profit and equity participation was expanded to include every employee.

Magna's unique corporate culture is one of the main reasons for its success. At the heart of this culture is an operating philosophy based on profit sharing between the three driving forces of the business: investors, employees, and management. This principle is enshrined in Magna's Corporate Constitution, which pre-determines the percentage of annual profits shared by each group.

Magna International Inc.

Magna's unique corporate culture helps bring together and develop a superior calibre of human and manufacturing resources

A percentage of the profits allocated to employees is also used to purchase Magna stock on their behalf, making each employee a shareholder with a real stake in the success of the company. In fact, ever since the introduction of the Employee Profit and Equity Participation program in 1976, Magna has grown at the remarkable average rate of approximately 30 percent per year.

In addition to the Corporate Constitution, the company also has an Employee Charter of Rights, guaranteeing, among other matters, competitive wages, a safe and healthful working environment, and fair

eventually expanded into the production of automotive stamped parts following an initial order to produce metal brackets for GM sun visors.

One of the main reasons for the company's rapid growth has been Magna's strategy of building small factories in order to foster a close working relationship between managers and employees and maintain an entrepreneurial environment. Still another reason for Magna's growth was the company's decentralization of

treatment. A key feature of the Charter of Rights is the Magna Hotline, a toll-free number which employees can call if they have any concerns or if they feel their rights have been violated.

As a corporation which focuses on innovations in both its human resources and automotive technologies, Magna International will continue to be a business pioneer and a corporate achiever for many years to come.

Syncrude
Working to Secure Canada's Energy Future

Aerial view of Fort McMurray, Alberta

Dragline working in the Syncrude mine

Photos, courtesy, Victor Post Photography

competitive source of alternative energy right in their backyard. At about $15.00 (Cdn.) a barrel, Syncrude's operating costs are comparable to the finding and production costs of new conventional oil sources.

The Syncrude product is high quality light, sweet crude — among the best low-sulphur oils in Canada. Furthermore, the production potential of the total oil sands deposits in Alberta could be as high as 1.7 trillion barrels.

The key to recovering this huge source, says Syncrude chairman Tom Vant, is more research and development. While some 200 billion barrels of oil are recoverable using present extraction techniques, Syncrude's owners, a consortium of the Alberta government and several energy companies, are forming research alliances with governments and academia to realize the full potential of the oil sands.

Indeed, since 1973, Canadian production of conventional oil has decreased by an astounding half-million barrels a day. And in the past two years alone, production has fallen a further 85,000 barrels a day.

In September, 1992, Syncrude passed the 600 million barrel production mark of synthetic crude oil. But, says Newell, a continued development of the oil sands will require "significant capital investment from strong, long-term, focused investors, supportive governments and continued innovation in technology."

There's no question that oil will continue to be the world's major source of energy well into the next century. In Canada, Syncrude, with its record of even lower operating costs, and continuous improvements in production, safety, environmental performance and productivity, leaves us well positioned to secure our energy future.

Syncrude Canada Ltd. is the world's largest producer of high quality light, sweet synthetic crude oil and is Canada's largest industrial sector employer of native people. The company is a joint venture owned by Alberta Energy Company Ltd., Alberta Oil Sands Equity, Canadian Occidental Petroleum Ltd., Gulf Canada Resources Limited, HBOG-Oil Sands Limited Partnership, Imperial Oil Resources, Mocal Energy Limited, Pan-Canadian Petroleum Limited, and Petro-Canada. The company's Mildred Lake mining, extraction and upgrading operation is located 40 km north of Fort McMurray, Alberta.

CANADA could switch to synthetic crude oil and be oil self-sufficient for more than 200 years if its oil sands resources are developed further.

As the world's largest producer of synthetic crude oil, Syncrude Canada Ltd. already supplies 12 percent of total crude oil production in Canada, or more than 65 million barrels of oil per year.

As Syncrude president Eric Newell notes, "Moving beyond a heavy reliance on foreign energy makes perfect sense for Canada. Unpredictable foreign suppliers and sporadic price fluctuations leave us too vulnerable. And if an energy shortage were to occur, the consequences would be disastrous."

Newell said it's time Canadians realized there is a

CHRYSLER CANADA LTD. in 1993 enjoyed one of the most successful years in its 68-year history.

The company's net sales of a record $13.6 billion were 43 percent higher than the previous record $9.5 billion in net sales reported for 1992. Pretax earnings of an all-time record $418.8 million, compared with a $64.2 million loss in 1992, represented a year-to-year turnaround of $483 million. Earnings from operations increased from $65.8 million in 1992 to a record $379 million in 1993. The company's assets increased by $1 billion — from $3.1 billion in 1992 to $4.1 billion at year-end 1993. Shareholders' equity increased from $1.1 billion to $1.4 billion at year-end 1993.

During 1993 the company increased its share of the Canadian vehicle market for the third consecutive year, from 16.8 percent in 1992 to 19.1 percent in 1993 — the company's highest level of penetration in 17 years. Chrysler's dealers across Canada delivered 226,819 cars and trucks in 1993, an increase of 11.0 percent over the 205,071 vehicles they sold in 1992.

Chrysler's three vehicle assembly plants in Canada built an all-time record 643,356 cars and trucks in 1993, an increase of 38.5 percent over the previous record 464,403 vehicles Chrysler Canada produced in 1992.

Chrysler Canada accounted for nearly 30 percent of all Canadian auto industry production and is now building close to three vehicles in Canada for every one it sells here.

For the second consecutive year, Chrysler's minivan plant in Windsor, Ontario, in 1993 built more than 300,000 Dodge Caravan and Plymouth Voyager MagicWagons in a single year. A third production shift was added in January 1994 to keep up with record-breaking sales of Chrysler's minivans in the United States and Canada. The company is currently producing a record 1,342 minivans a day around the clock, six days a week.

Chrysler Canada's sales of a record 67,396 minivans in 1993 were the highest for any year since Chrysler introduced these industry-leading vehicles a decade ago.

In March 1993, the company announced a major capital investment in excess of $600 million to retool the Windsor Minivan Plant to build Chrysler's all-new, third-generation "NS" minivans beginning in the second quarter of 1995.

Chrysler's Bramalea Assembly Plant in Brampton, Ontario, built more than 250,000 of the company's award-winning "LH" cars — the Chrysler and Dodge Intrepid, Chrysler Concorde, Eagle Vision, Chrysler New Yorker, and Chrysler LHS — in 1993, the plant's first full year of production.

The company's Pillette Road Truck Assembly Plant in Windsor began production of the redesigned full-size 1994 Dodge Ram vans and wagons early in 1993. The Pillette Road plant produced nearly 85,000 Dodge Ram vans and wagons during 1993.

Chrysler Canada Ltd.

Building Canada

Factory-fresh Chrysler LHS drives off Final Assembly Line in Chrysler Canada's Bramalea Assembly Plant in Brampton, Ontario. The Bramalea plant produces daily nearly 1,000 of Chrysler's award-winning "LH" cars on two shifts

A wholly-owned subsidiary of Chrysler Corporation of Detroit, the Chrysler Corporation of Canada Ltd. was incorporated in Windsor, Ontario, in June 1925. The new company had 181 employees and built 4,474 cars in its first year. Today, Chrysler Canada employs more than 14,000 Canadians at its three vehicle assembly plants and three component manufacturing plants and offices and parts depots across Canada.

The company's more than 600 dealers from coast to coast sell Chrysler, Dodge, Plymouth, Eagle, and imported Colt passenger cars and Dodge and Jeep light-duty trucks and sport/utility vehicles.

G. Yves Landry was appointed President and Chief Executive Officer of Chrysler Canada Ltd. effective January 1, 1990. Born in Thetford Mines, Quebec, Mr. Landry joined Chrysler Canada in 1969.

The same pioneer spirit that steered Microsoft Corporation to become the world's largest software manufacturer has made Microsoft Canada Inc. the premier supplier of PC systems and applications software in Canada.

More than ten years have elapsed since the introduction of the personal computer. Now, the power of personal computing reaches over 100 million people worldwide, and Microsoft has helped propel that growth.

Not surprising, when you consider that Microsoft is the "MS" in its MS-DOS operating system — the industry standard platform on which millions of personal computers are based. It is also the springboard for Microsoft's Windows systems software and its powerful, yet easy-to-use application software products including Microsoft Word and Excel.

Microsoft Canada started with just 10 employees in 1985. By 1990, the company had grown to 83 employees, and each year since, increased by 50 percent to its present staff size of over 300.

Microsoft Canada maintains a strong presence across the country, from its 75,000 square foot head office in Mississauga, to regional offices in Quebec City, Montreal, Ottawa, Toronto, Winnipeg, Calgary, and Vancouver.

Microsoft Canada operates from a truly Canadian

Microsoft Canada Inc.
The World's Largest Software Manufacturer

perspective marketing English and French products in all major software categories, including desktop applications, PC systems and networking products.

Recently, Microsoft entered the home software category and introduced Microsoft Home. Microsoft Home products are comprised of four distinct categories: Personal Productivity products offer users tools for managing finances, like Microsoft Money, and managing tasks at home and for family, such as writing letters, with Microsoft Works. Multimedia Library products, like Cinemania, give users reference works with not only text, but also multimedia elements such as rich graphics, full motion video, sound and animation. Games products, like Microsoft Golf, are engaging and fun to use, providing users with a challenging way to test their skills. Kid's Creativity products, like Creative Writer, let kids explore an inspiring new world.

Training is also a key focus for the company. The Solution Providers program, established in 1992, provides training and information to key partners such as value-added resellers, consultants, developers, and training companies. Members of the Microsoft Solutions Provider program design, develop, deploy, and support business solutions using the latest information technology. Through this program, Microsoft has established partnerships with a range of third party solution providers who provide customized applications, integration, technical support, training, and other services for Microsoft products.

Microsoft has a vision for the future of personal computing: a goal to evolve the existing PC standards to include new capabilities such as compound documents, object-oriented file systems, distributed file systems, handwriting recognition, and multimedia. That is, to unify all of the sources of information in our lives toward truly achieving a point where we have access to "Information at your fingertips."

Canada is already well established as a world leader in software development. As Microsoft Canada continues to grow, it will introduce a worldwide mission to ensure Canada continues to set the pace, standards and innovation for many years to come.

Microsoft head office, Mississauga, Ontario

Vestcap Investment Management Inc.

The Right Time, the Right Place....

VESTCAP was incorporated in May 1988 to provide highly personalized and attentive investment management services to individuals, trusts, and estates. It was originally founded to answer a need, namely to establish an investment counselling firm for a small group whose members had attained financial self sufficiency. Since then the company has grown by 2,400 percent, and continues to attract the attention of many others who appreciate the philosophy, style, and care Vestcap has to offer.

The key "Vestcap Difference" is its experience in global asset structuring, its real emphasis on personal contact, a completely personalized portfolio approach, and its consistently reliable performance results.

Starting with a macro view of world economics, Vestcap next analyzes business trends, then North American conditions, finally making its sectoral selection in order to arrive at a cohesive list of securities suitable for its customized portfolios. To minimize risk and to produce returns in excess of risk-free alternatives, a balanced portfolio discipline is employed on a priority basis. Continual monitoring of economic and business forecasts allows the Vestcap team to adjust its asset allocation as conditions warrant. Vestcap's preoccupation is the search for value-oriented securities.

One hundred percent owned by its five principals, totally independent of all other financial institutions, this investment counselling firm makes investment decisions without bias. Its portfolio managers use a team approach that combines over one hundred years of experience in portfolio management with

the discipline that flows from a team's decision-making process. This group of multi-talented individuals, with backgrounds in economics, political science, engineering, communications and law, is dedicated to maintaining Vestcap's ideal. The professional managers have spent all of their careers in the industry.

To provide intelligent investment counsel to clients, to preserve and enhance their capital and to increase their purchasing power is the mission of Vestcap.

*Roger S. Glassco,
Vice President*

*A.R. Deane Nesbitt,
Member of the Board*

*M. Nugent Schneider,
President*

*Albert E. Matthews, Jr.,
Member of the Board*

Leo S. Frank, Vice President

Vestcap's new headquarters are located at One Queen Street East, Toronto

Photographs, courtesy, Peter Caton

Imasco

A Tapestry of Canadian Success Stories

With busier lifestyles and demographic changes, customers require more flexible and accessible financial services. Canada Trust's EasyLine is one of the most innovative telephone banking services available anywhere

A former bank branch, the two-storey Shoppers Drug Mart at the intersection of Yonge and King, in downtown Toronto, is unique and very spacious for a drug store in the city centre

Imperial Tobacco's leaf processing operations in Aylmer, Ontario have been upgraded to meet the highest possible standards and ensure efficient operations

I MASCO LIMITED, with headquarters in Montreal, is one of Canada's largest corporations. It was formed in 1970 to diversify Imperial Tobacco Company into other consumer markets.

Hallmarks of Imasco's growth have been investing in outstanding organizations and furthering the dreams of entrepreneurs. Each Imasco company is an important thread of success woven into the corporate tapestry. Imperial Tobacco, Shoppers Drug Mart, and Canada Trust are such success stories. Each illustrates Imasco's driving spirit: responding to consumer needs with the

highest quality goods and services while helping to build strong communities.

Imperial Tobacco Company: The Origins of Imasco
Imperial Tobacco Company was incorporated in 1912 when the Canadian tobacco industry was still in its infancy. It began as a consolidation of two Montreal companies and over its eighty-year history has acquired many other tobacco businesses.

During World War II, Imperial embarked on a goodwill program of distributing its cigarettes to Canadian troops abroad, which also served to keep brand loyalty alive. The war stimulated Canadian economic growth and, during the post-war boom, Imperial constructed additional plants in Ontario and Quebec. Its engineers began experimenting with machinery for processing leaf tobacco which was subsequently licensed to manufacturers around the world.

In the early seventies, TV and radio advertising of tobacco products were discontinued, and Imperial decided to channel some of its advertising and promotion budget into support for professional sports events and the arts. This support grew over the years and continues to this day.

By 1980, Imperial's *Player's* brand had become Canada's most popular cigarette and the company was the country's undisputed industry leader.

Today, Imperial Tobacco continues to flourish, led by the two largest selling domestic cigarette brand families, *Player's* and *du Maurier*. The company employs over 2,700 people in all phases of the industry, from the purchase of raw tobacco leaf to the distribution of final products.

Shoppers Drug Mart: Joining Forces with a Force

When scarcely 20 years old, Murray Koffler inherited two neighbourhood drug stores in Toronto. He went to pharmacy school, learned the heart of the business, then proceeded to redefine it. The end result was Shoppers Drug Mart.

With typical bold strokes, Koffler revamped the concept of the twentieth century "drug store" in Canada by ripping out the soda fountain and emphasising the dispensary, requiring his pharmacists to wear starched white coats as a symbol of their professionalism. To that he added consumer-oriented approaches in merchandising and promotion. In the mid-'50s, he began acquiring other drug stores and organized them around a then-novel franchising concept: pharmacist "associates" would own and operate their own stores within the system and share in the profits. The concept turned out to be a cornerstone of the chain's success.

In 1962, Koffler's 17-store chain became known as Shoppers Drug Mart. It went public, and major expansion occurred through acquisition and mergers in the '60s and in the '70s. Upon entering the chain, stores typically doubled their previous year's profits.

When it was time to sell his business, Murray Koffler chose Imasco largely because of its strong financial position but also because he liked Imasco's tradition of sponsoring worthy Canadian causes. A philanthropist in his own right, Koffler had seen to it that Shoppers had an established reputation as a leading educator on health issues as well as a supporter of hospital fundraising.

Shoppers Drug Mart continues to grow and develop under Imasco's ownership. In today's Shoppers, pharmacists serve as health advisors and are important liaisons between physician and patient. It's a far cry from soda fountain days!

Canada Trust: Helping to Build a Community

In 1986, Imasco acquired Canada Trust, one of the largest financial institutions in Canada. The company had its origins in the frontier days of Canada as the Huron & Erie Savings and Loan Society (H&E), a "building society" established in 1864 in London, Ontario, then the country's western edge. Formed by 25 London businessmen, the H&E was instrumental in shaping a stable and prosperous community.

Through building societies, people would pool their savings to finance the purchase of land by others. Innovative rules allowed borrowers to pay back their debts in monthly instalments of principal plus interest. The concept was ideally suited to the development of pre-confederation Canada. Capital was scarce in those days, for banks handled only commercial accounts, and people literally stashed their savings under mattresses.

Loans which enabled farmers to buy their land were H&E's dominant business for many years, and stories abound about the travelling valuators who had to conquer near impassable terrain on horseback to make their reports. In 1898, H&E acquired General Trust Corporation of Calgary which led to the formation in 1901 of an H&E subsidiary named Canada Trust.

The depression brought on difficult times, made more so in the prairies by drought and the subsequent abandonment of land and loans. The company supported its beleaguered customers, advancing money for seed, sometimes accepting harvested crops as payments on mortgages. Not surprisingly, profits dwindled and did not regain their 1930 level until 1950.

The outbreak of World War II began an economic recovery and, by 1946, it was clear that if the company was going to grow, it would have to acquire other trust companies with good business volumes. This it did, and it also entered the field of corporate pension fund administration. By 1957, the company's two names began to meld into one corporate image, Canada Trust.

Over the course of the '60s and '70s, Canada Trust emphasized personal financial services and developed its well-earned reputation for friendliness and convenience. And through its active residential mortgage program, the company is staying true to its early mission of helping Canadians invest in their own communities.

THE CANADIAN ASSOCIATION FOR COMMUNITY LIVING is one of Canada's ten largest charitable organizations. With over 40,000 members across Canada, it works with and on behalf of people who have been labelled mentally handicapped and with their families.

The mission of the Canadian Association For Community Living is to develop a welcoming, supportive community for all Canadians. Whether one has a mental handicap, develops one, or cares about someone with a

changed. I sometimes wonder who is truly handicapped. Mandy accepts us all with our limitations and narrow-mindedness and we accept Mandy for what she is: a child who is funny, determined, and in my view, extremely courageous." *The mother of Mandy's best friend in Saint John, New Brunswick.*

"Amanda will live a normal life. I think we can provide her with the education and the know-how ... we want her to be able to go out on her own, get a job,

The Canadian Association for Community Living

Robert, Sandra, and Robin shop for groceries in their local supermarket. Happiness is being self-supporting and having "keys of our own"

Harold, William and Margaret enjoy a backyard barbecue with neighbours and friends. They are living successfully in the community after residing in institutions for many years

possibly get married and lead a normal life, because she is a normal person. She is just a little slow in learning things...." *Tom Henke, Relief Pitcher, Texas Rangers, whose daughter, Amanda, has Down Syndrome.*

"If all the support systems are in place and the teacher's focus is positive, teachers and students alike grow and benefit from the (integration) experience." *Margaret Murray, teacher.*

handicap, the work of the Canadian Association for Community Living will ensure that people with mental handicaps are given the assistance they need to be active members of the community.

In a truly integrated society, divisions between people dissolve and the winners are each of us individually and collectively.

"I dream of Daniel taking an apple to his teacher, of seeing him in a school play, and of him bringing home his report card. These are very ordinary things, but for the family of a child (with a mental handicap), these are dreams that bring unexplained joy." *L. Carson, Fredericton, New Brunswick.*

"My personal views on integration have greatly

"When I was younger they put people like me in institutions, not on jobs. Since I was a slow learner, no one gave me a chance. Now I have a job that I really love and my boss is happy because I am good at my work. People called mentally handicapped can do a lot of jobs very well when someone gives them a chance." *Barry Smith, Usher, Roy Thomson Hall, Toronto, Ontario.*

"I am Peter Park. I existed in an institution for 18 years. I started living in 1978. I feel that I would never have made as many friends as I have if I existed in an institution. I work and got married after a while; now we live happily and can use resources in the community that anyone can." *Peter Park, People First of Canada.*

Thanks to the generous support of Horn Abbot Ltd. this profile was made possible

IT has been said that a journey of 10,000 miles begins with a single step. For UPS that saying neatly describes the simple but ambitious origins of what is now the world's largest package distribution company.

In 1907, Jim Casey, a resourceful teenager who believed in perfect service for a fair price, founded UPS in Seattle. Casey began his delivery service with foot messengers. As the business expanded, the company put those messengers on bicycles. Times changed, and cyclists were transformed into drivers, commanding a huge fleet of trucks that grew larger and in some cases "piggybacked" onto railroad cars. Ultimately, UPS launched its air service.

UPS's Canadian journey also began with a single step. When UPS came to Canada in November of 1974, the company was, literally, a one-man show operating

UPS serves every address in Canada and more than 185 countries and territories

out of a 10 x 10 sq. ft. office in the basement of a hotel just outside Toronto. The company's first revenue — 27 cents — was earned even before it was officially in business when a hotel guest asked that a parcel be taken downtown.

Today, UPS serves every address in Canada and more than 185 countries and territories. Striving to maintain a financially strong company, UPS delivers millions of packages, while continuing to offer high

quality service at competitive rates.

UPS has evolved from a company offering essentially one product with little emphasis on technology and limited modes of transportation, into a worldwide enterprise with a wide range of products, using advanced technology and many different types of transportation.

Customer service is the moving force behind the evolution of UPS. The company is committed to anticipating and meeting its customer's needs. In September 1993, for example, the company activated Canada's first nationwide cellular data transfer network, enabling customers to receive immediate tracking information about their shipments. For the first time in Canada, businesses relying on the predictable delivery of goods to stay competitive are able to track packages using the pinpoint accuracy of cellular technology.

United Parcel Service Canada Ltd.

The World's Largest Package Distribution Company

UPS strives to work with its customers confronted by a wide range of modern distribution problems. Using advanced logistics management, UPS assists corporate clients with all aspects of the movement of their goods from warehouse management to industrial engineering. With its advanced technology, UPS helps its clients improve their inventory turnover, eliminate the need for paperwork to track the flow of goods, electronically provide shipment information to U.S. and Canadian Customs — ahead of actual shipments — to speed customs clearance and save time.

From its earliest days, Canada, geographically vast, has depended on reliable, predictable transportation for survival. The country's origins are inextricably linked with its history as an international trading partner, and transportation linking east with west helped bring Canada together as a country. Today, Canadian business still depends on the reliable, predictable transportation of goods, both domestically and internationally. UPS, truly a pathfinder, is committed to help Canadian customers to meet their transportation needs, now and in the future.

Procter & Gamble

THERE was great excitement, back in 1915, when Procter & Gamble selected the City of Hamilton, Ontario, as the site of its first plant outside the United States. It is said that the plant's original 75 employees were so proud of their new company that they paraded truckloads of the first soap production through the City streets for all to see. One of those products, Ivory, soon became a household name and to this day remains Canada's leading bar soap.

The employees' pride and optimism were well founded. Today, P&G Canada employs about 4,000 people and has annual sales exceeding one billion dollars. It is estimated that at least one of P&G's more than 100 high-quality consumer products can be found in every household in the country — market leaders that include Tide laundry detergent, Bounce fabric softener, Cascade dishwashing detergent, Crest toothpaste, Scope mouthwash, Pert Plus shampoo, Oil of Olay moisturizer, Pampers paper diapers, Always feminine hygiene products, Crisco shortening and Duncan Hines cake mixes. In addition, the company produces a number of products for commercial and industrial use.

P&G Canada's General Offices are located in North York, Ontario, part of Metropolitan Toronto. Its manufacturing operations have expanded to six plants, five in the province of Ontario and one in Quebec. Sales offices are located in Halifax, Montreal, Toronto and Calgary. The recent acquisitions of Norwich Eaton, now P&G Pharmaceuticals (in 1984), Richardson-Vicks (1985), Noxell Canada (1989), Shulton Canada (1990), Max Factor Canada (1991)

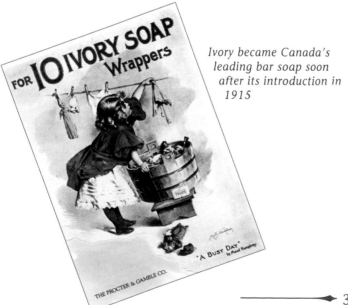

Ivory became Canada's leading bar soap soon after its introduction in 1915

and Facelle Canada (1991), have considerably expanded P&G's presence in the health care, beauty care and paper products fields, with respected brand names such as Pepto-Bismol, Vicks, Cover Girl, Noxzema and Royale.

The Procter & Gamble Company, headquartered in Cincinnati, Ohio, was established in 1837 when William Procter, a candlemaker, formed a partnership with his brother-in-law James Gamble, a soap maker. Neither could have foreseen that their small business, with just $7,000 in capital, would evolve into a highly respected transnational organization with annual worldwide sales of almost $30 billion and 106,000 employees in more than 50 countries. Indeed, even though they were men of vision who always had their eyes on the future, the founders would have had difficulty believing that their company would become the world's preeminent marketer, a leading advertiser and supporter of basic research and product development in many of the countries in which P&G operates.

What is the secret of P&G's success? Why have thousands of employees gladly spent their entire careers with the company? Why has this business grown and prospered over more than 150 years through often adverse conditions, including major wars, severe depressions, and ongoing cultural and global change?

Part of the answer lies in the operating principles instilled in the organization by the founders and reinforced by the generations of employees who succeeded them — basic principles such as a dedication to providing consumers with superior products at a fair price, and an organizational culture which fosters honesty and integrity, hard work, pride of accomplishment, being the best in what it does, and doing what is right for the long-term health of the business.

P&G's success and growth can also be attributed to its creation of innovative new products that meet consumer needs, and its continual improvement of existing products' performance standards. Three good examples are Tide, Crest, and Pampers. Tide, the first heavy-duty synthetic laundry detergent in Canada, was hailed as a "washday miracle" when it was introduced in 1948. Crest, the first fluoride toothpaste, was regarded as a "Triumph over tooth decay" in 1962 and the first fluoride toothpaste whose effectiveness was recognized by the Canadian Dental Association. Pampers paper diapers, introduced in 1972, greatly improved the quality of paper diapers and helped to move them into the mainstream of baby care. Over the years, each of these products, as well as the other P&G brands, have continually been improved.

Given the scope of its operations, P&G Canada affects the lives of many groups of people, including its employees, customers, suppliers, business associates, and Canadians at large. With this awareness, the company strives to balance each business decision so that it will be fair and reasonable for each group affected.

P&G recognizes the vital importance of continuing employment and its ultimate tie with the strength and success of the business. The company seeks to employ the best people it can find without regard to race, gender or any other difference unrelated to performance, and to promote, from within the organization, on the same basis. It encourages and rewards individual innovation, personal initiative and leadership. At the same time it promotes teamwork across disciplines, divisions and geography in order to get the most effective integration of the ideas and efforts of its diverse people. The development of individuals is maximized through training and coaching, and managers are evaluated, in part, on their record in developing subordinates. P&G also strives to maintain a caring culture, one which encourages candid, two-way communication at all levels and involves employees in the decisions that affect their lives.

Procter & Gamble seeks to benefit the country and the communities in which it operates by providing financial support to leading Canadian universities in the form of capital grants, and by supporting student conferences and other endeavours. In addition, the company provides financial help to more than 200 worthwhile organizations in a variety of fields, including health care, the arts and charity.

Building environmental quality is another area

It is estimated that at least one of P&G's more than 100 consumer products can be found in every household in Canada

where P&G makes every effort to be a responsible corporate citizen. It is widely recognized as a leader in environmental activities and is helping to lead the development of meaningful and sustainable environmental innovation.

Part of the company's strong image stems from numerous initiatives supported by a Corporate Environmental Quality Coordination Team. Formed in 1989, the Team's mandate is to minimize the impact of P&G's products, packages and processes on the environment. One of the first policies it initiated involved the development of an integrated approach to solid waste management that includes, in order of priority: source reduction, reuse, recycling, composting, and as a final alternative, landfill.

Two examples of source reduction initiatives are the introduction of Enviro-Pak packages and the conversion of its paper diapers from thick to thin.

Enviro-Pak is a refill pouch which encourages the reuse of conventional plastic bottles. Introduced by P&G in 1989 for Liquid Tide laundry detergent, Downy fabric softener, Ivory Liquid dishwashing detergent and Mr. Clean all-purpose cleaner, the Enviro-Pak has since been expanded to several other P&G brands. With plastic resin savings of 65 to 85 percent per refill pouch, the growing success of Enviro-Pak has provided an estimated annual reduction of more than seven million plastic bottles, representing almost 400,000 kilograms of plastic resin.

P&G was an industry pioneer in the conversion of paper diapers from thick to thin through the use of an absorbent gelling material. This move resulted in a reduction of the volume of used diapers going to landfills by 50 percent and packaging material by over 90 percent.

P&G is forging toward the next century with plans to make the company's future even more successful than its past through a firm commitment to its values, technologies and high-quality people.

In addition to playing a major role in the production and supply of cement and concrete to Ontario's construction industry, St. Lawrence Cement has another story to tell. It is one that takes place behind the scenes where innovative technological achievements and ground-breaking research have led to new hope in addressing some environmental concerns.

St. Lawrence Cement began operations in 1954 in Quebec but soon expanded into Ontario with the addition of its plant in Clarkson (Mississauga), Ontario, in 1956. Today St. Lawrence Cement is recognized as the largest cement producer in eastern Canada and the

St. Lawrence Cement

An overview of St. Lawrence Cement's Mississauga plant, the largest cement plant in Canada

northeastern United States. The company also ranks as the second largest cement manufacturer in the country.

Its products are found in a number of installations throughout Ontario. From the newly constructed Terminal 3 building at Pearson International Airport to major highways such as the 427 and 401 in Toronto, from banks and apartment buildings to refineries to generating stations, St. Lawrence Cement's products are part of everyday life for most Ontario residents.

With 5 cement plants, 33 cement distribution terminals, 58 ready-mixed concrete plants, 27

quarries and sand pits and 2 construction companies, St. Lawrence Cement is divided into three separate operational divisions: Quebec and the Maritimes, Ontario, and the United States. Serving over 15 million Canadians and 60 million Americans, the company accounts for more than 25 percent of the total capacity of the cement produced in Canada.

Since its opening, St. Lawrence Cement has continued to grow and has now developed into a full, vertically integrated group by acquiring aggregate quarries and plants for manufacturing concrete products and materials.

However, it is the company's Mississauga operation that has established a worldwide reputation as a technological leader and outstanding corporate citizen. It is here that, on several occasions, history was made in the industry.

From the day of its official opening, the Mississauga plant was lauded for its technological capabilities in waste reclamation. Its new dust-collection equipment between the kilns and the stack was designed to collect and feed the waste dust back into the firing end of the kilns for reburning.

When the facility was expanded in 1968, its new preheater kiln was the first large preheater kiln ever installed in North America. In fact, at that time it was the largest in the world.

In the mid-1970s pioneering efforts of an outstanding technical staff led to even further recognition worldwide.

The technical people at the company saw the potential of cement kiln technology for the utilization of organic waste for fuel. Since temperatures in the kilns can reach as high as 2100 degrees celsius with a retention time of six seconds, technicians saw the kiln as an ideal process for the destruction of waste. In 1976 St. Lawrence Cement in Mississauga began groundbreaking research — with the full support of the Ontario

Ministry of the Environment, Environment Canada, and the U.S. Environment Protection Agency — into the destruction in its kilns of chlorinated organic wastes.

The results of these tests have influenced waste management efforts on a global scale. Plants in Europe and the U.S. have drawn upon the technology to the extent that there are now literally hundreds of cement operations used as waste destruction sites worldwide. Cement companies in Canada are following the same trend, examining waste destruction efforts for tires and municipal solid waste.

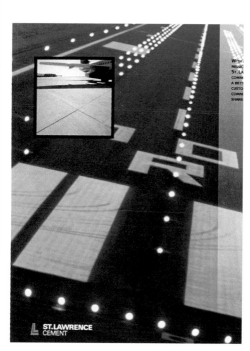

St. Lawrence Cement is supplying the cement to produce the concrete for this immense oil drilling platform to be used for the Hibernia Oil project off the coast of Newfoundland

St. Lawrence Cement's affiliate construction company, Dufferin Construction, has been the main contractor for the construction of runways at Toronto's Pearson International Airport

Other significant developments include the utilization of kiln waste dust in three areas: neutralization and consolidation of acid waste at tanneries, steel plants, and metal plating; extraction of potassium and sulphates for chemical use; and pelletization as fertilizer filler and for Kitty Litter. The company has also developed the utilization of industrial wastes in cement production in four major applications: petro coke for partial fuel replacement; pelletized Blast Furnace Slag as addition to concrete; waste lubricating oil as fuel; and silica fume addition for production of high strength concrete used in construction of oil drilling platforms.

These research efforts have been well recognized by industry experts. In 1978 the Chemical Institute of Canada awarded the company its highly prized Environmental Improvement Award.

St. Lawrence Cement's commitment to improving the quality of life for its employees and the communities its serves is also reflected in its ongoing financial and moral support to local health, cultural, and education programs. For example, the company developed an extensive training course for Junior Achievement called the Business in Action (BIA) Workshop. Funded and organized by St. Lawrence Cement, this two-day training program has become a much anticipated and highly coveted annual prize for outstanding Junior Achievers.

St. Lawrence Cement was also a key contributor to the Mississauga YMCA project and has funded the efforts of numerous historical and conservation groups in the area. It has been publicly recognized for many of its programs in support of local environmental efforts. In 1975 the SOTAS (Save Our Trees and Streams) Award was presented to the company for its landscaping at the Mississauga plant, while the reclamation of an old quarry in Milton into a landscaped park has received international recognition.

Community relations have always been important to St. Lawrence Cement. Information sessions, public meetings, newsletters, and open houses reinforce the company's extensive communication efforts and led to its presentation by the Mississauga Board of Trade of the 1989 Outstanding Business Achievement Award.

While continuing to provide improved products for the construction industry, St. Lawrence Cement will retain its ongoing commitment to environmental and community issues. Through continued research and technological advancements and the forward-thinking corporate philosophy that has characterized its past endeavours, St. Lawrence Cement promises to maintain its role as an industry achiever –in more ways than one.

Midland Walwyn

Growing with Canada

IN A TIME when only change seems constant in the financial market place, it is reassuring to reflect on the unusual length and breadth of Midland Walwyn's history. A Company that has been an integral part of the evolution and development of Canadian capital markets, Midland Walwyn is now one of the nation's pre-eminent financial services organizations serving the individual investor.

While the names Midland and Walwyn are relatively recent in origin, the date of the Company's creation extends back to 1883. In that year, Augustus Nanton, a promising young stock broker from the Toronto offices of Osler & Hammond, was asked to travel west to Winnipeg. There, the Scottish principals of that company were assured, financial services would soon be in demand.

Forty-two years later, he completed his leadership of the company as Sir Augustus Nanton of the thriving firm of Osler, Hammond & Nanton, a diversified provider of financial services, to become president of the Dominion Bank, later to become the Toronto Dominion Bank.

From that impressive beginning, other important predecessor firms joined the long line of distinguished Canadian investment companies to form the present-day Midland Walwyn. Names like Walwyn Fisher, Midland Securities Limited, McCuiag Bros., Nay & James, Gardiner & Company, Cochran Hay & Co., and S.J. Stodgell & Co. In 1964, Osler, Hammond & Nanton itself merged with Midland Securities and other venerable names like Macrae and Company, Atlantic Securities, Mead & Co. and Doherty Roadhouse soon joined the fold.

In 1990, Midland Walwyn Capital Inc. was created at a time of unprecedented deregulation in the Canadian financial services industry. The

Well into its second century of service to Canadian investors, Midland Walwyn is a fixture in Toronto's bustling financial district. From its headquarters in BCE Place the company is expanding its operations in Canada and abroad

MIDLAND WALWY

new corporate structure combined the disparate yet complementary strengths of four companies, Midland Doherty Financial Corporation, Walwyn Inc., the Scotia Bond Company and Dean Witter Reynolds (Canada) Inc.

And today, more than 110 years after the formation of that first investment firm, there are almost a thousand Midland Walwyn Financial Advisers in more than 82 offices across Canada and internationally. From the first office in Winnipeg, the Midland Walwyn family has grown into one of Canada's largest financial services organizations serving the individual investor.

The Company has established itself as an industry leader with innovative products and a commitment to service as the basis for long-term client relationships. Its growing clout in institutional, fixed income and investment banking circles, as well as its expansion into innovative money management activities like the Hercules and Atlas no-load mutual funds families, have marked Midland Walwyn's rise in industry prominence in the 1990s. The Company now manages more than $17 billion dollars in assets for more than 300,000 individual Canadians as well as institutional investors. With new headquarters, located in BCE Place, at the heart of Toronto's financial district, the Company has one of the most technologically-advanced trading and sales facilities in the Canadian industry.

From this new vantage point, Midland Walwyn looks to the future with characteristic enthusiasm. In addition to its predominant Canadian presence, important alliances have been formed with several American investment firms to provide its clients with investment opportunities in the expanded North American free trade market.

Through changes and challenges of all kinds — economic, technological, regulatory and social — Midland Walwyn has helped Canadian investors for more than 110 years and has grown from its regional beginnings to become a major force in the Canadian financial services marketplace.

Augustus Nanton, himself, would be proud.

On Midland Walwyn's vast trading floor, buy and sell orders are communicated instantly through a state-of-the-art computer network that facilitates the trading of millions of dollars in Canadian and foreign securities daily

MIDLAND WALWYN

BLUE CHIP THINKING™

ON APRIL 20, 1970, in Rexdale, Ontario, the first Canadian Radio Shack store opened, signalling the start of a new era in Canadian consumer electronics. Twenty years later, more than 800 Radio Shack outlets are a part of the everyday lives of Canadians coast to coast.

Radio Shack's unique retail success is rooted in its philosophy of offering Canadians leading-edge electronic products at affordable prices. This offering, combined with the company's commitment to put the customer first with superior service and support, has established Radio Shack as Canada's largest electronics chain.

It was that same philosophy of exceeding consumer needs and expectations that proved successful for Radio

another 102,000 square feet.

In 1978, Radio Shack constructed its present head office facility. It covered 300,000 square feet which included a large distribution centre, a fully equipped garage, a spacious truck yard and extensive office space. In 1987, the distribution centre was expanded by another 100,000 square feet.

The 1990's marketplace will present unique challenges to all Canadian retailers and Radio Shack has taken significant steps to remain at the forefront of the industry. The company has repositioned itself as a multiple niche retailer offering broader and deeper assortments in specific niche markets. Radio Shack is aggressively reaching out to potential new customers through innovative advertising programs,

Radio Shack Canada

The Better Choice — Guaranteed

Radio Shack stores are a familiar sight in cities and towns across Canada

Shack U.S.A. Starting in Boston, in 1921, Radio Shack grew from a fledging local retail operation to a multi-billion dollar retail giant.

Expanding Radio Shack U.S.A.'s retailing principles to the Canadian market soon brought the company exciting growth.

Radio Shack stores have been firmly established all over the country from Vancouver Island to Newfoundland and from the 49th parallel to the Yukon and Northwest Territories. Radio Shack is as visible in small rural communities as it is in large urban centres. Some 398 of its 858 Canadian locations are authorized dealer outlets conveniently located in Canada's smaller but vital centres.

Radio Shack's head office, located in Barrie, Ontario, was constructed in 1970. It originally covered 40,000 square feet and was expected to contain growth for five years. However, two years later, as a result of unprecedented growth, the original building was expanded to cover 123,750 square feet. In 1975, the company had to rent additional space, adding

while protecting its existing loyal customer base. The company is experimenting with new retail formats and has placed greater emphasis on sales force training to ensure that it continues to provide exceptional customer service.

Today Radio Shack employs more than 2,300 Canadians and carries a broad range of consumer electronics products including audio and video, computers and computer software, electronic kits and games, communications products and electronic accessories. The company is committed to marketing quality products at fair prices, providing customers with excellent service and maximizing shareholder value.

Radio Shack is a wholly owned subsidiary of InterTAN Inc., an international company with retail operations in Canada, Australia and the United Kingdom. In total InterTAN Inc. operates 1,700 retail stores and dealer outlets. InterTAN Inc.'s operational headquarters are located in Barrie, Ontario, just minutes away from Radio Shack Canada's head office.

From its beginning, in 1853, as a small freight-forwarding company moving goods across the Canada/U.S. border from its office in Hamilton, Canada West, American Express has grown into a leading provider of travel related and financial services. Today, the name is synonymous with quality service, security, worldwide recognition and a proven tradition of meeting customer needs.

American Express in Canada delivers business and consumer travel services through 47 American Express

airline points, travel packages, lifestyle and entertainment experiences with participating American Express partners throughout Canada and the world. In addition, Front of the Line ticket access means Canadians can enjoy the best seats to the most sought after entertainment and sports events coast-to-coast.

Canadian corporations rely on American Express to provide a full range of travel management services. The Corporate Card offers extensive Cardmember benefits and provides unique management information

American Express *A Tradition of Outstanding Service*

Canadian headquarters, Markham, Ontario

Foyer of Canadian Regional Operating Centre

Travel Service Offices, 40 Representative Offices and 8 Business Travel Centres. A global network of more than 1,700 travel service locations in 120 countries means Canadians are assured of superior service wherever they go.

The American Express Travellers Cheque, invented over 100 years ago, still provides travellers with the safest cash substitute and comprehensive emergency features which ensure security and peace of mind — features like hand-delivered refunds virtually anywhere in the world.

The American Express cards — Personal, Gold, and Platinum — are accepted across Canada and around the globe and provide a wide range of personal financial expense management, travel and entertainment services. Canadian cardmembers enjoy the most unique rewards program — Membership Rewards. The program includes

®

systems to assist companies in monitoring and controlling business and travel expenses.

With business success comes responsibility. Each year the American Express Foundation provides financial support in the areas of community service, education, and cultural programs. The Foundation selects projects that make a difference to the quality of life in communities where its employees and customers live and work. American Express supports and encourages employees to embrace the value of good citizenship, contributing time, expertise, and resources to community service organizations.

Coast-to-coast, every day, the 2,000 employees of Amex Canada Inc. and Amex Bank of Canada take pride in their achievement of providing customers from around the world with outstanding service.

Bridgestone/Firestone Canada Inc.

BRIDGESTONE/FIRESTONE CANADA INC. is a leading tire manufacturer/marketer and offers a broad range of high quality tires for passenger cars, public transit vehicles, trucks, and aircraft.

The company was established in March 1990 as a wholly owned sales and marketing subsidiary of Bridgestone/Firestone Inc. of Nashville, Tennessee,

independent dealer network of 600 outlets, including three wholly owned subsidiaries: Crown Tire Service Ltd., Service de Pneus CTR Ltee., and Crown Tire Service (Atlantic) Canada Ltd.

The Firestone division also has an extensive independent distributor network of more than 970 outlets, runs 110 Firestone Automotive Centres and supplies

Callaway Corvette fitted with Bridgestone's Run flat Technology tires

and is among the group of companies owned by the Bridgestone Corporation, which has a worldwide emphasis on technology, marketing, and service.

Bridgestone/Firestone Canada Inc.'s corporate headquarters in Mississauga, Ontario, were opened in May 1990 and the company operates distribution centres in Mississauga, Vancouver, Winnipeg, and Montreal.

In 1992, Ed Hyjek was appointed President and CEO of Bridgestone/Firestone Canada Inc. and later the same year, was recognized as "Chief Executive Officer of the Year" by Bridgestone/Firestone, Inc.

Bridgestone and Firestone brand tires are manufactured at a leading-edge plant in Joliette, Quebec. A textiles plant in Woodstock, Ontario, manufactures nylon yarns, resins and woven tie cords.

Bridgestone products are distributed through an

more than 672 Ford dealerships across the country.

The company's commitment to innovation, quality, and community involvement is reflected in the Bridgestone motto: "Serving Society with Products of Superior Quality," and through the reputation of Bridgestone products.

Bridgestone off-the-road tires are popular worldwide for superior cost-per-hour enjoyment and the company's aircraft tires are used by more than 100 international airlines.

In Canada, sophisticated breakthrough products like Blizzak, a new snow tire ensuring the best traction in the worst of winter driving conditions, introduced in 1992, and the runflat tire heralding the end of the spare tire, introduced in 1993, will ensure Bridgestone/ Firestone Canada Inc. builds on its leadership position and enhances competitiveness.

Royal Doulton Canada Limited

Dedicated To Excellence Through People And Products

ROYAL DOULTON CANADA LIMITED is the largest importer and distributor of giftware and tableware in Canada. Established in 1956 with a staff of 13, the company has expanded to an eight-acre site in Scarborough, Ontario, with 275 employees. There, product development, marketing, sales, administration, and distribution work together as a team to serve a coast-to-coast network of domestic and hotelware representatives.

Royal Doulton Canada Limited is a subsidiary of Royal Doulton plc in Stoke-on-Trent, England, which encompasses the famous ceramic brand names, Royal Doulton, Royal Albert, Minton, Royal Crown Derby, and Beswick which together total more than 1,000 years of history and tradition.

In 1988, Royal Doulton proudly acknowledged the accomplishments of Terry Fox with the production of a limited edition character jug. Pictured in the studio in Stoke-on-Trent, England, Betty Fox discusses the clay model with modeller Bill Harper

Canada is the most significant export market for Royal Doulton products per capita. These products enjoy the most popularity in Canada second only to the United Kingdom itself. To provide the best service to customers, Royal Doulton Canada Limited operates showroom facilities in Montreal and Vancouver and has a national sales staff of Domestic and Hotelware representatives. In addition, numerous retail stores operate under the name "The Royal Doulton Store" in major centres across Canada.

Royal Doulton Canada Limited's mission statement reads, in part, "through our marriage of artistry and craftsmanship, Royal Doulton offers the finest china and crystal in the world." Although Royal Doulton Canada Limited takes pride in the level of respect which its famous brand names have earned, the company is committed to continuously improving its products and service to exceed customers' expectations. The company's leadership role in this industry is a result of marketing efforts to the bridal

consumer, first-class merchandising support to each authorized dealer, response to the information technology requirements of customers, and a dedication to excellence through people and products.

Employees are proud to work for Royal Doulton Canada Limited in an environment that encourages innovative contributions to improving service. The company is committed to the community and environment and has implemented the use of new packaging loosefil which is both recyclable and biodegradable. Corporate financial support and product donations are extended to numerous national and regional charitable and arts organizations. In 1988 Royal Doulton was especially proud to honour the tenth anniversary of Terry Fox's run in support of cancer research by producing a character jug of his likeness in a limited edition of three. One of the jugs was auctioned for $32,000 with all proceeds going to Canadian cancer research.

The imagery of Canada has been commemorated in numerous ways through Royal Doulton products. The founding of Quebec in 1608 by Samuel de Champlain; the formation of the Dominion of Canada in 1867; landmarks such as Lake Louise and Niagara Falls; indigenous wildlife; the centenary of The Royal Canadian Mounted Police and even the maple tree have all been depicted on Royal Doulton wares. Many of these subjects are sought after by enthusiastic and patriotic Canadian collectors who scour antique markets and auctions to add to their collections.

Royal Doulton Canada Limited is proud to play a part in Canadian history and remains dedicated to enhancing the quality of life for loyal Canadian customers.

Philip Environmental Inc.

PHILIP ENVIRONMENTAL INC. is a fully integrated by-product management and environmental services company based in Hamilton, Ontario, with operations throughout Canada and the United States. The company has achieved rapid growth in recent years through a number of acquisitions in Canada and the U.S. Philip is Canada's largest recycler of commercial and industrial waste, and one of North America's leading integrated environmental service companies.

Philip is a "made in Canada" success story. The company was founded by two brothers, Allen and Philip Fracassi in the early 1980s with a vision of treating one industry's waste as another industry's raw material. Under their continuing leadership, the corporate objective is to maximize the use and value of industrial waste streams through mid-processing and reuse of recycled materials in industrial applications. Some examples include recycling of foundry sands and iron-bearing wastes from the steel industry and waste lime from sugar refining for use as raw material in the cement industry. Ongoing research and development continues to support maximizing diversion of waste from landfills through the development of new technologies and markets for recycled products.

The company is organized under four "Pillars" of operation including Solid Waste, Chemical Waste, Resource Recovery, and Environmental Services.

Solid Waste includes industrial, commercial, and municipal recycling and disposal. Chemical Waste

includes processing and recycling involving alternative fuel programs for waste oils and solvents and chemical and physical treatment for chemical wastes and industrial wastewater. Resource Recovery includes recycling of solid and liquid metal bearing wastes for reclamation of copper, brass, tin, aluminum ferrous metals and plastics.

Environmental Services include a full range of environmental and technical recycling services including site and waste auditing, lab services, site remediation, risk assessments, emergency response, groundwater and hydrogeological studies and geotechnical engineering. Philip operates the largest emergency response network in Canada.

Through Philip Utilities Management Corporation, the company provides research, development and operational capabilities in municipal and industrial water and wastewater treatment.

Philip operations are governed by the company's environmental policy, seeking to maximize diversion of waste from landfill, minimize environmental impact of operations and establishing community involvement in areas where Philip has operations. The company undergoes regular internal and external environmental audits and an annual external environmental audit to ensure strict adherence to the highest environmental standards. Philip has an excellent environmental "track record" for which the company has won numerous citations and awards.

Edward Gajdel, Longside Image

Allen Fracassi, President and Chief Executive Officer and (r) Philip Fracassi, Executive Vice President and Chief Operating Officer. In the background, Philip Metal Recovery Industries, the only detinning operation in Canada and a leading processor of post-consumer cans

CANADA'S leading biotechnology research company, Connaught Laboratories Limited is the country's largest producer of biological products for human health. Its vaccine sales to the United States, Europe, Asia, and Africa make it known worldwide.

Named in 1914 after the Duke of Connaught, son of Queen Victoria, and Governor-General of Canada, 1911-1916, the laboratory was largely the result of the efforts of Dr. John FitzGerald, a pioneer in producing serums and anti-toxins. With the outbreak of World War I, Connaught, as a part of the University of Toronto, produced vaccines against diphtheria, smallpox, typhoid, tetanus, and rabies. Following the discovery of the hormone insulin by Drs. Banting and Best at the University of Toronto in 1921, it became the world's first manufacturer of insulin and remains a leading supplier of it through Connaught Novo Nordisk Inc.

In the 1940s Connaught was the first company to develop large scale methods to produce penicillin and a decade later worked closely with Dr. Jonas Salk to be the first mass producer of inactivated polio vaccine. Connaught also assisted Dr. Albert Sabin in developing an oral polio vaccine.

Excellence and in 1992, the Gold Award for Marketing.

In 1989 Connaught became a member of the Pasteur Mérieux family of companies, a biological organization with traditions going back to Louis Pasteur. Pasteur Mérieux Connaught is a part of the Rhône Poulenc global organization.

The major focus of Connaught's research is on developing new and improved vaccines. Current R&D priorities include a genetically engineered version of the Human Immunodeficiency Virus (HIV), as well as respiratory syncytial, parainfluenza and the influenza viruses

Connaught Laboratories

Excellence in Biologicals for a Healthier World

Connaught's connection with the University of Toronto ended in 1972 when it was reorganized as a fully integrated commercial research and manufacturing company by the Canada Development Corporation. Six years later Connaught expanded its operations into the United States with the purchase of facilities in Swiftwater, Pennsylvania. By 1987 the company had developed a new technology that led to a conjugate vaccine against Haemophilus influenza type b, a major cause of infant meningitis. Marketed as ProHIBiT®, the company has received a Gold Award for Innovation at the 1989 Canada Awards for Business

which cause respiratory infections in young children and the elderly.

Its emphasis on research places Connaught in the top 20 companies among the leading 500 companies in Canada. More than 15 percent of Connaught's total sales worldwide is earmarked for research and development — more than $50 million in 1994 as the company's projected sales for the year are expected to reach $341 million.

Connaught is committed to its vision — *Excellence in Biologicals for a Healthier World* — and its commitment to protect people around the world from disease.

OVER a century ago, two young American pharmacy graduates established in England a company whose aim was to discover and market new medicines to promote human health and improve the quality of life.

Today, the global British-based company, Wellcome PLC., is represented in Canada by Burroughs Wellcome Inc., which bears the names of the founders — Silas Burroughs and Henry Wellcome.

Burroughs Wellcome Inc.

Proud of the Past: Committed to the Future

State-of-the-art manufacturing facilities

Focused communication sets the pace for the Burroughs Wellcome team

the first drug RETROVIR*Pr (zidovudine) to slow the progression of the AIDS virus.

The company is also known for its development of the first marketed lung surfactant EXOSURF NEONATAL*Pr (colfosceril palmitate) used in neonatal respiratory distress syndrome.

Additionally, Wellcome has a strong commitment to anaesthesia, having produced a heritage of surgical muscle relaxants including the development of curare-like compounds.

Subsequent newer compounds TRACRIUM*Pr (atracurium besylate) and NUROMAX*Pr (doxacurium chloride), discovered over the years have made significant contributions to anaesthesia and have led to Wellcome's dominant role in this field.

Wellcome's discoveries have been significant. In the very few times the Nobel Prize for Medicine has been awarded to pharmaceutical researchers, no less than five have gone to researchers associated with Wellcome. These included laureates, Drs. George Hitchings and Gertrude Ellon whose pioneering work paved the way for advances in modern cancer therapy.

Burroughs Wellcome Inc. is located in Kirkland, Quebec, a suburb of Montreal. Since its inception in 1906 the company has grown to be both a major competitor and leading producer of pharmaceuticals in the Canadian marketplace.

The company's founders chose the unicorn as its corporate symbol for good reason. Although mythical, it is inextricably linked to the power to heal and cure. These ideals are maintained in the Wellcome world, and notably in Burroughs Wellcome Inc., through innovative research, a strong sense of community support, and provision to the future through education.

Wellcome is well known for its research heritage. Significant lifesaving breakthrough drugs were discovered in the areas of leukemia, bacterial, and viral infections, and malaria. In fact, the early transplantation of kidneys was made possible by IMURAN*Pr (azathioprine), an invention of Wellcome's scientists.

Recent Wellcome discoveries have been in the treatment of herpesvirus infections ZOVIRAX*Pr (acyclovir) which include illnesses such as genital herpes, chicken pox, and shingles. It also pioneered

Wellcome research will be directed towards improved therapies in lung and breast cancers, epilepsy, and stroke. Moreover, the Canadian company will strive to be a key generator of clinical research data to support new drug entities for worldwide markets.

The company believes medical care cannot remain isolated from social and educational issues. It must work closely with both health providers and the people affected by disease through programs which support them.

An example of this commitment is Positive Action, an international commitment to education and care issues in HIV/AIDS. In this regard, Burroughs Wellcome Inc. has supported grants for AIDS walks to raise money for AIDS service organizations, as well as provide them with information services. The company also supports educational materials for consumer groups.

Burroughs Wellcome Inc. continues its commitment to the training of future health professionals through providing grants and bursaries. Such is Burroughs Wellcome Inc. Proud of its past. Committed to its future.

Wellcome

FLAT, unleavened breads were all that mankind knew until 3000 BC when, allegedly, an Egyptian baker set aside some dough forgetting to place it on the fire. The growth of yeast cells caused the dough to expand dramatically. Adding this "sour dough" to his regular batch, the baker produced an aerated, light-textured loaf which soon became a luxury not intended for common consumption.

By 200 BC, the Romans had invented their own leavening and fermenting agents. And when Europeans

Fleischmann's Yeast

arrived in North America, they brought with them baking techniques little changed from ancient Roman times. Maintaining uniformity of the yeast creation process was difficult because the environment of nineteenth century homes could not be controlled. In 1868, brothers Maximillian and Charles Fleischmann revolutionized both home and commercial baking with the development of Fleischmann's Yeast, the first compressed yeast sold in North America.

Legend declares that

By the end of the last century customers had become familiar with the freshness-preserving, tin-foil wrapping with the bright yellow label. Today Fleischmann's Yeast is the market leader in North America with high brand awareness and a very loyal consumer following

Charles Louis Fleischmann, a visitor to New York in 1865, so disliked the bread consumed by Americans that he returned home to Budapest, isolated a quality strain of yeast and returned to New York City with the vial in his vest pocket. Establishing Fleischmann & Company, the brothers created an extensive distribution system. Initially, Charles Fleischmann distributed his yeast cakes in a hand-held basket going from house to house. Success through advertising and promotion led to a growing demand and eventually delivery by horse-drawn carriages. Refrigerated rail cars serviced more than 1,000 bakeries in the 1880s. By the turn of the

century, over 30,000 bakeries and 225,000 grocers were similarly serviced. Freshness was so important that there was never more than one week's requirement of yeast in the entire country.

In June 1929 The Fleischmann's Yeast Company absorbed four smaller corporations: Royal Baking Powder Company, E.W. Gillette Company Ltd. of Canada, The Widlar Food Products Company, and Chase and Sanborn, Inc.. Together these companies formed Standard Brands, Incorporated.

Throughout the years the Fleischmann's Brand has continued to stand for innovative techniques. During World War II Fleischmann's Laboratories developed strains of yeast containing large amounts of vitamin B1, enabling white bread to be "enriched." An "active dry yeast" which did not require refrigeration permitted the army to ship and store large quantities of yeast overseas for troops. In the 1980s, the company developed "Quick-Rise Yeast" which allowed bread to rise 50 percent faster.

In addition to product advancement, Fleischmann's has cultivated the baking art itself with recipe dissemination programs, a toll free 1-800 Baker's "helpline," and grassroots support through rural Country Fair sponsorships and baking contests.

By 1986 Specialty Brands had purchased the Fleischmann's Yeast product line. Specialty Brands' family includes other famous names such as Allen's, Spice Islands, Blue Ribbon, Dromedary, Dec-A-Cake, French's ® and Schwartz.®

A plant in Lasalle, Quebec, produces all of the company's Canadian retail yeast requirements as well as industrial and food service applications. Opened in 1928, the plant currently employs 83 full time staff and has seen significant volume growth in the late 1980s and early 1990s. This ensures for Canadians excellent baking results into the next century and beyond.

French's ® and Schwartz ® are trademarks of Reckitt & Colman Inc.

MacMillan Bloedel Limited

A Canadian Forest Industry Pioneer

THREE founding British Columbia companies — the Powell River Company, Bloedel Stewart and Welch, and the H.R. MacMillan Export Company — were each built by visionary men who foresaw the need to provide quality paper and wood products to millions of people around the world.

In 1908 American entrepreneurs, Dr. Dwight Brooks and Michael Scanlon, saw that Powell River, north of Vancouver, was the perfect location for a newsprint mill. The Powell River Company turned out the first roll of newsprint manufactured in B.C. in 1912. It soon became one of the world's largest newsprint plants and today is credited with introducing the first self-dumping log barge to B.C.

Another visionary, Julius Bloedel, a Seattle lawyer, realized the enormous potential of B.C.'s softwood forests. In 1911 he and two partners, John Stewart and Patrick Welch, began acquiring large blocks of Vancouver Island forests. Their Franklin River camp soon became one of the world's largest logging operations. Here, in the 1930s, the Canadian industry saw its first steel spar and chainsaw. In 1938, Bloedel Stewart and Welch became the first logging company in the province to plant seedlings in a logged-over area.

The H.R. MacMillan Company was created by one of Canada's great pioneers, Harvey — better known as H.R. — MacMillan, B.C.'s first Chief Forester who had gained considerable experience in world lumbering circles during World War I. With his good friend Whitford Van Dusen, another forester, he incorporated a company in 1919 to sell B.C. lumber products to foreign markets. In 1924 they established a shipping company that would become one of the world's biggest charter companies. Their acquisition of extensive forest lands laid the foundation for today's program of intensive forest management.

Each company experienced continued expansion until mergers in 1951 and 1959 brought them together to create one of world's most fully integrated forest products companies. Initially MacMillan Bloedel operations were concentrated in coastal B.C. Starting in the 1960s, the company expanded across North America as well as to Europe and the United Kingdom. Acquisitions and construction activities over the years have given MB worldwide assets of more than $4 billion. Today, the company's marketing and distribution activities ensure

Parallam parallel strand lumber is one of several composite wood products developed by MacMillan Bloedel researchers making the company a leader in this field

MacMillan Bloedel has had its own tree improvement centre since 1970 to ensure superior seedlings and strong healthy forests

wood and paper products reach people worldwide.

Emloyees today pride themselves in being leaders. MB research people have developed a range of new, environmentally-friendly products and processes aimed at getting the highest possible return from the forest resource. In the area of scientific forest renewal, employees are dedicated to forestry practices based on achieving the best total use of the forest for everyone and ensuring that harvested trees are replaced for future generations.

Building on a rich tradition of always planning for the future, MB employees are ready to take the company into the next century.

The Prudential Insurance Company of America

Eighty-five Years of Canadian Achievement

THE PRUDENTIAL was founded in Newark, New Jersey, in 1873, as the Widows and Orphans Friendly Society. It officially began business in 1875 when the name was changed to The Prudential Friendly Society.

The Prudential Insurance Company of America has been part of the Canadian financial scene since 1909, when offices were opened in Hamilton, London, Stratford, Toronto and Montreal.

At the end of 1909, The Prudential was operating in 25 cities across Canada with 125 staff managers and 422 agents who sold $11 million of insurance and helped build assets of $250,000. By 1929, The Prudential was among the leading insurance companies in Canada.

Sales in Canada had reached almost $108 million by the company's 75th birthday. The time had come for a Canadian head office. On Friday, December 1, 1950, employees attended the official opening of the Canadian head office, located at King and Bay Streets in downtown Toronto. In 1985, the Canadian head office moved to The Consilium, a joint venture project in Scarborough, Ontario, where it is now located. The Consilium complex includes three office towers with plans for a fourth.

The Prudential Insurance Company of America is one of the largest financial institutions in the world. In Canada, The Prudential employs more than 2,800 people in its head office in Scarborough, Ontario, and in over 100 offices from coast to coast.

The company offers a full range of group and individual life, health, home, auto, travel and disability insurance as well as investment products such as RRSPs, RRIFs, mutual funds, fixed-term investments and commercial and residential mortgages. It also has an extensive real estate portfolio.

The Prudential's major real estate investments include 95 Wellington West,

a 330,000 square foot office building in downtown Toronto; the Twin Atria Building in Edmonton; and The Consilium, a joint-ownership, mixed-use project in Scarborough's City Centre. The company also has a minority ownership position in Bentall Corporation. The Prudential's Property Investments Department also manages real estate assets for institutional clients.

The company has an investment portfolio in Canada of close to five billion dollars containing various government and corporate bonds. The security investments department specializes in corporate, public and private placement debt obligation and in common stock investments on behalf of the company's insurance and pension operations.

The Prudential's Canadian Head Office opened at King and Bay Streets in downtown Toronto in December 1950. The occasion also marked The Prudential's 75th anniversary

The Consilium, the present location of The Prudential's Canadian Head Office, opened in Scarborough, Ontario, in 1985. The project includes three towers, with plans for a fourth

W.C. Wood Company Limited

1994 Top Team at W.C. Wood Company

O N DECEMBER 6, 1896, when Wilbert Copeland (Bert) Wood was born, Ontario farmers like his grandfather John and his uncle Charles were still clearing land for farming. Bert was raised on that farm in Luther Township until 1909 when (again like many Ontarians) his family trekked to Saskatchewan where they took a homestead.

Bert Wood graduated in the early '20s from the University of Saskatchewan in Agricultural Engineering and joined Massey-Harris in Toronto where he worked as a research engineer on Massey's new farm machinery until the Great Depression forced Massey to lay him off in 1930.

Wood saw the introduction of electric power across rural Ontario as an opportunity for a new business and founded W.C. Wood Company Limited in February 1930 to manufacture electrical farm equip-ment. His first product was an electrically powered grain grinder which would save farmers the necessity of having to transport grain from the farm to the feed mills for grinding and back to the farm for feed. He had parts for his grinder cast and tooled at a local machine shop, assembled them on the back porch of

his landlady's house and with the $150.00 he received from a Brampton-area farmer for his first grinder he established his new business.

Wood rented an empty candy shop on Howard Park Avenue in Toronto, bought a lathe and machined the castings for his own electric grinders. From this one-man shop, the company developed over the next 64 years into Canada's leading freezer producer and the largest Canadian-owned appliance manufacturer.

By 1934 W.C. Wood Company had moved to a larger factory on Dundas Street north of Bloor in Toronto where it expanded its electrical farm equipment line to include an oat roller, a farm milking machine, and a farm milk cooler. It was the refrigeration system designed for milk coolers that got W.C. Wood Company into its first electrically operated farm freezer in 1938. Little did the founder realize at that time that this product would be a stepping stone on the path from farm equipment to appliance manufacturer.

In 1941 the company moved from Toronto to a 25,000 square foot factory at 123 Woolwich Street in Guelph, where for the next 15 years it grew and prospered expanding the facility to 40,000 square feet. By 1956 another move was necessitated and the company acquired the Taylor Forbes property and moved its manufacturing facility to 5 Arthur Street South where an existing 90,000 square-foot plant allowed the company to continue to grow over the next few years. By 1963, additional space was needed and the first of many additions was undertaken which resulted in the company owning two Guelph plants by 1985, totalling 600,000 square feet. By this time, the company's total manufacturing was devoted to appli-ance production, chest and upright freezers, compact refrigerators, compact kitchens, humidifiers, dehu-midifiers, and rangehoods. More than 95 percent of the total production was for the domestic market with the remaining being shipped to the United States, South America, Europe, Asia, and the Caribbean.

By 1985, however, free trade was in the air and the company began focusing on a North American market with all the opportunities that lay south of the border. Initially all United States sales were of Canadian-made product. However, by 1988 it became apparent that higher value added costs in Canada would necessitate a U.S. facility to serve this U.S. market.

Twelve months were taken to study 40 communities in 6 states, and finally in late August 1989, the company announced the selection of Ottawa, Ohio, as its choice for its U.S. manufacturing facility. In early September 1989 ground was broken on an alfalfa field to construct a new 137,000 square foot factory to manufacture upright freezers for the North American market. Equipment started to arrive at the new plant in January 1990, tool proving commenced in March, and first production came off the lines in late April.

The new plant has provided three benefits to the corporation. It has allowed the company to take advantage of significantly lower operating costs. It has allowed the company to reduce its exposure to exchange rates by exporting back to Canada upright freezers to offset a significant surplus of U.S. funds generated by the exporting from Canada to the U.S. of chest freezers. Most importantly, it also gave the company a U.S. presence that enhanced the

opportunities for the company to expand its U.S. sales. The result of all this was that while certain production was being transferred from Canada to the U.S. employment continued to grow in both countries.

Over the years, the company has received many awards from various sources for its products including the National Industrial Design Award in 1955 presented by C.D. Howe, numerous customer recognition awards for customer responsiveness, quality, and supplier/customer partnership as well as an "A" for Achievement Award from the Ontario government recognizing the world leadership provided by W.C. Wood Company for energy efficiency in its products.

In 1977 the company produced its one millionth freezer and by 1983 the company had reached the two million mark in its appliance production. In June 1991 the company on both sides of the border celebrated its five millionth appliance.

W.C. Wood Company is still a privately owned Canadian company with its owners continuing to work in the business. Its objective is to see that at the end of each year its suppliers, customers, employees, and shareholders are each a little better off. It looks forward to the challenges of a tri-lateral trade agreement between Canada, the United States, and Mexico. It will continue its focus on productivity, quality, customer responsiveness, integrity, and organizational effectiveness combined with a strong financial foundation.

Grandfather John Wood and Uncle Charlie, in 1897, clearing family farm where W.C. Wood was born

W.C. Wood, Founder of the Company

ELIZABETH ARDEN INC., an international, multimillion-dollar corporation, was founded by Florence Nightingale Graham in the early part of the twentieth century when female entrepreneurs were a rare commodity. Small but indomitable, with luxurious red-gold hair, Graham was a connoisseur of fashion with flawless taste and exacting standards from which she never wavered.

Born in Woodbridge, Ontario, in 1884, Graham was inspired by her namesake to study nursing. As a student she recognized the link between physical health, massage, and the maintenance of healthy-looking skin. At age 24, Graham immigrated to New York. By 1910 she had opened a small Fifth Avenue Salon, creating her own skin treatment preparations and giving facials. During this early period Graham chose Elizabeth Arden as her professional name. Soon christened the "little Canadian woman with the magic hands," Arden easily established a loyal clientele.

As the salons with their famous red doors opened throughout the United States, Europe and the Far East, Arden's commitment to perfection in formulas, packaging and services established her company as a leader in the beauty business.

retexturize the skin, making it firmer, smoother and softer. The revolutionary, biodegradable, single-dose gelatin capsules offer easy application for the consumer. The make-up category has also continued to grow with the launch of such products as the Flawless Finish Foundation Collection, and Lip Spa, the first lipstick ever to contain water.

The fragrance category represents an enormous source of prestige for Elizabeth Arden. In addition to Blue Grass, which has maintained steady sales since its 1936 launch, Red Door was added to the Elizabeth Arden fragrances in 1989. With the development of a fine fragrance division, Parfums International, the company is represented on fragrance counters worldwide with such leading brands as Chloé, Lagerfeld for Men, Fendi, Fendi Uomo, Elizabeth Taylor's Passion for Men, Elizabeth Taylor's White Diamonds, and the Elizabeth Taylor Jewel Collection.

Treatment, makeup and fragrance. In all categories the "little woman with the magic hands" has made a lasting mark and has left an unprecedented legacy to be carried well into the twenty-first century and beyond.

Elizabeth Arden Inc.

As Chairman of the Board and Director of all Arden Enterprises, Elizabeth Arden continued to supervise the production process and, until her death on October 18, 1966, inspired such new ideas as the first brown-toned (Burnt Sugar) and blue-toned (Cyclamen) lipsticks and the use of lightwear plastic jars as packages for skin cream.

Throughout the 1970s and 1980s, the Elizabeth Arden Research Laboratory continued to produce landmark products. In 1974, Visible Difference Refining Moisture-Creme Complex, the first of what the *New York Times* called the "super creams" appeared on the market. Visible Difference was the first product in the cosmetics industry to actually document skin penetration. Following four years of research, the Millenium line of cell renewal products was introduced. Millenium products work on and within the epidermis to accelerate the natural cell renewal process.

Scientific breakthroughs continue at Elizabeth Arden during the 1990s. Ceramide Time Complex Capsules and Ceramide Eyes Time Complex Capsules work to

Sunflowers. Elizabeth Arden's newest fragrance. An exhilarating fragrance that recharges the senses, renews the spirit and creates a mood all its own

This 71,000 square foot high-tech property located in Vancouver is indicative of the ten million square feet of industrial properties in the portfolio

Scotia Place is a 550,000 square foot office building located on the main downtown intersection in Edmonton

Morguard Investments Limited

making Morguard the largest manager of tax-exempt real estate in Canada.

Morguard operates nine regional offices across Canada where property management, appraisal, leasing and accounting functions are performed, and complements its internal real estate expertise through the use of external consultants, including architects, engineers, lawyers, brokers, appraisers, and general contractors. When called upon, these professionals provide the highest level of expertise available in each of the markets that Morguard operates.

Morguard's Office, Industrial and Shopping Centre operations departments are responsible for day-to-day management of the properties which comprise the investment portfolio. The economy of scale associated with the operation of a 21 million square foot portfolio allows Morguard to provide a level of service which is unavailable elsewhere in the industry.

The growth in the size of the managed portfolio during the past 17 years serves as testimony to the successful relationship that Morguard continues to enjoy with its clients and tenants.

The Morguard managed investment portfolio has approximately 30 percent of its assets in office properties, 34 percent in retail, 24 percent in industrial, 11 percent in mixed use, and 1 percent in development sites.

This balance has allowed investors to participate in the service, consumer product, and industrial sectors of the economy and has been proven to be risk adverse and profitable.

Portfolio diversification by geographic location, reflecting population base and strength of the local economy, is as important as diversification by property type.

Current strategy has resulted in 30 percent of the portfolio in Victoria and Vancouver, 11 percent in Edmonton and Calgary, 6 percent in Saskatchewan and Winnipeg, 36 percent in Toronto, 7 percent in Ottawa and 10 percent in Montreal.

M ORGUARD INVESTMENTS LIMITED is a full-services, real estate investment management and development company which offers value added financial products to institutions wishing to invest profitably in Canadian property.

The company purchases, develops, manages and sells assets on behalf of its clients, endeavouring to provide each of them with a well-diversified, expanding, investment portfolio.

Morguard also serves the accommodation needs of Canadian business, by providing well-located, superior managed office, industrial and retail space in target markets. While pursuing its business goals, Morguard stresses innovation and intelligent risk-sharing in all of its endeavours, bound by the balanced interests of tenants, investor clients, employees and shareholders. Morgard is owned 80 percent by The Metropolitan Life Insurance Company and 20 percent by management.

Morguard established itself as a major force in the Canadian real estate industry in the late 1960s and early 1970s, through the placement of mortgage investments on behalf of Canadian pension funds and other institutions.

In 1975, Morguard pioneered the concept of tax-exempt real estate equity investment for Canadian pension funds and created Pensionfund Realty Limited, a company it has managed since inception. Currently Morguard manages $1.8 billion of real estate on behalf of the company's institutional clients.

The leasable area of the client portfolio is some 21 million square feet, housing over 2,500 tenants,

MERCK FROSST CANADA INC. is Canada's largest fully-integrated pharmaceutical company. Its more than eleven hundred employees are engaged in the discovery, development, manufacture, marketing and sales of prescription and over-the-counter pharmaceutical products.

Most corporate activity takes place at the company's Kirkland, Quebec, headquarters, just outside Montreal. Regional offices are based in Vancouver, Calgary,

Merck Frosst

Canada's Largest Fully-Integrated Pharmaceutical Company....

Merck Frosst facility in Kirkland, Quebec

Winnipeg, Edmonton, Toronto, Ottawa, Quebec City and Halifax.

Merck Frosst's roots in Canada stretch back nearly a century. The chemist Charles Frosst and four associates, including William S. Ayerst and Frank W. Horner, founded Charles E. Frosst & Co. in Montreal in 1899. The famous numbered analgesics such as 217® and 222® were the company's first products .

By the mid-twenties, the company was entirely family-owned. That same decade, Frosst became the first producer of synthetic vitamin D in Canada. The company's reputation as a leader in research was bolstered in the mid-1940s when Frosst pioneered the field of nuclear medicine with the development and commercialization of the first radioactive pharmaceutical products for sale in Canada and abroad.

In 1965 Charles E. Frosst & Co. joined Merck & Co., Inc. of Whitehouse Station, New Jersey, whose history began with a German pharmacy acquired in 1668 by Friedrich Jacob Merck. The Merck family founded the American firm in 1891 and established a branch in Montreal in 1911. Towards the end of World War II, Merck & Co. Ltd. was producing penicillin in the first deep fermentation unit to be operated in the Commonwealth.

Merck continued to grow rapidly in the post-war period, merging with Sharp & Dohme in 1953 and then with Charles E. Frosst & Co. in 1965. In the late sixties, a Merck Frosst team in Montreal scored a pharmaceutical first with the discovery of timolol maleate, marked as

BLOCADREN® (for the treatment of high blood pressure) and TIMOPTIC® (for glaucoma).

The Merck Frosst Centre for Therapeutic Research is the largest biomedical research facility in the country and employs more than 150 world class scientists. Since 1976 Merck Frosst researchers have been the lead team in the world in leukotriene research, naturally occurring substances implicated in respiratory diseases. Merck Frosst scientists are developing compounds that may one day represent breakthrough therapies for the treatment of asthma and other respiratory conditions.

Merck Frosst is also active in the communities it serves, particularly in the area of supporting and promoting science and science education. The company hosts dozens of field trips for students, has developed a program which sees Merck Frosst scientists visit local high schools to talk about the research they do, and is engaged in an ambitious nation-wide co-op student program. In addition to numerous other scholarships, research grants and university faculty sabbaticals, Merck Frosst also provides scholarships to pharmacy and medicine students across the country, research fellowships to medical and pharmacy schools and is a corporate sponsor of the Federal Government's Canada Scholarships Program.

As the pre-eminent pharmaceutical company in Canada and as part of the world's leading pharmaceutical company, Merck & Co., Inc., the Merck Frosst name stands for superior research for superior products and for a highly desirable working environment.

217®, 222® - Trademark Merck Frosst Canada Inc.

BLOCADREN, ® TIMOPTIC® - Trademark Merck & Co., Inc./Merck Frosst Canada Inc., R.U.

KODAK came to Canada in 1899 and first located on Colborne Street in downtown Toronto. A staff of 10 cut and packed film and paper, fitted lenses and shutters to cameras and mixed chemicals.

Three years later the company moved to King Street West where it eventually built three buildings — the last in 1908. By that time, the manufacture of film, paper and mounts was already under way and the staff had grown to 108 persons.

Over the years, Kodak's operations in Canada have expanded substantially. Kodak Canada is the nation's

Kodak Canada Inc.
Manufacturing in Canada for the World

only manufacturer of photographic products and the leading supplier of imaging products for photography, health care, document management, printing and publishing, and the motion picture industry.

Since 1913, Kodak Canada's headquarters and manufacturing facilities have been located on a 20-hectare site in Metropolitan Toronto, with regional offices in Montreal and Vancouver, and district offices in major cities. The more than 2,000 Canadians who are Kodak Canada, market, distribute, service and support products from coast- to-coast as well as man-ufacture a wide variety of photographic products designed to meet the imaging needs of Canadians.

Kodak Canada has earned the world mandate to produce micrographic film for Eastman Kodak and also manufactures a major portion of the company's EASTMAN Color Print film, the film used for projection in movie theatres. Exports of micrographic and motion picture film are a substantial portion of Kodak Canada's business.

Kodak Canada's world class manufacturing opera-tions have earned two international citations: Class A MRPII (Manufacturing Resources Planning), the first of the Eastman Kodak companies in the world to move to this standard company-wide; and registration to ISO 9000 standards for the company's Manufacturing and Supply, and for its Customer Service and Customer Equipment Services Divisions.

Kodak Canada's ability to meet the criteria for these demanding benchmarks reflects the dedication of Kodak Canada people to the Quality Leadership Process (QLP) which allows employees at all levels to assess and improve the quality of the products and

services they provide. Working in teams, employees define their customers, identify customer expectations and develop strategies to meet or exceed those expectations.

Kodak's goal is to continue its world leadership in images. That means a commitment to expanding the utility of film — the internationally-recognized standard of excellence for image capture. It also means combining the best features of film with the unique capabilities of electronics to define a new paradigm of excellence in images and imaging.

Film coating control room

Kodak has harnessed photographic and electronic technologies to provide customers with innovative products for every imaging need — capture, manage-ment, display and storage. The emphasis is on devel-oping effective solutions for the customer's application rather than simply placing the product.

In the 1990s "images" mean more than just pictures and the needs of Kodak's customers are, indeed, diverse. Governments, institutions and businesses of all kinds look to Kodak for products and programs to solve the challenges of information management.

Photographers, photofinishers, cinematographers, printers and publishers look to Kodak to lead them into the world of imaging made possible by the merging of traditional and digital technologies.

Similarly, in the world of medicine and health care, Kodak continues to take a leading role in diagnostic imaging with an expanding portfolio of leading-edge products.

Kodak Canada's leadership means it will continue to set new standards of quality, performance and reliability — that is the Kodak Canada commitment to its customers.

Home Hardware Stores Limited

Bringing a World of Products to Canadians

"...part of the Canadian scene"

Dealers on Parade

HOME HARDWARE STORES LIMITED is a Dealer-owned company, controlled and operated by independent hardware, building supply, and furniture Dealers across Canada.

The company was founded in 1964 by Walter Hachborn, Henry Sittler and a small group of independent hardware retailers who wished to serve their communities and compete successfully with large chain organizations. Their aim was to puchase products for less, eliminate the middleman's profits and develop an equity in the company in relationship to their purchases. By banding together and working collectively toward the common cause, they have achieved their goal of preserving the independent Dealer.

There are about 1,000 stores. They are located in every province and territory of Canada. Annual retail sales exceed 1.25 billion dollars and Dealers are served from four major distribution centres. The Home Office is located at one of these, in the village of St. Jacobs, Ontario, just north of the city of Waterloo. Home is conscious of its responsibility as a corporate citizen and supports community and national interests by offering stable employment and opportunities for staff development and advancement. It is Canadian in its objectives and supports Canadian industry wherever possible, thereby creating employment and strength in the Canadian economy.

Home Hardware's mission as a completely Dealer-owned company is to supply quality products and services and offer programs to operate efficient stores, which will provide the consumer with competitive prices and superior service.

The company has one of the largest and most modern paint and chemical manufacturing plants in Canada. Its Beauti-Tone paint products consistently rank among the top quality brands in the country and are sold in all Home Hardware locations.

Home Dealers have the advantage of controlling their own destiny. The company is owned by the Dealers it serves and is controlled by a Board of Directors elected from among the Dealers and representing every region of Canada. Among the management and staff are skills in every field: buyers, marketers, merchandisers, operational specialists, financial and accounting professionals.

Home Hardware's program begins with consistent, low-cost distribution. Merchandise cost is among the lowest in the industry because of the systems and volumes purchased by the company. This purchasing power has become worldwide through the company's affiliation with Le group Ro-Na Inc. operating in the province of Quebec, HWI of the United States and Interlink International Inc., which is an organization of 18 dealer-owned member companies located throughout North America, Europe, South Africa, Australia and New Zealand.

A Canadian corporate achiever, Home Hardware truly brings a world of products and services to Canadians of all walks of life in cities and towns from sea unto sea. The big yellow trucks and distinctive HH logo are a friendly part of the Canadian scene.

Color Your World

Canada's Best Paint & Wallpaper Value...
We Guarantee It!

EACH year Color Your World employees help millions of people decorate and beautify their homes. Whether Canadians need paint, wallcoverings, window treatments or just decorating advice, there is one clear choice — Color Your World.

Canadian owned and operated, Color Your World is truly a Canadian story of achievement and success. The company began as a small paint store on Toronto's College Street in 1912. For many years its claim to fame was household paints. They offered the country's widest paint selection with excellent quality and prices. During the 1970s and 1980s the company also became the largest retailer of wallpaper in Canada. Today these paint and wallpaper lines are complemented by the finest selection of window treatments available.

Color Your World operates over 300 retail stores along with research, manufacturing and distribution facilities in both Toronto and Vancouver. As well, over 35,000 commercial painters, architects and maintenance contractors depend on the high quality of Color Your World products to meet their maintenance or decorating requirements.

Color Your World's record of success is the result of a total organizational commitment to customer service.

Every one of its 1,500 plus employees and franchisees is required to graduate from an intensive customer service training program. Graduates must pass the 128-hour course with a minimum grade of 80 percent. This training program has been acclaimed by the Ontario Ministry of Skills Development and designated as a college credit course.

Thanks to the high standards of customer service, Color Your World can offer the Ultimate Guarantee. This revolutionary guarantee assures customers that they will be fully satisfied with the product quality, the price and, most importantly, the calibre of service. If a customer is dissatisfied, for any reason, with the quality of their service they will receive a credit note equalling 10 percent of their purchase.

Color Your World's customer service record is rivalled by its rich tradition of product innovations. Some examples include the environmentally friendly Eco Logo products and the country's first high gloss latex paint. Another exciting development is Color Magic. This computer system can display paint and wallpaper in a wide variety of room settings. Customers can now visualize how different patterns and colors will appear in a room before they buy.

Color Your World employees are dedicated to giving the decorating customer the very best quality, superior service, the lowest prices and the widest selection. It all adds up to value for the customer and it is the reason why Color Your World's slogan reads as it does:

Color Your World — Canada's Best Paint and Wallpaper Value! We Guarantee It!

The North West Company Inc.

The new Tomorrow Store concept (introduced in Nelson House, Manitoba, 1993) offers a superior shopping environment custom-designed for each community it serves

THE business of the Company is one of the longest continuing enterprises in the world, tracing its roots back to North American's first trading post, established on the shores of James Bay in 1668 — where a NORTHERN store is still operating today. The original North West Company was a partnership of Montreal-based entrepreneurial traders formed in 1779. Between 1779 and 1821, The North West Company "Wintering Partners" travelled inland from the St. Lawrence River and the Great Lakes vigorously competing against the Hudson's Bay Company and venturing westward to the Pacific Ocean. In 1821 the two companies amalgamated under the Hudson's Bay Company name, creating a fur trade monopoly that covered one quarter of North

The North West Company is involved with community concerns like sports, good nutrition (with its Healthy Living Program), the Stay-in-School campaign, literacy, and other native programs and associations

America. Throughout the 1800s and into this century, the enterprise continued under the Hudson's Bay Company ownership until the assets of The Northern Stores Division were acquired by the employees and a group of new investors in 1987. In 1990 the Company renewed its link to the past and re-established its identity as an independent retailer by changing its corporate name to The North West Company, and the trading name of its retail operations to NORTHERN.

Only five years old, the new company crossed the international border by acquiring Alaska Commercial Company and Frontier Expeditors in 1992. Headquartered in Anchorage, AC Company is the largest retail chain in rural Alaska; FEI is a wholesaler serving smaller, independent retailers.

Today The North West Company is the leading retailer of food, family apparel, and general merchandise in small, northern communities. The company also applies its unique heritage and knowledge of the North by operating complementary businesses which include the Inuit Art Marketing Service, Hudson's Bay Blanket Division, Fur Marketing Division, Heritage Marketing Division and Transport Igloolik. With its head office, Gibraltar House, in Winnipeg, Manitoba, the company's staff of 4,000 operate over 150 stores across northern Canada and more than 20 in Alaska. It is the largest private sector employer of aboriginal people in Canada.

A new distribution centre, complete with the latest in warehousing technology, is located in Winnipeg and provides stores with food and general merchandise. The company's Montreal-based ship, the *MV Aivik*, brings goods to stores throughout the eastern Arctic. As well, customers are serviced by the company's three annual "Selections" catalogues, which are also translated into Greenlandic and distributed to 20,000 homes in Greenland.

The North West Company continues to live up to its "Enterprising" motto. New locations are opened, facilities upgraded and new services — such as fast food, banking and travel — constantly introduced. It has come a long way since those first trading posts, and while The North West Company carries its heritage proudly, it is still making history today.

Ward Associates

Information Technology Staffing for the 21st Century

WARD ASSOCIATES is an innovative Canadian Staffing company serving the needs of the Information Technology community through consulting and staffing services. The goal of Ward Associates is to offer excellent service and the highest of integrity to the business community while maximizing the potential of individuals and corporations alike.

Peter J. Ward, president and founder of Ward Associates, believes that "the world around us is quickly realizing that the resolute answer to providing the competitive edge in today's technological trends is skill. This skill must be made available 'just in time' with a predictable high quality and level of productivity. The less social, political and off-target distractions the better. This skill, moreover, is delivered only by PEOPLE."

Information and knowledge are not only the foundation but true tangible assets for the beckoning future. Since 1978 Ward Associates has positioned itself with a veritable "gold mine" of information germane to the Information Technology professionals who are moving into and shaking the "new economy." As Nuala Beck, a leading Canadian economist, claims in her recent number one best seller, *Shifting Gears*, the engine of the '90s and beyond is the "chip." The cheaper the microchip gets, the faster we go, and the further we go!

Ward has quickly been accepted as a "benchmark" or "model" to the Information Technology world of staffing. A sophisticated tracking system integrated to a unique service-driven delivery process in a true team environment completes Ward's impressive infrastructure.

Ward Associates correctly offers a unique blend of Information Technology Consulting and Strategic Staffing Initiatives with one purpose: to allow clients to focus truly on their respective core businesses while having the flexibility to react quickly to new market opportunities or fluctuating business cycles without costly repercussions.

The company with a dream to be the best has grown from a small staff of three some 16 years ago to over 200 contract consultants and core staff with sales in 1994 approaching $18 million. New offices are planned to facilitate an expanding national media presence and a growing request for services across Canada.

Ward's success is no secret: this all-Canadian company unconditionally treats others as they themselves would want to be treated. Ward's corporate commitment reinforces this philosophy: "Provide the best IT solutions; Provide the best service and valuable advice; Contribute to our industry and community. We challenge each other to develop an enjoyable, fulfilling, prosperous workplace."

P.J. (Peter) Ward actively supports NAPS (National Association of Personnel Services), APPAC (The Association of Professional Placement Agencies and Consultants), NACCB (The National Association of Computer Consultant Businesses, CIPS (The Canadian Information Processing Society), York Technology, and the Christian Business Men's Committee.

P.J. (Peter) Ward, founder, Ward Associates, preparing for the 21st century

Knob Hill Farms

Canada's Pioneer of Regional Food Marketing

KNOB HILL FARMS is a "proud to be Canadian" chain of retail and wholesale food outlets based in and around Metropolitan Toronto. Privately owned and operated by its founder, Steve Stavro, it has grown to be known as Canada's largest independently owned food retailer.

This is quite remarkable because Knob Hill Farms has achieved this distinction with just ten stores — but they are not your normal, garden variety supermarkets. Stavro has been a leading pioneer of the "think big" school of food marketing. Over 30 years ago, he was trailblazing the way with his regional marketing approach for today's trend in warehouse style retail outlets.

Back in 1962, he opened his first Knob Hill Farms *Food Terminal* in the suburban Markham area of Toronto, which he quickly enlarged to 60,000 square feet. This was huge for then because the average supermarket of the major chains was under half that size. Many people in the industry thought Stavro had gone overboard, especially when he added a large tent outside in the summer months. But, Stavro was on to something it took other retailers years to see.

Today, Knob Hill Farms' locations go as big as 340,000 square feet. That jumbo Food Terminal is in Cambridge, Ontario, about one hour west of Toronto, and is the largest "food only" retail outlet in the world — offering one-stop shopping for meats, fresh produce, and groceries, plus an in-store bakery and fresh fish market.

Another fact which makes this success story even more phenomenal is that Stavro started Knob Hill Farms in the early 1950s as a single open-air fruit and vegetable market in Toronto's east end, across the road from his father's grocery store.

As fate would have it this store was near the original Woodbine racetrack, and this triggered one of Stavro's later involvements in the world of sport. When young Steve delivered groceries on his bicycle from his father's store to the stable area, he developed a love for thoroughbred horses, and vowed one day he would own horses. Today, his Knob Hill Stable is one of Canada's finest thoroughbred racing operations, and he occasionally races horses at top U.S. and European tracks.

Also in the sporting vein, another Stavro lifelong passion has been soccer. A top player in his youth, Steve spent large sums in the 1960s trying to popularize the professional game in Canada, and says Knob Hill would be much more successful today if soccer hadn't taken so much of his time then away from the food business.

In the 1960s, Steve also got involved in Major Junior Hockey, sponsoring a team in the Metro Jr. League. This turned out to be the beginning of a long and strong friendship with well-known Toronto sportsman Harold Ballard, who eventually became the major owner and CEO of Maple Leaf Gardens.

In 1981, Stavro went on the Board of Maple Leaf Gardens, and in 1990 when Ballard died, Stavro was named as one of the three executors of the estate. Ballard's will made provision that any of the executors could purchase the estate's shares in Maple Leaf Gardens and Stavro exercised that option. Thus, today Knob Hill Farms and Steve Stavro find themselves in control of the fabled Maple Leaf Gardens, and the Toronto Maple Leaf hockey club — two venerable institutions in Canada's illustrious sporting heritage.

Stavro believes that to be successful in business you should stick to what you know. He knew food because he grew up working in the family store. His father, Atanas Stavro, left the Macedonian highlands in Greece right after Steve, his second son, was born in 1927, and came to Canada to make a better life for his family. Wife, Tsveta, and sons, Chris and Steve, joined him in 1934, after he got established with a small butcher shop in Toronto's

Harold Ballard, the man who got Stavro involved in hockey, poses with Steve and Sally, and operatic tenor Luciano Pavarotti at a charity function in their home

At Knob Hill's Wholesale outlet in Scarborough, restauranteurs and food retailers shop on motorized carts beneath gigantic Canadian and Provincial flags

Knob Hill Farms Cambridge/Waterloo Food Terminal sits on a 25-acre site. The 340,000 sq.ft. store serves the immediate and surrounding communities

east end. When the family arrived, they lived above the store, and later a daughter, Gloria, was born.

Theirs was a "mom and pop shop" in today's terms — and when a cousin who worked there quit, Steve left school and went to work with his dad. He had completed grade ten with good marks, but he was needed in the family store.

In the 1940s, Steve started promoting his "think big" ideas when he talked his father into buying a nearby store twice the size, which had been gutted by fire. After his father paid for it and the refurbishing, he was not happy with Steve for talking him into this expensive move. However, when it opened and did more than twice the business, Atanas realized that young Steve had a gift for merchandising.

It was across the road from this store where Steve, with older brother Chris, set up an open-air fruit and veg-etable stand, and called it Knob Hill Farms — the name of a then popular brand of California produce. Within a few years, they expanded Knob Hill Farms to nine loca-tions — three more open-air markets, and five small supermarkets.

But, once again Steve's "think big" ideas came into play and brother Chris, not wanting to go along, decided to go into real estate investments. Steve then sold off all the small locations and put all his eggs in one basket — a large Food Terminal, as he described it. There were all sorts of naysayers, telling him it would never work. But the rest is food marketing history. Subsequently, he opened large Food Terminals in Pickering, Mississauga, Oshawa, North York, Cambridge, Scarborough, and three in Toronto.

Even with many large locations and hundreds of employees, Stavro's Knob Hill Farms is still a family style

Benburb, Canada's Horse of the Year in 1992, is led into the winner's circle by owner Stavro, and trainer Phil England. The jockey is Richard Dos Ramos

Stavro with jockey Lloyd Duffy and soccer immortal, Sir Stanley Matthews. Steve brought Matthews to Canada to play for his Toronto City soccer team. He liked Canada so much he stayed several years

operation. Steve, often accompanied by his wife Sally, visits several of his Knob Hill locations daily. Three of their four daughters work in the business, and Steve thinks of his long-term employees as extended family. He prides himself on being a hands-on operator, and has no thoughts of retiring.

Today, warehouse outlet style retailing is becoming more and more popular, but the visionary merchant, the pathfinder who started it all with his Knob Hill Farms Food Terminals, was Steve Stavro — food entrepreneur *par excellence.*

Shunning the spotlight, Stavro avoids interviews, remembering his father's advice "Let your work speak for itself." But if you do get him to talk about business, he always points out that Knob Hill's success was only possible because Canada provided a stable society and a free enterprise economy. That's why Stavro says Knob Hill Farms will forever be known as a *"proud to be Canadian"* company.

THE FOUNDER OF MENTHOLATUM, Albert Alexander Hyde, was born in Lee, Massachushetts, in 1848. In 1865 he moved to Kansas and lived out his life in Wichita, a raw frontier town. After he lost the fortune he had

The Mentholatum Company of Canada

The Mentholatum management team: Rick Gazzola, Sales & Marketing Manager, Greg McCaughey, Field Sales Manager, Len Dowsett President, Judy Salomons, Controller

menthol, long extolled by the Japanese as a remedy for many ailments. He studied its healing effects and spent four years working with doctors, chemists and druggists to develop the remedial emollient he had originally envisioned. He named it " Mentholatum."

The name proved effective. It was pleasant to the ear, easily remembered, and noted the two main ingredients: menthol and petrolatum. The distinctive name also set

A.A. Hyde, known for his strong convictions, made it his life's work to distribute the wealth he had accumulated

accumulated in banking and real estate, he entered into a modest partnership with two other men to form the Yucca Company which began selling a fine soap based on the oil of the yucca plant. Soon other products followed, including fly paper, cough syrup and silver polish. The company was guided by Hyde who had experience in financial matters; the others developed and sold products. In 1890, Hyde bought out his partners as the company could not support three families, Mr. Hyde's numbering eleven children by 1899!

Between 1890-1894, Mr. Hyde developed the most well-known and successful of all the Yucca Company products, Mentholatum Ointment.

Hyde had become intrigued by the properties of

it apart from other home remedies of the time which were usually linked to someone's name and touted as "a secret." Before long Mentholatum was singled out for particular mention among the many products of the company and it was often used in print as a generic rather than a trade name.

Hyde sold the product door to door and sought personal endorsements of his product's effectiveness. Testimonials poured in, many ailments were listed for treatment in the sales literature — one of the greater claims being for relief of piles, a common complaint.

The company was one of the first in North America to employ travelling salespersons and two were women, one an osteopath, Doctor Ella Veazie.

By 1906, the years of struggle were over and the Yucca Company had grown from a small regional purveyor of soaps and toiletries to become the manufacturer of a patent remedy with nationwide sales. A factory was opened in Buffalo, New York. It became The Mentholatum Company.

Charlie Hyde, son of "A.A." Hyde, opened, in 1906, a Canadian subsidiary known as "Mentholatum Inter-American Inc." and constructed a 10,000 square-foot, two-story building on the present site in Fort Erie, Ontario.

With his sons managing the businesses, Hyde devoted more and more time to his life-long interest in philanthropic pursuits, supporting any organizations that he believed contributed to the growth of the Kingdom of God on earth. The Boys Club of America, the Y.M.C.A. or any missionary requesting help would receive money and Mentholatum. Because of this product donation to missionaries in Africa and the Far East, Mentholatum ointment became the product of choice for anyone suffering from a cold or skin irritation and became known worldwide as "the Medicine Chest in a Jar." In Africa there is no word for ointment; "true Mentholatum," is the brand product and "Mentholatum" is generic for other companies' products.

Today Mentholatum products are sold in over 150 countries. In Canada, the company continued to grow under the leadership of C.H. Hyde until 1933 when he was succeeded by General Manager Mr. G.H. Stratton Sr. followed by his son, G.H. Stratton, Jr.

By 1974 Mentholatum Inter-American had become The Mentholatum Company of Canada, Limited as a stand-alone subsidiary. In 1983, Mr. L.G. Dowsett became President and General Manager.

Under Mr. Dowsett's leadership, many new products have been acquired, the most notable being "Deep Cold Therapy" which is used in relief of arthritis and muscle aches. It is the only analgesic ever endorsed by the Canadian Chiropractic Association; it has become the mainstay product leading to record high sales and profits. The Canadian operation is also being advanced with creative product packaging, including a jar sized for professional use, a pump action dispenser and a new aerosol — for action in the action sports. A Canadian adaption of another Japanese product "Softlips" promises also to be a success story.

"Len" Dowsett's leadership has been recognized beyond the company as well. He recently served as president of the Nonprescription Drug Manufacturers Association of Canada, and continues to actively participate in its annual Golf Tournament.

In 1988, Rohto Pharmeceuticals Co. Ltd. of Japan, which had a trademark licensing agreement with Mentholatum since 1975, acquired the company and all its subsidiaries. Yasuhiro Yamada, as CEO, leads the present campaign with "Quality Health Care Worldwide" as its logo.

A.A. Hyde would have been proud of the growth and prosperity of his "brainchild" whose products include Deep Heating Rub and Lotion, Mecca Ointment, Fletcher's Castoria, and Smug Denture Cushions, among others. He died in 1935 at the age of 87, having no accumulated wealth and true to his philosophy "we are not here to lay up worldly treasures but to be of service."

Deep Cold Therapy used for relief of arthritis and muscle aches is the only analgesic ever endorsed by the Canadian Chiropractic Association

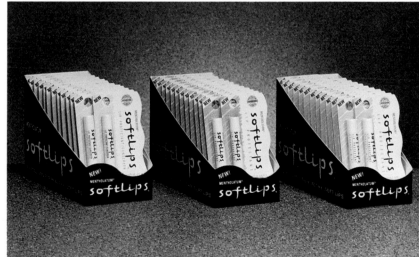

Soft Lips, another adaptation of a remedial Japanese product, is the newest addition to the soothing, healing line-up

Integral Consulting Inc.

A Full Service EDI Consulting Firm

AS THE WORLD MARKETPLACE becomes more accessible, problems of language become major obstacles between trading partners. Computer technology, one of the major components facilitating the everyday business transactions between corporate trading partners, can suffer many difficulties in translation. This is where Integral Consulting Inc. plays a vital role. Established in 1986, Integral Consulting Inc. has an unfailing commitment to understand the needs of the IBM mid-range market place and to provide superior products, services, and knowledge of the highest level for the satisfaction of their customers.

President and CEO Emma Perlaky and her husband arrived in Toronto from Hungary with 20 years experience in the business sector, but less experience speaking English. They dared to dream of a branch operation back in Hungary which could provide a service to both national and international clients. Their dream materialized beyond all expectations when they were able to contract with giant IBM in developing EDI (Electronic Data Interchange) software and, significantly, the production unit with the Serial #1 of the AS/400 series in the forward-looking EDI process was presented to Integral with a plaque recognizing their contribution.

A major challenge facing the founders was to research two problem areas: 1) the personal requirements of the new bosses and 2) how to express the problems (and solutions) in English.

Their talent and logic were applied successfully and led to many more joint projects with IBM. The firm has evolved on a planned, controlled basis, building gradually a staff of 16, including the involvement of the Perlaky family, possessing skills of application and marketing in a forward-looking atmosphere. The logo is an eye-catching combination of the calculus symbol for Integer and a C for Consulting, "The Power of 1 (ONE)."

Customers include local and international organizations. A three-year partnership with VE-Integral KFT of Hungary is a joint venture with Volan Elektronica Rt. also of that country. Marta Visontai, managing director of the Hungarian branch, and her colleagues offer technical and business expertise on various platforms including IBM PCs and the AS/400. They adapt existing western software to meet that country's accounting and tax requirements, ensuring that the user interface is translated into Hungarian. They also design, code and/or enhance software applications for financial, sales and marketing, human resources, transportation and manufacturing sectors. Another valuable service is in helping newcomers to get established in the Hungarian way of doing business.

Electronic Data Interchange (EDI), the enabling technology for fundamental change between trading partners, now encompasses the globe. "We are EDI change masters. We orchestrate all aspects of a successful EDI program on time and on budget," says Mrs. Perlaky. And along with all of this, she finds time for woodcarving, reading and collecting antiques.

Emma Perlaky, President and CEO

International VERIFACT Inc.

World Leader in PIN Technology

INTERNATIONAL VERIFACT INC. (IVI), a publicly owned corporation based in North Toronto, designs, develops, manufactures, and markets customized electronic point-of-service terminals and related equipment. Its customers include banks, retailers, computer and health care industries in Canada and the United States.

In just over ten years of operation, a blue-ribbon clientele has been cultivated from Quebec to California. The company's reputation has been enhanced by a high level of product quality, data security, and reliability, as well as ground-breaking research and development.

Founded in 1983, the company became a major player when, in 1985, a single contract with Lucky Stores Inc. of California marked it as North America's largest supplier of debit card terminals and developer of electronic payment systems.

The staff is a dynamic team of highly trained engineers, software designers, and sales personnel, as well as manufacturing and administrative employees.

The V2000, introduced in early 1992, has set the standard for quality and value among debit/credit point-of-sale terminal systems. The V2000 and the creative new C2000 family of products will be the most important revenue producers for International VERIFACT for the foreseeable future.

While much of the revenue growth came from the use of VERIFACT products in the rollout of the Interac direct payment (debit) program, many important additions were also made to the North American customer base, especially in the United States where much of the company's future growth is expected to occur.

VERIFACT has a strong and debt-free balance sheet which gives the company the freedom to aggressively approach the many new and emerging markets for intelligent debit/credit terminals. In the past year VERIFACT made a number of turnkey production and assembly arrangements with major companies so that it may concentrate on what it does best: matching the needs of customers to the very latest in technology.

In the past year International VERIFACT:

• increased sales dramatically through its participation in the INTERAC direct debit program sponsored by Canada's major banking and financial institutions;

• introduced four members of the new C200 family of products, all easily programmable through the industry standard ANST "C" based language;

• reinforced its reputation as the standard-setter in secure transactions;

• established a sales organization in the United States with headquarters in Scottsdale, Arizona;

• welcomed several new institutional shareholders;

• added more than $8 million to working capital as a result of the exercise of warrants issued in February, 1992.

George Whitton,
Chairman and Chief
Executive Officer

International VERIFACT's product line serves a broad range of customers who have come to expect reliability and up-to-the minute technology in electronic funds transfer and point-of-sale systems

On April 26, 1993, the next generation paper company arrived in Canada. Unisource Canada, with the promise of helping its customers outperform their competition, debuted as the most extensive, single-source distributor of fine papers, graphic supplies, industrial products and system solutions in Canada.

Operating as Unisource Canada East and Unisource Canada West, the company services the country from regional headquarters in Montreal and Vancouver. It is

Unisource Canada, Inc.
One Name ... One Vision ... One Source

Unisource Canada, Inc., Richmond Hill, Ontario

the result of a major acquisition engineered in September 1992 by Paper Corporation of America, North America's largest marketer and distributor of fine papers and industrial products. PCA, an Alco Standard company headquartered in Wayne, Pennsylvania, has 330 locations, more than 9,000 employees and US $4.5 billion in annualized sales.

The acquisition involved three Abitibi-Price distribution companies: Barber-Ellis Fine papers, Price Daxion and Inter City Papers. At the same time, PCA also acquired Crown Paper, a major distributor of industrial packaging, janitorial products and printing papers. These companies were combined with PCA's Smith Paper of British Columbia to form Unisource Canada.

Management of Unisource Canada realized that the new company would never be able to rest solely on its size. Yves Montmarquette, President of Unisource Canada East, said that being part of the largest distribution network

in North America brings with it a serious obligation to customers. "We are and will continue to be customer advocates," he stated. "Our entire organization must meet and work with customers; that's our number one priority."

"Our goal is straightforward: to make it easier for our customers to do business by providing a single, one-stop source for their printing and packaging needs," explained Don Cook, president of Unisource Canada West. "The companies that form Unisource Canada are dominant forces in their marketing areas and now, as a single source supplier, plan to provide a level of expertise, inventories, products, and customer service unequalled in Canada."

Beginning with revenues of nearly $925 million, Unisource's 40 distribution centres, more than 25 specializing in fine paper, represent $900 million of inventory, 2 million square feet of warehouse space and employ 1,800 people.

Relying on advanced technology as the backbone of its national distribution network, Unisource is able to manage all order processing, product replenishment, inventory control, storage and receiving, delivery, accounts payable and management reporting on behalf of the customer. Customer service is one of Unisource's biggest assets....

To meet customers' needs, Unisource has developed a "market specialist" program by calling on advertising agencies and corporate communication departments to learn the needs of graphic artists and designers.

Overall, Unisource sees significant growth opportunities in the web, graphic arts, silk screen, bookbinding, and business communications paper market segments.

With the single source concept, maintaining inventories large enough to meet customers' needs is critical. Inventory in a Unisource warehouse includes a diversity of coated and uncoated papers, carbonless papers, cut size papers, laser speciality papers, specialty text and cover grade papers, envelopes, as well as graphic and printing supplies.

The single source concept that showcases Unisource as a Canadian corporate achiever redefines the way of doing business for the graphics arts industry throughout Canada.

Catelli Pasta

As Old as Canada Itself

Carlo O. Catelli

IN 1867, while a new nation was declaring itself to the world, Carlo Onerato Catelli (Charles Honoré Catelli) was taking the first step in the founding of a great corporate presence in Canada's future economic prosperity. The young Italian immigrant opened a pasta outlet on Rue Saint-Paul in old Montreal.

New Italian immigrants settling in that city provided a ready market for pasta. By 1908 the demand was great enough for a joint venture between Mr. Catelli and other Montreal businessmen —thus C.H. Catelli Ltd. was created.

In 1939, the aging facilities on Rue Bellechasse were no longer suitable. The company opted to settle on a site at 6890 Rue Notre-Dame Est where it still continues operation. Expansion into the canned spaghetti and canned spaghetti sauce markets followed.

Within a decade, Catelli Ltd. established branches in other parts of Canada, the first at Lethbridge, Alberta. In the mid fifties the company, now named Catelli-Habitant, became a subsidiary of Ogilvie Flour Mills Company Limited, Canada's largest flour-milling industry. The purchase of Dyson Limited, famous for pickles, with plants in Manitoba and Ontario, enabled Catelli to continue the many traditional Dyson family recipes.

In 1968, Catelli Habitant became a subsidiary of John Labatt Limited. The corporate names Catelli Limited and Ogilvie Mills Limited were, by 1971, designated to their respective companies.

The '80s saw further expansions with corporate Catelli comprising four operating divisions: Catelli Products Group, Habitant Jarred Products Group, Catelli U.S. Group (New Hampshire), and United Maple Products. Catelli employed more than 1,200 people throughout Canada and the northeastern United States.

Products included pasta, pickles, sauces, soups, puddings, syrups, jams, marmalades, and flour. Product growth was engineered by franchise building, geographical expansion, new product development, increased sales to the food service industry and private and generic label markets, and related corporate acquisitions.

Catelli's largest single investment remains in pasta. Pasta production employs the largest number of people and is the main contributor to the company's profitability.

In June 1989, Borden Inc., a United States multi-food manufacturer, purchased Catelli and eventually sold off its subsidiaries. Borden today maintains a strong hold over the Canadian pasta manufacturing operations.

In 1991, 20 million dollars was invested in renovating the Montreal plant, thereby doubling its production capacity.

Created in 1972, the sunshine/rainbow Catelli logo projects Catelli's corporate image and broad spectrum of products with an optimistic and positive symbol.

Facing the future with optimism is the real legacy of Carlo Onerato Catelli: a man who took a simple idea, a single product, and the most rudimentary equipment and created an enterprise which emerged as a conglomerate of considerable proportions in modern-day food processing technology.

The 1930s Catelli delivery fleet in Montreal

Human Resources Technologies Inc.

"Touching the Spirit of Human Resources"

Over the last two decades, as businesses have fought not only for profitability and growth, but often for survival, business leaders have been heavily investing in information systems to control and understand their real costs for doing business. Management information systems have enabled corporate leaders to make informed corporate decisions because of the availability and accuracy of operational data.

With vision based on business intuition and depth of human resources experience, Dr. Shayne Tracy, in 1988, developed HUMAN RESOURCES INFORMATION SYSTEMS stating "the time is upon us when corporations will be looking to have complete, accurate, available live data on their greatest resource. Information systems to give decision making data on this investment in human resources will be on the next wave of technological development."

Human Resources Technologies Inc. is a privately owned, all-Canadian company based in Oakville, Ontario. In the six years since inception, its trademarked products *Super HR* and *Super Trainer* have been independently evaluated in the market as "the two leading PC based HRIS Software products in Canada." *Super HR* is a Human Resources management information system that tracks all employee information such as work histories, benefits and salary administration, training, performance reviews and job descriptions. Additional features include succession planning, health and safety, absenteeism control, recruitment and applicant tracking. As well, the system allows the user to manage information required by government legislation such as Pay Equity and Employment Equity.

Super Trainer is an award winning Training Administration System that enables trainers to manage all training activities and generate management reports and cost-benefit statements.

Each year substantial allocations of capital have been poured back into the research and development of new products and enhancements including responding to the ever changing legislation of the various governments. The company, as a pathfinder, has grown consistently over the years to reach the point where there are now 350 installations. The company's reputation continues to grow due to the ease of data input, information retrieval and powerful reporting capabilities. In addition, the company is moving the technology to include innovative features in the areas of personnel assessment and selection, and performance feedback.

The great value of technology is in its ability to consolidate information in a timely manner to allow management to have clarity of vision in its decision making. HR Technologies, in addition to providing software solutions for human resources executives, also provides consulting services in the areas of "performance management, organizational development, leadership training and executive recruitment."

Human Resources Technologies Inc. is a human resources company, run by human resources professionals, and provides relevant services and technology for clients with 50 to over 10,000 employees. With this understanding of the HR function, HR Technologies adopted the theme "Touching the Spirit of Human Resources" to help maintain its perspective that all aspects of its operation is to be contributing to the enhanced productivity and well-being of Canada's workforce — our greatest treasure.

As the key principals of Human Resources Technology Inc., Shayne Tracy, left, and Richard Booth, right, are committed to serving clients by bringing know-how human resources technology to Canada's business community

The Golden Griddle Corporation

Celebrating 30 Delicious Years

Golden Griddle Family Restaurant, 345 Bloor St.E., Toronto, Ontario

W hat was started by entrepreneur Harold McDonnell on May 2, 1964, as a small 60-seat restaurant at the corner of Redpath and Eglinton Avenues in central Toronto has become one of Canada's most popular chain of family restaurants.

Golden Griddle Family Restaurants, now more than thirty years old, serves millions of customers each year throughout most major cities in Ontario.

Its history, moreover, is not just one of serving a wide variety of delicious homestyle breakfast, lunch and dinner entrees. It also exemplifies a tradition that includes a dedication and a personal commitment to serving the many communities where this proud, all-Canadian family restaurant chain has chosen to locate.

Golden Griddle franchisees, suppliers, and customers are always busy helping to raise funds for Golden Griddle Children's Charities, a non-profit charitable foundation dedicated to assisting needy children.

The franchisees of Golden Griddle Family Restaurants are proud to be a part of a great Canadian foodservice tradition proclaiming: "Golden Griddle.... We're not fast food — we're great food fast."

GiGi, the Golden Griddle Mascot widely used to promote Golden Griddle Children's Charities

GOLDEN GRIDDLE

GOLDEN GRIDDLE CHILDREN'S CHARITIES

IS A FOUNDATION THAT FUNDS AGENCIES AND OTHER CHARITIES THAT HELP NEEDY CHILDREN

WON'T YOU PLEASE HELP US?

KPMG

More than 150 years in the making...

THE LARGEST professional services firm in Canada, KPMG is a business accustomed to change. From modest beginnings in Montréal in 1840, the firm has constantly expanded, today employing some 5,000 Canadians in more than 70 offices from coast to coast. Nearly 100 firms in large and small communities from the Atlantic to the Pacific coast have joined forces over the past 150 years to build a dynamic, full-service organization that encompasses KPMG Peat Marwick Thorne, chartered accountants, and KPMG Management Consulting. The firm provides a complete range of audit, consulting, financial advisory and tax services to business, public sector, and not-for-profit organizations.

Many of Canada's pioneer enterprises are KPMG clients. The Bay, George Weston, and Rogers Communications are a few of the prominent names on a client list that reaches into virtually every facet of Canadian life and commerce. The firm's more than 55,000 clients include a large share of Canada's biggest and best-known companies, the largest number by far being owner-managed enterprises.

These clients are innovative, entrepreneurial, and action-oriented — and they expect the same from KPMG's personnel. Excellence in auditing or accountancy is not enough in today's marketplace. The stereotypical accountant, pouring over legers with one hand on a calculator, has given way to a diverse range of professionals committed to providing creative solutions to client problems and opportunities.

The entrepreneurial spirit that has propelled KPMG forward is apparent today in the way the firm services the individual needs of its diverse clientele. KPMG's practice groups focus on the needs of specific Canadian industries — from banking to mining, from automobile dealerships to hospitality and tourism. Their mission: to assist clients in addressing the latest operational, financial, regulatory and marketing issues affecting their organizations.

Opportunity lies within any change. As organizations look for new ways of doing business in the nineties, KPMG has emerged as a sought-after advisor whether the situation calls for downsizing, expansion, or streamlining for competitive advantage. To help clients turn change into opportunity, KPMG has been a leader in embracing new approaches and at the

A cartoon of the 1880s showing Canada as a rapidly growing young nation surrounded by envious nations

forefront in entering new service areas. For example:

• The firm has put more than a dozen accountants, engineers, and management consultants to work in the environmental area, helping clients address risk, comply with new law and take advantage of tomorrow's opportunities.

• Acting for lenders, regulators or troubled companies themselves, KPMG's corporate recovery specialists have been involved in some of the most

Towards 2000

sophisticated restructuring exercises that have, in recent years, taken place in Canada.

• KPMG consultants are assisting organizations to develop new costing systems using activity based management to measure performance. New management techniques, new capital, more automation and computer systems usually mean that the allocations based on the historical labour component are misleading.

• With corporate fraud on the increase and financial litigation becoming more complex than ever, KPMG developed the largest forensic and investigative accounting practice in Canada as an aid to assist clients in combating and protecting themselves against everything from kickbacks and wrongful dismissals to management frauds, stock market manipulations, and even arson.

Just as entrepreneurial clients have "gone global," so too has KPMG become their global advisor, with a service network that reaches across Canada and stretches worldwide. First among accounting firms to complete a global merger, KPMG is the world's leading professional services organization with a network of over 800 offices in more than 130 countries. By thinking globally and delivering locally, KPMG brings worldwide knowledge to bear on client concerns.

To succeed in a time of change, limits must be stretched and old assumptions challenged. KPMG professionals are advising Canadian entrepreneurs to pursue aggressive growth around the world, establishing new

international markets for Canadian products and their strategic acquisitions of operations outside Canada. To meet the information needs of its clients, many of KPMG's surveys are international in scope — such as its in-depth reports on international fraud and corporate environmental reporting, perceptions of business leaders on the implications of NAFTA and its authoritative analysis of global cross-border merger and acquisition activity. KPMG is a true pathfinder....

Looking toward the twenty-first century, KPMG's aspirations are reflected more than ever in the firm's mission statement: "We will be the recognized leader in providing personalized, objective professional services. We will strive relentlessly for the success of our clients through teamwork, innovation, and access to firm-wide expertise."

INDEX

Abbott, Scott   216-219

Abbott, Dr. Maude   112-113

Aitken, W.M.;Lord Beaverbrook   166-169

American Express   383

Amiens & Gen. A.W. Currie   160-161

AMJ Campbell Van Lines   348

Ann of Green Gables   99,   230-233

Arbor Memorial Services   361

Arden, Elizabeth   162-165

Ashevak, Karoo   25

Ashevak, Kenojouak   27

Ashland Chemical Canada Ltd.   355

Atkinson, Joseph   88-91

Babcock & Wilcox Industries Ltd.   353

Ball, Michael   98

Banting, Dr. Frederick   10-13, 72

Barker, Col. William   53

Beauchemin, Pierre   206-207

Beck, Adam   318-321

Bell, Alexander Graham   210-215

Best, Dr. Charles   10-13, 263, 300

Bethune, Dr. Norman   58-63

Bibb, Henry   267

Bigelow, Dr. Wilfred G.   234-237

Bishop, Col. William Avery   50-53

Bombardier, J. Armand   224-227

Botterell, Dr. Harry   296-299

Boxing   194-199

Bridgestone/Firestone Canada Inc.   384

Brookfield Development Corporation   363

Brown, Dr. Alan   71,72,74,75

Burns, Tommy   195

Burroughs Wellcome Inc.   388

Burton, Dr. Eli   258-261

Bush Pilots   76-81

Callaghan, Dr. John   234-7

Campbell, Kim   205

Canadian Comic Creators   20-23

Canadian Pacific Railway   28-31

Canadian Association for Community
    Living   374

Casgrain, Thérèse   203

Catelli Pasta   409

Charlottetown Festival   96-99

Chrétien Jean   7, 8-9

Choice Hotels Canada Inc.   366

Chrysler Canada Ltd.   369

CIBA Vision   354

Color Your World Inc.   399

Connaught Laboratories Limited   387

Counsell, Dr. John   296-299

Country Style Donuts   358

Cunard, Samuel   180-183

Currie Gen. A.W.   160-161

Cyr, Louis   46-47

de la Roche, Mazo   308

Desbarats, Georges-Edouard   14-15

Dickens, Clennell "Punch"   77-81

Digital Equipment of Canada Ltd.   362

Dominion of Canada General Ins.   360

Dixon, George "Little Chocolate"   194

Dixon, Franklin W.   92-95

Drake, Dr. T.G.H.   72,74,75

Dressler, Marie   312, 316-317

Edison, Thomas Alva   304-307

Edmonton Grads   285

Electron Microscope   258-261

Eli Lilly Canada Inc.   349

Eliot, Elmina   89

Elizabeth Arden Canada Inc.   394

Evans, Matthew   304-7

Fairclough, Ellen   205

Falconbridge Nickel Mines   270,272-3

Fenerty, Charles   290-291

Fessenden, Reginald   42-45

Fife, David   245

Fleming, Sir Sandford   34-37

Ford Motor Co. of Canada   346

Foster, Hal   20-23

Fridolin   240,241

Frye, H. Northrop   252-253

Gélinas, Gratien   240-241

Geological Survey of Canada   157,159

Gesner, Abraham   136-139

Gingras, Dr. Gustave   132-135

Gisborne, Frederic Newton   148-151

Golden Griddle Corporation, The   411

Gould, Glenn   170-173

Green, Lorne   97

Hammell, Jack   328-329

Haney, Chris   216-219

Haney, John   216-219

Hanlan, Edward ("Ned")   82-83

Heart Pacemaker   234-237

Herbert, Ruth   74

Henson, Josiah   264-267

Heparin   262-263

Herbert, Ruth   74

Hillier, Dr. James   258-261

Hiram Walker   359

Hollywood Stars   312-317

Home Hardware Stores Limited   398

Hoodless, Adelaide Hunter   250-251

Hopps, Jack   235-7

Horn Abbot   218-219, 374

Hospital For Sick Children
         66-71, 72-75, 188-191

Human Resource Technologies Inc.   410

Humphrey, John Peters   114-117

Ice Hockey   322-327

IMASCO   372

In Flanders Fields   33

Insulin   10-13

INCO Limited   268-271, 364

Integral Consulting Inc.   406

Interforest Ltd.   344

International Verifact   407

Inuit Art   24-27

Ipeelee, Osuitok   25

Irving, K.C.   174-177

Jameson, Anna   201

Johns, Dr. Harold E.   186-187

Johnson, Pauline   48-49

Joubin, Franc   254-257

Journey's End Corporation   366

Jousse, Dr. Al;   296-299

KPMG   412

Karsh, Yousuf   118-121

Knob Hill Farms Limited   402

Kodak Canada Inc.	397	
Kraft General Foods Canada Inc.	350	
Langford, Sam	197	
Leacock, Stephen	286-289	
Leger, Paul-Emile	152-155	
Leggo, William	14	
Leggotype	15	
Lindsley, Thayer	270, 272-273	
Logan, William E.	156-159	
Lonergan, Bernard	208-209	
Longboat, Tom	100-101	
MacKay, John	187	
MacLennan, Hugh	238-239	
MacLeod, Dr. J.J.R.	10-13	
MacMillan Bloedel Limited	390	
MacMillan, H.R.	308-311, 390	
Magna International Inc.	367	
Maple Syrup	220-221	
Massey, Daniel	84-87	
Massey, Hart	84-87	
May, Wilfred "Wop"	76-81	
McClung, Nellie	204	
McCollip, Dr. Bertram	10-13	
McConachie, George "Grant"	80-81	
McCrae, John	32-33	
McCurdy, J.A. Douglas	212-214	
McFarlane, Leslie	92-95	
McIntosh Apple, The	110-111	
McKenna, Seana	98	
McLaren, Norman	140-143	
McLarnin, Jimmy	196	
McLennan, John	122-125, 261	
McLuhan, Marshall	178-179	
McMaster, Elizabeth,	66, 70	
McNaughton, Gen. Andrew G.L.	126-127	
Mentholatum Co. of Canada,	404	
Merck Frosst Canada Inc.	396	
Michener, Roland	209, 327	
Microsoft Canada Inc.	370	
Midland Walwyn Capital Inc.	380	
Mohawk Skywalkers	64-65	
Molson Companies, The	338	
Montgomery, Lucy Maud	230-233	
Moodie, Susanna	201	
Morguard Investments Limited	395	
Municipal Trust	365	
Murdoch, James Y.	274-277	
Murphy, Emily	200	
Murray, Dr. Gordon	262-263	
Mustard, Dr. William	188-191	
Naismith, James A.	280-285	
National Research Council	125,127,259,260,295	
Nickel	268-271	
Nobel Prize	11,13,229	
Noranda Mines	274-277	
North West Company, The	400	
Oaks, Harold "Doc"	73-81	
Ontario Hydro	318-321, 352	
Oonark, Jessie	26	
Osler, Sir William	128-131	
Pablum	68, 72-75	
Page, Percy	285	
Parr Traill, Catherine	201	
Patch, John	278-279	
Pearson, Lester B.	228-229, 327	
Peel, Paul	54-57	
Penfield, Dr. Wilder	330-333	
People's Republic of China	58,59,63	
Peterson, Oscar	144-147	
Philip Environmental Inc.	386	
Pickford, Mary	312-313	
Power Corporation of Canada	342	
Prebus, Dr. Albert	258-261	
Prince Valiant	20-23	
Procter & Gamble Inc.	376	
Prudential Insurance Company of America	391	
Quebec Wood Sculpture	16-19	
Radio Shack	382	
Reid, T.M. "Pat"	77	
Reid, Pat	77	
Rogers, E.S. ("Ted")	334-335	
Royal Bank of Canada	343	
Royal Doulton Canada Limited	385	
S.C. Johnson and Son, Limited.	356	
St. Lawrence Cement	378	
Saunders, Sir Charles	242-245	
Schadd, Mary Ann	267	
Schrum, Gordon M.	124,125	
Schuster, Joe	20-23	
Selye, Dr. Hans	222-223	
Shatner, William	97	
Shaw Festival	96-99	
Shearer, Norma	314-316	
Sifto Canada Inc.	340	
Sifton, Sir Clifford	184-185	
Simcoe, John Graves	264-5	
Smith, Donald; Lord Strathcona	31, 34	
Smith, Dr. Ivan	187	
Solandt, Omond	300-303	
Specialty Brands	389	
Stowe, Dr. Emily Howard	202	
Stowe-Gullen, Dr. Ann Augusta	203	
Stratford Festival	96-99	
Strong, Maurice	7, 308	
Summerfeldt, Dr. Pearl	74	
Superman	20-23	
Syncrude Canada Ltd.	368	
Thompson, John Fairfield	271	
Tiktak, John	24	
Tisdall, Dr. Frederick F.	72-75	
Toronto Star, The	20,88-89	
Trivial Pursuit	216-219	
Turnbull, Wallace R.	292-295	
Tyrrell, Joseph	102-105	
Underground Railroad, The	264-267	
Unisource Canada Inc.	408	
United Parcel Services Canada Ltd.	375	
United Nations	114-118, 228	
Vanier, Jean	246-249	
Vanier, Georges	246	
Vanier, Pauline	246	
Vestcap Investment Management	371	
Villeneuve, Gilles	38-41	
Villeneuve, Jacques	41	
W.C. Wood Company Limited	392	
Ward Associates	401	
Werner, Ed	216-219	
Willson, Thomas "Carbide"	192-193	
Wilson, J. Tuzo	106-109	
Women's Rights	200-205	
Women's Institutes	250,251	
Woodward, Henry	304-307	
Zhongde, Liu	7, 63	